Oscar Wilde as a Character in Victorian Fiction

Also by the same author

'The Law According to Oscar Wilde', *The Wildean* 22 (January 2003)

'Isola's Ghost: A Long Lost Sister in Oscar Wilde's Fairy Tales', *In-Between: Essays and Studies in Literary Criticism* 10.2 (September 2001)

'Homoeroticism and the Child in Wilde's Fairy Tales', *The Wildean* 19 (July 2001)

'Stevenson's Life Before the South Pacific', *The Beach of Falesá' in Context: A Collection of Essays* (Adelaide: Flinders University Press, 1999)

Oscar Wilde as a Character in Victorian Fiction

Angela Kingston

OSCAR WILDE AS A CHARACTER IN VICTORIAN FICTION
Copyright © Angela Kingston, 2007.

All rights reserved. No part of this book may be used or reproduced in any manner whatsoever without written permission except in the case of brief quotations embodied in critical articles or reviews.

First published in 2007 by
PALGRAVE MACMILLAN™
175 Fifth Avenue, New York, N.Y. 10010 and
Houndmills, Basingstoke, Hampshire, England RG21 6XS
Companies and representatives throughout the world.

PALGRAVE MACMILLAN is the global academic imprint of the Palgrave Macmillan division of St. Martin's Press, LLC and of Palgrave Macmillan Ltd. Macmillan® is a registered trademark in the United States, United Kingdom and other countries. Palgrave is a registered trademark in the European Union and other countries.

ISBN-13: 978–0–230–60023–2
ISBN-10: 0–230–60023–9

Library of Congress Cataloging-in-Publication Data

Kingston, Angela.
   Oscar Wilde as a Character in Victorian fiction / by Angela Kingston.
     p. cm.
   ISBN 0–230–60023–9
   1. Wilde, Oscar, 1854–1900—In literature. 2. Authors, Irish, in literature. 3. Authors in literature. 4. English fiction—19th century—History and criticism. I. Title.

PR5823.K63 2007
828'.809—dc22
                                                     2007011739

A catalogue record for this book is available from the British Library.

Design by Newgen Imaging Systems (P) Ltd., Chennai, India.

First edition: December 2007

10 9 8 7 6 5 4 3 2 1

Printed in the United States of America.

I awoke the imagination of my century so that it created myth and legend around me . . .

> Oscar Wilde, *De Profundis*

For all those readers and writers
with Wilde imaginations

Contents

List of Plates xi

Acknowledgments xiii

Introduction 1

1 Aesthete 1877–1890 15
George Fleming (Julia Constance
   Fletcher): *Mirage* (1877) 17
Walter Besant and James Rice: *The Monks of
   Thelema* (1877) 22
A. T. D.: 'O'Flighty' (1879) 25
George Bernard Shaw: *Immaturity* (1879) 27
Rhoda Broughton: *Second Thoughts* (1880) 41
Anonymous: *Ye Soul Agonies in Ye Life of
   Oscar Wilde* (1882) 46
Mrs (Rosa) Campbell Praed: *Affinities:
   A Romance of To-day* (1885) 48
Mrs (Mary) Humphry Ward: *Robert Elsmere* (1888) 57
Henry James: *The Tragic Muse* (1890) 61
Marc-André Raffalovich: *A Willing Exile* (1890) 73
Arthur Conan Doyle: *The Sign of Four* (1890) 78

2 Decadent 1891–1895 93
Marie Corelli: *The Silver Domino; or,
   Side Whispers, Social and Literary* (1892) 95
Ella Hepworth Dixon: *My Flirtations* (1892),
   The Story of a Modern Woman (1894),
   'The World's Slow Stain' (1904) 101
Arthur Cunliffe: 'Ossian Savage's New Play' (1893) 111
Max Beerbohm: 'A Peep into the Past' (1893 or 1894) 115
Richard Le Gallienne: 'The Woman's
   Half-Profits' (1894) 121

Arthur Conan Doyle: 'The Greek
   Interpreter' (1894), 'The Empty House' (1903)   123
John Davidson: *Baptist Lake* (1894)   130
G. S. Street: *The Autobiography of a Boy:
   Passages Selected by His Friend, G. S. Street* (1894) 135
Robert Hichens: *The Green Carnation* (1894)   138
Robert Buchanan and Henry Murray:
   The Charlatan (1895)   148
Ada Leverson: 'Suggestion' (1895)   153

3   Pariah 1896–1900   **157**
Ada Leverson: 'The Quest of Sorrow' (1896)   159
Aubrey Beardsley: *The Story of Venus
   and Tannhäuser* (1896)   160
Mabel Wotton: 'The Fifth Edition' (1896)   169
Richard Le Gallienne: 'Brown Roses' (1896)   173
Bram Stoker: *Dracula* (1897)   174
John Strange Winter (Henrietta Stannard):
   A Seaside Flirt (1897)   184
Frederic Carrel: *The Adventures of John Johns* (1897)   189
Grant Allen: *Linnet: A Romance* (1898)   193
Joseph Conrad: 'The Return' (1898)   200
Mrs (Rosa) Campbell Praed: *The Scourge-Stick* (1898)   207
Cyril Arthur Edward Ranger Gull: *The Hypocrite* (1898),
   Miss Malevolent (1899)   210
Curtis Yorke (Susan Richmond Lee):
   Valentine: A Story of Ideals (1899)   221

Conclusion   **225**

**Appendix: Oscar Wilde as a Character in Fiction,
   1900–2007**   **233**

Notes   247

Index   291

Plates

1	Wilde photographed in 1882, aged 27	85
2	The 'Professor of Aesthetics' photographed in full aesthetic mode in 1882	86
3	Undated photograph of Wilde's wife Constance	87
4	Wilde photographed in 1882	88
5	Detail from photograph taken at the country house of Jean and Walter Palmer, September 1892	89
6	Illustration for 'The Decadent Guys' in *Punch*, November 10, 1894, by Bernard Partridge	90
7	Wilde and Lord Alfred Douglas c. 1893	91
8	Aubrey Beardsley's illustration 'The Toilet'	92

Acknowledgments

The wide scope and integrity of this study would not have been possible without the generous assistance and support of many Victorianists in Australia and around the world. I have been able to complete this work in a timely fashion thanks to financial support from the George Fraser Scholarship—thanks George, wherever you are.

I would like to thank Dr David Smith for his steady encouragement and countless pieces of invaluable advice. I am also grateful for the continuing support of the University of Adelaide English Department. For showing me where to begin, I am obliged to Karl Beckson, Michael Seeney, David Rose, and members of the *Victoria* list, the electronic conference for Victorian Studies. The electronic journal *The Oscholars* and the print journal *The Wildean* have also been invaluable sources of information and consultation.

I am particularly indebted to the following people for giving me the benefit of their specialized knowledge, identified in brackets: Stephen Calloway, James G. Nelson and David Wilkinson (C. A. E. Ranger Gull), Helen Debenham (Rhoda Broughton), Nicholas Grene and Tony Gibbs (George Bernard Shaw), Peter Morton (Grant Allen), Michael Seeney (Henrietta Stannard), and Talia Schaffer (Bram Stoker). I must also single out Peter Vernier (Wilde at Oxford), whose generosity and thoughtfulness know no bounds, and David Rose (Oscar Wilde and G. B. Shaw), for his assistance in securing copies of Shaw's *Immaturity* manuscript from the National Library of Ireland. Thanks also to The Society of Authors, acting on behalf of the Bernard Shaw Estate, for permission to quote from the *Immaturity* manuscript.

I owe a great deal to the librarians from all the libraries I have consulted, especially Alan Keig and Jodie Ottewell from the Barr Smith Library, for their tenacious pursuit of rare Victorian texts. The assistance of Bruce Whiteman, Scott Jacobs, Jennifer Schaffner, and Suzanne Tatian at the William Andrews Clark Memorial Library in Los Angeles has been a godsend and the staff at The British and Bodleian Libraries have been consistently friendly and helpful. Mark Samuels Lasner must also be thanked for access to his personal collection of Wilde manuscripts.

I am very grateful to Carolyn Stott and Bruce Whiteman for providing translations for French references and Tom Wright for paving my way to the Clark Library in Los Angeles. I would also like to express my gratitude to Patrick Allington for proofreading the manuscript.

Thanks must also go to Ida Sherriff, Rosalynne, Bill and Amanda Kingston, and Lisa, Jo, Zach, and Ben Allevi for their unwavering support. Finally, heartfelt thanks to Kathy Fogarty, Elizabeth Auricht, Kelly McGorm, Nicole Sabbadin, Kate Howell, and George Oates for their precious friendship and innumerable acts of random kindness, and to Simon McGuire, for his love and belief in me.

Introduction

> Art has not forgotten [Thomas Griffiths Wainewright]. He is the hero of Dickens's *Hunted Down*, the Varney of Bulwer's *Lucretia*; and it is gratifying to note that fiction has paid some homage to one who was so powerful with 'pen, pencil and poison'. To be suggestive for fiction is to be of more importance than a fact.
>
> Oscar Wilde, 'Pen, Pencil and Poison'

As countless critics have observed, and as the preceding quote suggests, the late nineteenth-century author Oscar Wilde regarded his own life as an artistic subject. Indeed, he considered that '[t]o become a work of art is the object of living'.[1] Such categorical statements were frequently made by Wilde and explain the writer's determination to put his genius 'into his life' rather than into his work—a resolution he famously confided to André Gide.[2] Wilde's fascination with the vagaries of image and identity is reflected in the preoccupation with masks, mirrors, and portraits in his literary works. Just as Wilde strove to foster psychological complexity and ambiguity in his writings, he also consciously endeavored to cultivate diversity in his own character with the intention of becoming a symbolic figure, capable of inspiring endless interpretation. With this goal in mind, Wilde astutely exploited the burgeoning media and consumer culture of his time to become a conspicuous public personality.[3] Terry Eagleton recently summarized Wilde as 'a man who saw himself as clay in his own hands'.[4] Indeed, Wilde refused to fix or 'fire' his personality into any definite form and endeavored to maintain a fluid, malleable identity, consistently rejecting notions of an underlying 'authentic self'. Consequently, Wilde presents a mass of contradictions to those who would try to pin him down; he was at once an Irishman with Republican sympathies who courted the English aristocracy, a Protestant who was deeply fascinated by Catholicism, an effete dandy capable of besting the burliest athletic opponent (in conversational *or* physical combat), a socialist and an elitist, an optimist and a cynic, a husband, a father and a lover of men.

While Wilde's complexities can perhaps be attributed to his singular nature as much as to his premeditated design, there can be no doubt that he deliberately set out to inspire the imagination of his era. Near the end of his life, Wilde reflected that he had been ultimately successful in achieving this end:

> I was a man who stood in symbolic relations to the art and culture of my age. I had realized this for myself at the very dawn of my manhood, and had forced my age to realize it afterwards. Few men hold such a position in their own lifetime and have it so acknowledged . . . [I] showed that the false and the true are merely forms of intellectual existence. I treated Art as the supreme reality, and life as a mere mode of fiction; I awoke the imagination of my century so that it created myth and legend around me—[5]

Wilde's many appearances as a character in the fiction of his contemporaries substantiate his claim to have stimulated the artistic imagination of his era. Indeed, Wilde's ambition to 'become' a work of art was realized faster and more literally than even he could have anticipated. In the space of twenty-three years—from his first foray into public life to his death in 1900—no less than thirty-seven discernible portraits of Wilde appeared in novels and short stories by his peers. Truly, as Wilde states above, 'few men hold such a position in their own lifetime'. His refusal to take a definite shape clearly left many contemporary authors unable to resist the temptation of molding him themselves and offering their satisfyingly 'complete' Oscar Wildes to a reading public consumed with curiosity about the elusive man behind the self-fashioner.

This book, a survey and analysis of this remarkable corpus of fiction, produced by a broad cross-section of Victorian authors, will be of particular interest to the modern scholar who seeks to understand Wilde's contemporary context. Surprisingly, this extensive and illuminating source material has gone largely unexploited by academics. Though critical studies examining the Wildean portraits in the better-known fictions, such as Bram Stoker's *Dracula*, Henry James's *The Tragic Muse*, and Robert Hichens's *The Green Carnation*, have appeared sporadically, many of these stories, even those by authors as familiar to Victorianists as George Bernard Shaw, Max Beerbohm, and Aubrey Beardsley, have been overlooked and forgotten.[6] Several scholars have hinted at the value of this 'buried treasure', much of which has been gathering dust in rare book libraries. John Stokes observed in 1996 that 'a complete history of representations of Wilde remains to be written', and Robert Tanitch recently offered an expansive and fascinating survey of dramatic representations of Wilde.[7] Thus far, however, portraits of Wilde in novels and short stories have not been considered in an extensive, discrete study. While the 'complete history' of such works suggested by Stokes is beyond the scope of this study, what is offered here is a comprehensive analytical review of those that appeared during Wilde's lifetime, which aims at completeness. That the relatively small chronological period considered here can yield a book of this nature is both a testament to the magnitude of Wilde's impact upon the art of his age and the richness of the largely unmined resource material.

The substantial number of fictional depictions that appeared immediately after Wilde's disgrace came as a surprise to the present writer, especially in light of the previously held belief, articulated by Michael Seeney in 1996, that 'Following the trials there was an understandable recession in the Wilde fiction industry . . . The rebirth of Wildean fictive treatments comes in the nineteen-thirties'.[8] This study identifies no less than twenty-eight novels and short stories appearing between Wilde's trials and 1930. While the more superficial portraits have been included here in the interests of thoroughness and are only briefly examined, complex portraits such as those offered by George Bernard Shaw, Henry James, and Robert Hichens provide ample material for detailed analysis.

This book is divided into three parts, reflecting three chronological periods that correspond with distinct phases in Wilde's public life: 1877–1890 (Aesthete), 1891–1895 (Decadent), and 1896–1900 (Pariah). Under these headings subtitles listing individual authors and works are provided for ease of reference. Analysis is confined to works originally published in English. Although the focus of this study is on portraits of Wilde in Victorian literature, a brief summary of Wilde's posthumous fictional life appears in the Conclusion, and an annotated bibliography of twentieth- and twenty-first-century fictions featuring Wilde as a character can be found in the Appendix. Although this study is limited to prose fictions in the traditional sense of novels and short stories, it must be stated that many other creative interpretations of Wilde have appeared both during his lifetime and after his death: dramatic works, films, poetry, lyrics, cartoons, comics, and visual art works, some of which are mentioned passim here.

In critiquing each fiction, I have attempted to indicate the strength of the resemblance of the fictional character to Wilde, ascertain if and how the author was acquainted with him and investigate how this relation is reflected in their work. I have also endeavored to determine whether the portrait was ever acknowledged by the author or Wilde and in what manner. Where I have found existing commentaries on the Wildean element in these stories, I have included a summary of relevant critiques in addition to my own analysis; where no other critiques are mentioned, the reading is a new one offered for the first time by the present writer.

The combined Wildean portraits presented here offer a composite picture of Wilde that is unusually complete. We see Wilde in all modes and in all settings: at home and at university, at art exhibitions and dinner parties, at séances and country weekends, in London and abroad, single and married, at work and play, even on horseback! Thirty years after Wilde's death his friend Robert Ross reflected, 'As in the fable of a gold and silver shield [in which two knights argue over the color of a shield only to discover that it is silver on one side and gold on the other] every one received entirely different impressions [of Wilde] according to the method of their approach and the accident of acquaintance'.[9] The thirty-five fictions analyzed here certainly vindicate Ross's claim.

The nature of the authorial connection to Wilde varies widely in these works. There are Wilde's intimates (Max Beerbohm, Richard Le Gallienne, and Ada Leverson), friends (Robert Buchanan, Arthur Conan Doyle, Julia Constance Fletcher, Robert Hichens, Rosa Praed, George Bernard Shaw, Henrietta Stannard, and Bram Stoker), acquaintances (Rhoda Broughton, C. A. E. Ranger Gull, and Henry James), friends who became enemies (Aubrey Beardsley, Marie Corelli, and Marc-André Raffalovich), fellow aesthetes and decadents (Beardsley, Beerbohm, Ella Hepworth Dixon, Fletcher, Le Gallienne, Leverson, Raffalovich, G. S. Street, and Mabel Wotton), fellow journalists (Grant Allen, Beerbohm, Frederic Carrel, Dixon, Fletcher, Ranger Gull, Hichens, Le Gallienne, Shaw, and Street), fellow socialists (Allen and Shaw), authors with reputed homosexual leanings (Corelli, Hichens, James, Le Gallienne, Praed, Raffalovich, and Stoker), *Yellow Book* contributors (Beerbohm, John Davidson, Dixon, James, Le Gallienne, Leverson, and Street), contributors to Wilde's magazine *The Woman's World* (Corelli, Dixon, Fletcher, and Praed), 'New Women' (Broughton, Dixon, Leverson, Praed, and Stannard), spiritualists (Doyle, Praed, and Stoker), and Oxbridge undergraduates ('A. T. D.' and Arthur Cunliffe). Two authors have totally resisted identification (A. T. D. and the author of *Ye Soul Agonies in Ye Life of Oscar Wilde* [1882]), hence the nature of their relation to Wilde remains unknown.

Just as fascinating as these authors' relationships with Wilde are the plethora of interconnections between the authors themselves; there is very often only one degree of separation between them. For example, Raffalovich was a good friend and patron of Beardsley, who in turn was a frequent visitor to the home of Ada Leverson, who also entertained Hichens and Beerbohm, and of course, Wilde. 'Fictionalizing Oscar' was certainly a popular pastime within his own circles.

While it is the lack of any existing study of this kind that has inspired this book, several general reference works dealing with *romans à clef* and other examples of 'real' people in fiction have appeared, several of which give examples of fictional Oscar Wildes.[10] Most of these offer only two or three examples; the most extensive list, in William Amos's *The Originals: Who's Really Who in Fiction* (1985), lists only five. As several of these works offer rare critical overviews of the use of real characters in fiction and identify the broader issues and complexities involved in this type of portraiture, it is worth taking a moment to consider their approaches and conclusions here. Alan Bold, editor of *True Characters: Real People in Fiction* (1984), has noted that

> [s]ome of the most celebrated characters and incidents in literature are modeled on actual originals and events and an awareness of these has an intrinsic interest . . . The real people might be . . . ordinary people writ enormously large by the author. Or they might be so spectacularly larger than life that they demand artistic attention.[11]

As the present study demonstrates, Wilde clearly falls into Bold's latter category. Amos concurs with Bold's estimate of the intrinsic interest of such works and avers that fictional portraits are often unfairly dismissed as a result of their inevitable mingling of author and subject, an issue that is addressed below. Amos also refers to the academic notion that identifying such portraits speaks of a 'vulgar curiosity', but convincingly argues that 'literature cannot be divorced from its raw materials . . . people'.[12] Amos and other commentators highlight the fact that the author often feels impelled to heavily disguise or deny whole or partial 'real-life' portraits, preferring the reader to conclude that 'all characters are created solely from the imagination, forged only on the anvil of the writer's genius'.[13] Amos points to Leo Tolstoy, Charles Dickens, Somerset Maugham, George Meredith, H. G. Wells, Evelyn Waugh, Agatha Christie, and Graham Greene as notable pretenders in this regard.

Although some of the authors examined here, such as Marie Corelli and George Bernard Shaw, denied their borrowings from life, most of Wilde's fictionalizers, including Rosa Praed, Arthur Cunliffe,

Max Beerbohm, and Robert Hichens, openly acknowledged their fictional sketches of Wilde. The prospective increase in book sales to be gained by producing a portrait of the controversial aesthete appears to have been an enticement in this respect; consider the following review of Praed's Wildean novel *Affinities* from the *Saturday Review* of April 4, 1885:

> Novelists are more and more getting into the habit of employing personalities, of turning romance into a kind of fictitious Society journalism. Consequently readers more and more look out for personalities . . . To make people say 'Vere Plantagenet is meant for So-and-So, you know', or 'Miss Brown is really Miss Jones', may get a novel talked about for a month—[14]

Concerns about accusations of libel were commonly dispelled with physical disguises and assumed names. In the fictions discussed here, Wilde becomes shorter, thinner, fairer, balder and bearded and goes by such startlingly original names as Esmé Amarinth, Cyprian Brome, Caradoc Gobion, Baptist Lake, Hyacinth Rondel, Ossian Savage, Thaddeus Sholto, and Florian Wood.

That these fictional Oscar Wildes are effectively composite creations—part Wilde, part imagination, and part authorial reaction to Wilde—will quickly become apparent to the reader of this book. However, far from being a reason to disqualify these characters as objects for serious analysis, the compound nature of these portraits serves to provide a uniquely truthful, intimate picture of Wilde's relation to his world. Wilde's grandson and esteemed Wilde scholar Merlin Holland recently argued that today's academics are often too preoccupied with the factual minutiae of Wilde's life and writings to see the forest for the trees. Holland particularly calls attention to the important contextual material to be found in early biographies and reminiscences of Wilde by his associates, despite their frequently personal and 'impressionistic' qualities:

> each in their way [bring] Wilde briefly back to life as they saw him, each more or less flawed by modern standards but even the flaws adding a dimension to the picture . . . there is much that is unique in these personal appraisals. Treated with caution, weeded of self-interest, they remain an invaluable source—[15]

The 'personal appraisals' discussed in this book are also unique and have defied categorization. They do not fit into the genre of 'historical fiction' in the traditional sense, in that the authors lived alongside their subject; in many ways they are more like a form of subjective biography. However, having extensively examined the Wildean fictions presented here I am in agreement with Holland that such personal, 'impressionistic' works provide an invaluable context for reading Wilde. Of course, Holland's qualifying statement—that such works must be interpreted 'with caution' and with an eye for authorial influence—also applies to fictional portraits. For this reason the present writer has endeavored to provide as much relevant historical information about the authors of these works and their relation to Wilde as possible, alongside close readings of their work. The resulting commentary constitutes a type of communal biographical framework that supports and consolidates the textual analysis. This historical framework also allows a unique appreciation of the composition of Wilde's social and professional milieus, and, by extension, of the influence of those milieus on Wilde as an author and as a personality.

Promoting an appreciation of these factors is particularly important in light of the modern critical practice of viewing Wilde as 'one of us'; a perception that has worked as much to obscure as to reveal him. This point of view is a relatively recent one; until the 1960s and 1970s, Wilde was generally marginalized and dismissed by academics as a minor writer, a trivial aesthete, and a sexual reprobate. The increasingly serious scholarly attention given to Wilde in the latter half of the twentieth century can be largely attributed to two factors: the first publication of his letters by Rupert Hart-Davis in 1962, and the radical revision of traditional approaches and areas of study in literature that took place from the 1960s. Once armed with new epistolary source material, a license to go where no literary critic had gone before and, from 1987, with Richard Ellmann's ground-breaking biography, modern critics swarmed to Wilde. To their collective delight they found that, with his intelligent and subversive observations on the complex, fluid nature of art, individuality, sexuality, gender, culture, and representation, Wilde had preempted the axial questions being posed by postmodern literary theorists.[16] Because these questions were yet to be answered, Wilde emerged from his relative obscurity to become a cultural prophet and what Matthew Sweet has called an 'honorary Modern'. As Michael Bronski has observed, 'the contemporary reconstruction of any historical figure always happens in response to a current public need'.[17] Modern commentators began to speculate that Wilde's deceptively trivial epigrams might conceal the answers to the questions we were asking in our own *fin-de-siècle*. This suspicion, combined with a new appreciation of Wilde's radical liberalism in the face of Victorian intolerance, makes him appear more familiar to us than his contemporaries. As Sweet puts it, Wilde seems 'too ironic, too desiring, too like us to be considered a bona fide Victorian'.[18] Merlin Holland has highlighted the fact that Wilde's 'modern face' often leads people to assume that he lived well into our century, perhaps as a contemporary of Noël Coward in the 1920s.[19] Richard Ellmann goes so far as to claim that Wilde 'belongs to our world more than to Victoria's', essentially because

> [w]e inherit his struggle to achieve supreme fictions in art, to associate art with social change, to bring together individual and social impulse, to save what is eccentric and singular from being sanitized and standardized, to replace a morality of severity by one of sympathy.[20]

So, regardless of the fact that Wilde *was* a son of the nineteenth century and never lived to see the twentieth, we have adopted him for ourselves. By the 1990s, there was an unprecedented level of academic and popular interest in the writer, which has only continued to grow. Wilde has captured the cultural imagination and assumed iconic status like no other Victorian. We have reinstated his lost celebrity; we call him by his first name and we have put his words and image on T-shirts, tea-towels, and greeting cards. We have revisited his life and works with a plethora of books, plays, and films. In the year 2000, which marked the centenary of Wilde's death, a myriad of commemorations, exhibitions, and academic conferences were held around the world. However, if our contemporary enthusiasm for Wilde has virtually overturned his undeserved reputation as a lightweight wit and sexual deviant, it has also worked to remythologize him, most notably as a protomodernist oracle, born before his time.

The potential academic pitfalls of reading Wilde as 'one of us' have been effectively demonstrated by Alan Sinfield and Matthew Sturgis, with regard to the frequent misinterpretation of Wilde's sexual identity. Sinfield, a queer theorist, has convincingly argued that 'Wilde and his writings look queer because our stereotypical notion of male homosexuality derives from Wilde, and our ideas about him'.[21] Sinfield avers that neither Wilde nor the Victorians saw Wilde as a homosexual but as an aberrant heterosexual who indulged in homosexual acts—an important distinction. Sturgis also notes that most Victorians did not read the effeminacy of the aesthetes and decadents as 'homosexuality': '[i]t was seen, rather, as a phenomenon of the age, which found its concomitant in the increasing masculinity of women'.[22] These findings are supported by fictions such as Joseph Conrad's 'The Return', Grant Allen's *Linnet*, and C. A. E. Ranger

Gull's *The Hypocrite*, books published after Wilde's trials that paint him as a philanderer who preys on women. While neither Wilde nor his contemporaries appear to have regarded the author as a 'homosexual' man, this has not prevented many critics from taking Wilde's homosexual 'identity' as a given, erroneously critiquing his words and actions by modern sexual mores.[23] In order to avoid this practice and read Wilde authentically, we must continue to research the social, political, and ideological intricacies of his world. No matter how familiar he appears to us, Wilde must be read as a historical figure in a historical context.

In order to do this, the modern scholar must first negotiate a profusion of twentieth- and twenty-first-century interpretations of Wilde. The author's perpetual elusiveness and eminently adaptable personality have led all manner of theorists to claim him as their own. Literary and cultural critics in the areas of gender studies, queer theory, performance theory, aesthetic theory, women's studies, cultural criticism, textual scholarship, reader response criticism, Irish studies, religious studies, theater history, and philosophy have all offered divergent definitions of Wilde, according to the specific concerns of their individual fields.[24] Though this study's essentially biographic approach to Wilde in fiction offers a series of close readings that rely on no one theoretical approach, it does resemble new historical criticism. Although this study places more emphasis on the presence of the author in the work than most new historicists would allow, its focus on the social, historical, and political influences on the production of the texts, its use of unconventional, marginal historical material to cast new light on a historical figure, and its juxtaposition of this material with existing historical information, can all be read as part of a new historicist approach.

In many ways, however, this is also a humanist study, which disclaims the formalist theories of Michel Foucault and Roland Barthes, promulgated in the 1960s and 1970s, which assert that the author is 'dead' in the work. In denying this philosophy I am in accord with many modern scholars, such as Melissa Knox, who avers that the wide influence of such theories has resulted in the unfair dismissal of biographically based studies as 'nonliterary and noncritical' by many academics.[25] Knox also asserts that this is a particularly mistaken practice with regard to Wilde, who repeatedly foregrounded the correspondences between his art and his life, correspondences that continue to incite academic debate. For such a writer, Knox astutely observes, 'intensive biographical scrutiny remains indispensable'.[26]

A notable dissenter from this view is Ian Small, who adamantly rejects many of the early biographical studies of Wilde by his contemporaries, on account of their subjectivity, personal involvement, and frequent failure to discriminate between anecdotal, partial, and factual evidence.[27] These characteristics also occur in many of the fictions presented here; certainly these texts often tell the reader as much about the author as about Wilde. However, as Knox has observed, such personal, subjective studies are valuable precisely because 'they were written by people who knew Wilde well, and who had occasion to observe events in his life that helped to transform his personal and literary styles'.[28]

Of course, fiction, which is by definition subjective, should never be mistaken for biography or history, but when considered with a view to its limitations it can certainly act as a valuable supplement to historical knowledge. As Thomas Carlyle put it, history thrives on 'stern accuracy in inquiring' *and* 'bold imagination in expounding and filling-up'.[29] It must also be remembered that the study of history has been influenced by the same fragmentation of traditional concepts of truth and knowledge that has affected literary and cultural criticism. Modern historians now embrace a broad range of new approaches and perspectives, particularly social ones. Biographies that embrace subjectivity and fictional methods are also becoming increasingly common and widely endorsed. The modern, more comprehensive approach to historical subjects is encapsulated by K. Jenkins, who avers that

> the past and history are not stitched into each other such that only one historical reading of the past is absolutely necessary. The past and history float free of one another . . . the same object of enquiry can be read differently by different discursive practices.[30]

The discursive possibilities afforded by fiction are certainly exciting ones in Wilde's case; the fictional portraits presented here, though often reinforcing our notions of what is Wildean, also offer some extraordinarily candid and illuminating observations of Wilde that are rarely found in more traditional historical sources. These works capitalize on fiction's ability to focus on the emotional and the individual, and as a result are able to provide a uniquely intimate, human picture of Wilde, unmitigated by the constraints of 'historical' reportage. This feature of fiction is a particularly valuable one with regard to Wilde, as, owing to his ignominious downfall, many authentic nineteenth-century reactions to him were stifled, effectively smothered when he became an 'unmentionable' in polite society. Subsequently, overly decorous Victorian standards of propriety worked to prevent nearly all but the most disparaging public commentary on the disgraced author. Luckily, many contemporary authors took advantage of the more liberal medium of fiction, which allowed them to depict and comment upon their controversial counterpart freely. Such fictions constitute a valuable resource not least because they contain remarkably unrestrained reactions to the ineffable Wilde, from authors living in one of the most 'restrained' periods in history.

A close reading of these works also fulfills a partial but valuable historical/biographical function in that, at the simplest level, the commonalities of their Wilde portraits assume a degree of authenticity merely by their frequency, substantially supporting or negating assumptions made in traditional histories or biographies (as demonstrated above with relation to Wilde's sexuality). Moreover, the extensive use made of little-known secondary material in this book, particularly memoirs by minor writers, has resulted in the unearthing of some long-buried, valuable historical information about Wilde that casts a new light on his personal and professional life. (Less than half of Wilde's fictionalizers discussed here are mentioned in Richard Ellmann's *Oscar Wilde*, the most definitive and comprehensive biography to date.) The following pages include previously unpublished insights into the nature of Wilde's relationships with women and his complex relationships with George Bernard Shaw and Henry James. There is even a hint of an unsuspected romantic connection with the contemporary artist Louise Jopling.

We can reasonably assume that Wilde himself would have supported the expansive, poststructuralist approaches to history outlined above. As Neil Sammells has noted, Wilde's belief that 'we should rewrite history' and his consistent 'championing of the inauthentic', effectively sanctions the more self-conscious, subjective ways in which he has been represented.[31] Wilde constantly derided the public's taste for objective realism. He contended that facts had 'no intellectual value' and reveled in blurring the lines between fact and fiction in his writings and conversation. Indeed, this is one of the characteristics that make Wilde appear so familiar in our own age of 'genre blur'. He aspired to be a 'cultured and fascinating liar', with 'the wit to exaggerate' and 'the genius to romance'.[32] Wilde would habitually offer his own imaginative versions of history, with titles like *The True History of Anne of Cleves* or *The True History of Androcles and the Lion*. Thomas Wright, a collector of Wilde's spoken stories, highlights the latter's belief that 'every interpretation that was artistically realized was "true"' and that many versions of a historical tale were possible.[33] Wilde's opinion on this subject is encapsulated in the quotation at the beginning of this Introduction and is one that Wilde repeatedly asserted:

> 'The truth about the life of a man is not what he does, but the legend which he creates around himself. I have never paraded the streets of London with a lily in my hand . . . That legend merely indicates the impression that I have made on the masses, and it indicates the nature of my temperament better than what I have (actually) done . . . Legends should never be destroyed. It is they which help us catch a glimpse of the genuine face of a man'.[34]

Other writings by Wilde on this topic include his lengthy undergraduate essay 'The Rise of Historical Criticism', in which he defends the fictitious elements in the histories of Thucydides, Sallust, Livy, Tacitus, and Polybius. In 'The Decay of Lying', he praises Herodotus, Cicero, Tacitus, Mallory, Marco Polo, Cellini, Casanouva, Napoleon, Defoe, Boswell, and Carlyle for their merging of fact with fiction, contending that all kept facts either 'in their proper subordinate position, or else entirely excluded [them] on the general ground of dullness'.[35] In 'The Portrait of Mr. W. H.', he offers an alternative reading of the life of Shakespeare and, as Wright has noted, Wilde's characters were often suggested by his friends: Ernest Dowson inspired 'The Poet in Hell' and Robert Ross suggested 'St. Robert of Phillimore'.[36] Wilde was also not averse to drawing upon his own character to give life to the protagonists of his novel and plays; his Lords Wotton, Illingsworth, Darlington, and Goring all display recognizably Wildean qualities.

One can equate Wilde's preference for imaginative interpretations of people and history with his preference for Impressionism in art. Indeed, Wilde himself often compared Impressionism to good fiction.[37] Just as he considered more realistic paintings to be failures because of their inability to 'stir the imagination'—asserting that they rather set 'definite bounds to it'—Wilde disapproved of the unimaginative depiction of reality in literature. In painting and writing, Wilde believed that 'life and nature may sometimes be used as a part of Art's rough material but . . . they must be translated into artistic conventions'.[38] We know that Wilde could be relatively thick-skinned about unsympathetic characterizations of himself, as long as he felt they were 'artistic'. His willingness to be identified with Rosa Praed's startlingly demonic version of him in *Affinities* (1885), discussed in Part 1, testifies to the strength of his convictions in this regard.

Of course, it is doubtful that Wilde would have viewed all of the fictions in this study as works of art; he publicly disparaged the writings of several writers included here and it is true that the quality and style of these works varies widely. Moreover, many are parodies and satires that cruelly caricature Wilde, a man who acerbically referred to caricature as 'the tribute which mediocrity pays to genius'.³⁹ For the most part, however, Wilde patiently endured the parodies and satires that made sport of him, recognizing that any publicity was good publicity, and relying on the opportunity to present himself in a more favorable light once the world was looking. (A notable exception was Wilde's response to one of the works examined in Part 2, Robert Hichens's *The Green Carnation* (1895). Wilde recognized the real danger this novel posed to his reputation and departed from his usual good-natured tolerance of such works to publicly denounce the book.) Dennis Denisoff makes the point that some parodies and caricatures may well have worked in Wilde's favor. Although Denisoff states that parody is often used as a weapon to undermine the legitimacy of perceived cultural threats, he also notes that many parodists of aestheticism 'attempted to modify or revamp the subject while acknowledging its beneficial contributions to contemporary culture'.⁴⁰ This study examines caricatures and parodies of both types described by Denisoff, and his theories are specifically discussed in relation to Robert Hichens and Ada Leverson in the following pages.

Dangerous or advantageous, parody or psychological portrait, 'potboiler' or 'high brow' fiction, all of the works examined here are unique artistic and historical documents charting the course of Wilde's remarkable career through the 1880s and 1890s. Moreover, the largely unmined primary and secondary material has both yielded valuable new evidence for some existing perceptions of Wilde and revealed many significant details and connections that had previously 'fallen through the cracks'. The result is a study that, whatever other functions it performs, contains much previously unpublished information on Wilde and his world. I will give the last words of introduction to Wilde himself; I like to think that his reaction to this work might resemble his response to Mabel Wotton's *Word Portraits of Famous Writers* (1889):

> Few of the word-portraits in [this] book can be said to have been drawn by a great artist, but they are all interesting, and [the author] has certainly shown a wonderful amount of industry in collecting her references and grouping them . . . it is a delightful book . . . and by its means one can raise the ghosts of the dead, at least as well as the Psychical Society can.⁴¹

1
Aesthete 1877–1890

'I say, my dear fellow, do you mind mentioning to me whether you are the greatest humbug and charlatan on earth, or a genuine intelligence, one that has sifted things for itself?'

Nick Dormer to Gabriel Nash,
in Henry James, *The Tragic Muse*

In April 1877, the 22-year-old Oscar Wilde was thoroughly enjoying a cultural tour of Greece and Rome as one of a party led by his old Trinity College professor Reverend Dr John Pentland Mahaffy. However, he was traveling without leave from his Oxford college, Magdalen, and on his return he was promptly suspended for this impertinence. The young Wilde, ever the opportunist, decided to make the most of this unexpected recess by sampling the delights of the London season. He made his London début with a splash, attending the opening of the Grosvenor Gallery on the first of May in a spectacular coat cleverly designed to resemble a cello. The Prince of Wales, William Gladstone, and John Ruskin were present at this event. Though he soon resumed his studies at Oxford, Wilde's successful appearance at the Grosvenor opening and his bold review of the exhibition for the *Dublin University Magazine* mark the beginning of his career as a self-styled 'Professor of Aesthetics'. Remarkably, Wilde's parallel career as a character in fiction began almost simultaneously; within months of the Grosvenor opening, he had made memorable appearances in two novels. As it was Wilde's distinctive aesthetic style that first captured the imagination of contemporary authors, it is appropriate to begin this study with a brief review of that aestheticism.

It must first be noted that Wilde's early aesthetic attitude was the result of a synthesis of pre-existing modes of aestheticism with his own unique style. Aestheticism per se had emerged on the European continent in the early nineteenth century and embraced the principle of 'art for art's sake', a phrase that embodied the belief that it was not the place of art to instruct on social, political, or moral matters, but rather to exist autonomously. While this view of art was expounded in various ways by Immanuel Kant, Johann Schiller, Friedrich Schelling, and Johann Goethe in Germany and by Samuel Taylor Coleridge, Leigh Hunt, and Arthur Hallam in England, aesthetic philosophy first became popular in France with the writings of Benjamin Constant, Victor Cousins, and a new breed of novelists and poets who strongly influenced Wilde. These included Theophile Gautier (*Mademoiselle de Maupin*, 1835 and *Èmaux et Camées*, 1852), Charles Baudelaire (*Les Fleurs du Mal*, 1857), and Joris-Karl Huysmans (*À Rebours*, 1884). Add to the philosophies of these authors various elements from the teachings of Mahaffy and Wilde's Oxford mentors John Ruskin and Walter Pater, and one begins to glimpse something resembling Wildean aestheticism c. 1877. Mahaffy instilled Wilde with a life-long love of all things Greek, Ruskin extolled the beauty of the Italian Renaissance period and insisted that art must be a part of day-to-day life, and Pater advocated living a life of intense experience and sensation: 'To burn always with [a] hard gemlike flame, to maintain this ecstasy, is success in life'.[1]

The young Wilde also admired the quasimedieval aestheticism of the Pre-Raphaelite Brotherhood—the first exponents of English aestheticism from 1848—and their revolt against the contemporary canons of art and literature. It was this movement, along with other protoaesthetic groups, such as the Syncretics and the Spasmodics, that first inspired fictional portraits of aesthetic figures, with books like W. E. Aytoun's *Firmilian* in 1854 and Charles Kingsley's *Two Years Ago* in 1857. The 1870s saw the appearance of a long line of outrageously self-indulgent, effeminate, beauty-worshipping poets and painters in fiction, well before Wilde became the self-appointed figurehead of the British aesthetic movement. Amongst these characters are Ambergreen and Thornicroft in Mrs Margaret Hunt's *Thornicroft's Model* (1874), Henry James's eponymous *Roderick Hudson* (1875), and Mr Rose in W. H. Mallock's *The New Republic: or, Culture, Faith and Philosophy in an English Country House* (1877). However, from 1877 onward, as Wilde quickly became the face of British aestheticism, many fictional aesthetes began to bear an unmistakable resemblance to him.[2] Some of these early Wildean characterizations draw heavily upon pre-1877 aesthetic fictions and stereotypes and possess traits such as solemness, mercenariness, humorlessness, and heartlessness that by all reports were uncharacteristic of Wilde. The early fictions that more accurately reflect the particular style of aestheticism that Wilde developed at Oxford—an aestheticism that, despite its ostentatious trappings of lily-love and blue and white china, was definable by its genial good humor and healthy self-parody—are usually written by those who had the opportunity to observe Wilde at close quarters.

George Fleming
(Julia Constance Fletcher)
Mirage (1877)

One writer whose portrait of Wilde was based on close observation was his first 'fictionalizer', the American novelist, short-story writer, playwright, and translator Julia Constance Fletcher (1853–1938). Fletcher gave Wilde a memorable part as Claude Davenant in her three-volume, semiparodic novel *Mirage*, which was published, like her popular romance *The Nile Novel* (1876), under the pseudonym George Fleming.[3] The 20-year-old Fletcher had befriended Wilde and his Oxford colleague William Bouncer Ward when they were traveling in Italy with Professor Mahaffy; Fletcher spent some time horse-riding with Wilde and Ward in the Campagna.[4]

Mirage charts the adventures of the sensitive, cultured, and clever Constance Varley and her companions as they travel on horseback through Syria and Palestine. Fletcher incorporated the Wildean Davenant into her story as one of Varley's travel companions. Despite the speed with which she did this—the novel appeared in bookshops only months after they met in Italy—Davenant is a convincing, fully realized picture of the young Wilde. He is witty, insouciant, sagacious, and enigmatic, with an unmistakably Wildean physiognomy:

> That face was almost an anachronism. It was like one of Holbein's portraits, a pale, large-featured individual: a peculiar, an interesting countenance, of singularly mild yet ardent expression. Mr. Davenant was very young—probably not more than one or two and twenty; but he looked younger. He wore his hair rather long, thrown back, and clustering about his neck like the hair of a medieval saint. He spoke with rapidity, with peculiarly distinct enunciation; he spoke like a man who has made a study of expression. He listened like one accustomed to speak.[5]

Fletcher's Davenant displays all the intellectual enthusiasm and egotism of an unseasoned Oxford youth. He is wholly consumed by his own deliberations, at one point being so distracted as to forget to guide his horse. Davenant also delivers Pater-like paeans to intense emotions and sensations, rhapsodizes on the subject of ancient Greece, and spouts Pre-Raphaelite-style poetry in a distinctive voice redolent of Wilde's:

> 'I wrote some verses for your fan, for your Japanese fan, the other day,' he said dreamily; and after a moment, and as no one answered, he began to repeat some lines, half to himself, and in a low and singularly well modulated voice:
>
> > 'A flowery fan for a white flower hand
> > (*White cranes flying across the moon*)—
> > A breath of wind from a windless land—
> > A breath in the breathless noon.
> > Flowers that blossom—a wind that blows
> > (*White cranes sailing across the sky*)—
> > A sigh for the light love, the love that goes,
> > A flower for the loves that die!'[6]

Richard Ellmann has noted the echo in these verses of Wilde's ballad 'The Dole of the King's Daughter', written the previous year:

> What do they there so stark and dead?
> (There is blood upon her hand)
> Why are the lilies flecked with red?
> (There is blood on the river sand.)[7]

Fletcher's depiction of Wilde's Paterian pronouncements strikes a particularly authentic note. We know that Wilde discussed Pater's teachings with Fletcher; in a letter to Ward in July 1877, Wilde asks his friend for the 'name and address of Miss Fletcher . . . I have never sent her some articles of Pater's I promised her'.[8]

It is generally considered that Wilde's undergraduate travels served to hone his distinctive style of aestheticism to some degree and this is reflected in *Mirage*. As Ellmann observes, Fletcher's novel reflects Wilde's discovery of topographical symbols and cultural artifacts to encapsulate his aesthetic creed.[9] Davenant revels in the 'sumptuous life' and the 'splendid use of color and material' in the East, spending his last penny on an ancient piece of silk.[10]

Davenant also shares the young Wilde's fascination with Roman Catholicism, particularly his aesthetic, archaic conception of it; he is chiefly preoccupied with 'religious picture-frames and [the] "sincere" effects of painted glass'.[11] He identifies the 'Venus of the Greeks and the Virgin of the Italians' as the 'two stars of the material and the spiritual life'.[12] Indeed, to his companions, Davenant seems to encapsulate all the mystery of early Christianity; he appears to them as 'an early Christian brought down to date—and adapted—like a restored Church'.[13] Despite all his aesthetic excesses, however, Fletcher's Davenant has many Wildean charms; the comments made by the American Ferris most likely represent Fletcher's own assessment of her Oxford friend: 'Claude is a good sort of fellow . . . in spite of all his nonsense. He strikes me as a sort of epitomized Europe . . . I am curious to see if he will accomplish any thing. He has talent'.[14] Fletcher appears to have been diverted by the wit that underlined Wilde's aesthetic posturings, which is reflected in Davenant's drolleries:

> '[My sister's] house is pure Elizabethan, and they have furnished it with Louis Quinze chairs—those gilt things, with legs, don't you know. I'm sorry, for I was very fond of my sister . . . Still I do go down there every autumn for a few days, to shoot. Last year I shot the dog,' he added mildly.[15]

While Fletcher gives full scope to the aesthetic undergraduate's charms, she also gives a voice to those critical of aestheticism in the protestations of Mrs Gard, an embittered clergyman's wife:

> 'I have heard those young men talk of their carpets and their pictures, and laugh at this, and sneer at that, and talk of the proper understanding of life—Life! There is not one of you who knows what the word means. You call yourselves artists; I say you are nothing but lookers-on—people who stand by and weigh and criticise—'.[16]

The effect of Gard's comments is somewhat undermined, however, by her rancorous and narrow-minded nature. As the above commentary suggests, Davenant emerges as a largely sympathetic character.

Fletcher also offers us an entirely congruous picture of Wilde's early relations with women. Although Varley charms Davenant—he thinks that 'there is the unsatisfied soul of a poet in [her] nature'—the latter does not court her, quickly perceiving that she is in love with his friend Denis Lawrence.[17] He offers her instead 'a secret homage of [delicate and elusive] sentiment'.[18] Davenant's 'artistic' appreciation of Varley is typical of what we know from other sources as Wilde's distinctly asexual reaction to beautiful women; Davenant compares Varley to 'rare and exquisite Venetian glass—some thin, priceless, wave-tinted marvel of beauty'.[19] It is possible that Fletcher experienced this type of admiration from Wilde first-hand. Davenant's pronouncements on the subjects of love and marriage are also redolent of Wilde's; after placidly contemplating the prospect of marriage 'in the manner with which he would have discussed some old picture', Davenant philosophically concludes: 'There are many other emotions I wish to experience before I marry—emotions absolutely necessary to the artistic consummation of a life'.[20]

Shelley Salamensky has averred that such statements from Davenant may have been intended to suggest Wilde's sexual preference for men, a conclusion that appears to stem more from hindsight than from any evidence in *Mirage*.[21] I must also disagree with Salamensky's assertion that Fletcher implies Wilde had pedophilic inclinations. The only possible supporting text for Salamensky's reading is a scene in which Davenant comments on the beauty of a 'half-grown' Arabic boy who is acting as a model and assistant to his artist friend Lawrence. However, the context in which Davenant's brief comment is made hardly supports the suggestion of a pedophilic attraction. When the boy comes looking for Lawrence, Davenant drolly suggests that Lawrence invite him in to alleviate the sparseness of his friend's recently dismantled home:

> [Davenant] came in and looked about him disconsolately. 'I hate these changes. I wish I had not come in to spoil my old impression. Do have that boy in Lawrence. He's got a beautiful face, I noticed, and it will be something to look at,' with a reproachful glance at the bare walls.[22]

This is the only reference that Davenant makes to the boy, and it is a rather thin piece of evidence for asserting that Davenant (and by implication Wilde) had pedophilic tendencies. (Biographical evidence points to the likelihood that Wilde was most sexually attracted to physically mature young adults.[23]) Moreover, it is not Davenant but his friend Lawrence who plans to take the boy with him on his travels and there is no doubt cast over his motivation for doing so.

Mirage received a measure of critical acclaim and was favorably reviewed by Henry James (another fictionalizer of Wilde discussed in this section) in the *Nation* on June 7, 1877. James declared that, despite 'excessive slightness of subject and an unbusiness-like way of telling the story', '*Mirage* strikes us as very clever indeed'. He praised the novel's 'great charm of description . . . fineness of observation . . . wit in the conversations [and] constant facility and grace of style'. Despite making some disparaging remarks on the trend toward extravagantly aesthetic heroes in American fiction—reflecting his personal distaste for the excesses of aestheticism—James cannot help but admire Fletcher's portrait of Davenant: 'The sketch of the young Oxford neo-pagan, Davenant, is really brilliant'.[24] James, having attended the opening of the Grosvenor Gallery where Wilde had made his London debut just over a month before, most likely recognized Davenant as a portrait of Wilde. It is interesting to speculate that Fletcher's novel may have 'planted the seed' in James's mind for his own 1890 portrayal of Wilde in *The Tragic Muse*.

Salamensky argues, somewhat strangely in light of her dual homosexual/pedophilic reading, that Davenant 'woos' Varley and that this reflects 'a fantasy of being loved by Wilde'. Here, Salamensky may be closer to the mark; it does appear that Wilde harbored some romantic feelings toward Fletcher. He confided to Ward in August 1877 that Fletcher 'writes as cleverly as she talks: I am very much attracted by her in every way'.[25] Ward also stated in *Oscar Wilde: An Oxford Reminiscence* (1954) that the romantic nature of Fletcher's broken engagement to a Lord Wentworth had excited both their interests.[26] After their time together in Italy, Wilde continued to correspond with Fletcher and he dedicated his Newdigate Prize–winning poem 'Ravenna' to her in 1878. Upon winning the coveted award Wilde received the following letter of congratulations from Fletcher, which also announced her impending visit to Oxford:

> Mr. George Macmillan has told me the news about the Newdigate and I am so pleased—and so proud of you. I have been all this while trying to dis-entangle our engagements [Fletcher was traveling with her stepfather] so as to find 3 clear days for Oxford. We shall go up Sunday [emphasis in the original] morning by a train that leaves Paddington at 10 o'clock—and stay until Tuesday night. Can you send a card with the name of the hotel where we had better stop? And will you, if you see him, tell Mr. Pater of our arrival? I should write to him but I don't know how to sign myself. Mr. Benson sends most cordial congratulations.[27] I am so [emphasis in the original] glad. Yours always, Dudu Fletcher.[28]

The familiar 'Dudu' and expression of pride in Wilde's achievements indicate that the Fletcher/Wilde friendship was blossoming; it also appears that Wilde facilitated a meeting for Fletcher with Pater, the mentor he had encouraged her to read.[29] From all appearances, Wilde seemed to have been pleased with his depiction in *Mirage*. In his dedication of 'Ravenna' to Fletcher, Wilde deliberately identifies her as his friend and the author of *Mirage*, which suggests that he saw the publicity potential in fictional portraits from the first.

The Wilde/Fletcher friendship was to stand the test of time. Wilde continued to support Fletcher's writing career: as an editor he published her novel *The Truth about Clement Ker* as a serial in *The Woman's World* in 1888, and we know that he attended the first night of one of her plays shortly before his fall from grace.[30] A copy of *Mirage* was listed among Wilde's effects sold at an auction after he was declared bankrupt in 1895.

WALTER BESANT AND JAMES RICE
The Monks of Thelema (1877)

In the same year that Fletcher published *Mirage*, Walter Besant (1836–1901) and James Rice (1843–1882), coauthors of a series of popular novels that Rice conceptualized and Besant largely wrote, published their satirical fiction *The Monks of Thelema*.[31] Besant's and Rice's book documents the experiences of the 'brethren' of the Abbey of Thelema, a type of aesthetic commune devoted to the pursuit of 'high culture'. One of the brothers of this order is the distinctly Wildean Paul Rondelet, a recent graduate from Oxford, who has acquired a taste for Pater, Ruskin, Rossetti, Whistler, and modern French poetry. At Oxford, Rondelet also became a self-appointed 'Prophet' of the New Paganism, one who 'may now be found in London ... loung[ing] about sales of china ... and [worshipping] at the Grosvenor Gallery'.[32] While Rondelet wears a superficial disguise, comprising a moustache and a gratuitous eye-glass, his other physical characteristics and mannerisms are clearly borrowed from Wilde:

> He was rather a tall man, with a droop in his head; and he had long white fingers, which played plaintively about his face while he sat. He spoke in a low voice, as if exhausted by the effort of living among humans—[33]

As this book will demonstrate, large, white hands and a resonant, well-modulated voice in a Wildean character are often indicators that an author had observed Wilde first-hand. Rondelet's aesthetic attire is also characteristic:

> He was elaborately got up: a studied simplicity reigned in his neat and faultless dress; his grey kid gloves, the hat which was not too new and yet not too shabby, the plain black silk ribbon which did duty for a tie ... his smooth cheeks ... his dark hair parted down the middle with an ambrosial curl, half an inch long over his white brow, spoke of quintessential taste.[34]

Like the young Wilde, Rondelet has become widely known by his first name, writes Pre-Raphaelite poetry and is proficient in Greek, but has yet to prove himself in print. Unlike Julia Constance Fletcher, Besant and Rice paint an unsympathetic portrait of the young Wilde, often scathing in its satire. This appears to be due to the authors' lack of sympathy with the aesthetic movement; aesthetes are harshly depicted in the novel as an elitist 'school of prigs'. One of the characters in *Thelema* avers that proponents of aestheticism demonstrate

> 'the effect of too much cultivation on a weak brain . . . These young men have nothing new to say, and yet desire greatly to seem to have something new. So they invent a sort of jargon, and call it the only language for the expression of "higher thought!"'.[35]

Rondelet is selfish, conceited, and mercenary, with no scruples about taking advantage of his friends. His Oxford College is identified as 'Lothian', and Rondolet is a Lothario in every respect. He repeatedly passes off the ideas of others as his own and is referred to by members of his order as 'Brother Parolles', after the boastful, insincere pedant and pretender of Shakespeare's *All's Well that Ends Well*. True to Wilde's own definition of fiction in *The Importance of Being Earnest* ('[t]he good [end] happily, and the bad unhappily'),[36] Rondelet's attempt to create an elitist aesthetic journal fails miserably and he suffers a ritual humiliation at the hands of the woman he intended to marry for money. At the close of the novel Rondelet is forced to resign himself to the previously unthinkable; writing for the 'common herd' in the *Daily Press*.

Wilde appears to have taken Besant's and Rice's swipe at himself and the aesthetic movement with characteristic good humor and held no grudge against them. He told an American reporter five years later that he considered Besant and Rice 'great writers' and he referred to Besant in September 1887 as a writer 'of a very distinguished order'.[37] Indeed, Besant was well known as a man of letters, a novelist in his own right, a scholar, a philanthropist, and a driving force in professionalizing British letters and administering the Society of Authors. The lesser known Rice was a Cambridge graduate who was called to the bar in 1871. Rice met Besant through his short-lived publication *Once a Week* and their literary partnership lasted ten years until Rice's death in 1882.

It appears that Wilde was acquainted with Besant at some point. Coulson Kernahan records that 'about the time when Wilde's star was culminating' he heard him tell a story in which he spoke intimately of Besant, using his Christian name.[38] However, in a letter to J. S. Little on August 1, 1888, regarding the unsatisfactory seating arrangements at a Society of Authors dinner, the following comment from Wilde on Besant does not appear friendly: 'it would perhaps be too much to expect that the universal benevolence of Besant should condescend to details [like seating arrangements]. For philanthropy so wide as his, fiction is the proper place'.[39] Possibly Wilde was reacting to Besant blocking his election as a member of the Savile Club; in 1888 the latter entered his name in the Candidates' Book of the Club to speak on Wilde's proposed membership.[40] A further comment on Besant by Wilde in 1890s 'The Critic as Artist'—that 'Providence and Mr. Walter Besant have exhausted the obvious [subjects for creative writing]'— also appears to suggest that Wilde's formerly high opinion of Besant had dwindled substantially.[41] Wilde later reviewed this statement in a letter to the editor of the *Pall Mall Gazette* on August 27, 1891, but only to acknowledge the 'regrettable' fact that

> [o]ne has merely to read the ordinary English newspapers and the ordinary English novels of our day to become conscious of the fact that it is only the obvious that occurs, and only the obvious that is written about.[42]

Whether or not there was some 'bad blood' between the two men, Wilde would have been unimpressed with Besant's increasing proclivity for writing realistic, moralistic, and didactic fiction after Rice's death. In 1900, while writing of being seen by a former friend with a handsome male companion, the disgraced Wilde compared the old friend's 'terrible' judgmental smile to something out of 'one of Besant's novels'.[43] He could have made a similar comment about Besant being knighted in 1895, the same year that Wilde was convicted and imprisoned for 'gross indecency'.

* * *

The year after *The Monks of Thelema* was first published, Wilde graduated from Magdalen College with a rare double first and the above-mentioned Newdigate Prize for poetry. In the following year, 1879, he moved to London into lodgings with his artist friend Frank Miles. On his arrival in London, Wilde embarked upon a major self-promotion drive, determined to be noticed by the right people. The artist Louise Jopling recalls Wilde paying her a visit around this time with a large snake twisted around his neck.⁴⁴ Such extraordinary antics, combined with his sparkling wit and engaging conversation, soon won Wilde a place in London's elite intellectual and artistic circles. He met Gladstone, Asquith, and Balfour and befriended James Whistler, Lillie Langtry, Ellen Terry, and Sarah Bernhardt. Wilde was at first famous for being famous. The Polish actress Helen Modjeska found his celebrity remarkable: 'What has he done, this young man . . . that one meets him everywhere? Oh yes he talks well, but what has he done? He has written nothing, he does not sing or paint or act—he does nothing but talk. I do not understand'.⁴⁵

As many commentators have observed, Wilde's slowness to exercise his literary powers, combined with his self-confessed devotion to self-creation and dramatization, had the unfortunate initial effect of his being widely lampooned as a literary lightweight or a fraud. As Arthur Nethercot notes, 'He had advertised his poses so successfully that almost no one would believe that anything he said or did could be genuine'.⁴⁶ In the 1877 burlesque *The Grasshopper*, Wilde was satirized in a dance routine alongside James Whistler and Frank Miles. In James Albery's 1880 satiric play *Where's the Cat?*, he was mercilessly parodied as the aesthetic writer Scott Ramsay.⁴⁷ Most conspicuously, Du Maurier's *Punch* drawings poked fun at Wilde with the poet Jellaby Postlethwaite and his friends Maudle the painter and Prigsby the art critic (the last two also often bore resemblances to Whistler and Swinburne). Although Du Maurier publicly averred that Postlethwaite was not specifically a caricature of Wilde, the public certainly took him to be one. Wilde himself professed to believe that he was the original of Maudle and that Postlethwaite was a composite of his aesthetic friends.⁴⁸ Leonée Ormond and others have persuasively argued that Du Maurier did not imitate Wilde but that the latter cleverly assumed aspects of the Du Maurier characters in order to capitalize on the publicity.⁴⁹

A. T. D.

'O'Flighty' (1879)

The year 1879's 'O'Flighty', which appeared in the *Oxford and Cambridge Undergraduate's Journal* on February 27, is the first of three satires included in this study that were written by Oxford undergraduates. The author was identified only as A. T. D. and—to the present writer's knowledge—has never been positively identified.⁵⁰

The story is set in Oxford where we first see the aesthetic student Henton out walking with his pragmatic friend Montacute, the narrator. During their stroll, Henton is surprised to see O'Flighty—a play on Wilde's middle name 'O'Flahertie'—fraternizing with the 'ultra-Philistine' Deakin. (It is later revealed that Deakin and O'Flighty met at a lunch at Magdalen College—Wilde's *Alma Mater*—where O'Flighty had remarked: 'how hard it is to live up to the level of blue china', alluding to a famous remark of Wilde's from that period.) Henton introduces O'Flighty, who is wearing 'a yellow overcoat, soft hat, and rather untidy hair', to Montacute, who already knows of the aesthete by reputation.[51] Thrown together with O'Flighty and at a loss for conversation, Montacute makes reference to the news of the day: the British invasion of Zululand. O'Flighty languidly expresses his indifference to the subject, adding in response to Montacute's question that he has not checked that day's telegrams posted at the Oxford Union Society: 'I never look at telegrams . . . what they say is mostly untrue, and they really are so very uninteresting'. O'Flighty goes on to complain of the lack of 'Higher Culture' in an army that would fight with savages painted in red and yellow; Henton facetiously suggests that olive green might be less disagreeable. When O'Flighty goes on to lament the offensive smell of primitive tribes, the unaesthetic Deakin sarcastically proposes that O'Flighty

> 'purchase a few cases of eau-de-Cologne or otto of roses, and send them with a polite note to the Zulu: "Private—I beg your pardon,—Major General O'Flighty presents his compliments and the accompanying few bottles of essence to King Cetewayo, and requests that he will see that his men's handkerchiefs are properly scented before going into action". But I forgot; they probably haven't any. Nevermind, he might administer it anyway, inside or out!'[52]

Deakin also suggests that O'Flighty might send Cetewayo a poem 'on a sheet of vellum with serene mediaeval illuminations, beginning with O'Flighty's lines: "Mighty indeed thy glory, yet to me, / Barbaric King!"' These are lines from Wilde's poem 'Ravenna', which won the Newdigate Prize the year before 'O'Flighty' was published.

Henton proceeds to read a poem he has written about the fleeting nature of youth and happiness that meets with an unenthusiastic reception from his listeners. When Montacute ventures that he found the meaning of the poem difficult to discern, O'Flighty avers that '[t]rue poetry has no meaning'. When Deakin declares that Rossetti's poetry is immoral, O'Flighty is incensed. The aesthete insists that 'the true poet must be immoral', asserting, '[w]hen men and women have attained to the Higher Culture they will be able to receive Rossetti, but not before'. The philistinic Deakin also fails to appreciate O'Flighty's favorite 'Early Florentine School' of art and likes to sing drinking songs. When Deakin begins to sing a song of his own composition O'Flighty can stand no more and quickly escapes unnoticed. By way of explanation, Henton says,

> 'I don't think O'Flighty cares much for vocal music . . . I went with him to a concert last year. I think it was one of Russell's, anyhow the singing was very good, and he seemed to be listening attentively, at least he kept his eyes on the singer all the time, but when she had finished, he said in a distressed tone, "How dreadful it is to have to look at a woman with such a painfully unaesthetic pose!"'[53]

Whoever A. T. D. may have been, 'O'Flighty' offers a rare insight into how Wilde was perceived by his Oxford contemporaries and effectively illustrates the myth making that surrounded him from his earliest days of celebrity. Like Besant and Rice in *The Monks of Thelema*, A. T. D. was also somewhat prophetic about Wilde's future in journalism. O'Flighty conjectures that 'if it comes to the worst [after taking my degree] I think I shall write for the *Times*'. Although Wilde never wrote for that publication, his career as a journalist during the last half of the 1880s certainly kept the wolf from the door before the spectacular success of his society plays.

George Bernard Shaw

Immaturity (1879)

Wilde's fourth fictional manifestation appeared courtesy of a fellow young Irishman in London, George Bernard Shaw (1856–1950). In 1879, the 23-year-old Shaw, who was two years younger than Wilde, included a portrait of the latter as Patrick Hawkshaw in his first novel, *Immaturity*.[54] Although this book remained unpublished until 1930, by which time it had been partially revised by the mature Shaw (despite his avowal to 'make no attempt to correct the work of the apprentice with the hand of the master'[55]), it is included here in accordance with its first date of completion. However, as some of Shaw's later emendations did relate to the character of Hawkshaw, both the original manuscript and the 1930 published version will be considered here.

In 1879, the young Shaw was yet to win the recognition as a playwright, critic, and novelist that he was later to achieve. Having abandoned his job as a clerk in a Dublin estate office, Shaw had moved to London in 1876 and promptly embarked upon a rigorous program of self-education, largely conducted at the British Museum's Reading Room, while living on a family allowance. *Immaturity* was Shaw's first attempt to make his mark in the literary world, and he began work on it just three months after Wilde first settled in London in December 1878. Contemporary publishers were unimpressed by its alternately serious and satirical depictions of English society, written in a style that Stanley Weintraub has called 'reminiscent of Dickens and anticipatory of Gissing'[56]; it was rejected by ten publishing houses between November 1879 and October 1881. Nicholas Grene observes that while the book, with its Dickensian influences and inter-linked subplots, conforms to the conventions of the multivolume Victorian novel, the original manuscript is 'heavy-handed . . . formal [and] full of long and contorted sentences'. The published version that appeared some fifty years later, edited by the more experienced Shaw, is noticeably more polished.[57]

To Shaw scholars, the main interest of the novel and its preface is autobiographical. As is the case with many first novels, the protagonist— in this instance the earnest, diligent, and plain-speaking clerk-turned-secretary Robert Smith—is clearly derivative of the author. Smith, like Shaw, detests his prosaic clerical life and eventually breaks away from it, but never loses the pragmatic outlook imbued by his early experience. While Smith is Shaw's principal self-portrait in *Immaturity*, the industrious artist Cyril Scott and the eminently practical seamstress Harriet Russell also display Shavian attributes. Russell lives in Smith's Islington boarding house and he first regards her as a romantic interest; but love fails to blossom. The two boarders become friends and are eventually drawn into the same circle of aesthetic poets, painters, and philosophers via their respective associations with Halket Grosvenor's country estate, Perspective Park. Smith becomes secretary to Grosvenor's friend, an Irish MP, and Russell, through Grosvenor's housekeeper, meets and marries another of Grosvenor's friends, the artist Cyril Scott. At Perspective Park, Grosvenor plays host to regular aesthetic gatherings of 'promiscuous composition':

> felt hats, tweed and velveteen clothes, long hair, music on Sundays, pictures of the nude figure, literary women, and avowals of agnosticism . . . free expression of opinion [prevailed]—[58]

Just as there is more than one character in *Immaturity* who demonstrates a Shavian influence, there is also more than one personality who displays aspects of Wilde at these aesthetic gatherings. Among the Easter Sunday assemblage at Perspective, we briefly glimpse

Macartney, an 'Analysis of Genius man', with Wilde's 'studied negligence of pose', 'sonorous voice', and 'studied phrasing and accent'. We also see the affected, long-haired poet Bolingbroke, who plays a piano piece in the form of a 'study for the loose wrist'.[59] However, it is the poet, journalist, and exponent of aestheticism Patrick Hawkshaw who represents Shaw's most unequivocal and complex portrait of Wilde. Hawkshaw is known as a 'fine gentleman' and is a prominent member of the Perspective circle. Despite his Irish name, Hawkshaw calls himself an Englishman and is a lazy, gossipy charmer full of 'poetic nonsense' who has a passion for 'pagan deities' and all things Greek. Hawkshaw's sonnets, such as his 'The New Endymion', are lauded by Grosvenor's set (Wilde's composed his poem 'Endymion' in 1878, the year before Shaw began work on *Immaturity*). As with the young Wilde, recently arrived in London, there is much conjecture in artistic circles as to what the talented young Hawkshaw will do next. Grosvenor recounts the rumor that Hawkshaw will 'edit the Elizabethan dramatists', but in fact the aesthete's next undertaking is to be a controversial interpretation of Hamlet.[60]

He is often talked about, yet Hawkshaw, like Wilde, is not universally admired. Like Helen Modjeska, at least one of Grosvenor's guests is bewildered as to the young Hawkshaw's claim to fame and accepted authority on subjects 'which have baffled the maturest intellects'. The unaesthetic and plain-speaking Irish MP Woodward thinks him an untalented and impertinent young 'puppy'. Excerpts from Hawkshaw's Greek translations are considered by one aristocratic dowager to be '[un]fit to be read in a respectable house', and the poet's frequent use of compound adjectives divides his listeners 'between admiration for his genius and regret that they had been induced to listen to him'.[61] Wilde-like, Hawkshaw easily disarms his detractors with his friendly banter, lavish compliments, and affable compliance with the harshest criticisms.

For every detractor, however, Hawkshaw has a gushing disciple to hang upon his every Wildean pronouncement: 'your [peacock blue] dress . . . was a daydream'; '[w]hat an accursed thing it is to have relatives!'; 'I am always in earnest until three o'clock, when I assume my cap, bells, and cardcase'.[62] In stark contrast to Smith and the semi-Shavians Scott and Russell, the thought of hard work makes Hawkshaw shudder. He speaks proudly of never having worked steadily in his life, being too sensitive a creature to endure the 'spectre [of] Drudgery', and he is philosophically resigned to a life of debt.[63]

Perhaps the most Wildean of Hawkshaw's utterances are his cynicisms on the compromising effect of marriage upon the individual; many of these are inspired by the impending wedding of Scott and the seamstress Russell. Hawkshaw's relation to Russell is of particular interest here. At first wary of the dispassionate and utilitarian dressmaker, who is immune to his whimsical charms, Hawkshaw is soon won over by her staunch individuality and intellectual sagacity. The Shavian Russell also comes to appreciate Hawkshaw's admirable qualities of good humor and tolerance, despite her aversion to his studied triviality. This aspect of the Russell/Hawkshaw relationship accurately reflects the actual relationship between Shaw and Wilde, which is examined below.

It is Hawkshaw's conduct in relation to another woman, the notorious flirt and socialite Isabella Woodward, daughter of the Irish MP, which casts the harshest light upon his character. Heavily in debt because of his extravagance during the London season, Hawkshaw engineers a romance with Woodward, already a friend, with a view to marrying her for her money; a scenario that had already been devised for a Wildean character by Besant and Rice in *The Monks of Thelema*. Hawkshaw appears to have succeeded in this design when Woodward encourages his attentions and gives him jewelry in order to alleviate his immediate financial difficulties. However, Woodward soon tires of Hawkshaw's fulsome professions of love and practice of trading on the strength of their relationship. When she severs their attachment, Hawkshaw quickly devises a way to simultaneously protect his social standing, solve his financial difficulties, and revenge himself on Woodward by writing an allusive poem, 'A Song of Bent Branch and Broken Laurel', in which the central character, a version of himself, is the victim of a woman's treachery. Henceforth, in order to promote gossip and book sales, Hawkshaw shrewdly assumes the demeanor of a 'broken man' for public appearances. One of his followers describes the transformation:

> 'No more arty ties and all that. He has set up a suit of dead black, long skirts, broad collars, and a black stock. His coat and head look as if a brush hadn't touched them for six weeks. No gloves; and for all that you can see of his cuffs, he might as well have no shirt. He is a regular scarecrow; and he has turned miser as well; travels third class; walks long distances; and comes into a drawing room with boots on as big a gas meters, all splattered with mud'.[64]

To complete the melancholic effect, Hawkshaw publishes his poem 'in a black kid cover bearing neither ornament nor inscription . . . [with leaves] of rough, heavy paper with untrimmed edges'.[65] The book is issued as an expensive 'limited' edition. After Hawkshaw succeeds in making Woodward's 'treachery' the talk of the town, society cannot snap up his book fast enough, and the poet makes a massive profit. Despite this windfall, however, it is only when Mr Woodward offers to buy back his daughter's jewelry that Hawkshaw redeems it from the pawnbrokers and returns it, with the barefaced lie that the gems had never left his possession.

Such unsavory revelations about Hawkshaw's character appear to have their root in Shaw's early mistrust of Wilde. It is not known when Shaw and Wilde first met. In his essay 'My Memories of Oscar Wilde', included as an appendix in Frank Harris's 1916 biography *Oscar Wilde: His Life and Confessions*,[66] Shaw could not recall any contact in Ireland, although, like most Dubliners, he knew of the Wilde family.[67] It is possible that Shaw was inspired to create the character of Hawkshaw after observing Wilde at the British Museum Reading Room, where Shaw was in the habit of writing. Wilde applied for a reader's ticket there on March 1, 1879, the very same month that Shaw began work on *Immaturity*.[68] Shaw and Wilde met at least once at one of Wilde's mother's 'at homes' in London between 1879 and 1885; Shaw recalled that Lady Wilde was good to him in those 'desperate days'. Shaw also referred to his sister Lucy's 'innocent conquest' of both Oscar and his brother Willie; Wilde attended Lucy's 'wedding tea' in November 1887.[69]

Wilde's and Shaw's early meeting at the home of Wilde's mother, related by Shaw in his appendix to Harris's book, appears to have set the tone for future relations between the two men. Shaw recalled, '[Wilde] came up and spoke to me with an evident intention of being specially kind to me. We put each other out frightfully; and this odd difficulty persisted between us to the very last'.[70] In *Immaturity* this uneasy relationship is reflected in an uncomfortable scene between Smith and Hawkshaw, when both men meditate 'on the power that each possessed in disconcerting the other'.[71]

The 23-year-old Shaw's portrait of Hawkshaw suggests that as a young man he felt a degree of resentment and suspicion toward Wilde, two years his senior, that was symptomatic of a latent rivalry. In order to understand Shaw's reaction to Wilde, one must appreciate that, in light of their common aspirations and significantly divergent natures, a sense of competition between the two men was perhaps inevitable. In 1879, both Shaw and Wilde were young Protestant Dubliners attempting to establish a literary reputation in London. Both were egotistical individualists and paradoxical humorists. Both were to become eloquent public speakers and witty subverters of conventional Victorian mores who were continually mocked in the press. Both worked as reviewers; from 1885 to 1888 their unsigned reviews in the *Pall Mall Gazette* were often mistaken for each other's.[72] Both developed an interest in Socialism; Wilde attended a meeting of Shaw's Fabian Society on July 6, 1888. Robert Ross later told Shaw that this Fabian Society meeting inspired Wilde to write 'The Soul of Man under Socialism' (1891). (Shaw also produced an idiosyncratic tract on Socialism, 'The Quintessence of Ibsenism' [1890], which probably influenced Wilde's essay.[73]) Both also promulgated controversial ideas about dress; Shaw's being ostentatiously practical, Wilde's ostentatiously flamboyant. Finally, both were to win acclaim as London playwrights in the 1890s.

One might conclude from this striking list of similarities that Shaw and Wilde would be 'kindred spirits'; however, one must also consider their equally remarkable catalogue of contrasts. Shaw's upbringing was impoverished and middle class; Wilde grew up in the elitist milieu of Dublin's fashionable Merrion Square. Shaw left school at 15 and took charge of his own education; Wilde emerged from the prestigious Magdalen College at Oxford with a double first and the illustrious Newdigate Prize. Shaw felt shy and awkward among society, and always considered himself an 'outsider'; Wilde placed himself at the center of every social gathering and quickly charmed his most strident critics. Shaw, intensely public spirited, utilized literature to propagate strongly held beliefs and induce change. Wilde, unabashedly selfish, purported to value style over substance and habitually mocked those who dispensed 'good advice'. Shaw took many years to earn his reputation by sheer determination and hard work; the indolent Wilde achieved fame with a combination of audacious self-publication and brief bursts of productivity. That Shaw should feel some resentment toward Wilde under these circumstances is not surprising, especially in 1879; in that year Wilde had become the talk of the town less than a year after graduating from Oxford, whereas the disadvantaged and industrious Shaw had yet to make any impact on his adopted city (and in fact did not make a regular income from his pen until 1885).[74] As Shaw reflected in 1916, 'Oscar seems to have said: "I will love nobody: I will be utterly selfish; and I will be not merely a rascal but a monster; and you shall forgive me everything"'.[75] Hawkshaw's lackadaisical approach to work, starkly contrasted with that of the hardworking artist Scott, reflects Shaw's sense of injustice at Wilde's early success. Scott complains,

> 'It is all very well for Hawkshaw, who turns out cheap wares by priming himself up now and then for a desperate fit of working, and gets credit for it all the moment it is before the public, to take things easily. It is

very different with me; for I have drudged year after year until I have very little patience left for anything but work. If it was easy work, that could be dashed off by the help of a few tricks in a fit of enthusiasm, like his poetry, a man might keep his nerves robust at it'.[76]

Shaw's envy of Wilde can also be glimpsed in Smith's reaction to Hawkshaw's charismatic power. Smith, who is highly 'conscious of his own deficiencies in polite intercourse', envies Hawkshaw's 'careless gaiety', and he wonders at the poet's composure before delivering his translation of a Greek play to a crowded society drawing room: 'the mere imagination of having to accomplish [this task] made Smith's knees knock together'.[77]

Hawkshaw also displays the exaggerated arrogance that Shaw always disliked in Wilde and delighted in debunking. Shaw described Wilde in 1916 as 'a very prime specimen of the sort of fellow-townsman I most loathed . . . the Dublin snob'.[78] Patrick Hawkshaw is certainly an elitist; when he learns that the artist Scott is in love with the working-class dressmaker Russell, he automatically assumes that there can be 'no question' of marriage; the Shavian Smith promptly rises to Russell's defense and praises her as 'an exceptional woman' that Scott would be lucky to marry.[79]

Shaw's resentment of the young Wilde's burgeoning celebrity, and growing reputation as a commentator on the arts, is frequently evident in *Immaturity*. Shaw felt that Wilde was ill-qualified as an arbiter of artistic taste and believed his own claim to this role was a more justified one: 'Wilde started as an apostle of Art; and in that capacity he was a humbug'.[80] Wilde's pronouncements on music, which he knew relatively little about, particularly irritated Shaw, who prided himself on his musical knowledge and later earned a reputation as one of London's most respected music critics at the *World*. In *Immaturity* it is revealed that Hawkshaw's musical knowledge is limited, despite his pretensions of wisdom on the subject.

Shaw's advocacy of temperance is also reflected in the artist Cyril Scott's disgust at Hawkshaw's frequent consumption of alcohol. When Hawkshaw bemoans his lack of funds and motivation to write, Scott encourages him to curb his drinking. Hawkshaw, who habitually drinks before breakfast, replies that '[b]randy is absolutely necessary to make my ideas flow . . . Better live ten years drunk and write a hundred poems, than sixty years sober and compile soullessly for the publishers'.[81] As an old man Shaw referred to Wilde's death at 46 as the price he paid for 'Immortality as a Talker on Alcohol'; whereas he, always abstemious, was still active at 83 years of age.[82]

Richard Dietrich notes that the Wildean Hawkshaw is also unfavorably contrasted with the Shavian Smith in his relations with Isabella Woodward:

> Hawkshaw's letter [to Isabella] is a florid affair . . . betraying a weakness of character that disgusted her. [A letter from Smith to Isabella], on the other hand . . . [is] a business-like and matter-of-fact account . . . [which] reveals to Isabella the unusual probity of her father's secretary, whereupon she begins 'a new romance [with Smith], based on respect for virtue'.[83]

Dietrich also sees a comparison between Wilde and Shaw in the latter's contrasting of Hawkshaw's and Scott's divergent approaches to art:

> Scott's posing is the result of an aggravated pride and sensibility, behind which there is real talent, whereas the posing of Hawkshaw is the result of an incorrigible, if entertaining, dishonesty. Scott is earnest where Hawkshaw is gaily deceiving. Scott plays the role of artist in order to defend himself against doubts of his talent, whereas Hawkshaw assumes the disguise of artist purely for the delight of impersonation and its social rewards.[84]

This habit of comparing himself (or a fictional substitute) with Wilde (or a fictional substitute) and emerging the 'better man' reflects Shaw's simultaneous identification with, and rejection of, Wilde. This may also be inferred by the name Shaw chose for his Wildean poet. The addition of the word 'hawk' in front of Shaw's own name has led Michael Holroyd to suggest that Shaw saw Wilde as a version of himself 'gone wrong'. The word 'hawk' can imply a rapacious person or someone who relates gossip too freely; Shaw's Hawkshaw displays both of these traits.[85] Dietrich reads the 'hawk' in Hawkshaw as an indicator of Shaw's disapproval of the type of artist who commercially 'hawks' his artist status, rather than letting his work speak for itself.[86] On the other hand, the word 'hawk' can also evoke the impression of power and far-sightedness, traits that Shaw would have undoubtedly glimpsed in the young Wilde.

There is very little physical description of Hawkshaw in the first published version of *Immaturity* (1930). What description there is conforms to the common practice of deflecting potential accusations of libel by giving the derivative character contrasting attributes—Hawkshaw has a 'slight figure . . . and voice no more than ordinarily resonant'—while including enough distinctively Wildean characteristics to suggest a portrait. Shaw's poet speaks 'rhythmically' and wears a conspicuously Wildean costume: 'a long black coat, dove-coloured trousers, primrose gloves, and a bronze-hued scarf, fastened by a brooch representing a small green beetle with red eyes' (Wilde often wore a green scarab ring). Hawkshaw also has Wilde's 'refined affectation' and distinctive manner of looking languidly through half-closed eyes.[87]

There is considerably more physical description of Hawkshaw in the original manuscript for *Immaturity*. In addition to making many minor improvements to the text in 1930, Shaw also decided to cut two chapters from the original manuscript, as significant portions of these pages had been eaten by mice![88] An inspection of the rodent-ravaged sections of the manuscript, currently held in the National Library of Ireland, reveals that—although the damage to the two chapters is extensive—there is a lengthy scene featuring Patrick Hawkshaw and Cyril Scott that remains intact.[89] The scene in question appears in the original chapter XII, when Hawkshaw visits Scott's studio. When the artist opens the door to Hawkshaw, Shaw provides the extensive physical description of the latter than is lacking in the 1930 published version. Hawkshaw is described as

> a man of about thirty years of age [Wilde was then 25], very thin with long hair, and effeminately handsome features in which refinement and intelligence were contrasted with brutishness in the mouth, and languor in the eyes. He was taller than Cyril Scott, but as the latter grasped his white damp hand in his own knotty brown one, the superior energy of the artist became remarkably apparent.[90]

The long hair and effeminately handsome features, the duality of noble upper and grosser lower facial features and the white hands are all redolent of Wilde. Once inside Scott's studio, Hawkshaw proceeds to complain about the effrontery of an actor who has presumed to question his interpretation of Shakespeare's *Hamlet*. Hawkshaw's assertion that the only function of an actor is 'to lend his substance to the embodiment of a poet's thought' recalls Wilde's similarly dismissive comments about actors, whom he frequently referred to as 'puppets'.[91]

During the course of their conversation, Scott frequently criticizes Hawkshaw's drinking (Hawkshaw argues that he is 'never drunk, and some of the greatest poets alive are never sober') and finds further fault with Hawkshaw's poetry, which he contends is repetitious in form and in its incessant depiction of dream-like, unrealistic women: 'brass and clay creatures with serpents in [their] hair, and feet that weave spells, and deadly cruel eyes, and bestiality in proportion to the brandy you drink before writing'. Hawkshaw, in response to Scott's suggestion that he has never cared about an actual woman in his life, asserts that it is his romantic mistreatment at the hands of women that has driven him to drink: 'Look at me. Look at what I am, at what they have left me'. When Scott avers that 'no such woman ever existed', Hawkshaw flippantly replies: 'You have been reading a lot of reviews, or you are going to be married' (Scott is indeed about to be married to Harriet Russell).[92] Hawkshaw appears to delight in baiting the serious Scott in this manner:

> 'When I see you lying on your back there half asleep, destroying yourself with liquor, I feel as if it would be an act of charity to sting you to display a flash of real feeling, in order to let you know what real feeling is like' [said Scott].
> 'Ah!' said Hawkshaw, with a languid smile, 'what a glorious thing it is to be young. I assure you it quite rouses me only to contemplate your obstreperous energy. Have you any more brandy?'[93]

Hawkshaw's parting words to Scott in this scene are particularly interesting. When Scott takes a last shot at Hawkshaw's poetry, Hawkshaw offers to write a poem for Russell 'in my old milk and water style, which you used to swear by when we were both friendly obscurities'.[94] Perhaps here Shaw was recalling their early Dublin days; the Shavian Scott, who is so irritated by the Wildean Hawkshaw, is strangely softened by this allusion. Perhaps it was this connection that compelled the older Shaw to cut this scene from the final version of the novel in 1930; it is, after all, a scene that could easily have been transposed into another chapter. Alternately, after the Wilde scandal of 1895, Shaw may have felt uncomfortable about including Scott's suggestion that Hawkshaw had never cared about a woman, particularly in light of the fact that one of Wilde's sons from his marriage to Constance was still living in 1930.

As for Shaw's revisions regarding Hawkshaw in the non-nibbled portions of the original manuscript, there are relatively few, mostly of a minor nature.[95] There are, however, some alterations to the text that reinforce Hawkshaw's Wildean origins. For example, Shaw gave Hawkshaw several more *mots* on such typical Wildean subjects as individuality, the middle classes, the English education system, and married life. One such addition reads: 'our tragedy [as artists is that we] are unique and beyond class; but we all have middle class relatives, especially wives'.[96] Another alteration may also be telling. The 'Greek tragedy' recited by Hawkshaw in chapter VIII of the 1930 published text was formerly specified as 'Oedipus' in the original manuscript. This may have been intended by the young Shaw as a tongue-in-cheek allusion to Wilde's close relationship with his mother, which he witnessed first-hand at Lady Wilde's 'at homes'. Of course, this can only be speculated upon, but Shaw must have had some reason for removing the reference in 1930; it is possible he thought better of a youthful joke that was in questionable taste.

Were we to take Shaw at his word in his 1921 preface to *Immaturity*, which leaves the reader with the impression that no significant alterations have been made to the original text, we would be misled in more than the nature of Shaw's revisions. Shaw's prefatory essay also contends that, while '[m]any of the characters in this novel [owe] something to persons I [have] met', there is only one character who is an actual portrait, that being the artist Cyril Scott, who Shaw avers was based on the landscape painter Cecil Lawson.[97] In fact, there are at least two other 'actual portraits' in the novel. Apart from his distinctive portrayal of Wilde, Shaw later admitted that the character of a dancer with whom Smith becomes smitten—Bernardine di Sangallo—was an outright depiction of Ermina Pertoldi, a dancer Shaw admired in the 1870s.[98] He even decided to dispense with the alias and revert to the dancer's original name in the published version of the book. Shaw explains his reluctance to identify the originals of his characters in the 1930 preface to *Immaturity*, postulating that if he did this the historical person would be identified with the fictional character until their 'dying day, with heaven knows how much more scandalous invention added to account for my supposed intimate knowledge of [their] character'.[99] It was most likely the prospect of 'scandalous invention' regarding his relationship with the disgraced Wilde that deterred Shaw from ever identifying Wilde's likeness in *Immaturity*, as he later did with the portraits of Lawson and Pertoldi.

It is also possible that Shaw was reluctant to identify Wilde in his first novel because of the unsympathetic nature of the portrait; in spite of all of Shaw's objections to Wilde, he grew to respect the latter's talents and courtesies to him as the years went by. Shaw once said that although he was 'in no way predisposed' to like Wilde, the latter *earned* his regard.[100] Descriptions of some of their meetings—Shaw estimated that there were not more than twelve before Wilde's death—contain glimpses of fellow-feeling, often stemming from the ability of both men to laugh at themselves. Shaw recalled a pleasant chance meeting at a naval exhibition in Chelsea in February 1890, which diffused much of the tension that had characterized their previous interactions:

> I don't know why I went or why Wilde went; but we did; and the question of what the devil we were doing in that gallery tickled us

both. It was my sole experience of Oscar's wonderful gift as a raconteur . . . for once our meeting was a success; and I understood why Morris, when he was dying slowly, enjoyed a visit from Wilde more than from anybody else—[101]

Shaw's opinion of Wilde appears to have improved significantly from the mid-1880s; he was particularly impressed when Wilde was the only literary man in London bold enough to sign a controversial 1887 petition he had drafted, proposing a reprieve for the Chicago anarchists sentenced to death for rioting the year before. 'It was a completely disinterested act on his part; and it secured my distinguished consideration for him for the rest of his life'.[102] Shaw also appreciated Wilde's respect for his talents, at a time when the rest of London was treating Shaw as something of a joke:

> Wilde on his part made a point of recognising me as a man of distinction by his manner, and repudiating the current estimate of me as a mere jester. This was not the usual reciprocal-admiration trick. I believe he was sincere, and felt indignant at what he thought was a vulgar underestimate of me; and I had the same feeling about him.[103]

Shaw returned Wilde's courtesy by defending the latter against his critics and publicly professing his admiration for Wilde's stylish and amusing reviews and society plays, with the single exception of *The Importance of Being Earnest*, which he thought heartless (Shaw conceded, however, 'the force and daintiness of [the play's] wit').[104] Shaw later stated that '[c]omedy: the criticism of morals and manners *viva voce*, was [Wilde's] forte. When he settled down to that he was great'.[105] Shaw grew to see his countryman as an ally in the fight against British philistinism and its drama: '[o]ur school is the Irish school; and Wilde is doing us good service in teaching the theatrical public that "a play" may be a playing with ideas instead of a feast of sham emotions'.[106] The two men exchanged presentation copies of their books and Shaw sent Wilde tickets for the first night of his play *Arms and the Man* on April 21, 1894.

Three extant letters further demonstrate the respectful relationship that grew between the two men. The first, from Wilde to Shaw, is postmarked February 23, 1893 and refers to Shaw's 1891 publication, *The Quintessence of Ibsenism*, the central tenets of which probably influenced Wilde's 'Soul of Man under Socialism' as stated above:

> My dear Shaw, You have written well and wisely and with sound wit on the ridiculous institution of a stage-censorship [Shaw was one of the

few British writers to publicly protest the banning of Wilde's *Salomé* from the London stage in 1892]: your little book on Ibsenism and Ibsen is such a delight to me that I constantly take it up, and always find it stimulating and refreshing: England is the land of intellectual fogs but you have done much to clear the air: we are both Celtic, and I like to think that we are friends: for these and many other reasons Salomé presents herself to you in purple raiment. Pray accept her with my best wishes, and believe me, very truly yours, Oscar Wilde.[107]

In his reply, dated February 28, Shaw relates that he has yet to receive the volume of *Salomé* ('I expect her to arrive a perfect outcast, branded with inky stamps, bruised by flinging from hard hands into red prison vans') and further reflects on the evils of British censorship:

we have to half fight down, half educate up, if we are to get rid of Censorships, official and unofficial. And when I say we, I mean Morris the Welshman [who both Shaw and Wilde admired] and Wilde and Shaw the Irishmen; for to learn from Frenchmen is a condescension impossible for an Englishman.

I hope soon to send you my play 'Widowers' Houses', which you will find tolerably amusing, considering that it is a farcical comedy. Unfortunately I have no power of producing beauty: my genius is the genius of intellect, and my farce its derisive brutality. Salomé's purple garment would make Widowers' Houses ridiculous; but you are precisely the man to appreciate it on that count.

I saw Lady Windermere's Fan in its early days, & have often wished to condole with you—since nobody else did—on the atrocious acting of it . . . I hope you will follow up hard on that trail; for the drama wants building up very badly; and it is clear that your work lies there. Besides, you have time and opportunity for work, which none of the rest of us have. And that reminds me of the clock; so farewell for the moment. GBS.[108]

A letter from Wilde to Shaw, postmarked May 9, 1893, indicates that Wilde did receive a presentation copy of *Widowers' Houses*, which had received a lukewarm reception the year before. Wilde paid Shaw the compliment of ranking *Widower's Houses* with his own more successful plays:

My dear Shaw, I must thank you very sincerely for Op. 2 of the great Celtic School. [Wilde had previously referred to his *Lady Windermere's Fan* as 'Op. I of the Hibernian School'.] I have read it twice with the keenest interest. I like your superb confidence in the dramatic value of the mere facts of life. I admire the horrible flesh and blood of your creatures, and your preface is a masterpiece—a real masterpiece of trenchant writing and caustic wit and dramatic instinct . . . When are you coming to the Haymarket? [Where Wilde's *A Woman of No Importance* was playing.] Sincerely yours, Oscar Wilde.[109]

Notwithstanding such friendly missives, Wilde was well aware of the personal and philosophical disparities between himself and Shaw. Wilde frequently ragged Shaw for his foibles, most famously alluding to his countryman's habit of disconcerting people with his blunt questions and tactlessness with his quip that Shaw '[had] no enemies but [was] intensely disliked by all his friends'.[110] When Frank Harris asked Wilde what he thought of Shaw, Wilde reportedly replied,

> 'a man of real ability but with a bleak mind. Humorous gleams as of wintry sunlight on a bare, harsh landscape. He has no passion, no feeling, and without passionate feeling how can one be an artist? He believes in nothing, loves nothing, not even Bernard Shaw, and really, on the whole, I don't wonder at his indifference'.[111]

Despite this chaffing, Shaw demonstrated his regard for Wilde by being one of the few men of letters who publicly championed the disgraced decadent after his conviction in 1895. He drafted petitions advocating leniency for Wilde during his prosecutions and imprisonment (which failed to win significant support) and defended Wilde against Max Nordau's attack on him in *Degeneration* in the New York *Liberty* on July 12, 1895. Although Shaw, in 1916, somewhat harshly referred to the postprison Wilde as 'an unproductive drunkard and swindler' (epithets that incited angry responses in print from Wilde's friend Robert Harborough Sherard),[112] in the next sentence Shaw went on to say that Wilde's writings demonstrated that he was not 'a selfish or base-minded man'.[113] While he disapproved of Wilde's wayward postprison life, Shaw continued to proclaim Wilde's talent in reviews and articles when the latter's name was anathema; in 1897 he bravely proposed Wilde's name for a projected 'British Academy of Letters' in the *Academy* magazine.[114] He also continued to send the disgraced Wilde copies of his books and Wilde returned the favor. Shaw was particularly moved by Wilde's postprison appeals to improve conditions for children in English jails (far more than he was by *De Profundis*[115]), and in an article that appeared in German in Vienna's *Neue Freie Presse* in 1905, Shaw criticized English society for its unjust treatment of Wilde, asserting that

> [o]ur present day morality is repugnant . . . Wilde's claim to greatness rests on the fact that our morality could not fool him, and the moralists

of his time could neither break him nor dishonor him. He held fast to his pose to the very last, because it was an honest pose. For that very reason it has been unspeakably annoying to English morality which, too, is a pose, but without the benefit of the excuse of being an honest one.[116]

Reflecting upon their association on August 9, 1939, Shaw wrote to Alfred Douglas, 'I did not dislike Wilde; and I don't think he disliked me'.[117] When asked shortly before his death whom he would most like to meet, Shaw replied, 'I do not want to talk to anybody, alive or dead, but if I craved for entertaining conversation by a first-class *raconteur*, I would choose Oscar Wilde'.[118] Despite their barbs at each other's expense, it is clear that the two men came to regard each other with respect and understanding. This is perhaps why Shaw was not content to let *Immaturity*'s Patrick Hawkshaw stand as his only fictional portrait of Wilde. Gary Schmidgall has convincingly argued that the character of Peter Keegan, a defrocked priest in Shaw's play *John Bull's Other Island*, completed four years after Wilde's death, is a more sympathetic portrait of Wilde. Schmidgall reads Keegan, a philosophic, melancholy humorist, as an 'act of penance for the caricature in Patrick Hawkshaw'.[119]

Rhoda Broughton

Second Thoughts (1880)

The year after Shaw completed his first version of *Immaturity*, Rhoda Broughton (1840–1920), one of several 'New Woman' authors considered in this study, published her novel *Second Thoughts*, which features a portrait of Wilde as the poet Francis Chaloner.[120] Broughton had moved to Oxford with her sister in 1878, Wilde's final year as an undergraduate at Magdalen. At 38 years of age, Broughton, the niece of Irish writer Sheridan Le Fanu, was a novelist of some notoriety. Her novels were a combination of social satire and sensationalism; the unrestrained actions of her rebellious heroines were modeled on the New Woman and incited a degree of controversy. It was thought that Broughton moved to Oxford 'to sketch University foibles'. Her sharp wit soon won her a place in university social circles and she established a literary salon, although she was frequently snubbed by those who disapproved of her work.[121] Broughton's biographer Marilyn Wood states that Broughton

> proved more than a match for Oscar Wilde who, not relishing the idea of having a rival who might out-talk and out-epigram him, declined to send her any more invitations to his own parties.[122]

Broughton's friend the novelist Margaret Woods contended:

> [n]either [at Oxford], nor later, was [Wilde] equal to encounters with Rhoda Broughton, who . . . loathed him.[123]

As the witty center of a band of literary admirers, it is certainly possible that Broughton was viewed as a rival by Wilde. Broughton counted Matthew Arnold, Thomas Hardy, Anthony Trollope, Walter Pater, and Henry James among her friends and invitations to her later 'at homes' in London and Headington Hill were keenly sought after. However, it is also likely that Broughton and Wilde experienced a 'personality clash'. Broughton appears to have alienated Wilde with her conventional morality and propensity for malice; she was described by various observers as arrogant, tart, temperamental, and disposed to sarcasm.[124] Marilyn Wood persuasively argues that Broughton's portrait of the Wildean poet Francis Chaloner in *Second Thoughts* was an act of revenge on Wilde for a social snub. Broughton appears to have felt such slights deeply; Michael Sadleir relates that she was prone to 'fits of almost morbid depression' on this account and Ethel Arnold recalls Broughton remarking, 'I can't forget those early years of my life [at Oxford], when those from whom I had every right and reason to expect kindness and hospitality showed me nothing but cold incivility. I resent it still, *and I shall resent it to my dying day* [emphasis in the original]'.[125]

It seems that Broughton was not invited to more than one of Wilde's Oxford soirees; however her friend Margaret Woods was. The nature of Broughton's portrait reflects the fact that the author did not know Wilde well. With only second-hand access to the vagaries of Wilde's personality (through Woods, who also disliked him[126]), Broughton's Wildean character became fragile, melancholic, and humorless:

> Chaloner does not laugh . . . he never does. Life never turns the comic side of her face towards him. He is of the same mind as—was it Châteaubriand who said that not only had he no keen sense of wit, but that it was positively disagreeable to him?[127]

This description certainly does not resemble the undergraduate Wilde we have come to know through his letters and the recollections of his Oxford contemporaries—whatever the deficiencies of the young aesthete, wit and humor were not lacking. Of course, it is also possible that Broughton and Wood saw a side of Wilde that he did not present to other contemporaries, one that does not fit our existing picture. Whatever the case, we can confidently mark Chaloner as a fictional portrait of Wilde: he is clearly recognizable with his long hair, 'early Byzantine face', distinctively decorated rooms, love of Pre-Raphaelite poetry and Paterian desire for 'a larger life' with 'passionate pulsations'; at one point he suggests to the heroine Gillian Latimer that they 'burn like a pure and gem-like flame upon one altar'.[128] Chaloner's conversation is unmistakably Wildean, echoing the elaborate, ornamental language that Wilde was both celebrated and criticized for. He tells Latimer that his poetry should be read to the 'low pale sound of the viol or virginal: with a subtle perfume of dead roses floating about, while the eye is fed with porphyry vases and tender Tyrian dyes'![129]

Unsurprisingly, Broughton's portrait of the young aesthete is a hostile one that clearly reflects her dislike of Wilde—Chaloner is insensitive, egotistical, and never suspects Latimer's 'sincere desire for his absence'.[130] (As in *The Monks of Thelema* and *Immaturity*, it is once again suggested that the Wildean character's courting of the heroine is prompted by her financial status.) Broughton's description of Chaloner's rooms in *Second Thoughts* corresponds exactly with contemporary reports of Wilde's rooms at Magdalen, complete with delicate Japanese china, unfinished paintings on easels, and a single lily in a blue vase. Broughton's description of this décor clearly signals her disapproval of the aesthetic style; like her protagonist Gillian Latimer, Broughton was of a more conservative bent. The unfinished Pre-Raphaelite portraits in Chaloner's studio are described as 'sickly virgins and diseased Aphrodites', all being representations of the same 'livid, dislocated woman ... carrot-headed, thumb-nosed, sunk-chested—almost always backed by sunflowers, and invariably swaddled in unwholesome draperies'.[131] Richard Ellmann has observed that Chaloner's two portraits of Venus and Hylas highlight 'the sexual ambiguity of aesthetic young men'.[132] In contrast, the rooms of the manly, straight-talking, hardworking hero of the novel, Doctor John Burnet, which are dismissed by Chaloner as 'ungraceful' and 'un-Greek', contain 'bold design and lively colours', curtains of a 'good strong undeniable blue', and a 'first-class' drawing room suite. Latimer remarks, 'One has of late years such a surfeit of cholera blues and livid greens, that one begins to long for magenta and arsenic back again ... I find it a refreshing change from sunflowers and peacock's eyes'.[133]

Wilde certainly had reason to dislike Broughton, and he appears to have retained his early aversion to her. As a reviewer for the *Pall Mall Gazette*, he published a scathing denouncement of Broughton's novel

Betty's Visions on October 28, 1886. George Bernard Shaw, who, as related above, reviewed for the *Pall Mall* at the same time as Wilde, recalled that 'the barbarous amusement of skinning minor poets [and other writers] alive' was prevalent at the time, and often inspired 'deadly vendettas'.[134] Wilde's review of Broughton's work could conceivably fall into this category:

> No one can ever say of [Rhoda Broughton] that she has tried to separate flippancy from fiction, and whatever harsh criticisms may be passed on the construction of her sentences, she at least possesses that one touch of vulgarity that makes the whole world kin.[135]

It is true that, despite her compelling plots and character depictions, Broughton's fiction is frequently melodramatic and sentimental; moreover, her style and grammar are often poor. Wilde's review concluded, 'In Philistia lies Miss Broughton's true sphere, and to Philistia she should return'.[136] Clearly, Wilde thought as little of Broughton as she thought of him. Margaret Woods, who always maintained that Wilde resented her friend's superior wit, wrote in 1941,

> The last time I met Oscar was at a Private View of the Royal Academy; he then said that he had lately come across Rhoda Broughton and found her tongue as bitter as ever; which meant, no doubt, that he had been as the French say, completely *roulé* by her lightning wit, to which he had no ready retort.[137]

Did Broughton's 'lightning wit' really leave Wilde at a loss for words, or did he merely object to the poor quality of her writing and her 'bitter tongue'? Unfortunately, in the absence of new evidence, we are unlikely to ever know the answer to this question.

* * *

It is worth pausing at this point to mention two theatrical productions that lampooned Wilde and the aesthetic movement in 1881, reinforcing the unfavorable image of Wilde presented by Besant, Rice, and Broughton. The first of these was *The Colonel*, by F. C. (Francis Cowley) Burnand, in which Wilde is blatantly parodied as the self-important 'transcendental genius' Lambert Streyke, founder of the 'Aesthetic High Art Company'. This parody is a particularly severe one; Streyke is revealed to be an unscrupulous confidence trickster who takes advantage of a titled friend in order to live the high life. The following comments made by the drama critic for the *Illustrated*

Sporting and Dramatic News apparently refer to a statement made by Wilde at the premiere of this production:

> The modern Aesthete is rather a gorgeous creature; and as a well-known, amiable, and very long-haired Aesthete observed on the first night, had he been called in he could have given the management some valuable hints as to how aestheticism might be corporeally burlesqued.[138]

Burnand, a contributor to *Punch* from 1863, took up its editorship in the same year that *The Colonel* was first performed. Like Besant, Rice, Shaw, and Broughton, Burnand took a dim view of the aesthetic craze. R. G. G. Price avers that Burnand and his *Punch* cartoonist Du Maurier were equally to blame for that publication's perpetual stereotyping of contemporary art, artists, and aesthetes like Wilde. Apart from the Du Maurier characters mentioned above, Wilde's other incarnations in *Punch* included the Wilde-eyed poet, Oscuro Wildegoose, Ossian Wilderness, and Drawit Milde.

The satire from the *Punch* camp was soon to be eclipsed by that of Gilbert and Sullivan's comic opera, *Patience, or Bunthorne's Bride*, which premiered at the Opera Comique on April 23, 1881. *Patience* remains the most enduring dramatic parody of early Wildean aestheticism. Central to the plot is the rivalry between the aesthetic poets Reginald Bunthorne and Archibald Grosvenor, both of whom resemble Wilde, particularly Bunthorne, who declares,

> You must lie upon the daisies and discourse in novel phrases of your complicated state of mind,
> The meaning doesn't matter if it's only idle chatter of a transcendental kind.

Reinforcing the 'aesthetic sham' image that had been promulgated by previous fictions and satires, Bunthorne blithely confesses to the audience that he is 'not fond of uttering platitudes / In stained glass attitudes' and that his 'mediaevalism' is actually 'affectation / Born of a morbid love of admiration'. Bunthorne also invokes a popular legend about Wilde while imparting advice on how to succeed as an aesthete: 'Though the Philistines may jostle, you will rank as an apostle in the high aesthetic band / If you walk down Piccadilly with a poppy or a lily in your medieval hand'.[139]

Despite Bunthorne's obvious resemblance to Wilde, Gilbert maintained that his aesthetes were composites, and indeed, apart from their similarities to Wilde, they also suggest Whistler, Rossetti,

Swinburne, and Ruskin. However, in the ostentatious Bunthorne the public saw only Wilde, and by the time the production was taken to America in 1882, Bunthorne's more Whistlerian characteristics (dark curls, a white lock of hair, a moustache, and an eye glass) had been relinquished for Wilde's long brown locks and gestures. Wilde followed his usual practice of referring to the satire with an air of amused tolerance and attended the premiere in London and a performance in New York. Wilde's star was on the rise; he had just published his first edition of poetry, *Poems* (1881)—a controversial selection of suggestive, sensual poems of the 'fleshly school'—and the Prince of Wales had asked to meet him, remarking, 'I do not know Mr. Wilde, and not to know Mr. Wilde is not to be known'.[140] In an inspired move, Wilde accepted Richard D'Oyly Carte's offer to lecture on aestheticism alongside the touring company of *Patience* in America in 1882. The media hype surrounding his visit to America and Canada that year has been well documented. The lecture tour stands as a remarkable achievement in self-promotion, with Wilde riding on the backs of his parodists and detractors to increase his fame and spread his aesthetic creed.

Anonymous

Ye Soul Agonies in Ye Life of Oscar Wilde (1882)

The Americans were quick to follow the English example of satirizing Wilde. The popular press, which featured many of *Punch*'s Du Maurier cartoons ridiculing the aesthetic movement before Wilde's arrival, published many similar caricatures and articles lampooning him once he had arrived in the country. A short satirical booklet, entitled *Ye Soul Agonies in Ye Life of Oscar Wilde*, appeared while Wilde was touring and told the story of his life in a similar style to *Patience*. Published privately by an anonymous author with illustrations by Charles Kendrick, *Ye Soul Agonies* constitutes an illuminating record of the American take on the British 'Professor of Aesthetics'. Most of the American satires mimicked those imported from England, poking fun at Wilde's preoccupation with lilies and sunflowers and his lack of literary output. The author of *Ye Soul Agonies* avers that Wilde composed his first poem at age 4:

> The sun is yellow,
> The sky is blue;
> And I am four,
> That's quite too-too.[141]

Interestingly, the author displays a surprising knowledge of Wilde's Portora and Trinity College history. He contends that Wilde's tutor at the latter institution, Professor Mahaffy, was jealous of his brilliant student and was glad to be rid of him when he won his Oxford scholarship. The author has Mahaffy writing from Trinity College Dublin to John Ruskin at Oxford:

> MY DEAR RUSKIN . . . I send you Oscar Wilde. Look out for your Stones of Venice. He'll pulverise *them*, and then he'll pulverise *you*. He kicked up no end of a *dust* here. Tibi. [emphasis in the original]
> The MAHAFFY.[142]

Ruskin effusively replies to Mahaffy that Wilde is 'the missing link between the past and the future of Art', that 'the bridge had been built, and its keystone was Oscar'; a reference to Ruskin's famous Hinksey Road Campaign.[143] (Wilde reportedly 'broke many stones' for the Hinksey Road and was supposed to have been 'specially invited to fill [Ruskin's] barrow, and to help him trundle it down the plank'.[144]) The Paterian philosophy of 'intense sensations' adopted by Wilde is also mocked with an illustration of an Oxford don beating a bending Wilde with birch twigs; the caption reads: 'Ye work of an Ancient Master fills him with exquisite pain'.[145]

Wilde and the Prince of Wales are depicted as great 'pals', and in one passage Queen Victoria and her companion Mr Brown urge Wilde to write a poem about the Albert memorial. By this time Wilde and the Prince of Wales often met in society and Wilde told an acquaintance in Dieppe in 1897 that he had met Queen Victoria and admired her appearance and regal bearing.[146]

Ye Soul Agonies also contains many passages that poke fun at Wilde's high opinion of his literary abilities and his place among the London literati:

> Alfred Tennyson, on hearing of Oscar's arrival [in London], fled to the Isle of Wight and set to work on a poem on the Zulu War, which he named 'Charge of the Dark Brigade', in contradistinction to his 'Charge of the *Light* [emphasis in the original] Brigade'. Browning commenced reading Johnson's Dictionary upside down, with a view to coining words, and Rossetti bought a job lot of goose-quill pens and some paper that had been injured by water at a fire. As for the minor poets, they borrowed 'fivers' where they could and went out of the country.[147]

* * *

After completing his American tour, Wilde spent some months in Paris working on a play—*The Duchess of Padua* (first produced as *Guido*

Ferranti by American actor Lawrence Barrett in New York in 1891)— before returning to England in 1883. Upon his return it was soon noted that Wilde had abandoned the distinctive aesthetic costume for which he was renowned, in favor of a new look inspired by Parisian fashions. William Gaunt describes the change:

> Gone were the velvet breeches, the silk stockings and the page-like mop of hair, the medieval soulfulness, the Pre-Raphaelite yearning. Instead there appeared the *flaneur* of the boulevards, a gay cosmopolitan, sipping absinthe, smoking scented cigarettes, and dressing the part of the dandy, the continentalized dandy on the model described by Baudelaire . . . after Bunthorne came Beau Brummel.[148]

The initial fervor and pretensions of the aesthetic fad had abated, and the sophisticated 'Wilde of the second period' had arrived. Once back in Britain, Wilde embarked upon another lecture tour, speaking mainly on interior decoration and his American experiences. When he was not lecturing, Wilde wrote articles and reviews for journals, including the *Pall Mall Gazette*, the *Saturday Review*, and the *Court and Society Review*. In November that year he became engaged to Constance Lloyd, the daughter of an Irish barrister, whom he married in 1884. Wilde's relationship with his new wife appears to have fired the imagination of his next fictionalizer, Mrs (Rosa) Campbell Praed.

Mrs (Rosa) Campbell Praed
Affinities: A Romance of To-day (1885)

The novelist, journalist, and playwright Mrs (Rosa) Campbell Praed (née Murray-Prior, 1851–1935) was the first Australian-born novelist to win international fame.[149] Praed grew up in the Queensland bush, the daughter of a pastoralist who later became a politician in Brisbane. Three years after marrying Arthur Campbell Praed and enduring the harsh conditions and isolation of his Port Curtis station, the Praeds migrated to England in 1876, where Rosa began to write as Mrs Campbell Praed. Australian settings and political themes feature frequently in her writings,[150] as do tales of the occult and risqué plots featuring troubled marriages. Praed's own marriage was not a happy one; she later separated from her husband to live with her friend Nancy Harward, possibly in a lesbian relationship.[151]

The Praeds moved to London around 1882 and Rosa soon became well known in artistic and political circles. She began to incorporate many of her new famous friends and acquaintances into her fiction: Ellen Terry, Ada Rehan, Arthur Conan Doyle, Mrs Lynn Linton, and Lady Colin Campbell are all thinly disguised in her writings.[152] So too, is Oscar Wilde, who appears as Esmé Colquhoun, the central male character of her 1885 novel, *Affinities: A Romance of To-day*, a work that also contains fictional portraits of the artist Louise Jopling (as Christine Borlase) and the theosophist Madame Helena Blavatsky (as Madame Tamvasco).[153] Although the school of theosophy is never mentioned by name, it is this movement and contemporary London's fascination with it that constitutes the background to Praed's novel. Late nineteenth-century theosophists studied Hindu and Buddhist teachings on such paranormal topics as mesmerism, clairvoyance, and astral body experiences. The Theosophical Lodge in London, established by Anglo-Indian journalist Alfred Percy Sinnett, quickly became popular with many members of 'Upper Bohemia' with a taste for new sensations, including Rider Haggard, Rudyard Kipling, Bram Stoker, Oscar Wilde, and his mother Lady Wilde.

Praed, a confirmed spiritualist and occultist, was a follower of the renowned theosophist guru Madame Blavatsky and held a theosophy meeting at her home on May 24, 1884 to introduce the new movement to London society.[154] This meeting inspired Praed to begin writing *Affinities*, which depicts theosophists as the 'New Pythagoreans' who 'hold the vulgar phenomenon of spiritualism in supreme contempt [preferring] a species of Indian jugglery which bases itself upon strictly scientific principles'.[155]

It is very likely that Wilde and his wife to be, Constance Lloyd, attended Praed's meeting of May 24. The couple shared a mutual interest in the occult; moreover, their influence is clearly discernible in Praed's *Affinities*. Wilde and Praed had many mutual friends in London's literary and theatrical circles and Praed was a frequent visitor to Lady Wilde's 'at homes'. Wilde also visited Praed's home to see plays performed privately there.[156] Praed admitted to taking notes from Wilde's conversation on such occasions and to drawing on these notes for the character of Esmé Colquhoun, an admission that makes Colquhoun of particular interest for our purposes.[157]

In keeping with the supernatural theme of the novel, the Wildean Colquhoun is first seen in a vision by Major Graysett, who has just returned from a long term of service in India to visit his friend Colonel Rainshaw's country estate. Almost immediately after Graysett's arrival, he experiences a disturbing vision in which he sees

> '[a] large man, very tall, and of great breadth of chest, with a way of tossing back his head so that attention was called to his statue-like

throat. He had a smooth-shaven face, rather classical features, and sensuous, Greek lips. He reminded me of a statue in the Louvre, I think of the young Alcides. There was a good deal of intellectuality in his face, and of fire in his blue eyes when he opened them fully, which did not seem to be his habit. The most striking thing about him was his hair. It was not red and it was not gold, but something between the two; and he wore it very long, and brushed back from his forehead.'[158]

Graysett sees a dying woman alongside this figure and is convinced that the man is the woman's husband who has plotted her death. To Graysett's surprise, he is introduced to the woman he saw in his vision, Judith Fountain, that night at dinner, where he also hears much talk of the poet Esmé Colquhoun, the aesthetic, Oxford-educated 'Apostle of the Beautiful'. Colquhoun has just returned from a successful lecture tour of the United States to lecture on his American experiences, just as Wilde had done two years before. (Wilde's meeting with Walt Whitman in America is referenced with Colquhoun's account of his visit with 'the [unnamed] greatest American poet'.[159]) Graysett meets Colquhoun, another visitor to Rainshaw's country house, in the following days and immediately recognizes the man in his vision. Moreover, Colquhoun is soon making advances toward Fountain, whom Graysett has fallen for himself and whom he feels bound to save from her vision-fate.

Apart from the physical similarities to Wilde described above, Colquhoun demonstrates many other Wildean characteristics. He is not only strong and proficient in such 'manly accomplishments' as horse-riding and shooting but can also be 'almost womanly' in his tenderness and affinity with the female sex. He talks cleverly 'as though he were being interviewed by a dozen newspaper editors', has a 'sonorous', 'liquid' voice and speaks 'with a good deal of emphasis and expression'. Like Wilde, Colquhoun rarely dances and he conducts himself with a 'serene self-complacency'.[160] His approach to life is conspicuously Wildean; Colquhoun is a worshipper of the ideal who is always seeking new sensations, and consequently he has a great interest in the supernatural. He is a self-confessed egotist ('if [the artist] were not a sublime egotist, he could not be a sublime artist') who has an opinion on every artistic subject.[161] In defending Wilde's literary heroes Gautier and Baudelaire, Colquhoun expounds his distinctively Wildean philosophy:

> 'What . . . is our mission—we writers—but to distil the essence of the Age? The critics tell us that we are complex, that we are psychological, that we are corrupt, that we are anatomists of diseased minds. We

reply: the Age is complex; the Age is corrupt; and the Society we depict is the outcome of influences which have been gathering through centuries of advancing civilisation. The men and women of the world have been refined from field flowers to exotics; the simple conditions of Nature are not for them . . . There is no room for Nature in London. She is too glaring, too crude, and London is essentially the pulse of civilisation—'.[162]

The very unaesthetic Rainshaw's reaction to Colquhoun's talk echoes that of many of Wilde's contemporaries:

'I must confess that his conversation is above the heads of a few of his audience; but some of his anecdotes, when the ladies are out of the way, are really very good, and quite broad enough to suit all comprehensions. I don't know that I should call his witticisms always refined. For the most part, however, I am obliged to take it for granted that he is an exceedingly clever young man. To me he appears like a wind-bag containing a few dried peas, which rattle considerably'.[163]

Colquhoun's public image upon returning from America also reflects the nature of Wilde's celebrity at that time. Although Colquhoun, like Wilde, generated an enormous amount of interest in the United States with his unique personality and aesthetic doctrines, Colquhoun is largely seen in England as a past 'idol of the hour'; this perception has been encouraged by the failure of his rather prosaic financial investment in a sawmill. Colquhoun reflects, 'It is a curious experience to be lauded as an Apollo on one side of the Atlantic, to be denounced as Society's last plaything, discarded and penniless, on the other'. He has also alienated certain important people with his sharp wit and as a result is occasionally 'cut' in society—an indignity he attempts to diffuse with the Wildean tactic of 'sublime indifference'.[164]

However, it is where Praed's portrait departs from a 'realistic' portrayal of Wilde that we see some remarkable developments. Wilde's charismatic personality, egotism, and celebration of the artificial combine to become something sinister in Praed's Colquhoun. Praed's is in fact the first of a long line of fictional Wildes to display preternatural characteristics. Hints as to Colquhoun's extraordinary nature and abilities are to be found in Praed's physical descriptions of the aesthete; his eyes have a ring of light around the pupil, his hair has the magnetic quality of cat's fur, and his face suggests a 'fallen Lucifer'. People find him 'both fascinating and repellent'.[165] Mrs Rainshaw voices her fear that Colquhoun has been influenced by an occult sect in America, where he learned how to use 'odic force' to

> '[absorb] into his own system all the vitality and will-force of any one peculiarly susceptible to magnetic influence, till the poor creature [loses] all individuality, and [becomes] a mere shell, galvanized into obedience by the will of its destroyer'.[166]

The occultist Judith Fountain proves to be highly susceptible to Colquhoun's fiendish powers, a fact that interests him almost as much as her wealth, and the pair are soon married. Although Colquhoun is not deliberately cruel to his wife, before long Judith becomes a mere 'shell' of her former self and a mental puppet to Colquhoun's puppeteer, suffering further agonies when she discovers that her husband does not love her but the artist Christine Borlase. Finally, in a fit of resentment at being kept from his true love Borlase, Colquhoun wills his wife to die, and the scenario of Major Graysett's early vision is realized. (Gabrielle Maupin Bielenstein has noted that the plot of *Affinities* is almost identical to Henry James's *The Portrait of a Lady*, published four years earlier in 1881.[167])

Affinities received mixed reviews from contemporary critics, who were largely unimpressed by its mystical melodrama and inchoate spiritualism. Colquhoun was immediately recognized as Wilde, and the critics delighted in disparaging his character:

> The villain is a poet and fop—much more a fop than a poet—who has been starring in America, and who has a reputation for uttering paradoxical futilities. This disgusting person, more or less a fortune-hunter, is also 'psychically' endowed with magical powers of will ... Mrs. Campbell Praed's scoundrel [combines] Mr. Du Maurier's Maudle with Mr. Sludge the Medium ... the psychical fop ... appear[s] to have been studied from [a] living [notoriety].[168]

Praed's publisher George Bentley was dismayed at the nature of her obvious portrait, and wrote to her on November 19, 1885:

> [i]n regard to Esmé, what you have to avoid is the imputation of anything that properly discredits a man. You have no right to draw a portrait so like Oscar Wilde that the public at once identify him, and then make this man do anything which society would condemn him for ... You may laugh at his fads, ridicule his theories, even speak of his love of dress ... [b]ut you must stop short of anything that throws a shadow of doubt upon his moral character or on his rectitude.[169]

Bentley must also have been concerned about Praed's depiction of the Colquhoun/Fountain union in light of Wilde's marriage to Constance Lloyd, a woman often described as submissive and acquiescent to Wilde, just a year before. Fountain has Constance's dreamy eyes, 'great quantity of golden brown hair', and 'rather thin, melancholy lips' (see plate 3).[170] Like Judith Fountain, Constance was a well-known devotee of occultism and theosophy. Constance was at one time a follower of Madame Blavatsky, but reportedly left the theosophy movement to join the more mystical Hermetic Order of the Golden Dawn.[171]

A comment made by Mrs Rainshaw about Colquhoun implies that Wilde's marriage to Constance, like his change of image soon after his return from America, was largely inspired by his declining celebrity:

> 'He is rather played out as a celebrity. People are getting tired of him, and the papers have been writing him down. It was quite necessary that he should take a new departure of some sort—cut his hair, grow a beard, or marry Sarah Bernhardt'.[172]

With her description of the popular interest in Colquhoun's marriage and his 'revamped' postmarital reputation, Praed clearly refers to the effects of Wilde's marriage:

> His admirers prophesied that under [these] purer and more favourable conditions of development his genius would soar to heights it had never yet attained. His detractors considered it advisable to commend the policy of a man who at the critical time of his career had been clever enough to secure the affection of a beautiful woman and the command of half a million of money.[173]

Colquhoun's attraction to Fountain's wealth reflects the common contemporary perception that Wilde married Constance for her money (an apprehension that has been convincingly disputed by Constance's biographer Anne Clark Amor[174]). Colquhoun, like Wilde, dedicates poetry to his wife and designs clothes for her that represent a major departure from her former style of dress. The new Mrs Colquhoun is described as follows as she enters an evening party:

> She was dressed after a fashion very unlike the conventional simplicity of her attire before her marriage. The rich velvet brocade falling in heavy folds about her figure, its sheen displaying gleams of dark red and flame colour, was made somewhat in the Italian style of the fifteenth

century, with full sleeves and stiff jewelled bodice cut low in front . . . her hair was now curled more elaborately—[175]

Compare this passage with Marie Belloc Lowndes's observation that, when at home, Constance Wilde

> dressed simply and in the type of frock which was beginning to be known as a tea-gown. But when she accompanied her husband to functions such as private views . . . she would appear in what were regarded as very peculiar and eccentric clothes. She did this to please Oscar and not to please herself.[176]

It is interesting that Praed paints the character based on Louise Jopling, Christine Borlase, as Colquhoun's true soul mate. Borlase and Colquhoun declare their love for one another but decide to sacrifice their love in order to pursue their respective artistic goals. Praed and Jopling were friends; Jopling painted Praed's portrait and presumably Praed consulted Jopling as she wrote her novel; she certainly collaborated with her in adapting *Affinities* into a play (although there is no extant record of the play having been performed).[177] As stated above, Jopling was also a good friend of Wilde's; in her memoir *Twenty Years of My Life: 1867–1887* (1925), she states that he was 'a constant visitor' to her house and was a 'most entrancing companion'.[178] Is it possible that Jopling harbored some romantic feelings toward Wilde and vice versa? Did their mutual friend incorporate their reciprocal feelings into her novel? Jopling mentions Constance Wilde several times in her memoir in a manner that may reflect some rivalry for Wilde's affections. Jopling contends that, when she asked Wilde how he came to love Constance, he replied, 'She scarcely ever speaks. I am always wondering what her thoughts are like'.[179] According to Jopling, she and Wilde enjoyed a superior rapport:

> One evening, at a party, I met the Wildes. He and I had much to say to each other. Mrs. Oscar approached us, looking exquisite in a dress the fashion of which just suited her. We both gazed at her admiringly. As she passed by, Oscar gave a deep sigh, and murmured half to himself and half to me: 'If only I could be jealous of her'![180]

Jopling also relates that she and Wilde were once among a group of guests who stayed at the country house of Jean and Walter Palmer; Constance was not present. A photograph of Wilde and Jopling standing next to each other at the Palmers, taken in September 1892, appears at plate 5. Another photograph taken at the Palmers, which

Jopling mentions in her reminiscences, also appears significant in this regard. Jopling writes,

> Mrs. Oscar had the reputation of not possessing a sense of humour, but I think she had it, in a subtle degree. She was not one of the party who was staying at the Walter Palmers'... Whilst [a] photographer [at the Palmers'] was posing us in the usual conventional manner, I said: 'Oh, do let us get up a scene! I will make love to Oscar, and you must all be shocked!' When Mrs. Oscar came to see me, I thought it would amuse her to see the photograph. All she said was, after looking at it for quite a long minute: 'Poor Oscar!'[181]

Certainly, the statements in Jopling's memoir could be read as reflective of a romantic interest in Wilde. It may be that Jopling felt, as a fellow artist, that she understood Wilde in a way Constance never could. Indeed, many contemporary observers noted that Constance seemed 'out of her depth' in Wilde's artistic milieu. The Jopling-based artist Borlase, however, is deeply entrenched in this world and understands that the Wilde-based Colquhoun is not well-suited to marriage:

> 'Applause and adulation are the breath of existence to you. The love and loyalty of one woman would never satisfy your nature, except under conditions which would enable you to take impressions from numerous other sources. You will secure for yourself these conditions... You require a thousand sensations in quick succession... You profess to worship the ideal; but in reality you are an utter materialist. You have all the weakness, all the inconsistency, all the greatness of a poetic nature.[182]

Borlase's words proved prophetic in relation to Wilde; the latter was soon to tire of domestic life with Constance and increasingly sought new impressions and sensations outside of his marriage. Did Praed draw Borlase's and Colquhoun's love from life? It is doubtful we will ever know, but the possibility is certainly a fascinating one.

While Wilde's enigmatic personality clearly fired Praed's imagination, the macabre nature of her portrait suggests that, in 1885 at least, she did not share her friend Jopling's affinity with him. It appears likely that Judith Fountain's first opinion of Colquhoun, before she falls under his mesmeric spell, reflects Praed's own opinion of Wilde:

> 'I have only a sort of curiosity about him. It is mixed with contempt, I think, although I admire him, and can realize the fact of his influence. I fancy that, if he were in earnest about his life, he might seriously

impress me. As it is, I seem to see through his artificiality, without in the least getting at his real nature. I have tried by way of experiment to read his thoughts, as I have often read those of other people, but have always failed. His mind is a blank to me'.[183]

If Praed did feel ambivalent toward Wilde, she seems to have maintained friendly relations with him. One passage in *Affinities* provides a possible insight into the nature of their conversations, and a rare example of Wildean commentary on Australia.[184] In light of Praed's admitted practice of taking notes from Wilde's talk, we can reasonably assume that Esmé Colquhoun's conversation with an Australian guest of Colonel Rainshaw's derives from a conversation between Wilde and the Australian Praed. When Rainshaw's guest remarks that Colquhoun would find colonial Australian life far too 'natural' for his taste, Colquhoun replies,

> 'to me there are but two terms, civilization and barbarism... Conventionalism is the worst form of barbarism. You [Australians] will strike your own keynote, and evolve harmonies in sympathy with your dazzling noon-day. I am a poet of the night—the night of city and *salon*—luxuriously illuminated, full of passionate sweetness, suffused with the voluptuous odour of perfumes. But for you, I am mute—an Australian Walt Whitman may perhaps lift you to a higher level than mine. At least you will not have to contend against the debasing influence of the Mediaevalists—the influence I am fighting'.[185]

True to his avowed preference for imaginative versions of real people in fiction, Wilde does not appear to have been offended by the fiendish nature of his portrait in *Affinities*. On the contrary, as Helen Reeves related to Praed, he seems to have reveled in the reflected notoriety it cast on him. In a letter to Praed, Reeves reproduced Wilde's response to questioning on Praed's portrait:

> 'Mrs. Praed gives you the face of a Greek God!'
> 'Of course! Just like me!'
> 'But she gives you a good figure!'
> 'Just like me!'

Reeves concluded, 'there was no taking the conceit out of him'.[186]

Despite the divided critical response to her novel, Praed was pleased with *Affinities*'s popular success, which she attributed to the 'portraits from life' that she included in the book. In the late 1920s she considered publishing a new edition of *Affinities* in light of the renewed public interest in Wilde and the theosophists; this never came to pass.[187] However, Praed was unable to resist drawing another fictional portrait of Wilde, including him as a character in her 1898 novel, *The Scourge-Stick*, discussed in Part 3.

In the three years following the publication of Praed's *Affinities*, Wilde proved himself to be much more than the 'aesthetic sham' depicted in some of the works discussed above. In addition to his journalism, he published a substantial number of short stories that were very well received, including 'The Canterville Ghost' (1887) and 'Lord Arthur Savile's Crime' (1887). He also assumed editorship of the journal *The Woman's World*, which formerly contained mainly fashion and society features, but which under Wilde's guidance was reconstituted to reflect more weighty feminist concerns and opinions. The year 1888 was to bring Wilde's greatest literary success yet: *The Happy Prince and Other Tales*, a volume of fairy tales of the type made popular by Hans Christian Andersen.

Mrs (Mary) Humphry Ward

Robert Elsmere (1888)

The year 1888 was also to see Mrs (Mary) Humphry Ward's (née Arnold, 1851–1920) greatest literary success, which came with the publication of her three-volume novel *Robert Elsmere*. The controversial novel documents a clergyman's philosophical struggle with orthodox Christianity and it won Ward, an active philanthropist, feminist, and intellectual, great acclaim among many of her contemporaries.[188] Among modern scholars, the book is widely regarded as a significant cultural document, reflecting the growing religious uncertainty of Victorians in the face of new evolutionary and historical knowledge. (The novel originally began as a pamphlet in defense of religious skepticism.[189])

Ward lived in Oxford from 1867 and married the Oxford don Thomas Humphry Ward in 1872. The couple remained in Oxford until 1881, maintaining a high profile in intellectual circles there. Readers of *Robert Elsmere* were quick to recognize portraits of the author's family and friends in the novel; examples of the latter are to be found in the Oxford tutors Langham and Grey, who are clearly based on Walter Pater and Thomas Hill Green. The Provost of St Anselm's also closely resembles Benjamin Jowett.[190] Ward only admitted, however, to the portrait of Green and 'a sketch among the minor characters'.[191] She was possibly referring to the poet Mr Wood, who appears briefly at a musical party given by Robert Elsmere's aesthetic sister-in-law Rose. Wood, despite his gratuitous eyeglass, is obviously modeled on Wilde, being

> the poet of the party, got up in the most correct professional costume—long hair, velvet coat, eyeglass and all. His extravagance, however, was of the most conventional type. Only his vanity had a touch of the sublime. Langham . . . heard him saying to an open-eyed *ingénue* beside him,—
> 'Oh, my literary baggage is small as yet. I have only done, perhaps, three things that will live.'
> 'Oh, Mr. Wood!' said the maiden, mildly protesting against so much modesty.
> He smiled, thrusting his hand into the breast of the velvet coat. 'But then,' he said, in a tone of the purest candour, 'at my age I don't think Shelley had done more!'
> Langham, who, like all shy men, was liable to occasional explosions, was seized with a convulsive fit of coughing, and had to retire from the neighbourhood of the bard, who looked round him, disturbed and slightly frowning.[192]

The wrapt attention of the *ingénue* invokes Wilde's popularity with the female sex; his reputation as an arbiter of taste for women was reinforced by his editorship of *The Woman's World* and he was a coveted companion of 'Professional Beauties' like Lillie Langtry and Patsy Cornwallis West. In *The Monks of Thelema*, Besant and Rice observe that men like Wilde were 'greatly believed in by certain women'.[193] Walter Besant declared Ward's representation of Wilde 'a sweet one', but a closer reading reveals that Wood and his clique are depicted as an undesirable, insincere lot, representing the lower end of the artistic social spectrum.[194] Rose's suitor Langham observes that

> the artistic acquaintance [Rose] gathered about her . . . contained a good many dubious odds and ends . . . Many of her friends in [his] opinion were simply pathological curiosities—their vanity was so frenzied, their sensibilities so morbidly developed.
> [Langham regarded certain men at the party as] belonging to a low type; men who, if it suited their purpose, would be quite ready to tell or invent malicious stories of the girl they were now flattering, and whose standards and instincts represented a coarser world than Rose in reality knew anything about.[195]

It is interesting that Langham, a portrait of Ward's friend Walter Pater, disapproves of Wood and his companions. Though Pater was a mentor to Wilde and expressed a qualified admiration for the latter's work, the aesthetic credo of the two men differed on many points and Pater did not always appreciate Wilde's appropriation of his philosophies. Pater was also far more cautious than Wilde and slower to apply his theories to life. (On hearing of Pater's death Wilde sardonically asked Max Beerbohm, 'Was he ever alive'?[196]) The timid Langham's disapproval of Mr Wood reflects Pater's distaste for Wilde's flamboyant aesthetic style. Despite Pater's and Ward's divergent intellectual priorities—he being largely concerned with the epicurean sphere of sensations, she with the ethical tradition—they shared a fascination with religious ideology and had a mutual respect for each other's work.[197] Ward, like fellow Oxford resident Rhoda Broughton, was of a conservative bent and she clearly preferred Pater's timidity to Wilde's flamboyance.[198]

Although there is no record of their meeting at Oxford, Ward could not have been unaware of Wilde's growing celebrity while he was at Magdalen, as they moved in the same social circles. We know, for example, that Ward and her husband were invited to a fancy dress ball at the home of George Morrell in May 1878 that Wilde attended.[199] However, Wilde is conspicuously absent from Ward's memoirs, *A Writer's Recollections* (1918), which includes a chapter on Oxford in the 1870s, when Wilde was a notable local figure. This is particularly curious in light of Ward's own account of her contemporary interest in aesthetic fashions:

[we] gave dinner parties and furnished our houses with Morris papers, old chests and cabinets, and blue pots . . . Most of us were very anxious to be up-to-date, and in the fashion, whether in aesthetics, in housekeeping, or education. But our fashion was not that of Belgravia or Mayfair, which indeed we scorned! It was the fashion of the movement which sprang from Morris and Burne-Jones.[200]

Ward and Wilde moved once more in the same circles in London during the 1880s. In his 1946 biography of Wilde, Hesketh Pearson records that Ward's husband (then a political-leader writer and art critic for the *Times*) and Wilde were among the same group of visitors at a Whistler exhibition.[201] During this period, Ward, like Wilde, was engaged in journalistic pursuits; both contributed to the *Pall Mall Gazette* and the *Saturday Review*. According to Ward's biographer John Sutherland, the Wards 'were by any standards a gregarious couple' and threw themselves into London's literary social life. Mrs Humphry Ward held a weekly salon for the London literati and the couple hosted many dinner parties, two of which were attended by the Wildes in 1886.[202] While there are no detailed accounts of these encounters, it appears that Wilde failed to impress Ward at these dinners; *Robert Elsmere*, written two years later, highlights her disapproval of Wilde's vanity and 'morbidly developed' sensibilities. Ward was not slow to support Wilde's prosecution for 'gross indecency' in 1895; she also urged his publisher John Lane to further persecute Wilde's associate Aubrey Beardsley.[203]

The fact that Ward and Wilde were not friends is hardly surprising in light of the former's renowned morality, which Wilde mocked in conversation with Frank Harris:

> 'I don't know why it is . . . but I am always matchmaking when I think of English celebrities. I should so much like to have introduced Mrs. Humphry Ward blushing at eighteen or twenty to Swinburne, who would of course have bitten her neck in a furious kiss, and she would have run away and exposed him in court, or else have suffered agonies of mingled delight and shame in silence'.[204]

Ward's aversion to Wilde may have been inflamed by such comments and by Wilde's cutting observations on her serious, realistic writings. Wilde often joked about the dull didacticism of *Robert Elsmere*; one of the characters in his essay 'The Decay of Lying' (1889) refers to the book as a 'deliberately tedious' 'masterpiece of the *genre ennuyeux* [boredom genre], the one form of literature that the English people seems thoroughly to enjoy'.[205] Another character in Wilde's essay states that although he is 'quite devoted' to the novel, he cannot treat it as a serious work, due to the fact that 'as a statement of the problems that confront the earnest Christian it is ridiculous and antiquated. It is simply Arnold's *Literature and Dogma* [by Ward's uncle Matthew Arnold, 1873] with the literature left out'. Significantly, he continues, 'On the other hand, it contains several clever caricatures, and a heap of delightful quotations'.[206] Horst Schroeder has noted that in one of the draft manuscripts of 'The Decay of Lying', instead of 'several clever caricatures', Wilde originally wrote 'one delightfully ill-natured caricature', surely referring to his own.[207]

* * *

In the year following the publication of *Robert Elsmere*, the appearance of Wilde's controversial short story 'The Portrait of Mr. W. H.' in *Blackwood's Magazine* (July 1889) marked a turning point in the public's perception of Wilde's sexuality. The story examines the theory that Shakespeare was enamored with, and addressed his sonnets to, a young male actor called Willy Hughes. Richard Aldington has noted that the essay contains allusions to a 'homosexual' poem by Virgil, which most educated men would have recognized and interpreted as 'an unequivocal declaration and an insolent defiance'. Aldington avers that these connotations prompted cautious men to start avoiding Wilde and his circle.[208] The breaking of the Cleveland Street scandal in September 1889, connecting Lord Arthur Somerset with a male brothel, also served to increase society's wariness of the aesthete.

HENRY JAMES

The Tragic Muse (1890)

A certain circumspection toward Wilde is certainly evident in Henry James's 1890 novel *The Tragic Muse*. This three-volume novel contains arguably the most complex psychological portrait of Wilde by a contemporary author, and consequently will be closely examined here. *The Tragic Muse* was first serialized in the *Atlantic Monthly* from January 1889 to May 1890 and appeared in book form in both England and America in June 1890, to mixed reviews. The novel explores the often opposing lures of love and ambition in charting the careers of Nick Dormer (a burgeoning politician who aspires to be a painter), his friend Peter Sherringham (a diplomat with a passion for the theater), and the object of Sherringham's affection Miriam Rooth (an aggressively ambitious actress). The Wildean character, Gabriel Nash, is an old Oxford friend of Dormer's and serves as the latter's artistic mentor, encouraging him to cast aside political ambition and pursue a career in art. Although other models have occasionally been suggested for Nash, this 'whimsical personage' is by common critical consent a fictional depiction of Wilde.[209]

Contemporary reviewers of *The Tragic Muse* made shrewd references to Nash's original. The *Athenaeum* of July 26, 1890 detected 'the suspicion of a male snob somewhere about—we will not say where, but he is present'.[210] Some reviewers were disparaging, clearly influenced by their reservations about Wilde. On October 3 the writer from the *Dublin Review* asserted that '[Nash's] artistic epicureanism is scarcely an exaggeration of the inanities indulged in by this modern type of humanity'.[211] Conversely, Wilde's admirers feted the portrait of Nash; in August an anonymous review in the *Dial*—edited by

Wilde's friends the artists Charles Ricketts and Charles Shannon—read, 'one of the characters claims the first place in our regard. Mr. Gabriel Nash, apostle of candor and exponent of the fine art of living, is so genially conceived a creation that the book is more than worth reading for his sake alone'.[212]

Like Wilde, James's character first comes to notice in his Oxford days, thanks to his 'genius for suggestive paradox' and 'wonderful [talk]'.[213] Nash has written 'a very clever book', has a passion for beauty, and propounds an aesthetic philosophy that is Pater refracted through Wilde: 'I've no *état civil* . . . Merely to be is such a *métier*; to live is such an art; to feel is such a career'![214] Nash defies all attempts at categorization by his contemporaries and refuses to be bound by Victorian conventions. He often refers to his fondness for other historical periods and exotic locations such as Cashmere, Granada, and Samarcand. Nash's means, profession, and address are all cause for speculation by his peers. Like many of Wilde's young acquaintances, Dormer declares himself a devoted disciple of Nash: 'I think whatever Nash thinks. I have no opinion to-day but his'.[215] The correspondences to Wilde continue; eternally sanguine and amiable, criticism from others is of no consequence to Nash. He happily pokes fun at his own idiosyncrasies, such as his early enthusiasm for china: 'we have our little phases, haven't we'?[216] Nash also 'lolls about' on divans, prefers the French school of painting and has an ambivalent relation to the dramatic arts in that, like Wilde, he derides the acting profession but frequents the theater and pays elaborate homage to leading actresses.

While James was careful to ensure that Nash did not physically resemble Wilde—he is 'of the middle stature', balding, and wears a beard—his personal and social attributes leave us in no doubt as to his original. The one physical Wildean attribute James does allow Nash is his voice, which has 'a conspicuous and aggressive perfection . . . He seemed to draw rich effects and wandering airs from it—to modulate and manipulate it as he would have done a musical instrument'.[217]

The Tragic Muse was not James's first appropriation of an aesthete for his fiction, nor was it to be his last. James first satirized aestheticism as early as 1876, with the title character in *Roderick Hudson*. Five years later, the aesthetic Gilbert Osmond in *Portrait of a Lady* (1881) writes a poem entitled 'Rome Revisited', most likely a fictional echo of Wilde's poem 'Rome Unvisited', published the same year.[218] 'The Author of "Beltraffio"' (1884) drew upon the domestic troubles of the aesthete John Addington Symonds and after *The Tragic Muse* James went on to explore the vagaries of aesthetic philosophy with

Mrs Gareth in *The Spoils of Poynton* (1897), Lambert Strether in *The Ambassadors* (1903) (whose name echoes that of 'Lambert Streyke' from Burnand's play *The Colonel*, discussed above), and in 1904's *The Golden Bowl*.[219] Of all his fictional aesthetes, however, Gabriel Nash is the most ambivalent portrait, and an examination of James's relation to Wilde provides some fascinating insights into the possible reasons for this.

One would be hard pressed to find two late Victorian personalities more different than Henry James and Oscar Wilde. James was conservative, serious, and self-effacing and found Wilde's flamboyance and flagrant self-publication highly distasteful. A letter written by Harriet Loring after entertaining both James and Wilde in Washington in 1882 highlights the contrast between the two authors:

> 'Laborious' describes [James] I think, his manners and conversation alike. He is always doing his level best and one can't help approving of him but longing for a little of the divine spark. Then we had Oscar . . . tights—yellow silk handkerchief and all. He is the most gruesome object I ever saw, but he was very amusing. Full of Irish keenness and humor and really interesting—[220]

A letter written by James to Isabella Stewart Gardner in January 1882, referring to the same function, reflects his antagonism toward Wilde. James writes of his disappointment after meeting at the Loring reception 'the repulsive and fatuous Oscar Wilde, whom, I am happy to say, no one was looking at'.[221] In light of Loring's testimony above, this appears to be a case of wishful thinking on James's part. In other letters from this period James refers to Wilde as 'an unclean beast' and a 'tenth-rate cad'.[222] Wilde temporarily charmed James in America when he told a reporter that 'no living Englishman can be compared to Howells and James as novelists', but when James called on Wilde to thank him for the compliment he found the young aesthete unbearably pretentious and patronizing. He particularly resented Wilde's inference that he was more a 'citizen of the world' than James.[223]

In addition to the difference in their personalities, Jonathan Freedman identifies three further factors that roused James's hostility toward Wilde. The first of these is their diverging interpretations of Pater's philosophies, which were formative influences for both.[224] The second is a sense of competition between the two men resulting from their common backgrounds and careers—both were men of letters and immigrants to England who simultaneously courted and satirized their adoptive society. Freedman finally points to James's jealousy of Wilde's theatrical success and public position as the leading 'Apostle of Aestheticism', a role to which James himself aspired.[225]

Freedman also refers to a possible factor that has fascinated many commentators on the relationship of James and Wilde, that being the former's latent homosexuality. Sheldon M. Novic states that James had 'love affairs, apparently only with men, but disapprov[ed] of promiscuity and of open homosexuality'.[226] This disapprobation is discernible in James's earlier fiction; Eric Haralson has noted that James's 1884 story 'The Author of "Beltraffio"' contains a 'strong suggestion . . . that [the] cult of perfervid aestheticism [in the story] constitutes a hotbed of dangerous male bonding'.[227] Freedman epitomizes the typical critical interpretation of James's response to Wilde when he highlights

> the excessively *personal* [emphasis in the original] quality of James's distaste for Wilde. James's own uneasy feelings about his sexuality, one might hypothesize, led him to see Wilde as the embodiment of his own impulses, and thus to demonize his double—to relieve himself of the burden of guilt or shame (or both) by denouncing Wilde's flamboyant and public flouting of sexual convention.[228]

As Ellmann has noted, Wilde's sexual recklessness, which steadily increased from the time of his first homosexual encounter, reportedly in 1886, through to the 1890s, posed a threat to practicing homosexuals: 'the tolerance of deviation, or ignorance of it, were alike in jeopardy because of Wilde's flouting and flaunting . . . James, foreseeing scandal, separated himself from this menace in motley'.[229]

It is often taken as a sign of James's softening toward Wilde that in 1888 James registered his name as a member of the Savile Club to speak at a meeting on the subject of Wilde's election as a member. However, as noted with regard to Walter Besant above, it is equally possible, and in fact more likely, that James registered his name in order to speak *against* Wilde's admission. James's frequent attempts to distance himself from Wilde are evident in his letters, especially after the latter's fall from grace. In a letter to Edmund Gosse in April 1895 James refers to Wilde's trials as 'hideous', 'sickening', and 'squalid', and asserts that Wilde 'was never in the smallest degree interesting to me'.[230] Although James thought Wilde's two-year sentence too harsh, when asked to sign a petition for the mitigation of the sentence he refused, replying through his friend Jonathan Sturges that 'the document would only exist as a manifesto of personal loyalty to Oscar by his friends, of whom [I] was never one'.[231]

Wilde's early remarks on James generally reflect their divergent approaches to literature. In reviewing another author's novel for *The Woman's World* in January 1888, Wilde obliquely refers to the burgeoning school of novel writing led by James:

> This school is not native, nor does it seek to reproduce any English master. It may be described as the result of the realism of Paris filtered through the refining influence of Boston. Analysis, not action, is its aim; it has more psychology than passion, and it plays very cleverly upon one string, and this is the commonplace.[232]

Wilde goes on in the same article to speak of the pleasure of finding another novel that reacts against this school: Lady Augusta Noel's *Hithersea Mere*. Wilde notes approvingly that Noel's novel 'suggests rather than explains' and is not concerned with the 'vivisection' of its characters.[233] In 'The Decay of Lying', published the year after this review, Wilde writes, 'Mr. Henry James writes fiction as if it were a painful duty, and wastes upon mean motives and imperceptible "points of view" his neat literary style, his felicitous phrases, his swift and caustic satire'.[234] There is no record of Wilde's opinion of his likeness in Gabriel Nash, however, we can reasonably deduce from these remarks that he would not have appreciated being put under James's fictional microscope.

Despite his criticisms of James's dispassionate, analytical style, Wilde did respect James's technical ability; Laurence Housman recalls Wilde remarking '[t]here are many things one ought to read which one is bound not to like: Byron, Wordsworth—even Henry James'.[235] Richard Ellmann records that James's *The Ambassadors* was on Wilde's last bookseller's bill.[236] A comment made by Wilde to his friend Robert Ross after reading 'The Turn of the Screw' in 1898 encapsulates Wilde's opinion of James's literary talents: 'I think it is a most wonderful, lurid, poisonous little tale, like an Elizabethan tragedy. I am greatly impressed by it. James is developing, but he will never arrive at passion I fear'.[237]

James's portrait of Nash in *The Tragic Muse* suggests that James had the same qualified respect for Wilde's literary abilities, despite his disparaging remarks about the man and his work. What is perhaps most interesting about Gabriel Nash is that, despite his discomfiting philosophies and unsettling effect on the central characters, James cannot bring himself to wholly condemn him. This was observed by the novel's earliest critics, such as the *Manchester Guardian* correspondent who noted that Nash's 'rank in the writer's estimation . . . is hard to fix'.[238] Later commentators have consistently expressed their surprise that James did not present a more scathing or satirical portrait of Wilde; indeed, at times the author portrays Nash almost fondly.[239] James's Nash belies his creator's protestation that Wilde was 'never in the smallest degree interesting' to him; James's examination of Nash's complex character is clearly an attempt by the author to come to terms with his mixed feelings about Wilde.

It has been noted by critics that much of Nash's philosophy, particularly with regard to the role of art and the theater in middle class, commercial society, corresponds with that of James himself.[240] Lyall Powers takes this as an indication that James effectively split himself into the characters of Dormer and Nash; he interprets Nash's physical attributes as further evidence of this.[241] However, I would argue that these correspondences are merely a reflection of the points on which Wilde and James *did* agree; in many ways they were on the same side against a 'Philistine' public, suspicious of art and artistic types. James, like Wilde, had little sympathy with this attitude, as he demonstrates when he mocks the conviction of Miriam's mother that 'the "aesthetic"—a horrible insidious foreign disease—is eating the healthy core out of English life'.[242]

It becomes clear as the novel progresses that Nash has both intelligence and literary talent, despite his relatively small output. This reflects James's opinion of Wilde; with all of James's criticism he would customarily concede that Wilde was gifted; he went to see the latter's plays, bought his books, and recorded some of Wilde's epigrams.[243] Richard Ellmann notes that there are various Wildean influences to be found in James's plays and Neil Sammells points to echoes of Wilde's *Dorian Gray* in James's 'The Figure in the Carpet' (1896).[244] In a letter to Edmund Gosse in April 1895 James refers to Wilde's career as 'nearly 20 years of a really unique kind of "brilliant" conspicuity . . . wit, "art," conversation'.[245] In another letter to Daudet on November 10, 1895, James asserts that if Wilde could survive and recuperate in prison he could still produce a masterpiece.[246]

The Tragic Muse imbues a sense of how James, 'laborious' in manner and in conversation, must have secretly admired the charisma and social skills of his aesthetic alter ego:

> [Nash] was perpetually in the field, sociable, amiable, communicative, inveterately contradicted but never confounded, ready to talk to any one about any thing and making disagreement (of which he left the responsibility wholly to others) a basis of intimacy.
>
>   . . . no recollection of him, no evocation of him in absence could do him justice.[247]

One also senses James's admiration in Nash's pronouncement:

> 'I talk; I say the things that other people don't, that they can't, that they won't—'.²⁴⁸

Nash certainly possesses many of Wilde's praiseworthy attributes. He encourages Dormer to pursue his dream of an artistic career, just as Wilde did for so many of his acquaintances, and demonstrates Wilde's empathy and generosity to those in need. Like Wilde, Nash has good taste and is 'an excellent touchstone'; his opinion carries 'the dignity of judgement [and] the authority of intelligence'.²⁴⁹ His unapologetic individualism is undeniably refreshing, as Nick Dormer observes:

> 'Most people have a lot of attributes and appendages that dress them up and superscribe them, and what I like [Nash] for is that he hasn't any at all. It makes him so cool . . . He doesn't shade off into other people; he's as neat as an outline cut out of paper with scissors. I like him, therefore, because in intercourse with him you know what you've got hold of—'.²⁵⁰

James also allows Nash to defend himself against the charges that were commonly directed toward Wilde, as demonstrated in the following conversation between Nash and Dormer:

> 'I say, my dear fellow, do you mind mentioning to me whether you are the greatest humbug and charlatan on earth, or a genuine intelligence, one that has sifted things for itself'?
> 'I do puzzle you—I'm so sorry,' Nash replied, benignly. 'But I'm very sincere. And I *have* [emphasis in the original] tried to straighten out things a bit for myself'.
> 'Then why do you give people such a handle'?
> 'Such a handle'?
> 'For thinking you're an—for thinking you're not wise'.
> 'I dare say it's my manner; they're so unused to candour'.²⁵¹

Nash denies his manner is 'affected':

> 'That's always the charge against a personal manner; if you have any at all people think you have too much.'
> 'I don't think it's so horrible, my disposition. But we've befogged and befouled so the whole question of liberty, of spontaneity, of good-humour and inclination and enjoyment, that there's nothing that makes people stare so as to see one natural'.²⁵²

Nash also denies he is impertinent: 'The only impertinence is aggression, and I indignantly protest that I am never guilty of *that* [emphasis in the original] clumsiness'.[253] These passages in the novel essentially constitute James defending Wilde against his detractors, of which he professed to be one. The following description of Dormer's reaction to Nash appears to epitomize James's dilemma:

> [Dormer] . . . had two states of mind in listening to Gabriel Nash; one of them in which he laughed, doubted, sometimes even reprobated, and at any rate failed to follow or accept; the other in which this contemplative genius seemed to take the words out of his mouth, to utter for him, better and more completely, the very things he was on the point of saying. Nash's saying them at such moments appeared to make them true, to set them up in the world—[254]

Of all the characters in *The Tragic Muse*, diplomat Peter Sherringham most effectively illustrates James's ambivalent reaction to Wilde. The aesthetic Nash holds a 'baleful fascination' for the conservative envoy, who feels 'a certain displeasure' at being unable to dismiss Nash as a bore. After declaring that Nash is 'impudent', Sherringham cannot help but feel 'guilty of an injustice—Nash had so little the air of a man with something to gain'. Sherringham feels petty when he is exasperated by Nash's perpetual good humor and unembarrassed inconsistency, and envies the aesthete his 'power to content himself with the pleasures he could get: [Sherringham] had a shrewd impression that contentment was not destined to be the sweetener of his own repast'.[255] Like Sherringham, one suspects that James, envious of Wilde's 'divine spark', 'would have been sorry to confess that he could not understand' the remarkable aesthete.[256]

James's portrait of Nash also suggests that the author was unnerved by the overt nature of Wilde's sexuality. Eric Haralson sees the novel as reflecting a 'delicate [balance of] homophobic and homophilic impulses'.[257] John Carlos Rowe has noted that Nash's name, being an amalgamation of the Elizabethan dramatists Gabriel Harvey and Thomas Nashe, evokes the bisexuality of many theatrical Elizabethan men.[258] Nash's sexuality is certainly shadowy; his androgyny mystifies his peers and he frequents the 'Anonymous' Club; the need for anonymity remaining conspicuously unstated. He emanates a 'morbid' air and his uncanny insights and persuasive powers add to a general sense of ambiguity and otherness. Dormer reflects that many people believe the comic press is 'restrained by decorum from touching upon the worst of [Nash's] aberrations'.[259]

Once again, our imaginations are left to supply the 'worst' type of aberration.

There are many more tangible hints at Nash's sexual inclination to be found in the text. Although we are not given an insight into his true feelings for Dormer, Nash talks to Dormer's sister 'only of Nick—of nothing else'.[260] When Nash tells Dormer that Miriam Rooth is in love, Dormer asks,

> 'Do you mean with you?'
> 'Oh, I'm never another man . . . I'm more the wrong one than the man himself'.[261]

The Tragic Muse is also the first of several novels discussed in this study to put the Wildean character between a woman and her man; Nash encourages Dormer to sever ties with his fiancé Julia Dallow, who disapproves of his artistic aspirations. J. H. Miller has noted that homosexuality in the novel often appears to be coded as a devotion to art.[262] Indeed, Nash's aesthetic philosophy, first communicated to Dormer at Oxford, has earned Nash a reputation as 'bad company', an 'evil genius' whose philosophy is 'poison'.[263] Nash 'convert[s]' Nick to the artistic life and the latter's studio becomes an 'unnatural spot'. Haralson describes the aesthete Nash as 'a fundamental affront to the heterosexualised order of things'.[264]

Like Praed's *Affinities*, James's *Tragic Muse*, in attempting to communicate the potent, yet elusive quality of Gabriel Nash's original, at times suggests a supernatural power. Nash's presence imbues a sense of 'the transient and occasional' and has a 'likeness to vapour or murmuring wind or shifting light'.[265] After hearing nothing of Nash for some time, Dormer imagines that he has 'melted back into the elements—he is part of the ambient air'.[266] Nash declares that he is prophetic and he is proven to be so. He also gives the impression that he is immune to illness and he reflects that he may be 'eternal'.[267] Lyall Powers reads Nash's angelic first name as symbolic of his role as a 'messenger of the god of art'.[268] Nash certainly presents some celestial qualities. Consider the following comment from Dormer, referring to one of the most fascinating episodes in the novel, his painting of Nash's portrait:

> 'Let me at any rate have some sort of sketch of you, as a kind of feather from the angel's wing, or a photograph of the ghost, to prove to me in the future that you were once a solid, sociable fact, that I didn't utterly fabricate you'.[269]

Dormer's attempt to capture something of Nash's essence by painting the latter's portrait proves to be curiously problematic:

> It struck [Dormer] that he had never *seen* [emphasis in the original] his subject before, and yet somehow this revelation was not produced by the sense of actually seeing it. What was revealed was the difficulty—what he saw was the indefinite and the elusive. He had taken things for granted which literally were not there, and he found things there (except that he couldn't catch them) which he had not hitherto counted in—[270]

James suggests that to 'pin down' Nash/Wilde, to scrutinize him, is to disarm him—to destroy his mysterious power. Nash under Dormer's analytical gaze is somewhat analogous to a sprite that has been captured in a jar and is slowly suffocating:

> [Nash] was uncomfortable, at first vaguely and then definitely so—silent, restless, gloomy, dim . . . Nick felt, accordingly, as if he had laid a trap for him . . . [he] guessed that what made his friend uncomfortable was simply the reversal . . . of his usual terms of intercourse. He was so accustomed to living upon irony and the interpretation of things that it was strange to him to be himself interpreted . . . From being outside of the universe he was suddenly brought into it, and from the position of a free commentator and critic . . . reduced to that of humble ingredient and contributor.[271]

Here James may strike at the core of Wilde's dislike of being 'vivisected' or 'unmasked'. In 'The Decay of Lying', where he argues that the artist should maintain a mask, Wilde states,

> It is a humiliating confession, but we are all made out of the same stuff . . . The more one analyses people, the more all reasons for analysis disappear. Sooner or later one comes to that dreadful universal thing called human nature.[272]

Unsurprisingly, Nash never returns for another sitting after being subjected to Dormer's debilitating scrutiny. Like the fairy tale creature, he must remain outside of the world of ordinary men in order to retain his glamor. The curious fate of Nash's incomplete portrait appears to confirm his supernatural nature. Dormer notes that after Nash's disappearance

> the picture he had begun had a singular air of gradually fading from the canvas. He couldn't catch it in the act, that the hand of time was

rubbing it away little by little (. . . as in some delicate Hawthorne tale), making the surface indistinct and bare . . . of all resemblance to the model. Of course the moral of the Hawthorne tale would be that this personage would come back on the day when the last adumbration should have vanished.[273]

The 'disappearing portrait' has inspired some diverse and fascinating critical interpretations. Rowe believes that 'James has caused Nash to "disappear" primarily to control the homoerotic passions and rhetoric that characterize his relationship with [Dormer]'.[274] Haralson interprets the projected return of Nash, when his image has finally faded from view, as reflecting the inevitable 'return' of suppressed homosexuality 'to haunt the heterosexual domain'.[275] Haralson also highlights the fact that Dormer jams the unfinished portrait into a corner, facing the wall, in order to continue with his heterosexual relationship and his artistic career.[276] Ellmann, on the other hand, sees Nash's strange exit from the novel as demonstrating the fact that 'aestheticism, being indifferent to concrete detail, could confer upon its followers only an illusory existence'.[277] Freedman highlights the obvious parallel between the transcendental qualities of Dormer's portrait of Nash and James's own fictionalization of Wilde. He notes that

> Nash's portrait is rendered 'bare of all resemblance to the model,' which is to suggest that it utterly masters, assumes, and remakes the identity of the individual it attempts to represent; it effaces the historical identity of that being by transmuting his image into the consummate perfection of the artistic image.[278]

Christopher Lane notes an interesting parallel between Nash's portrait and Dorian Gray's in Wilde's novel, observing that in both cases 'the characters' unfulfilled desire [is depicted] through their incomplete portraits. The portraits attempt to unite both the painter and the painted through art, within an acceptable limit of erotic expression'.[279]

Before leaving *The Tragic Muse*, the book's relation to *The Picture of Dorian Gray* must be further considered here. There has been some conflicting critical commentary on the question of how these two works influenced each other. As stated above, James's *The Tragic Muse* first appeared as a serial in the *Atlantic* from January 1889 to May 1890; that is, it was published just before *The Picture of Dorian Gray* was first printed in *Lippincott's Magazine* in July 1890. Both stories have an aesthete, an artist, and an actress as central characters; the actresses even share a common stage name—Vane—and both perform the role of Juliet. Moreover, both plots feature portraits that supernaturally change to reflect the sitter's fate.

Oscar Cargill was the first to comment upon these correspondences in 1957, although he did not draw the most obvious conclusion that Wilde had been influenced by James's work. Cargill argues that Wilde habitually spoke in public about his works in progress and that '[if James didn't] pick up . . . early knowledge of some of the substance of *The Picture of Dorian Gray* from the general repetition of Wilde's talk in London circles, there were several direct channels through which he might have got his information', such as Edmund Gosse (who was a friend of both James and Wilde's friend Robert Ross) and Joseph Marshall Stoddart, who commissioned Wilde's story for *Lippincott's*.[280] Cargill is convinced that James had only heard certain things about *Dorian Gray* and had not seen the actual text, remarking that if he had read it in full, 'he might . . . have implied graver limitations to his aesthete or have been repelled from using Wilde at all as a model'.[281] Cargill also cites emendations in *The Tragic Muse* when it appeared in book form in June 1890 (a month before Wilde's story appeared) as evidence of James's prior knowledge of Wilde's soon-to-be-published book. In particular, Cargill points out that Nash is described as a writer of verses in the *Atlantic* version of *The Tragic Muse*, whereas in the novel he is described as having written 'a very clever book': 'a sort of novel'. When pressed, Nick Dormer cannot specify exactly what type of novel Nash has written: 'Well, I don't know—with a lot of good writing'. Cargill argues that Dormer does not describe Nash's book because James had not yet read Wilde's *Dorian Gray*.[282]

Subsequent criticism has paid scant attention to Cargill's theory and has generally taken the alternate view that Wilde's novel was influenced by James's book. Jonathan Freedman goes further to suggest that James's hostility toward Wilde was exacerbated by Wilde's allusion to, and 'outright theft' from, his novel and that James's later novel *The Ambassadors* represents his revision of 'Wilde's redaction of his own text', committed 'with malice aforethought'.[283] Few seem prepared to accept that the correspondences between the two stories are coincidental. However, Kerry Powell's 1983 article 'Tom, Dick and Dorian Gray: Magic-Picture Mania in Late Victorian Fiction', which highlights the popular fascination with 'supernatural' pictures during this period, suggests that coincidence is also a possibility.[284]

With his portrait of Gabriel Nash, James was perhaps least true to his own philosophy on the use of real personalities in fiction. He averred in *The Art of the Novel* that in drawing upon life for fiction, the 'final savour [should be] constituted, but the primary identity destroyed', having been replaced by truth to a 'new life'.[285] However, as many other authors have discovered, Wilde's identity is too singular and conspicuous to be destroyed or disguised with a beard and a pseudonym. What 'new life' Wilde does acquire in James's novel is in his role as a repository for the author's conflicting responses to him. Nash's ambivalent depiction in *The Tragic Muse*, and his ambiguous departure from the book, demonstrate that James was unable to reconcile himself to a firm position on Wilde, in 1890 at least. The events of 1895 would provide him with a firmer base for his tenuous antipathy. However, James always acknowledged Wilde's talent, even after the latter's downfall. He also contributed to the support of Wilde's wife and children after the aesthete's disgrace and befriended his son Vyvyan in the early 1900s.

Marc-André Raffalovich

A Willing Exile (1890)

When Wilde first learned that his old Trinity colleague Edward Carson was to lead the prosecution against him during his trials in 1895, he reportedly told a member of his own legal team: 'No doubt he will perform his task with the added bitterness of an old friend'.[286] This could also be said of Wilde's next fictionalizer, Marc-André Raffalovich, who published *A Willing Exile* in 1890. Raffalovich's book was another highly personal fictional response to Wilde; the minor poet and novelist was a former friend who was fast becoming an enemy, and his novel clearly reflects the author's antagonism toward his subject. As was the case with James, Raffalovich's adverse reaction to Wilde appears to have been influenced by an anxiety about his own sexuality.[287]

Raffalovich was of Russian Jewish descent but he had been living in Paris before he emigrated to London in 1882. A man renowned for his physical unattractiveness, legend had it that his beautiful mother (who had a salon in Paris) sent him to London because she could no longer bear to look at his face! While he had his own literary aspirations, Raffalovich used the money he inherited from his wealthy banking family to carve a niche for himself as a patron of the arts in London, throwing lavish lunches and dinner parties for the artistic elite. Apart from Wilde, other distinguished guests who attended his receptions included Comyns Carr, Henry James, Louise Jopling, W. B. Maxwell, George Moore, and Walter Pater. Raffalovich had heard Wilde lecture about his travels in the United States and the two men became friends for a time in the 1880s.[288] However, Raffalovich became increasingly disgruntled with Wilde as their relationship continued, seemingly because of the latter's unapologetic egotism and the lack of caution he exercised in his private affairs. According to Raffalovich's article 'Oscar Wilde', published in *Blackfriars* in 1927, it was a chance comment from Wilde's wife Constance that proved to be the final straw for Raffalovich:

> Constance, who had always befriended me . . . said to me: 'Oscar says he likes you so much—that you have such nice improper talks together.' Was it a kindly warning, or just a mechanical repetition of his words? I was furious. I had imagined myself a privileged person, safe from his double-edged praise . . . I was innocent of what I called improper talks. I listened eagerly to his wit and wisdom and experience, to his store of unusual stories . . . but I had added nothing but what he called my blend of romance and cynicism, my boyish queries, my interest in all the Paolos and the Francescas. Looking back now his conversation must at times have resembled Dante's *Purgatorio*, Canto xxvi. I was furious: never again did I speak with him without witnesses.[289]

Raffalovich's overreaction to the word 'improper'—and his heated denial of contributing to conversations that could be interpreted as such—almost certainly reflect an anxiety pertaining to public speculation about his own sexuality. As a conservative man grappling with homosexual inclinations, Raffalovich, like James, could not afford to be seen as a friend of the flagrant and indiscreet Wilde.[290] We can reasonably assume that this was a major motivation behind Raffalovich's break with the playwright. Interspersed throughout Raffalovich's 1927 article are anecdotes intended to demonstrate Wilde's evil influence over him. Raffalovich relates that he was warned about associating with Wilde and repeatedly denies any fellow-feeling between them: 'everything he did or said annoyed me. He could do nothing right in my eyes'.[291] He speaks of being 'dragged' to a party at Tite Street, and expresses his wholehearted approval of Wilde's 1895 conviction for 'gross indecency'. Damning Wilde with faint praise, Raffalovich writes, 'I cannot remember his ever giving me bad advice. It is to his credit that he never did me any harm, and perhaps to mine that for years I detested him and his presence, and the traces of his influence'.[292] Such comments are typical of Raffalovich's lifelong quest to extricate himself from his former friend in the public eye.

As with Broughton, Ward, and James, Wilde may also have alienated Raffalovich with his review of the latter's work. Raffalovich's book of poems, *Tuberose and Meadowsweet*, was reviewed by Wilde in the *Pall Mall Gazette* of March 27, 1885. Altough the review was not entirely unfavorable, there was much in it to annoy Raffalovich:

> This is really a remarkable little volume, and contains many strange and beautiful poems. To say of these poems that they are unhealthy and bring with them the heavy odours of the hothouse is to point out neither their defect nor their merit, but their quality merely. And though Mr. Raffalovich is not a wonderful poet, still he is a subtle artist in poetry. Indeed, in his way he is a boyish master of curious music and of fantastic rhyme, and can strike on the lute of language so many lovely chords that it seems a pity he does not know how to pronounce the title of his book and the theme of his songs. For he insists on making 'tuberose' a trisyllable always, as if it were a potato blossom and not a flower shaped like a tiny trumpet of ivory. However, for the sake of his meadowsweet and his spring-green binding this must be forgiven him. And though he cannot pronounce 'tuberose' aright, at least he can sing of it exquisitely.[293]

In an indignant response to Wilde's criticisms, Raffalovich cited Shelley's identical pronunciation of tuberose; much to his consternation, Wilde blithely supplied a contradictory quotation from Shelley.[294]

As hard as Raffalovich worked to show that he and Wilde were not 'birds of a feather', he unwittingly provided us with considerable evidence to the contrary. For example, there is the unmistakable hint of personal resentment in his annoyance at Wilde's habit of 'selecting the youngest in any company and talking to him endlessly, turning his head ... for the mere pleasure of doing so, even though they were never to meet again'.[295] Raffalovich's recollection of a policeman who prevented him from witnessing one of Wilde's trials is also revealing:

> I wished to find my way to see this unheard-of spectacle of a twofold poetical justice, allured not only by the onslaught on Wilde, but by the flouting of Mrs. Grundy ... A *handsome youthful* policeman [my italics] stopped me: 'It is no place for you, Sir; don't go in'. 'Thank you; you are right', I murmured, and went away. This policeman, *fair, almost luminous, like the Archangel Raphael* [my italics], deserves from me this tribute.[296]

Rupert Croft-Cooke argues that Raffalovich's antagonism toward Wilde reflected his jealousy of Wilde's literary talent and celebrity.[297] (None of Raffalovich's poems, plays, or novels met with critical success.) Ian Fletcher has observed that 'from Wilde's point of view, [Raffalovich] was somewhat devoid of talent, not conspicuously witty, certainly not handsome and his sexual inclination not sufficiently marked'.[298] It may be that Raffalovich's main attraction for Wilde was his generous provision of epicurean delights for London's artistic set.

Raffalovich alleged that Wilde once told him, 'You could give me a new thrill. You have the right measure of romance and cynicism'.[299] Perhaps Wilde made a miscalculation in this assessment; there is little that would have thrilled him and far more cynicism than romance to be found in Raffalovich's *A Willing Exile*. Raffalovich appears to have had a considerable personal investment in the book; a friend observed at the time: 'André finished his novel and nearly made himself ill over it'.[300] Like his later novel *Self-seekers: A Novel of Manners* (1897), *A Willing Exile* is a satire on the superficial nature of fashionable society. A quotation on the title page from à Kempis imparts the moral of the story before it has begun, a moral that could not be further from Wilde's credo c. 1890:

> It is a great thing, and very great, to be able to do without all solace, both human and divine, and to be willing to bear this exile of the heart for the honour of God, and in nothing seek self, and not to have regard to one's own merit.[301]

Raffalovich's story charts the moral deterioration of the egocentric and obnoxious Wildean character, Cyprian Brome, who is the son of a *nouveau riche* manufacturer. Wilde's wife Constance also appears as Daisy Laylham, the heroine of the novel, who marries Cyprian, her first suitor, to relieve her family's financial difficulties (a twist on the usual scenario of the Wildean character marrying for money). We can reasonably assume that Daisy's wonder at her husband's antics is analogous to Constance Wilde's, the woman who befriended Raffalovich:

> Mrs. Brome, of course, knew many men. Cyprian was, or seemed to be, intimate with countless young or youngish men; they were all curiously alike. Their voices, the cut of their clothes, the curl of their hair, the brims of their hats, the parties they went to . . . Affectation characterised all these men . . . They were all gushers . . . Married . . . or unmarried, they gushed alike . . .
>
> Cyprian's cult for his own looks . . . increased . . . He lived with people who talked much about beauty . . . He had acquired the habit of comparing himself to every one he met and of debating who was better looking . . . He had two [bunches of] flowers . . . sent him every day, one before lunch, the other before dinner. His clothes much occupied him . . . sometimes Daisy, after having been away an hour, would find him and a chum still pursuing their analysis of another man's garments.[302]

In *A Willing Exile*, Raffalovich suggests that Wilde's charm is all calculation:

> [Cyprian] expressed moral sentiments gracefully at the right times— that is, at tea-time in some houses, and during meals in others; and he was very lenient to privileged offenders—[303]

Cyprian's increasing insensitivity and selfishness eventually drive Daisy into the arms of another man, Clarence Holford. The couple plan an elopement that is thwarted when Cyprian contracts a serious illness; soon after Holford also becomes ill after a fall from his horse. After some time Daisy realizes that Holford thinks more of Cyprian's wellbeing than her own, and the story ends with Daisy facing a bleak future attending to the needs of both uncaring invalids.[304]

It must be said that the style and plot of *A Willing Exile* are not of a high quality; as Brocard Sewell notes, 'fiction was not [Raffalovich's] medium; while [*A Willing Exile* and *Self-seekers*] attempt to satirize the superficialities of fashionable life, [they] do not escape triviality themselves'.[305] The commercial failure of the book may have contributed to the growing tension between Raffalovich and Wilde. Raffalovich probably felt envious of Wilde's growing celebrity, with *Dorian Gray* taking London by storm the year after the lukewarm reception of *A Willing Exile*. Raffalovich responded to Wilde's success with a sonnet against the latter's signature flower entitled 'The Green Carnation', first published in a London journal and then in Raffalovich's *The Thread and the Path* (1895). Raffalovich later described this sonnet as 'an important step . . . [a] public rejection of the whole set'.[306]

The rift between the two authors was cemented in 1892 when Raffalovich took up with Wilde's former constant companion, the poet John Gray, who felt he had been jilted by Wilde for Lord Alfred Douglas. Raffalovich was to remain Gray's friend, protector, and collaborator for some forty years. At the beginning of their friendship Raffalovich undoubtedly encouraged Gray to sever ties with Wilde (as he later encouraged the artist Aubrey Beardsley, who received a pension from Raffalovich, as related in Part 3). It is around this time that Wilde made some particularly cutting *bon mots* about Raffalovich, such as his famous comment about Raffalovich's somewhat extravagant entertainments: 'André came to London to start a salon, and has only succeeded in opening a saloon'.[307] (On his last visit to Raffalovich's for dinner Wilde arrived at the same time as five others, and said dryly to the butler 'A table for six, please'.[308]) Raffalovich avers in his 1927 article that finally Wilde would not sit next to him at the hair salon they both frequented: 'I became in that shop *somebody*—the customer who makes Mr. Wilde uncomfortable'.[309]

Raffalovich did not relinquish his role as a thorn in Wilde's side after the latter's fall from grace; less than three months after Wilde was imprisoned he published a forty-seven-page pamphlet in French entitled *L'Affaire Oscar Wilde*, which was reprinted the following year in a larger work on male homosexuality: *Uranisme et Unisexualité*. Croft-Cooke notes the 'high-minded disapproval' and 'pseudo-scientifically inquiring attitude' in this vituperative work, which argues for celibacy over the gratification of homosexual urges.[310] Raffalovich also provides some lurid details pertaining to Wilde's and Alfred Douglas's private lives and heaps censure on Wilde and English society:

> When I accuse him of criminality, I'm not concerned about the sexual acts of which he is accused, but of his personal role, of the influence that he had, and that he used so badly, of the youthful conceits that he perverted, of the vices that he so encouraged. English society is equally to blame . . . Wilde was encouraged and tolerated by English society . . . under the influence of vanity and impunity he ended up living a life that proved to be equally dangerous and daring for the public as for himself. He was a victim of himself, of society, of his friends. If he is to be pitied in his great misfortune, he should also be remembered as a national danger—[311]

The public's reaction to Wilde's trials undoubtedly affected Raffalovich's and Gray's future directions. Raffalovich converted to Catholicism the year after Wilde's conviction and reportedly organized masses to be said for Wilde and Alfred Douglas.[312] John Gray entered Scots College, Rome, in 1898 to prepare for the priesthood and was ordained in 1901; Raffalovich later followed him to Edinburgh and built St Peter's church, where Gray was rector for over twenty years and where Raffalovich regularly attended morning mass. Raffalovich purchased a home close to Gray's clergy house and saw Gray almost every day for twenty-seven years. Despite the frequency of their meetings, both men maintained an extraordinary formality in front of others.[313]

Arthur Conan Doyle
The Sign of Four (1890)

Wilde's next fictional appearance was alongside a character who ranks among the most famous in all English fiction: Arthur Conan Doyle's consulting detective Sherlock Holmes. Holmes and his protégé Dr Watson had made their first appearance in Doyle's *A Study in Scarlet* in 1887, first published in *Beeton's Christmas Annual* and then in book form the following year. The Edinburgh-born and educated Doyle (1859–1930) was at that time practicing medicine in Southsea. His *A Study in Scarlet* was not a runaway success; this was to come later for Doyle with the series of short stories about Sherlock Holmes that appeared in the popular *Strand* magazine from 1891. In the intervening period Doyle wrote another Holmes novel, *The Sign of Four* (1890), which features a portrait of Wilde as the aesthetic Thaddeus Sholto.

The Wildean characterization in this novel is of particular interest because Wilde himself was present at the novel's commission. The occasion was a dinner at the Langham Hotel in London on August 30, 1889, which was hosted by the American Joseph Marshall Stoddart, mentioned above as a mutual acquaintance of Wilde and Henry James. Stoddart represented and published Gilbert and Sullivan's works in the United States and had met Wilde during the aesthete's American lecture tour. Stoddart was in London promoting *Lippincott's Magazine* (which he edited) and he invited Wilde, Doyle, and an Irish MP named Gill to dinner. Stoddart may have felt apprehensive about bringing Doyle and Wilde together; the former was firmly conservative in his outlook, an 'establishment' man with traditional Victorian ideas about family and empire. However, Doyle, was also fair and broadminded and in his 1930 memoirs he recalls his dinner with 'the champion of aestheticism' as 'a golden evening'. Doyle's remarks on meeting Wilde at the Langham Hotel are worth quoting at length:

> Wilde to my surprise had read 'Micah Clarke' [Doyle's recent work of historical fiction] and was enthusiastic about it, so that I did not feel like a complete outsider. His conversation left an indelible impression upon my mind. He towered above us all, and yet had the art of seeming to be interested in all that we could say. He had delicacy of feeling and tact . . . He had a curious precision of statement, a delicate flavour of humour, and a trick of small gestures to illustrate his meaning . . . I remember how in discussing the wars of the future he said: 'A chemist on each side will approach the frontier with a bottle'—his upraised hand and precise face conjuring up a vivid and grotesque picture. His anecdotes, too, were happy and curious . . . The result of the evening was that both Wilde and I promised to write books for 'Lippincott's Magazine'—Wilde's contribution was 'The Picture of Dorian Grey [*sic*]', a book which is surely upon a high moral plane, while I wrote 'The Sign of Four', in which Holmes made his second appearance. I should add that never in Wilde's conversation did I observe one trace of coarse-ness of thought, nor could one at that time associate him with such an idea.[314]

Doyle was clearly charmed by Wilde, and the feeling appears to have been mutual. In addition to his appreciation of *Micah Clarke*, it has been suggested that Wilde was familiar with Doyle's other writings. John A. Hodgson has expanded upon Paul Barolsky's and Owen Dudley Edwards's conjectures that the Impressionist subtitle of Wilde's essay 'Pen, Pencil and Poison: A Study in Green', may have been inspired by Doyle's use of the same contemporary art jargon for the title of his first Sherlock Holmes novel, *A Study in Scarlet*.[315] Hodgson also believes that Wilde makes an allusion to *A Study in Scarlet* in *The Picture of Dorian Gray*, referring to 'the scarlet threads of life'—Doyle referred to the 'scarlet thread of murder'.[316] Wilde's letter of thanks to Doyle for his congratulations on *Dorian Gray* suggests that the former appreciated the latter's encouragement in the face of public censure:

> I do aim at making a work of art, and I am really delighted that you think my treatment subtle and artistically good. The newspapers seem to me to be written by the prurient for the Philistine. I cannot understand how they can treat 'Dorian Gray' as immoral. My difficulty was to keep the inherent moral subordinate to the artistic and dramatic effect, and it still seems to me that the moral is too obvious.[317]

As we have seen with many of the authors already discussed, the strong impression made by Wilde upon Doyle clearly compelled the latter to try to capture something of Wilde's essence in fiction. It has been observed that Doyle appropriated many historical personalities for his works; Samuel Rosenberg has identified portraits of Gustave Flaubert, Friedrich Nietzsche, Jean Racine, and George Sand, among others.[318] Doyle himself confirmed that Sherlock Holmes was based on Dr Joseph Bell, a consulting surgeon at Edinburgh Infirmary where the author was a medical student in the 1870s.

The Sign of Four was published in *Lippincott's* in February 1890 and in book form the same year. Thaddeus Sholto appears in the fourth chapter, and though he has some of the familiar physical blinds—baldness, different coloring, and an altered physique—he is clearly derived from Wilde. Doyle adds a jerky awkwardness and a thin, high voice to the disguise, but Sholto's remaining characteristics clearly point to his original, particularly his 'pendulous lip' and habit of passing his hand over his irregular, miscolored teeth as he speaks; a gesture that is often evoked in recollections of Wilde. Sholto's eyes are a 'weak, watery blue', a description that again fits Wilde, and which Doyle also gives to a later Wildean incarnation discussed in Part 2. Sholto, like several other fictional Wildes, gives the impression of extreme youthfulness despite being thirty years of age (Wilde was 36 in 1890) and an examination of

Sholto's handwriting reveals an 'irrepressible Greek *e*', a distinctive feature of Wilde's penmanship. Sholto's aesthetic tastes also mirror Wilde's contemporary preferences, as we discover when Sholto is first glimpsed in what he calls his 'oasis of art in the howling desert of South London'[319]:

> The richest and glossiest of curtains and tapestries draped the walls, looped back here and there to expose some richly-mounted painting or oriental vase. The carpet was of amber and black, so soft and so thick that the foot sank pleasantly into it, as into a bed of moss. Two great tiger-skins thrown athwart it increased the suggestion of Eastern luxury, as did a huge hookah which stood upon a mat in the corner. A lamp in the fashion of a silver dove was hung from an almost invisible golden wire in the centre of the room. As it burned it filled the air with a subtle and aromatic odour.[320]

Sholto favors expensive foreign wines and smokes an exotic 'Eastern' tobacco with a balsamic odor (Wilde had a fondness for Egyptian cigarettes). Sholto is also a talker, and his conversation is unmistakably Wildean:

> 'I am a man of somewhat retiring, and I might even say refined, tastes, and there is nothing more unaesthetic than a policeman. I have a natural shrinking from all forms of rough materialism . . . I live, as you see, with some little atmosphere of elegance around me. I may call myself a patron of the arts. It is my weakness . . . I am partial to the modern French school [of painting]'.[321]

Sholto's refined tastes extend to his Wildean wardrobe. Compare the following passage to the picture of Wilde taken by Napolean Sarony during Wilde's American lecture tour in 1882 (at plate 4):

> Our new acquaintance . . . produced from behind a curtain a very long, befrogged top-coat with astrakhan collar and cuffs. This he buttoned tightly up, in spite of the extreme closeness of the night, and finished his attire by putting on a rabbit-skin cap—[322]

Although various scholars have commented on the Wildean influence in *The Sign of Four*, none to my knowledge have noted this, one of the most conspicuous of clues. Wilde treasured the distinctive coat in the Sarony picture, and possibly wore it when he met Doyle in 1889.[323] Of course, Doyle may also have seen the Sarony publicity shots elsewhere, as they were widely distributed.

Despite his unmanly tendency to hypochondria and initial appearance of being rather callous and off-hand, Sholto proves to be an honorable and generous man, as Doyle perceived Wilde to be. Sholto stands against his greedy twin brother Bartholomew, insisting that they should include the daughter of their father's old collaborator in dividing their deceased father's estate (their father's collaborator went missing ten years before while staying at the *Langham* Hotel, the venue for the Stoddart dinner). Holmes commends Sholto on his unselfish conduct: 'You have done well, sir, from first to last'.[324]

Readers familiar with Wilde's biography will note the curious coincidence of Thaddeus Sholto's surname. The ninth Marquess of Queensberry, father of Alfred Douglas and the man who hounded Wilde into court, was John *Sholto* Douglas; even more curiously, *John* Sholto is the name of Thaddeus's father. The correspondences proliferate: when Thaddeus's father was alive he 'always employed two prize-fighters to act as porters' for him.[325] The Marquess, inventor of the 'Queensberry Rules' of boxing, also associated with pugilists and indeed used them at one time to intimidate Wilde on a visit to the latter's house. The John Sholto of Doyle's story also appears to have possessed Queensberry's infamous temper; Doyle relates that Thaddeus's father 'had suffered for years from an enlarged spleen'.[326] Remarkably in light of these concurrences, *The Sign of Four* was published a year before Wilde began to associate with Alfred Douglas or had anything to do with his father, according to Wilde's biographers at least. However, it is quite likely that Doyle knew Queensberry by reputation, as the author professed a 'keen relish for the manly art' of boxing. Indeed, Doyle may have befriended Queensberry at some point, given their shared view, recorded in Conan Doyle's memoirs, that it was '[b]etter that our sports should be a little too rough than that we should run a risk of effeminacy'.[327] One could hypothesize that Thaddeus Sholto, in addition to his obvious Wildean origins, may also incorporate something of the aestheticism of the Marquess's youngest son Alfred, who was moving in aesthetic circles in Oxford at this time. If this is the case, it represents an astoundingly coincidental amalgamation on Doyle's part.[328]

The fact that Thaddeus has an identical twin is also interesting. This could be an allusion to Wilde's brother Willie, whose close resemblance to his sibling was said to have prompted Wilde to pay his brother to wear a beard! The fact that Bartholomew is less sympathetic than Thaddeus might also imply that they are a division of Wilde into his 'good' and 'bad' sides; Doyle, like most others who met Wilde, was most likely won over by the latter's personality after being initially repelled by his apparent vanity and affectation. Indeed, Holmes reviews his first opinion of Sholto; he had initially concluded from the latter's handwriting that he was not a man of good character.[329]

Interestingly, Thaddeus Sholto is not the only character who bears a marked resemblance to Oscar Wilde in *The Sign of Four*. The great detective himself assumes a distinctly Wildean bent in this, his second appearance. In *A Study in Scarlet*, Holmes had already exhibited a pronounced egotism, a staunch individualism, and a 'bumptious style of conversation'.[330] In *The Sign of Four* he not only continues in this vein but also assumes a conspicuously Wildean style of speech. When it is revealed that Holmes is a published expert on tobacco, he coolly confirms that he has been 'guilty of several monographs'. Holmes later states: 'I never make exceptions. An exception disproves the rule'.[331] In addition to demonstrating a Wildean talent for epigram in the story, Holmes also displays signs of a bohemian or aesthetic inclination; he is knowledgeable about music, cocaine, and tobacco and keeps his tobacco in an exotic Persian slipper. Holmes also demonstrates Wilde's flair for table talk on any subject, a talent that Doyle had recently witnessed first-hand:

> Our meal was a merry one. Holmes could talk exceedingly well when he chose, and that night he did choose . . . I have never known him so brilliant. He spoke on a quick succession of subjects—on miracle plays, on mediæval pottery, on Stradivarius violins, on the Buddhism of Ceylon, and on the warships of the future—handling each as though he had made a special study of it.[332]

Note that Holmes discourses on the wars of the future, just as Wilde did with Conan Doyle at the Langham Hotel. It appears that Conan Doyle could not resist borrowing a little of Wilde's distinctive flair for his consulting detective.

As mentioned above, other scholars have also observed Wildean elements in Holmes. Ian Ousby has noted that in *The Sign of Four* Doyle directly employs 'the appurtenances which [d]ecadence made fashionable' and the decadent 'myth of the sensitive genius'. Ousby also highlights Holmes's aesthetic view of detection 'as an art to be practised for its own sake'. He goes on to speculate that Doyle probably wished to 'strike a topical note, and perhaps to gain a little of the publicity which Wilde and his colleagues were so adept at attracting'.[333] H. R. F. Keating avers that Holmes's desire to shock is a very Wildean characteristic, and one that was to epitomize the new decadence of the 1890s.[334] Owen Dudley Edwards highlights the famous incident at the beginning of *The Sign of Four*, where Holmes is revealed as a recreational morphine and cocaine user, as indicative of the detective's Wilde-like restlessness and recklessness: 'There was in him, as a fixed part of his character, that longing for change, stimulation, excitement which was leading his once solid age . . . down a long, long Gadarene slope'. (In discussing his drug use with Watson, Holmes remarks, 'I abhor the dull routine of existence. I crave for mental exaltation'.[335]) Paul Barolsky expands upon these themes and argues that Doyle 'disguised or domesticated the detective's aesthetic propensities, making them palatable to a vast, popular audience' (Ousby believes that this was more characteristic of Holmes's appearances after Wilde's trials in 1895).[336] Martin Priestman notes the Wildean overtones of Holmes's sexual isolation.[337] (In the 1894 Holmes story 'The Greek Interpreter', discussed in the following section, it is revealed that the detective has an 'aversion to women'.[338]) Karl Beckson has drawn attention to the contemporary, paradoxical tensions that are evident in Holmes's refusal to be pinned down to any one particular stance: 'At one moment challenging the force of evil represented by Professor Moriarty, at another coolly denying any noble motive, Holmes protests that his detection is a mental exercise, a way to keep himself entertained'. Like Barolsky, Beckson also notes that Holmes's didactic explanations of his method to Dr Watson are reminiscent of 'the annoyed artist endeavoring to explain his art to a blind public'.[339]

The Wildean characteristics that Holmes demonstrated in his second fictional outing were to stick. In 'A Case of Identity' (1892), he remarks, 'there is nothing so unnatural as the commonplace'.[340] In 'The Noble Bachelor' (1892), he avers, 'I read nothing except the criminal news and the agony column. The latter is always instructive'.[341] It may be that it is the uniquely Wildean component of Holmes' intriguing personality that has convinced so many of Doyle's readers that Sherlock Holmes was a real person. There have been several 'biographies' of Holmes written by admirers of the stories and many readers like to study Holmes's investigations as if they were historical accounts. Is it a credit to Conan Doyle's imagination that his characterization rings so true or rather to his ability to capture some of the essential qualities of a unique contemporary? There is an undeniable irony in the fact that Holmes, a character generally viewed by Victorian readers as a reassuring, heroic figure—a restorer of order—has so many attributes borrowed from one of the most mocked, maligned, and in many ways subversive figures of the late nineteenth century.[342]

Doyle was to draw on Wilde twice more in creating fictional characters for his Holmes stories: in 1894's 'The Greek Interpreter' and 1905's 'The Empty House'. When considered alongside *The Sign of Four*, these portraits constitute a fascinating record of Doyle's shifting view of Wilde as the latter moved from great success to humiliating disgrace; they are discussed in the following sections.

Plate 1 '[Claude Davenant was] a pale, large-featured individual . . . of singularly mild yet ardent expression . . . he wore his hair rather long, thrown back, and clustering about his neck like the hair of a medieval saint'.

George Fleming (Julia Fletcher), *Mirage* (1877), Wilde photographed in 1882, aged 27.

Plate 2 '[Francis Chaloner] lies back in a low chair by the fire, leaning his Botticelli head . . . against the cushion . . . and sighing'.

Rhoda Broughton, *Second Thoughts* (1880), The 'Professor of Aesthetics' photographed in full aesthetic mode in 1882.

Plate 3 '[Judith Fountain] had singularly lucid eyes, and rather thin, melancholy lips. Her smile was distant but engaging'.

Mrs (Rosa) Campbell Praed, *Affinities: A Romance of To-day* (1885), Undated photograph of Wilde's wife Constance.

Plate 4 '[Thaddeus Sholto produced] a very long, befrogged top-coat with astrakhan collar and cuffs. This he buttoned tightly up . . . and finished his attire by putting on a rabbit-skin cap'.

Arthur Conan Doyle, *The Sign of Four* (1890), Wilde photographed in 1882.

Plate 5 Detail from photograph taken at the country house of Jean and Walter Palmer, September 1892. Wilde and Louise Jopling stand behind George Meredith at bottom right.

"My dear Raggie, you are looking very well this afternoon."

Plate 6 Illustration for 'The Decadent Guys' in *Punch*, November 10, 1894, by Bernard Partridge.

Plate 7 Wilde and Lord Alfred Douglas c. 1893.

Plate 8 Aubrey Beardsley's illustration 'The Toilet', originally produced for his story 'Under the Hill', an expurgated version of *The Story of Venus and Tannhäuser*, which appeared in *The Savoy* of January 1896.

2

Decadent 1891–1895

'all the men who wore [green carnations] looked the same. They had the same walk, or rather waggle, the same coyly conscious expression, the same wavy motion of the head. When they spoke to each other, they called each other by Christian names. Is it a badge of some club or society, and is Mr. Amarinth their high priest? They all spoke to him, and seemed to revolve around him like satellites around the sun.'

Lady Locke, in Robert Hichens, *The Green Carnation*

As the year 1890 drew to a close, Wilde was poised to take the London literary scene by storm. The following five years were to see a meteoric rise in his celebrity. Publication of 'The Picture of Dorian Gray' in *Lippincott's Magazine* in June 1890 had already caused a stir, but its appearance in book form the following year was to have a prodigious effect, provoking a massive amount of media attention and controversy. Wilde's short story 'The Portrait of Mr. W. H.' had already inspired some conjecture about his sexuality; the publication of *Dorian Gray*, with its covert homosexual subtext, incited further speculation and censure. One reviewer of the story disparagingly remarked in the *Scots Observer* of July 5, 1890 that

> Mr. Wilde has brains, and art, and style; but if he can write for none but outlawed noblemen and perverted telegraph-boys [an allusion to the previous year's Cleveland Street scandal], the sooner he takes to tailoring (or some other decent trade) the better for his own reputation and the public morals.[1]

Of course, Wilde's increasingly intimate relationship with Lord Alfred Douglas, whom he is believed to have first met in 1891, did little to dispel public speculation.

The publication of *Dorian Gray* can be said to mark the beginning of the 'decadent' aesthetic period in England, the term 'decadent' having previously been used in relation to the darker style of French aestheticism, with its thinly veiled themes of perverse and forbidden pleasures such as homosexuality and sadism. Indeed, Wilde had long been a devotee of the French *décadents* Gautier, Huysmans, and Baudelaire, and his novel clearly reflects their influences. As Richard Ellmann notes, 'With its irreverent maxims, its catch phrases, its conversational gambits, its insouciance and contrariness, [Wilde's novel] announced the age of Dorian'.[2] Wilde reveled in his elevated celebrity status and presided over the English decadents from his table at the Café Royal, the ornately decorated French restaurant in Regent Street, already frequented by the French *décadent* poets Verlaine and Rimbaud.[3] William Gaunt describes Wilde's demeanor during this period: 'Bulky, brimming over with high spirits [Wilde] basked in triumph, in the new era, expanded with genial egotism'.[4]

Still greater success was to come. In 1891 Wilde also published his essay 'The Soul of Man Under Socialism', an acclaimed book of criticism entitled *Intentions*, a popular book of short stories (*Lord Arthur Savile's Crime and Other Stories*) and a second book of fairy tales (*A House of Pomegranates*). If there remained any doubt about Wilde's place as a star in the late Victorian literary firmament, it was truly quashed by the success of his society play *Lady Windermere's Fan* in 1892 and three further society comedies in the following three years. In playwriting Wilde found his true niche, successfully transferring his own sparkling drawing room banter to the stage. No matter what his contemporaries made of his singular personality, Wilde could no longer be dismissed as an unproductive, minor talent. After the triumphs of 1891 and subsequent years, Wilde's peers were forced to acknowledge that he was a literary force to be reckoned with.

Wilde's lack of literary output had made him an easy target for ridicule by earlier critics of aestheticism like Walter Besant and Rhoda Broughton; now disapproving authors had to countervail against Wilde's obvious talents in their fictional depictions of the aesthete. The 1890s Wilde could no longer be convincingly portrayed in fiction as a mere mouthpiece for the philosophies of Pater or frivolous aesthetic doctrines. The 'first phase' Wilde still occasionally appeared in fiction, perhaps because some authors still not did believe that Wilde was what Henry James suspected him to be—'a genuine intelligence'. As discussed above, Wilde's flamboyant individualism had alienated many of his more conservative contemporaries in the 1880s and this continued to occur in the 1890s. Indeed, Wilde was to supply his critics with even more grist for the mill. As his career flourished he became less mindful of public opinion and more reckless in his personal life. Many of the fictions that were to appear at the time of his greatest success contain subtle allusions to the 'darker' side of Wilde's decadence—his 'deviant' sexuality—a side already tentatively hinted at by James and Raffalovich.

MARIE CORELLI

The Silver Domino; or, Side Whispers, Social and Literary (1892)

Wilde's first fictional appearance in the English decadent period was in Marie Corelli's *The Silver Domino: or, Side Whispers, Social and Literary* (1892). Marie Corelli was the pen name of Mary Mackay (1855–1924), the best selling, highest paid fiction writer of her generation. An eccentric self-dramatist with a romantic temperament, she provoked almost as much conflicting opinion as Wilde himself.[5] A prolific author, Corelli's success is usually attributed to the substantial dose of sensational and mystical elements in her romantic novels. The conservative prejudices and prescriptive morality of her works also resonated with many middle-class readers.[6] Corelli's imaginative but uneven writing, most likely the result of a lack of formal education, was perhaps most accurately described by S. Boswin as 'a medley of good and very bad'.[7] Nevertheless, Queen Victoria, William Gladstone, and millions of English and Americans read Corelli's fiction.[8] Corelli, in any case, was convinced of her genius, despite suffering periods of agonizing insecurity, often induced by the savage ridicule of reviewers.[9] After a particularly harsh anonymous review of her novel *The Soul of Lilith* (1892) in the *Pall Mall Gazette*, Corelli's brother Eric Mackay confided to her publisher George Bentley that the review might be the last straw for Corelli and that she was considering giving up writing altogether.[10]

However, the spirited Corelli determined upon an alternate course of action. In April 1892 she began writing *The Silver Domino*, a satire lampooning many of the literary personages and critics of the day, with the express intention of 'putting them in their place'. She planned to publish the book anonymously and contrived to reveal her identity only when the book had been fêted by the critics who had previously derided her work. Unfortunately for Corelli, *The Silver Domino* is not an astute satire but an improvident, vituperative diatribe against everyone who had ever antagonized her in the literary and political worlds.[11] While the amount of early press attention the book received appeared to signal success, this was generated mainly by the anonymity of the author; initial guesses as to the writer's identity included W. E. Henley and the Rev. A. K. H. (Andrew Kennedy Hutchison) Boyd.[12] The more serious reviews condemned the book's spitefulness, sarcasm, and poor style.[13] The reviewer from the *National Observer* asserted on October 15 that

> the author is above all things anxious to impress the reader with the idea that he is Somebody, that he is on intimate terms with Everybody. He sets about it in the cheapest way possible . . . The style, a farrago of journalese, Carlylese, and inappropriate archaisms, is wretched.[14]

It was reported by the *Daily Chronicle* that friends of Oscar Wilde had visited the publisher of *The Silver Domino* to ask who had written the book.[15] It is no wonder that Wilde's associates were curious; Corelli had included a cutting portrait of Wilde and his wife in the chapter entitled 'Of the Social Elephant'. In this section, Wilde, who had become noticeably overweight, is caricatured as a tame elephant: 'a sort of grotesque pet of ours [who] moves slowly on account of his bulk'. Wilde's wife Constance appears as a fairy who 'manages' the elephant, sitting in a palanquin on his back. The elephant

> has a Trunk (or Intellectual Faculty) of the utmost delicacy and sensitiveness at the tip, and with this exquisitely formed member he is fond of picking up Pins.[16]

These 'pins' are later identified as

> Minute points of discussion having to do with vague subjects which (unless we could live on an Island of Dreams like the Laureate's Lotus-eaters) no one has any time to waste in considering . . . [17]

Corelli continues,

> [when his pins cease to interest him] . . . he shuts his blinking emerald eyes to outer things, and thinks. Then, rising with a mighty roar of trumpeting that blares across the old world and the new, he tears up the ground beneath his feet, and throws a Production—*i.e.*, a novel, or a play—in the face of his foes.[18]

The pretty, diminutive fairy wears aesthetic dress to please the elephant and does 'neither good nor harm' with her 'gossamer-discussion' on radical politics. Corelli avers that the fairy is 'infinitely more interesting than the Elephant himself'.[19] Corelli had expressed an interest in the aesthetic Mrs Wilde to her friend Bertha Vyver in a letter in the late 1880s.[20] A series of further observations on the elephant confirm that the pontificating pachyderm is a satirical portrait of Wilde:

> no one can be blander or more aware of his own value than the Elephant... Conscious of weight and ponderous movement, he nevertheless manages to preserve a suggestion of something indefinable that is 'utter'....[21]
>
> ... he thinks that if the 'masses' could only be brought to appreciate Colour as keenly as he himself appreciates it, the world would be both happy and wise, and would have no further need of law... He considers Nature *au naturel* a mistake. Nature must be refined by Art. *Ergo*, a grand waterfall would not appeal to him, unless properly illumined by electricity, or otherwise got up for effect [On visiting Niagara Falls in 1882 Wilde famously remarked that the Falls were 'the first disappointment in the married life of many Americans'.][22]

Corelli also makes a barbed reference to Wilde's early poetic aspirations and his lack of critical success in this regard:

> A strange spell was upon him, a wizard-glow of the light that blinds reviewers—Genius. He stood on the confines of a sort of magic territory... he was waiting for the proper person to come and cut off his head, or throw water over him, or something, and say—'quit thy present form and take that of a—' What? Well, let us say 'Poet', for example... But the magician who could or might have worked this change in him didn't turn up at the right moment, and so no one would believe he was anything *but* [emphasis in the original] an Elephant at last.[23]

Corelli suggests that Wilde's biting literary reviews reflect his frustration at failing as a poet:

> He broke into the newspaper shops and went rampaging round among the pens and the inkpots. He knocked down a few unwary authors whom he imagined stood in his way, and when they *were* [emphasis in the original] down, he stamped upon them.[24]

It soon becomes apparent that Corelli perceives herself to be a victim of Wilde's acrid reviewing style:

> I know perfectly well who it was that lifted me up a while ago in a journal that shall be nameless, and did his utmost to smash me utterly by the force with which he threw me down again...[25]

> He didn't know who I was then, and he doesn't quite know now, though I believe if I threw off my domino and showed him my features he would take to his old tricks again in a minute.[26]

No reviews of Corelli's work have been recorded as Wilde's. However, as Corelli suggests above, the work she refers to appears to have been written either anonymously or pseudonymously. It may also be that Corelli's resentment is an example of the misdirected acrimony that frequently resulted from anonymous reviews.[27] Nevertheless, Corelli clearly believed that an attack had been made, and the sense of betrayal this inspired (Wilde had formerly complimented Corelli on her work) may have proven the impetus for 'Of the Social Elephant'. Corelli relates that although the elephant seems harmless, he can be sly and malicious, and that 'society pets him as it pets all creatures of whom it is vaguely afraid'.[28] However, while Corelli appears to have been intimidated by Wilde, and clearly disapproved of his egotism, like many of Wilde's fictionalizers, she also demonstrated a reluctance to wholly condemn him. Despite her obvious grievance against him, Wilde clearly charmed Corelli, as the following passage demonstrates:

> I don't want to irritate him, because he is really a good creature; I would rather pet than goad him. He can be cruel, but he can also be kind, and it is in the latter mood that everybody likes him . . . as Elephant he is the living Emblem of Wisdom . . . I never heard of anyone yet who would venture to cast a doubt on his sagacity . . . his opinion on some things is always worth having, and when he picks up Pins his movements are graceful and always worth watching.[29]

Corelli also refers to the elephant's admirable 'buried' qualities, and in a later chapter names Wilde as 'a really clever man' and 'a born wit', despite his audacious borrowings from Molière and Rouchefoucauld.[30]

Wilde also appears in a poem in *The Silver Domino* that satirizes the literary personalities of the age, alongside Grant Allen, Matthew Arnold, Rhoda Broughton, Hall Caine, Thomas Hardy, W. E. Henley, Rudyard Kipling, William Morris, Henrietta Stannard, Algernon Swinburne, Alfred Lord Tennyson, and Mrs Humphry Ward. Corelli's ribbing of Wilde in this poem is relatively mild; she mocks his 'self-worship' and 'native brass' and entreats him not to leave England to reside in France. (Wilde had recently threatened to do this when the Censor of Plays refused to let him stage his play *Salomé* in London.[31])

In *The Silver Domino*, Corelli relates that she has fed the elephant 'many a time and oft with the sugared compliments he likes best',[32] and indeed there are several extant records of social meetings between Corelli and Wilde. Corelli attended Lady Wilde's 'at homes' where, as stated above, Wilde was a frequent guest, and we know that Wilde contacted Corelli on two separate occasions to congratulate her on her fanciful novels *A Romance of Two Worlds* (1886) and *Ardath: The Story of a Dead Self* (1889).[33] Corelli had sent Wilde a complimentary copy of the latter, most likely the one that was documented in Wilde's collection at the sale of his effects in April 1895.[34] It is not surprising that Wilde should have been an admirer of Corelli's early work; her preoccupation with the mystical and the exotic was one that he shared and his own highly decorative writing style had something in common with Corelli's overornamented, archaic prose. He told her, 'you certainly tell of marvellous things in a marvellous way'.[35]

Wilde and Corelli frequently moved in the same social circles; in the late 1880s, Corelli complained to a friend that Wilde had kept her talking 'no end of time' at a party in Upper Phillimore Place, and in 1889 both were present at a luncheon party given by Mr and Mrs Skirrow, which also included Robert Browning, Henry Irving, Ellen Terry, and Robert Buchanan.[36] At another party Wilde complimented Corelli on her style, congratulated her on her growing fame, and commented upon the power of celebrity: 'Such a lot of talking-about-you does more good than an infinite number of reviews'.[37] In June 1889, Corelli contributed an article entitled 'Shakespeare's Mother' to Wilde's *Woman's World*, which Wilde described as 'powerful' to an employee at the magazine.[38]

It is difficult to surmise exactly when relations between Wilde and Corelli began to sour, but this certainly appears to have happened. In 1892's 'Of the Social Elephant', Corelli still seems cautiously friendly toward Wilde, despite his perceived 'betrayal':

> He didn't hurt me [with his comments] though he tried; I got up from under his feet, and—offered him another Compliment. He took it—gracefully . . . Still, his eye is always on me—and mine on him—and we begin to understand each other.[39]

Whether or not he was responsible for 'smashing' Corelli in an anonymous review, at some point Wilde clearly stopped admiring her work; he most likely grew weary of the moralistic rhetoric that was an unfortunate adjunct of her writing.[40] There is no record of any reaction from Wilde's to 'Of the Social Elephant'. By 1895, friendly relations had certainly disintegrated, as indicated by Corelli's callous remark at the time of Wilde's trials: she complained that public interest in Wilde's demise had resulted in a drop in sales for her latest novel.[41] Wilde's response to a question from a prison warder during his subsequent incarceration, although amusing, clearly demonstrates his opinion of Corelli:

> 'Excuse me, sir, but Marie Corelli: would she be considered a great writer, sir? . . .'
> 'Now don't think I've anything against her *moral* character, but from the way she writes *she ought to be here* [emphasis in the original].'[42]

Wilde continued to mock Corelli in conversation after his release from prison. In a letter to his publisher dated January 9, 1898, Wilde jokingly alludes to the then 'open secret' of Corelli's authorship of *The Silver Domino*:

> the public like an open secret. Half of the success of Marie Corelli is due to the no doubt unfounded rumour that she is a woman.[43]

Corelli appears to have retained her grudge against Wilde long after his death. It was a spiteful letter from Corelli to Noel Pemberton Billing in 1918 that incited the latter to allege in court that a performance of Wilde's *Salomé* was endangering the British war effort, by virtue of the fact that the audience was susceptible to blackmail, because of the sexual peculiarities of the 'Wilde cult'.[44] Some might say that Corelli protested too much about Wilde's homosexuality; there has been speculation that Corelli herself was involved in a homosexual relationship with her friend Bertha Vyver, who wrote her memoirs in 1930.[45] This has never been confirmed, but the prospect that Corelli's ambivalent relation to Wilde, like that of James and Raffalovich, was mediated by her own sexuality, is an intriguing one.

While *The Silver Domino*, like most of Corelli's books, sold well despite the critics—reaching a twenty-second edition by 1894—there can be little doubt that she regretted its publication. While we cannot be sure if it widened the rift between Corelli and Wilde, it did result in the end of a cherished friendship between Corelli and her publisher Bentley and also terminated her association with Gladstone (she had satirized both in *The Silver Domino*). Rather than triumphantly claiming authorship of the book as she had planned, she was to publicly deny its authorship for the rest of her life.[46]

Ella Hepworth Dixon

My Flirtations (1892)
The Story of a Modern Woman (1894)
'The World's Slow Stain' (1904)

Wilde's next fictional representation appeared courtesy of the novelist and journalist Ella Hepworth Dixon (1855?–1932). The daughter of William Hepworth Dixon (editor of *The Athenaeum* from 1853 to 1869), Dixon's family's connections eased her entry into London's literary and artistic circles. At various times she counted such notables as Grant Allen, Max Beerbohm, Richard Le Gallienne, Edmund Gosse, Henry James, George Moore, Walter Pater, Robert Ross, and Ellen Terry among her friends. In such company it was inevitable that Dixon should encounter Wilde. In her 1930 memoir, *As I Knew Them: Sketches of People I Have Met on the Way*, Dixon recalls first meeting Wilde as a young man in the home of Justin McCarthy, and remembers being struck by his 'pontifical' announcements on Irish matters and his 'remarkable' voice, which 'made everything he said sound not only impressive but distinguished'.[47]

Dixon was a regular contributor of articles, short stories, and interviews to Wilde's *Woman's World* from 1888 to 1890.[48] In her memoir *As I Knew Them*, Dixon recalls *The Woman's World* as 'a magazine of splendid appearance' and states that she still possesses 'a most flattering letter from [Wilde] about a story I contributed to it ... to which he gave that unstinted praise which is so rare in Editors'.[49] Dixon clearly respected Wilde's artistic talents—she praised *Lady Windermere's Fan* for its wit and construction and referred to *The Ballad of Reading Gaol* as a 'masterpiece'[50]—however, she was less impressed by Wilde's personal charms: 'I am sure now [his voice] was one of Oscar Wilde's principal assets ... Otherwise he had not an engaging personality, being too much occupied with his own personal appearance and his carefully prepared paradoxes'.[51] We can more extensively gage Dixon's opinion of Wilde by her portrayals of him in not one, but three of her works of fiction: *My Flirtations* (1893), *The Story of a Modern Woman* (1894), and 'The World's Slow Stain' (1904).

My Flirtations was Dixon's first foray into novel writing and was a comic affair, each chapter comprising a satiric account of one of the narrator's (the appropriately named Margaret *Wynman*'s) past suitors. Perhaps because many of these portraits were drawn from obvious originals, and were often less than flattering, Dixon published the book under the pseudonym of her flirtatious protagonist. Though she was careful not to directly associate herself with the novel, in 1930 she dropped broad hints as to her authorship and displayed some pride in the book's success:

> [Robert Ross] . . . reviewed my [anonymous] first book . . . and announced that 'a new humorist had arisen'. The little volume certainly had a vogue among such formidable critics as Heads of Oxford Colleges and the like, while I remember the late Chief Justice Coleridge stopping me at a party . . . to tell me what he thought of it . . . I am sure its success (two editions) was largely due to the delightful illustrations by Mr. (now Sir Bernard) Partridge of *Punch*.[52]

Val Redmond, who appears in chapter 5 of *My Flirtations*, has been identified by several commentators as a fictional version of the 'first phase' Wilde, and will be discussed below. However, before examining Redmond, there is another character who derives from the 'second phase' Wilde who appears to have escaped detection; that is, the subject of the first chapter, Gilbert Mandell. Although Mandell has humble origins and is described as priggish, pessimistic, and a 'nervous host'—all characteristics antithetical to Wilde's—Mandell's remaining traits lead the reader to believe that these are merely 'smoke-screens', or perhaps tongue-in-cheek additions. Mandell is 34 years of age (Wilde was 39 when the book was published), a sophisticated man of fashion and a critic who has ingratiated himself with high society. He also enjoys acting as a cultural educator and arbiter of taste to the 'receptive' Margaret Wynman. Wynman describes Mandell as a very 'Superior Person' with the most complaisant manner. He lends her books by Pater, is enamored of aesthetic antiquities like Persian tiles, Japanese ivories, and illuminated manuscripts, speaks in paradoxes and loves to gossip about society: 'sometimes, when he was going to say something slightly malicious, he hesitated a little in his speech . . . because he was so delighted with what he was going to say'.[53] Like Wilde, Mandell respects intelligent women and endears himself to them with his deferential manner. Wynman's father laughs at Mandell's aesthetic excesses, but like many of Wilde's conservative contemporaries he has to admit that Mandell is a 'sharp fellow'. In addition, Mandell's social gatherings are attended by 'a handful of modish women, interlarded with thin, youngish-old men, who [spend] their lives criticising the critics'; a canny description of Wilde's immediate social circle.[54] (Dixon again refers to Wilde's 'youngish-old' male companions in describing Val Redmond's associates in chapter 5, discussed below.)

Mandell's physical attributes of 'middle-size', 'pink cheeks', and 'bald forehead' are part of Dixon's disguise; he can be more accurately identified by his 'fleshy and white' hands, which are so often described in recollections of Wilde.[55] Mandell's romantic hopes with regard to Wynman are ultimately dashed because she is irritated by his excessive complaisance and manicured hands, just as Dixon was annoyed by Wilde's 'pontifical' manner and habit of being 'too much occupied with his own personal appearance'.

In contrast to Gilbert Mandell, chapter 5's Val Redmond, at 22, is a much younger version of Wilde. He evinces the young Wilde's early enthusiasm for blue and white china, is 'indisputably "smart"', imperturbably cool, and has a following of young gentlemen who copy his neckties and buttonholes and call each other 'dear'.[56] Redmond also knows 'a great deal about clothes' and has 'a tendency to flout and pout', a talent for arranging flowers and excellent taste in décor. He enjoys the society of women and has passing enthusiasms for society beauties like Wynman, redolent of Wilde's fleeting passions for Lillie Langtry and Ellen Terry.[57]

While I cannot agree with Margaret Stetz that Partridge's illustration of Redmond confirms that he is based on Wilde—the illustrated Redmond is effeminate and well dressed but bears no other physical resemblance to Wilde—there can be little doubt about the inspiration for Val Redmond.[58] Dixon's joke of rephrasing and redirecting one of Wilde's most famous *bon mots* about André Raffalovich toward Wilde's own likeness, Redmond, is revealing, if not as effective as Wilde's original witticism. As related above Wilde once said of Raffalovich that he 'came to London to start a salon, and has only succeeded in opening a saloon'. Margaret Wynman's sister Christina remarks that 'Val Redmond's ambition was to start a *salon* in Sloane Street, but he has only succeeded, so far, in running a restaurant'.[59]

Dixon portrays Redmond as someone who has great potential to succeed, but whose comfortable circumstances and tendency to malicious gossip prevent him from living up to his potential. Dixon highlights Redmond's propensity to gossip several times, in such a way as to suggest that she herself may have felt slighted by Wilde in this regard.

> His intimate friendships lasted, on average, exactly six weeks. In other houses where they talk scandal it is usually about acquaintances, but in Val's drawing-room you generally heard his bosom friends deprived of their reputations . . . [to this trait] one may perhaps attribute the brief duration of Val's friendships.[60]

> One had an uneasy feeling that his devotion was only meant for dinner-parties; his little compliments were, like his bonbons, the accompaniments of the box he offered you at the play.[61]

That Wilde at some time extended his 'dinner-party devotion' to Dixon seems likely in light of a passage in Dixon's memoirs. She relates, 'a woman, to whom [Wilde] offered a verbal bouquet in passing, felt uplifted for the rest of the evening. I often met him at parties'.[62] It is true that Wilde's affectations, when combined with his transient enthusiasms for objects and people, often prompted accusations of insincerity. However, Margaret Stetz attributes Wilde's 'divergent idea of friendship' to his generally spontaneous and whimsical outlook, and notes that

> some of [his] most mutually satisfying connections were with women [like Ada Leverson] who shared his passion for novelty and whose temperaments put them at odds with the majority of their female acquaintances.[63]

Dixon does not appear to have been a woman of Leverson's type. Like Corelli, she seems to have channeled her dislike of Wilde's inconsistency into her fiction.

Dixon's ambivalent reaction to Wilde also appears to stem from her observation of his ambiguous sexuality and the unusual ambience surrounding him and his coterie. In describing one of Val Redmond's dinner parties, she notes that

> there was something strange and unusual not only about the guests, but the very dishes and the flowers . . . all the men were boys, though they appeared prematurely old, and all the ladies were elderly, though they, to be sure, looked unnaturally young.[64]

The repeated reference to young/old males contains the suggestion that extraordinary experience has made them old before their time. Her descriptions of the friendships between these men are also suggestive:

> one sometimes saw [Redmond's young male friends] giggling in corners, and calling each other by pet names . . . the young men constantly made each other little presents—[65]

Dixon highlights the reversal of gender roles in Redmond's circle, with women smoking while men refrained from the practice, implying an 'unnatural' state of affairs. Dixon also emphasizes the fact that only elderly women are present; women who are unsuitable as romantic candidates. Dixon's sketches of Mandell and Redmond in *My Flirtations* reflect Wilde's social nature, as do two of the characters in her next novel, a *Bildungsroman* entitled *The Story of a Modern Woman* (1894). The second book also reflects the professional relationship between Dixon and Wilde. As stated above, Dixon regularly contributed articles, short stories and interviews to the *Woman's World* during Wilde's editorship in 1888 and 1889. In *A Modern Woman*, Dixon again uses two separate characters, both editors, to depict various aspects of Wilde. The first is Mr Bosanquet-Barry, editor of *The Comet*, who appears at several society events; the second is the unnamed editor of *The Fan*, a women's journal of the same type as *The Woman's World*.

A Modern Woman charts the struggles of Mary Erle, an intelligent, educated woman who ekes out an existence by creative writing and journalism after the death of her father leaves her to fend for herself in a man's world. Dixon described the novel as 'somewhat gloomy' and expressed surprise at its immediate success, which resulted in the forging of many literary friendships:

> it caught on at once. Mr. T. P. O'Connor, ever generous to young authors, devoted the whole front page of his Sunday weekly to it; Mr. W. T. Stead made much of it in the *Review of Reviews*; it was translated into French and appeared in Tauchnitz, in the colonies and America, and was advertised by Messrs. Heinemann as one of 'the books of the year'.[66]

The first Wildean character to appear in *A Modern Woman* is Mr Bosanquet-Barry, the 27-year-old editor of the *Comet*. (Margaret Stetz argues that 'Barry' suggests an Irish persona and 'Bosanquet' an English one. The present writer perceives Irish/French resonances in the name. Either way, both possibilities suggest Wilde.[67]) Bosanquet-Barry is 'nice and hot from Oxford', with 'none of the old hackneyed Fleet Street ideas'. He first appears at a party hosted by Lady Jane Ives, wearing a buttonhole of Parma violets and accompanied by 'a pale-faced boy with tired eyelids'.[68] (Wilde's assistant editor at *The Woman's World*, Arthur Fish, recalled that Wilde often wore a buttonhole of Parma violets.[69]) Like his predecessor Val Redmond, Bosanquet-Barry is a malicious gossip, and he has 'a laugh which [is] not quite pretty'. He also has a 'fatuous smile', 'a somewhat spurious air of youth', and has 'picked up the editor's air of not meaning to allow anyone to detain him'. Erle's friend Alison thinks Bosanquet-Barry 'an odious youth' but tells Erle that she will have to know him if she wants to be an artist, as 'all the smart set are in love with him'.[70] The young editor frequently makes Wildean quips, such as his reference to 'the fatal error of being found out'.[71] Dixon provides another cursory disguise, perhaps again with tongue in cheek. Bosanquet-Barry possesses 'dazzlingly white teeth'; Wilde's teeth were discolored and he often held his hand over his mouth while speaking in an attempt to disguise them.

It is possible that Bosanquet-Barry's casual approach to commissioning articles reflects Dixon's frustration at a corresponding tendency in Wilde:

> Alison could hear Mr. Bosanquet-Barry, under the soothing influence of Lady Jane's excellent champagne, airily inciting Mary to write art criticisms for *The Comet*; a fact that Alison was certain he would forget the very next morning.[72]

If Dixon's portrait of Wilde in Bosanquet-Barry is unsympathetic, her portrait of his young, pale companion, Beaufort Flower, is even more so. Flower's description and his nickname, 'Beaufy', point to his original Lord Alfred Douglas, who was known as 'Bosie' and who by 1892 was a frequent companion to Wilde. Beaufort Flower demonstrates all of Douglas's worst traits as reported by contemporaries: he is 'spiteful', 'impertinent', 'vicious', 'tactless', and has a 'shrill', 'waspish' voice.[73] Dixon was clearly far from impressed by Wilde's choice of companion; her fictional portraits of Wilde appear mild by comparison.

The second Wildean character in *The Story of a Modern Woman*, the unnamed editor of *The Fan*, the women's monthly magazine, first appears in chapter 10: 'In Grub Street'. Like *The Woman's World*, the office of *The Fan* is located 'in one of the queer little squares out of Fleet Street'.[74] The name of the fictional magazine also has a Wildean resonance; Wilde's play *Lady Windermere's Fan* had been a smash hit just two years before. The editor of *The Fan* is 'a well dressed, supercilious-looking young man of thirty' with a 'rather affected voice' and 'smooth cheeks', who shares Wilde's preoccupation with fashion: 'I want [*The Fan*] to be quite the smartest thing out, and a real authority on dress and fashion. As to the dress part, I'm not afraid of that. I do it all myself'.[75] When the editor discovers that Erle has fashionable and aristocratic social connections he encourages her to write gossipy society articles about 'really smart' people, and to make her reports 'acidulous', 'sparkling', and 'just a wee bit malicious'.⁷⁶ Wilde was equally happy to have Dixon's interviews with celebrated personal friends for *The Woman's World*. Dixon's response to Wilde is discernible in Erle's reaction to her aesthetic editor:

> [Erle] felt vaguely uncomfortable as the supercilious editor's eye dwelt upon her, not feeling sure that he would approve of the shape of her sleeves, and being morally certain that he was by this time aware that her gown was not lined with silk.⁷⁷

Erle also experiences Dixon's frustration at being a woman in the masculine sphere of late Victorian publishing. Erle is kept waiting outside the *Fan* editor's office for twenty minutes while he has what appears to be a purely social meeting with a young male companion. The minutes tick slowly by while Erle listens to their 'guffaws of laughter', accompanied by the odor of cigarettes. When the editor discovers Erle's presence outside the office he becomes ill-at-ease recalling the nature of the preceding conversation (which is not described for the reader). Margaret Stetz points to this scene as typical of much of Dixon's writing, in that it highlights men's treatment of women as 'mere possessions and ornaments'.⁷⁸ This type of conduct in Dixon's Wildean editor is curious; it is generally thought that Wilde was not a perpetrator of such behavior toward women, especially in relation to his role at *The Woman's World*. Stetz asserts that Wilde's benevolent attitude toward women who worked in the arts was rare among contemporary men.⁷⁹ As his assistant editor Arthur Fish noted:

> [Wilde] secured a brilliant company of contributors [to *The Woman's World*] which included the leaders of feminine thought and influence in every branch of work . . . The keynote of the magazine was the right of woman to equality of treatment with man, with the assertion of her claims by women who had gained high position by virtue of their skill as writers or workers in the world's great field of labour. Some of the articles on women's work and their position in politics were far in advance of the thought of the day and [the general manager and the chief editor of Cassells] would call in at our room and discuss them with Oscar Wilde, who would always express his entire sympathy with the views of the writers and reveal great liberality of thought with regard to the political aspirations of women.⁸⁰

It is possible that Dixon allowed her dislike of Wilde's personal characteristics to influence her fictional depiction of his editorial priorities and practices. After all, Wilde did publish at least one short fiction by Dixon (entitled 'Murder—or Mercy? A Story of Today') and by her own report very generously gave this story 'unstinted praise'.

Dixon's final fictional portrait of Wilde falls outside of the chronological period of this study, however, it is included here as a significant postscript. Dixon's fifth and final fictional portrait of Wilde appeared in 1904, with the character of Gilbert Vincent in the short story 'The World's Slow Stain', included in Dixon's anthology *One Doubtful Hour and Other Side-Lights on the Feminine Temperament*. While Dixon's earlier characterizations of Wilde are hardly complimentary, this posttrial fictional portrait is even more trenchant.

'The World's Slow Stain' is a grim story about London socialite and 'New Woman' Adela Buller. Tired of her shallow and cynical artistic set, Buller accepts the marriage proposal of 'philistine' Anthony Mellingham, a man who jilted her ten years before, and whom she subsequently incorporated into a published novel as 'an insufferable cad and egoist', Mellingham being entirely ignorant of this work.[81] Buller's acceptance of Mellingham's proposal annoys her long-standing friend and occasional suitor, the jaded dramatist Gilbert Vincent. Vincent maliciously plants a copy of Buller's *roman à clef* in Mellingham's bag after the two are married; when the latter reads the novel on his honeymoon he immediately recognizes the scathing portrait of himself and the story closes with the couple contemplating a life of 'eternal rancour' together.[82]

Interestingly, in this story Dixon dispenses with the physical disguises that she employed for her former ersatz Wildes. The languidly cynical Vincent has 'a fat, white face, which expressed nothing in repose', conspicuously white hands and a 'soft, half-amused voice in which, in his capacity of successful dramatist, he was permitted to make the most outrageous statements'.[83] Dixon's physical descriptions of Vincent often reflect her disapproval of his disgraced original. Vincent's hands gesture with 'a curiously *un-English* movement [my emphasis]', the pallor of his face is 'uncanny-looking', and his smile is 'singularly unpleasant'.[84] As with her description of Mr Bosanquet-Barry in *The Story of a Modern Woman*, Dixon also includes another gibe about Wilde's unattractive teeth. In this instance, however, her comments reflect her knowledge of Wilde's 'crime': when Vincent smiles 'people [have] a brief vision of unclean things'.[85]

Vincent speaks deprecatingly of marriage, referring to it as 'a subtle form of revenge' and talks with a Wildean detachment about romantic feeling and sensations: '"I wonder . . . if it is possible I shall feel it if Adela really were to marry?"'[86] When Buller speaks passionately about a woman's place in nineteenth-century society, Vincent impersonally reflects,

> What excellent 'copy' she would make; what a capital type she would be on the stage; the young lady who is for ever hovering on the brink, but who has 'kept straight' all the same. Really he must try and make an exhaustive study of Adela.[87]

As it happens, Vincent is undeniably upset when Buller finally 'turns British matron' by marrying Mellingham:

> The thing was preposterous—it was worse, it was inartistic. He had been accustomed to drop in when he liked and read her scenes from his new plays (he was a man who was curiously dependent on feminine sympathy), even make love to her when he felt so inclined, and here was Adela the legal property of a blundering, idiotic British Philistine.[88]

While Dixon granted her Wildean character real feelings toward Buller, these feelings are shown to stem primarily from Vincent's selfishness; the same selfishness that leads him to spite Buller by alerting her husband to the existence of her novel, thereby ensuring her future unhappiness. Following Wilde's downfall the aesthete's egocentricity—which had always been a bugbear of his critics—was to be a powerful weapon in the hands of his detractors in fiction. A selfish and self-serving approach to women in the posttrial Wilde portraits, particularly in those written by women, may well reflect the widespread sympathy that was felt for Wilde's wife Constance in the wake of his disgrace.[89]

It is possible that the character of Adela Buller is partially drawn from life. Buller bears some resemblance to Wilde's friend Ada Leverson, another of his fictionalizers discussed below.[90] Like Leverson, Buller is a novelist who incorporates her associates into her fiction. She is also like Leverson in that she occupies a place at the center of London's artistic set, '[wears] her clothes with an air' and speaks in a habitually cynical drawl: 'There was a world of weariness, of disillusionment in her tone'.[91] Once a 'nice girl', Buller now devours decadent French novels and cannot remember how many advances she has received from admiring men (Leverson is believed to have had several affairs while she was married). In short, '[t]ime had besmirched her, year by year, with his horrible, corroding finger'.[92] However, Buller regrets the cynical worldliness she has acquired and embraces her marriage to Mellingham as an escape from it; it is only Vincent's spitefulness that prevents her from succeeding in this endeavor. As both were writers and journalists who moved in the same social circles, it is likely that Dixon was acquainted with Leverson and observed her friendship with Wilde. In light of the observations in 'The World's Slow Stain', it also appears likely that Dixon believed Wilde to be a bad influence on Leverson.[93]

By the time Dixon published her memoirs in 1930, her antipathy toward Wilde appears to have abated. In discussing her connection with Wilde in *As I Knew Them*, Dixon refrains from making any moralistic judgment of the aesthete and openly praises his talent. Dixon became a friend of Robert Ross, a well-known homosexual and devoted friend to Wilde who acted as his literary executor. She attended the wedding of Wilde's younger son, Vyvyan Holland, with Ross in 1913.[94] As Dixon observed, by that time the world had become a more tolerant place, with a 'broader outlook . . . deeper sympathy [and a] collective conscience'.[95]

* * *

As Wilde's career in fiction progressed, his literary career went from strength to strength. In the year after the release of Dixon's first book, 1893, Wilde published two plays (*Salomé* and *Lady Windermere's Fan*), wrote another (*An Ideal Husband*), and had *A Woman of No Importance* produced at the Haymarket Theatre. His growing fame was augmented by yet another caricature on the London stage, in Charles Brookfield's and Charles Hawtrey's *The Poet and the Puppets: A Travestie Suggested by Lady Windermere's Fan* (1893). In spite of the title, the play was more a parody of *Lady Windermere's* author; the 'vain, overbearing [and] inane' 'Poet of the Lily' was played by Hawtrey with Wildean apparel, mannerisms, and dialogue.[96] A contemporary reviewer said of the burlesque that

> the empty paradoxes of Mr. Wilde [were] very cleverly touched off, and the sham smart sayings were often very funny. It is perhaps a little too unkind in its suggestions against Mr. Wilde of plagiarism, and its hint that he is too keen in a bargain—[97]

After hearing of the planned production, and perhaps in mind of the enduring influence of *Patience* and other satires, Wilde appealed to the licenser of plays, E. F. S. Pigott, to be allowed to approve the script before it was staged. This was agreed upon. James Mackey Glover, who wrote the score for the play and was present at Wilde's perusal of the script, records that Wilde appeared to enjoy reading the burlesque and commented that he had been 'delightfully spoofed'. His only objection was to the poet protagonist being called 'Oscar' or 'Wilde'; he good-naturedly allowed the authors to use his lesser-known middle name: 'O'Flahertie'.[98] Wilde also allowed Brookfield and Hawtrey to appear in his play *An Ideal Husband* at the Haymarket in 1895. Brookfield repaid Wilde's largesse by conspiring with the Marquess of Queensberry to secure evidence against Wilde during his trials; he also invited the Marquess to a celebratory dinner on the day that Wilde was sentenced to two years' hard labor in May 1895.[99] Brookfield went on to become Examiner of Plays in 1912.

Arthur Cunliffe

'Ossian Savage's New Play' (1893)

The year 1893 saw another satirical portrait of Wilde published by an Oxford undergraduate, some fourteen years after the appearance of 'O'Flighty' by 'A. T. D.'. The short story 'Ossian Savage's New Play' was published on May 18 in the first edition of the appropriately named *Ephemeral*, an Oxford undergraduate publication issued for the duration of Eights Week, the University's annual intercollege boat racing festival. The inaugural issue of the *Ephemeral* also featured some unrelated gibes about Wilde's physical appearance ('Motto for Mr. O-sc-r W-ld-.—My face is my misfortune') and Alfred Douglas's magazine the *Spirit Lamp*.[100] The *Ephemeral* was edited by two Oxford students: rugby player Alfred Hamilton Grant (1872–1937) and his friend Arthur Cunliffe. The latter was the author of 'Ossian Savage', a deliberately provocative parody designed to capitalize on Wilde's presence in Oxford that month in order to increase sales of the *Ephemeral*. The editors were soon gratified; the famously quarrelsome Douglas took the bait and sent a sarcastic and belligerent letter to the editor, prompting what Grant called a 'full-blooded correspondence' for the rest of Eights week that ensured the *Ephemeral*'s success.[101]

Cunliffe's piece focuses on Ossian Savage, a celebrated playwright, poet, and wit, as he strolls down Piccadilly talking to himself about his next play, which the narrator predicts will add 'one more crown of *wilde*st, most luxuriant olive, to that head of his, which already threatened to strike the golden stars [my italics]'.[102] In depicting Savage's deliberations upon his new work, Cunliffe suggests that Wilde composed his comedies in a slapdash manner to a standard formula, with primary consideration being given to clever *bon mots* for a character based on himself:

> His play was progressing fast and well as usual, though it had not yet got a plot. The plot came afterwards in Ossian's plays with the 'finishing touches'. He had not yet conceived all his characters . . . for the present they were merely algebraical signs—x, y and z . . . z was becoming more and more definite every moment, developing as it [sic] was on old familiar lines into the imaginary picture of Ossian himself, fifteen years hence, with a title and an amazing career of vice. The interest centred round Lord Z, as it was bound to do, for Ossian's interests always centred round himself, his own ability, his own striking personality, and his own great-souled vices—[103]

Cunliffe's Savage laments the difficulty of equaling his former brilliance:

> 'I have said so many dreadful things about woman, and virtue, and youth, and the democracy, and the aristocracy', sighed the author wearily; 'I have hit the nail so often plump on the head, that it is really terribly difficult to be original'.[104]

Savage's projected dramatic dialogue makes a mockery of Wildean aphorisms:

> X. —'We women, Lord Z, have to live entirely in the Present: for we never have a Future, and we may not have a Past.'
> Y. —'Whereas as a matter of fact your thoughts are in the Past, and your hopes in the Future, while your despair is in the Present.'
> *Lord Z.*—'Women with a Past are alone interesting. Not to have a Past is, for a woman, what ignorance of the world is for a man. I had rather be a bad woman than a good man.'[105]

While the suggestions of vice, vanity, and desultory writing practices would perhaps have been enough to invoke the ire of Douglas, one particular passage appears to have given the most offense. The opening lines of the story refer to Savage as 'a man of a coarse habit of body and of coarser habits of mind'.[106] Douglas, in his sardonic letter to the editor that appeared on May 20, suggested that the *Ephemeral* had 'overstepped the limits of legitimate and good-natured chaff' with its description of Wilde and condemned the magazine's 'spiteful, offensive, and . . . dull' journalism:

> I feel sure that I may add to my own thanks, the thanks of my friend Mr. Oscar Wilde (or Ossian Savage, to adopt your witty and elegant

suggestion). You have discovered his secret in a wonderful way, and I only wonder that, now you know how it is done, you do not write a play yourself; it is very paying, and I should imagine that you will have little difficulty in acquiring the requisite 'coarse habit of mind'.[107]

Douglas's mistaken belief that it was Grant, not Cunliffe, who had written the article, aggravated his indignation; Grant was a personal friend and Douglas interpreted the story as a breach of their friendship. However, this mistake was rectified in the pages of the remaining issues of the *Ephemeral*, and Douglas received qualified apologies from both editors. Cunliffe's (anonymous) response in the *Ephemeral* of May 22 reads,

> I understand that it was the parenthetical clause in the first sentence of ['Ossian Savage's New Play'] . . . which chiefly provoked this violent onslaught . . . 'Ossian Savage, a man of coarse habit of body and of coarser habits of mind' . . . Is Lord Alfred Douglas quite sure that he has not misunderstood them? Possibly I took an unfair advantage of the two-fold use in English of the word 'habit' to compress the phrase; for in a skit where Oscar Wilde is called Ossian Savage one cannot write at large. May I paraphrase the objectionable sentence? 'Mr. Oscar Wilde is (in my opinion) a man of a corpulent habit of body; his mental tendencies are what the world (and . . . I agree with the world in this) is inclined to call "coarse" ' . . . I, as much as anyone else, am at liberty to form an opinion from the published works of an author as to what is the character of the mind that created them . . . [signed] The Editor who wrote 'Ossian Savage's New Play'.[108]

This resulted in a similarly qualified retraction from Douglas in the *Ephemeral*'s final issue of May 24:

> The explanation of the Editor who wrote 'Ossian Savage's New Play' certainly puts the affair in a new light. I misunderstood him, and though I still think that the sentence I objected to is in bad taste, I am able to acquit him of a deliberate intention to wound the feelings of myself or anyone else . . . I have heard Mr. Wilde accused of shallowness, of plagiarism, of preciosity in language, and of 'bad influence'; but this is the first time I have ever heard the word 'coarse' applied to his work . . . I can't help thinking that 'the Editor who wrote Ossian Savage's New Play' has either not read Mr. Wilde's books or has an imperfect knowledge of the English language. He has done the world an injustice.[109]

While we do not know whether Cunliffe read any of Wilde's books, he certainly appears to be familiar with Wilde's plays; his *Ephemeral* piece draws heavily on Wilde's dialogue for *Lady Windermere's Fan*, which premiered on February 20, 1892 and *A Woman of No Importance*, which opened just a month before the 'Ossian Savage' piece appeared. What little is known about Cunliffe has been gleaned from Grant's 1931 article in the *Cornhill Magazine*, recalling the days of the *Ephemeral*.[110] Grant records that Cunliffe, presumably an athlete who had '[t]itanic shoulders', first thought of producing a sensational magazine that would 'not only give scope to our literary talents but would also prove commercially profitable'. Cunliffe struck upon Wilde, who was then in Oxford visiting Douglas, as an 'obvious butt' for their literary japes, and proceeded to write the 'Ossian Savage' story. Grant remarked in 1931 that in 1893 Cunliffe's parody seemed 'quite new' and 'amazingly clever' for an undergraduate; however, he also referred to the piece as 'perhaps banal' and 'too ruthless'.[111]

Grant's change of heart may be attributable to the fact that Douglas induced him to meet Wilde at a dinner soon after the 'Ossian Savage' controversy died down. Wilde graciously made no mention of the *Ephemeral* satire when he met Grant but greeted him with 'a winning smile' and said 'I hear that you are called "Gragger" . . . But this is dreadful. It must not go on. We must find a new name for you, something beautiful and worthy and Scottish'. Later, Wilde playfully ragged Grant for smoking cigars instead of the aesthetic company's preferred gold-tipped cigarettes: 'How too terrible of you! But we shall call [your cigar] a nutbrown cigarette—and you shall smoke it'.[112] Just as the rugged young Grant was beginning to feel uncomfortable with such effusions from Wilde, the latter began to tell one of his famous stories about the early church, which held the undergraduate spellbound; Grant was hooked and returned to spend many more nights with Wilde and his coterie. On one occasion Grant and a friend even defended Wilde against some heckling passersby, by 'read[ing them] the Riot Act'. Wilde reportedly thanked them with open arms: 'You are magnificent—you are giants—giants with souls'.[113]

As Grant makes no mention of Cunliffe at these gatherings, we can reasonably assume that the author of 'Ossian Savage' was either not invited or unwilling to revise his opinion that Wilde was a man of 'coarse' mental tendencies. However Grant, who was later knighted after a distinguished career as a government official in India, cherished his *Ephemeral* experience primarily because it was instrumental in fostering his friendship with Wilde: '[Had] it not been for the *Ephemeral*, I should probably never have made the acquaintance of that strange personality—and I should thereby have missed an interesting and amusing interlude'.[114]

Max Beerbohm
'A Peep into the Past' (1893 or 1894)

Wilde's next appearance in fiction came courtesy of the journalist and caricaturist Max Beerbohm (1872–1956). Beerbohm became renowned for his clever caricatures of local personalities while he was still an undergraduate at Oxford in the early 1890s; he also joined Wilde's clique around this time. Beerbohm first met Wilde at a supper party given by his half-brother, the actor-manager Herbert Beerbohm Tree, in 1889. (In addition to his role as a Wildean aesthete in *The Charlatan*, Tree also lampooned Wilde with his roles in James Albery's *Where's the Cat?* and Francis Cowley Burnand's *The Colonel*, both discussed above.) Being an aesthetically inclined self-dramatist himself, Beerbohm was drawn to Wilde and watched him from a distance until April 1893, when the two men became friendly during rehearsals for Tree's production of Wilde's play *A Woman of No Importance*. Wilde was impressed by Beerbohm's critical, yet laudatory character piece on him in the *Anglo-American Times* of March 25, 1893, entitled 'OW by [Max Beerbohm masquerading as] an American'.[115] Beerbohm was soon invited to lunches, lectures, and the theater by Wilde and members of his circle.

Before he met Wilde the young Beerbohm had particularly admired *The Picture of Dorian Gray* and *Intentions*, especially the latter's controversial pronouncements on individualism, socialism, and realism in art. Wilde's early influence on Beerbohm's writing can be seen in the younger man's essay 'The Incomparable Beauty of Modern Dress', a satire on aestheticism, published when Beerbohm was at Oxford. Beerbohm's later writing also contains many Wildean resonances; Richard Ellmann has noted that Beerbohm's comic fantasy *Zuleika Dobson; or An Oxford Love Story* (1911) contains many echoes of *The Importance of Being Earnest* and *Salomé*.[116] J. G. Riewald has observed,

> The exact nature of [Wilde's] influence [on Beerbohm's writing] is often difficult to assess. It ranges from unconscious and conscious imitation to pastiche, and from pastiche to parody, overt or veiled, or even unconscious, and it may affect either the subject-matter, or the style, or both.[117]

When Beerbohm first met Wilde, after what the former called a 'long period of distant adoration and reverence', he was shocked to find the object of his veneration overweight and, on that occasion, unattractively inebriated.[118] Many of his undergraduate illusions were shattered, but Beerbohm, like so many others, was soon won over by Wilde's irresistible charm. In recollecting his early friendship with Wilde, Beerbohm later described the former's company as 'enchanting', calling him 'the greatest table talker of them all'. He recalled Wilde's conversation as being simultaneously 'spontaneous', 'polished', 'soothing', 'surprising', and 'brimful of intellectual theories and anecdotes'.[119] In a letter to Reggie Turner dated April 21, 1893, Beerbohm is clearly proud to relate Wilde's comments on his above-mentioned article in the *Anglo-American Times*:

> Oscar talked a good deal [at supper] about my article—said that he knew no other undergraduate who could have written it, that I had a marvellous intuition and sense of the phrase, that I must take to literature alone, and that my style was like a silver dagger.[120]

In light of his burgeoning friendship with Wilde and other literary and artistic figures like Arthur Symons, Ernest Dowson, Aubrey Beardsley, Lionel Johnson, John Davidson, William Rothenstein, G. S. Street, and Henry James, it is perhaps no surprise that the talented young Beerbohm was invited to contribute to the first number of the new *Yellow Book* (April 1894). The work that Beerbohm originally intended for this issue was a short satirical piece entitled 'A Peep into the Past', which offers a playfully predictive answer to the question posed by Besant and Rice in 1877's *The Monks of Thelema*: 'What will [the aesthetes] be like when they grow old'?[121] Beerbohm presents a tongue-in-cheek picture of Wilde as a portly old gentleman who has long since faded into obscurity, living the quiet life with his wife and two sons, solacing himself with Keats, Shakespeare, and reminiscences of his triumphs in a bygone era. As Michael Seeney has observed, 'in the light of later events, [this picture] becomes almost unbearably sad'.[122] Beerbohm eventually submitted a different article to the first *Yellow Book*, 'A Defence of Cosmetics', a burlesque of the exaggerated artificiality of the times (retitled 'The Pervasion of Rouge' in 1896). Presumably as a result of the Wilde scandal the following year, and Wilde's death in 1900, 'A Peep into the Past' was shelved by Beerbohm and did not appear in print until 1923.

'A Peep into the Past' is brimming with an insider's jokes about Wilde: the old man is now 'a glutton for work', 'an early riser', 'regular in his habits', and 'something of a martinet about punctuality'. He also enjoys walking and inexpensive cigarettes, has 'cut himself off from society', and prefers 'simple and unpretentious' décor—all of these traits, of course, presenting a comically stark contrast to the characteristics of the contemporary Wilde. Beerbohm continues in this vein: at dinner parties the elderly Wilde 'keep[s] a whole table perfectly serious, whilst he himself [is] convulsed with laughter', is still trying to get his play *Salomé* performed, has gone down in posterity not as a man of letters but as a journalist, is still wearing the costume of his heyday, and—as a final indignity—now wears a brown Georgian wig![123]

There are some friendly digs at Wilde's practice of avoiding tradespeople to whom he owed money, as well as a running joke about the relatively advanced age at which he first began playwriting. With regard to the latter subject, the narrator relates that he and other critics withheld their derogatory remarks about Wilde's plays out of respect for his remarkable display of 'senile enterprise'.[124] Beerbohm also refers to the famous incident after the opening night of *Lady Windermere's Fan* when Wilde shocked the audience by appearing on stage to address them after the play languidly smoking a cigarette. The narrator of 'A Peep into the Past' avers that Wilde had actually been somewhat 'dazed' at the time: '[we who knew him] noted with feelings of pity that in his great excitement he had forgotten to extinguish his cigarette, an oversight that the Public was quick to pardon in the old gentleman'.[125]

There are several passages in 'A Peep into the Past' that may explain Beerbohm's decision to withhold the piece from publication in the first *Yellow Book*. At one point, the narrator takes particular note of 'the constant succession of page-boys [to Wilde's house] which so startles the neighbourhood'.[126] Also, on being ushered into the old man's study, the narrator hears 'the quickly receding *frou-frou* of tweed trousers' before discovering a somewhat disheveled Wilde upon a sofa.[127] Beerbohm was well aware of Wilde's sexual proclivities, although it is generally believed that he did not share them. Beerbohm may have been concerned that these allusions might damage Wilde's already 'shady' reputation, a concern that had been made irrelevant by 1923. He may also have questioned the wisdom of publishing another passage in 'A Peep from the Past', which parodies the derivative nature of Wilde's writing. Beerbohm may have been concerned about offending his friend with his facetious summation of Wilde's *oeuvre*:

> the whole body of his signed work is very small—a book of parodies upon Rossetti, a few fairy-tales in the manner of Hans Andersen, an experimental novel in the style of Poe, a volume of essays, which Mr. Pater is often obliged blushingly to repudiate, a French play written in collaboration with M. Louÿs and one or two English ones in collaboration with Mr. G. R. Simms.[128]

While the general tone of the piece is one of friendly, playful satire, these passages may well have caused Wilde offense. It is also possible that Beerbohm showed Wilde the article in manuscript and was asked by his friend to abandon it. Wilde certainly expressed his displeasure at many of Beerbohm's illustrated caricatures of him, which mocked him mercilessly. Beerbohm, however, was largely unrepentant, not because his was a malicious personality but because he felt proud of his satiric talent.[129] Still, he clearly had some pangs of conscience about his uncanny ability to cut his subjects—often friends and acquaintances—down to size, particularly Wilde, as evidenced by the following statement made to his friend S. N. Behrman:

> 'One day, I found myself in the office of the police inspector who had arrested Oscar . . . The walls were covered with a grisly collection of criminal souvenirs . . . there among them, as though it were evidence against the inspector's latest malefactor, was one of my own caricatures of Oscar. I hadn't realized till that moment how wicked it was. I felt as if I had contributed to the dossier against Oscar; it gave me quite a turn. How did I come to do it? My hand did it, don't you know.' Max looked ruefully at his hand . . . His eyes had an expression of pain and bewilderment, as if he could neither understand nor explain the dichotomy in his art and in his nature.[130]

Beerbohm told Behrman: 'As a writer, I was kindly, I think—Jekyll—but as a caricaturist I was Hyde'.[131] As David Cecil notes, it is to Wilde's credit that he never begrudged or reprimanded Beerbohm for publishing his many 'wicked' Wildean caricatures.[132]

Wilde is obliquely parodied in several of Beerbohm's other satirical prose works. Beerbohm's final contribution to the *Yellow Book*, the story of 'The Happy Hypocrite: A Fairy Tale for Tired Men' (1897), published in book form the same year, lampoons *The Picture of Dorian Gray* and Wilde's fascination with masks, in the manner of a Wildean fairy tale. In Beerbohm's story, the depraved protagonist, Lord George Hell, who is compelled by love to wear a 'saintly' face mask, is transformed by love into George Heaven, magically transfigured to resemble the mask he wears. (Dorian Gray, who assumes the 'mask' of Basil Hallward's chaste portrait, is ultimately transformed by his evil deeds into a physical reflection of his true depraved self.) Karl Beckson has noted that Beerbohm's story was probably suggested by Dorian Gray's remark: 'Each of us has Heaven and Hell in him'.[133] Beerbohm sent Wilde a copy of *The Happy Hypocrite* upon the latter's release from prison; Wilde recognized the reference to *Dorian Gray* and, despite disliking 'the cynical directness' of the title, professed his delight with Beerbohm's 'wonderful and beautiful story', remarking, 'I had always been disappointed that my story had suggested no other work of art in others'.[134]

Beerbohm also satirically alludes to *Dorian Gray* in his poem 'Ballade de la Vie Joyeuse', which highlights the incongruousness of the hedonistic, amoral Wilde's employment of a moral conclusion for his novel: 'Even the author of "Dorian Gray" / Makes for his hero a virtuous mood'.[135] In January 1895, Beerbohm revisited Wildean aestheticism once more in the *Yellow Book* with the essay '1880', a 'futuristic retrospective' of the period 'now so far remote from us', along the same lines as 'A Peep into the Past':

> Beauty had existed long before 1880. It was Mr. Oscar Wilde who managed her *début*. To study the period is to admit that to him was due no small part of the social vogue that Beauty began to enjoy. Fired by his fervid words, men and women hurled their mahogany into the streets and ransacked the curio-shops for the furniture of Annish days.[136]

Wilde undoubtedly endured Beerbohm's frequent satirical jibes because he was particularly fond of him. The Oxford undergraduate impressed Wilde with his rapier wit and artistic talents; Wilde was also intrigued by Beerbohm's cool, enigmatic personality. (In a letter to their mutual friend Ada Leverson, Wilde wrote, 'Tell me, when you are alone with Max, does he take off his face and reveal his mask'?[137]) Beerbohm's imperturbability, maturity, and underlying conservatism prompted Wilde to remark that the gods had granted the young student 'the gift of perpetual old age'.[138] Wilde discouraged his young friend from collaborating with other authors, averring that Beerbohm was 'too individual a genius' to do so.[139] He also paid Beerbohm a comic tribute in the closing scene of *The Importance of Being Earnest*, by including the name 'Maxbohm' among a list of generals in the army directory.

As Wilde's star steadily rose, Beerbohm, like many others of Wilde's acquaintance, noticed a disquieting change in him:

> 'as Oscar became more and more successful, he became ... arrogant. He felt himself omnipotent, and he became gross not in body only ... but in his relations with people. He brushed people aside; he felt he was beyond the ordinary human courtesies that you owe people even if they are, in your opinion, beneath you'.[140]

He always publicly lauded Wilde's talent as an author and playwright, but Beerbohm's private correspondence during the years of Wilde's greatest success reveals his growing dissatisfaction with his friend's excessive egotism and recklessness. He wrote to Reggie Turner on

August 19, 1893 that Wilde had been unbearably fatuous during a meeting at the theater, and had left him feeling 'quite repelled'.[141] Later that year he referred to Wilde's appearance as being 'like one whose soul has swooned in sin and revived vulgar'.[142]

While Beerbohm remained a friend to Wilde throughout his 1895 trials,[143] imprisonment,[144] and after his release,[145] he subsequently kept his distance, concerned for his own reputation and those of his friends.[146] Wilde's dignified performance in the dock had made him rise once again in Beerbohm's estimation, but once Wilde was released and he showed no signs of renouncing his former recklessness, Beerbohm's exasperation resurfaced. He wrote to Turner on August 20, 1897, 'I hear that ass Oscar is under *surveillance* [emphasis in the original]—I suppose he is playing the giddy goat. Can't someone warn him to be careful'?[147]

Upon Wilde's death Beerbohm contributed money toward flowers for his grave and wrote a cautious but sympathetic tribute to Wilde in the *Saturday Review* of December 8, 1900, lamenting the loss to dramatic literature of a remarkable 'thinker . . . weaver of ideas . . . wit, and . . . master of a literary style'.[148] Beerbohm's reflections on Wilde in later years demonstrate his continuing fascination with the man. In his essay 'A Lord of Language' (1905), he reflects upon Wilde's recently published [and heavily expurgated] letter from prison, *De Profundis*. Beerbohm argues that the letter does not support the view that Wilde was 'gloriously transformed by incarceration'.[149] He contends that *De Profundis* is a creative essay by an artist, who is 'playing with ideas [and] emotions'.[150] In 1918, Beerbohm declined an offer to review the second edition of Frank Harris's *Oscar Wilde: His Life and Confessions*, which he saw as a 'raking-up of the old Sodomitic cesspool' and 'a disservice (howsoever well-meant) to poor old O.W.'s memory'.[151] Beerbohm's last recorded words on Wilde were delivered at the unveiling of a London Council plaque at Wilde's Tite Street house to commemorate the centenary of Wilde's birth in 1954. Beerbohm's tribute (written at 82 years of age) was read aloud by Sir Compton Mackenzie, and reflected fondly upon 'the delight of hearing Oscar Wilde talk'. Beerbohm wrote, 'To have heard him consoled me for not having heard Dr Johnson or Edmund Burke, Lord Brougham or Sidney Smith'.[152]

* * *

Satirical versions of Wilde continued to appear at regular intervals during the first half of the 1890s; May 1894 saw the publication of another undergraduate parody, this time a play in blank verse, entitled *Aristophanes at Oxford: O. W.* In a manner redolent of 1879's 'O'Flighty' by 'A. T. D.', the name that appeared under the title was 'Y. T. O.'. In the latter case the initials represented the last letters of the surnames of the three student authors: Leopold Charles Maurice Stennett Amery, Francis Wrigley Hirst, and Henry Alford Antony Cruso. In the preface to the play, the authors declare their

> honest dislike for 'Dorian Gray', 'Salome', the 'Yellow Book', and the whole of the erotic, lack-a-daisical, opium-cigarette literature of the day. Our attack, however, is one on principles and not on persons. We confess straight away that our Oscar Wilde is mainly a creation of our own fancy. We have never met the philosopher in question personally, or seen any-thing more of him than a distant back-view, and even that obscured by a throng of admiring Adonises.[153]

The rambling plot of *Aristophanes at Oxford* involves two contemporary Oxford students who encounter Socrates, Aristotle, and Thucydides, all recently escaped from Hades. The students, annoyed by the philosophy of the ancients, talk Wilde into collaborating with them in a plot to kill the philosophers, by trapping them under a canoe. The philosophers escape, Wilde is blamed for the plot and is sent to Hades accompanied by Charon and Cerberus. This farcical drama clearly reflects the authors' 'honest dislike' for Wilde's aesthetic affectations, as evinced by the following passage, in which a distressed Wilde exclaims,

> Oh! Oh! Salome! bring me some smelling-salts
> In a silver-lacquered bottle gemmed with beryl.
> An epigram! my spirit lamp for an epigram!
> I faint! I die . . .
> Ye spirits of Hedonism! help your priest![154]

There is no record of *Aristophanes at Oxford* ever being performed.

Richard Le Gallienne
'The Woman's Half-Profits' (1894)

Another lightweight literary work containing Wildean resonances published that year was *Prose Fancies*, a collection of tongue-in-cheek stories and articles by the journalist and minor poet Richard Le Gallienne (1866–1947). Le Gallienne was also a novelist, critic, reader of manuscripts for the Bodley Head, and a member of the Rhymers'

Club (a group of fourteen poets and associated writers and artists who met regularly between 1890 and 1895—Wilde occasionally attended their meetings). Le Gallienne had heard Wilde lecture at Birkenhead while still in his teens and as a young man mimicked Wilde's long hair and aesthetic dress. The two men became close friends from the late 1880s, after Le Gallienne sent Wilde a copy of his first volume of poetry. Their affectionate and effusive correspondence from this period suggests a mutual infatuation. Inscribed in a handmade copy of a poem he wrote for Wilde, entitled 'With Oscar Wilde, A Summer-Day in June '88', are Le Gallienne's words: 'This copy of verse I have made for my friend Oscar Wilde, as a love-token, and in secret memory of a summer day in June '88. R. Le G.'. In a later letter to Le Gallienne dated December 1, 1890, Wilde writes, 'I want so much to see you: when can that be? Friendship and love like ours need not meetings, but they are delightful. I hope your laurels are not too thick across your brow for me to kiss your eyelids'.[155]

Wilde and Le Gallienne's relationship seems to have cooled by the early 1890s, although they remained on good terms. In a review of Wilde's *Intentions* from this period, Le Gallienne praises Wilde's work as 'alive at every point' and 'refreshingly unsentimental', and goes on to laud the author as an insightful '<u>damascener</u> [Le Gallienne's emphasis] of thought'.[156] In February 1892, Wilde sent Le Gallienne and his wife two tickets to the premiere of *Lady Windermere's Fan* and later that year Le Gallienne defended the originality of Wilde's poetry in the *Daily Chronicle* (May 23). Le Gallienne continued to praise Wilde's work in the following year with a review of *Salomé* in the *Star* on February 22. Conversely, in 1893, Le Gallienne's poem 'The *Décadent* to His Soul' was interpreted by the poet Theodore Wratislaw as a satirical attack on Wilde. In the poem a toad-faced decadent, once 'an apple-cheek dear lad', corrupts his soul with strange new sins. The poem's narrator laments the decadent's decline: 'O let the body be a healthy beast / And keep the soul a singing soaring bird'.[157] When Wratislaw communicated his reading of the poem to Wilde, the latter reportedly remarked, 'It has always seemed to me that the finest feature of a fine nature is treachery'.[158]

However, there is little that seems treacherous and much that appears playful in 'The Woman's Half-Profits', one of the more whimsical pieces in Le Gallienne's *Prose Fancies* published the year after 'The *Décadent* to His Soul'. In this short story we find the 'self-enamoured' and 'distinguished' poet Hyacinth Rondel relaxing in his 'elegant new chambers . . . provided with all those distinguished comforts and elegancies proper to a success that may at any moment be interviewed'.

Rondel's walls, like Wilde's in Tite Street, have been decorated by Whistler and are adorned with portraits of leading actors and actresses and pictures by the latest artists 'hatched in Paris'. Like Wilde's, Rondel's bookcases are full of presentation copies from the authors: 'Mr. Rondel would as soon have thought of buying a book as of paying for a stall'. In this setting Rondel is unceremoniously accosted by his 'Muse'; the latter has decided she is entitled to half-profits from the poems she has inspired. In lieu of the money, the Muse is prepared to accept Rondel's hand in marriage or his death; Rondel chooses to settle with a check. The deflated poet, after contemplating his 'withered' laurels, '[goes] forth to seek a flatterer as a pick-me-up'.[159]

Hyacinth Rondel was to make one further appearance after 'The Woman's Half-Profits', in the short story 'Brown Roses' in Le Gallienne's second series of *Prose Fancies* in 1896, discussed in Part 3. Le Gallienne's portraits of Rondel were perhaps written in mind of Wilde's jest at the first night of *Lady Windermere's Fan*, as recounted by Le Gallienne in his book *The Romantic '90s*. Le Gallienne recalls a conversation with Wilde during the interval of the play:

> [Oscar said] '... you were very unkind to me in [your book *The Religion of a Literary Man*]', and he put on an air of deep grievance, 'most unkind!'
> 'My dear Oscar—' I began.
> 'Oh, yes, you were, and you know it,' he reiterated.
> 'I unkind to you!' I said, beginning to be really mystified.
> 'Most unkind. I could not believe it of you—so unkind to so true a friend.'
> So he continued to lure me on into a trap he had suddenly improvised for me ...
> 'Why, Oscar', I said at last, 'I don't know what you mean. Unkind to you in "The Religion of a Literary Man" ... why, I can't remember that I even mentioned your name in it.'
> Then he laughed out, with huge enjoyment of the success of his little stratagem:
> 'Ah, Richard, that was just it.'[160]

ARTHUR CONAN DOYLE

'The Greek Interpreter' (1894)

'The Empty House' (1903)

Arthur Conan Doyle, the author of 1890's *The Sign of Four* examined in the previous section, drew upon Wilde's persona for two more

Sherlock Holmes stories, the first appearing four years after *The Sign of Four*. As related in Part 1, the famous consulting detective continued to manifest Wildean characteristics in Doyle's works after 1890, including 1892's *The Adventures of Sherlock Holmes*. The *Adventures* also contains a possible reference to Wilde's aesthetic associates. In the story of 'The Red-Headed League', we encounter two somewhat effeminate criminals who invent the league of the title in order to perpetrate an ambitious robbery: the 'boyish' Duncan Ross and his aristocratic, haughty partner-in-crime John Clay. Several critics have noted the resonances of Wilde's friends Robert Ross and John Gray in these characters. (Duncan Ross also goes by the name of William Morris, another aesthetic acquaintance of Wilde's.) 'Silver Blaze' in the next collection of Holmesian short stories, the *Memoirs of Sherlock Holmes* (1894), also contains a character called Ross whose stable boy is covertly drugged with opium by a horse thief. Charles Higham reads this as a likely reference to the increasingly frequent appearance of young stable-hands in Wilde's circle.[161]

It is another short story from the *Memoirs*, however, 'The Greek Interpreter', that features an interesting Wildean personality: Holmes's enigmatic brother, Mycroft. Mycroft's intriguing description, mysterious occupation, and fleeting role in the Holmes stories have made him a fascinating figure to many of Conan Doyle's readers. It has been variously contended that Mycroft is in fact Albert Edward, the Prince of Wales, a former law clerk named Martin Hewitt, and, most remarkably, an anthropomorphic analogue computer![162] The present writer ventures to offer a Wildean reading of this character.

Before turning to Mycroft, it must first be noted that Holmes's increasingly Wildean qualities discussed above are also in evidence in 'The Greek Interpreter'. Holmes's comment to Watson in the story— 'I cannot agree with those who rank modesty among the virtues'—is particularly interesting in light of Doyle's recollection of a meeting with Wilde around this time:

> He asked me, I remember, if I had seen some play of his which was running. I answered that I had not. He said: 'Ah, you must go. It is wonderful. It is genius!' All this with the gravest face.[163]

It is also revealed in 'The Greek Interpreter' that the consulting detective has an 'aversion to women', something that Doyle had probably begun to suspect about Wilde in 1894.[164]

Despite his aversion to modesty, Holmes must admit that his brother Mycroft 'possesses [the faculties of observation and deduction] in a larger degree' than he does; a statement that astonishes Dr Watson, who had previously been unaware that Holmes had a brother at all.[165] Holmes goes on to relate that Mycroft is seven years his senior (Wilde was five years older than Doyle) and works as an auditor for several government departments. Holmes relates that his brother has a brilliant intellect, but is an 'armchair reasoner' who is typically too lazy to translate his thoughts into action, or to do more exercise than to walk around the corner from his lodgings to his workplace each day (Wilde's aversion to physical exertion was legendary).[166] The reader is further alerted to the possibility of a Wildean influence by Dr Watson's description of Mycroft's physique:

> Mycroft Holmes was a much larger and stouter man than Sherlock. His body was absolutely corpulent, but his face, though massive, had preserved something of the sharpness of expression which was so remarkable in that of his brother. His eyes, which were of a peculiarly light watery gray, seemed to always retain that far-away, introspective look which I had only observed in Sherlock's when he was exerting his full powers.[167]

Note Mycroft's 'light watery gray' eyes, redolent of the Wildean Thaddeus Sholto's 'weak, watery blue' eyes in *The Sign of Four*; Wilde's eyes were most consistently described as being light blue or gray.[168] In Mycroft's later appearance in 'The Bruce-Partington Plans' (1917), Doyle's further description of him appears to confirm a Wildean influence, particularly Wilde's uncanny ability to 'win over' with his intelligence and demeanor those who were initially repulsed by his physicality:

> the tall and portly form of Mycroft Holmes was ushered into the room. Heavily built and massive, there was a suggestion of uncouth physical inertia in the figure, but above this unwieldy frame there was perched a head so masterful in its brow, so alert in its steel-gray, deep-set eyes, so firm in its lips, and so subtle in its plays of expression, that after the first glance one forgot the gross body and remembered only the dominant mind.[169]

In 'The Greek Interpreter', Holmes and Watson visit Mycroft at the Diogenes Club at Pall Mall, which, according to Holmes, is 'the queerest club in London, and Mycroft one of the queerest men'.[170] In the story, the 'queerness' of the club relates to the fact that it 'contains the most unsociable and unclubbable men in town. No member is permitted to take the least notice of any other one. Save in the

Strangers' Room, no talking is, under any circumstances, permitted'.[171] This appears to be a satiric stroke by Doyle in the same 'topsy-turvy' vein as Beerbohm's 'A Peep into the Past'; Wilde being one of the *most* talkative and 'clubbable' men in London at that time. The name of Mycroft's club may also be a comic jab at Wilde. Diogenes was the ascetic founder of the Cynic sect at Athens (c. 400–c. 325 BC), a group that derided those who aspired, as Wilde did, to a life of epicurean luxury and ease.[172] This is also a likely possibility in light of Wilde's well-known interest in all things Greek. Indeed, Mycroft's association with the Greek interpreter, Mr Melas—a fellow member of the Diogenes whose case Mycroft passes on to his brother—also supports the likelihood of a Wildean subtext, as does Thaddeus Sholto's Greek handwriting in *The Sign of Four*.

Like Wilde, Mycroft can often be found at his regular haunts. While Wilde could usually be tracked down to his Tite Street address, the Albemarle Club, or the Café Royal, Mycroft can always be located at his Pall Mall lodgings, the Diogenes Club, or Whitehall. In many ways Mycroft's position at Whitehall could be said to resemble Wilde's at the Café Royal, as Holmes reveals in 'The Bruce-Partington Plans'. In that story we discover that, far from being a mere auditor working for the British government, Mycroft occasionally '*is* [emphasis in the original] the British government'[173]:

> 'Mycroft draws four hundred and fifty pounds a year, remains a subordinate, has no ambitions of any kind, will receive neither honour not title, but remains the most indispensable man in the country . . . He has the tidiest and most orderly brain, with the greatest capacity for storing facts, of any man living . . . The conclusions of every department are passed to him, and he is the central exchange, the clearing-house, which makes out the balance . . . his specialism is omniscience . . . he has made himself an essential. In that great brain of his everything is pigeon-holed and can be handed out in an instant. Again and again his word has decided the national policy—[174]

Wilde's mental agility and expert knowledge on a remarkable variety of subjects was often commented upon by his contemporaries, including Doyle himself, as related in Part 1. Considered in this light, Wilde's famous discourses from his table in the Café Royal, in which he proved himself to be an accomplished speaker on almost any subject, can be equated with Mycroft's role as a 'central exchange' or 'clearing-house' of thought and opinion. As Mycroft's words decided national policy, so Wilde's words set the tone for the English decadent movement.[175]

Mycroft appears briefly in two other Sherlock Holmes stories, in 1894's 'The Final Problem', where he masquerades as a brougham driver to assist Watson and Holmes in escaping Professor Moriarty, and in 1905's 'The Empty House', first published in *The Strand* magazine, where it is revealed that Mycroft has kept his brother in funds for three years while the rest of the world believed Sherlock to be dead. (Holmes had in fact been traveling under the guise of a Norwegian adventurer named Sigerson.) Although 'The Empty House' falls outside the period of this study, it will, like Ella Hepworth Dixon's 'The World's Slow Stain', be included as a relevant addendum, as it demonstrates Doyle's continuing fascination with the fallen decadent.

Doyle brought Holmes back from the dead in 'The Empty House' after much lobbying from readers and publishers. The narrative evokes strong shades of Wilde, who died three years before its publication. One of the characters presents too many of Wilde's unique characteristics to be overlooked, and the story appears to have been influenced by Wilde's *The Picture of Dorian Gray*, a novel that—as we have already seen—so impressed Doyle that he felt compelled to write to Wilde to congratulate him on it. In Doyle's story, Sherlock Holmes returns to London after three years of incognito adventures on the continent and foils an attempt on his life by substituting a wax image of himself as a decoy for his would-be assassin. That assassin, Colonel Sebastian Moran, is the one-time friend and associate of Holmes's most famous adversary, Professor Moriarty, who is now deceased. Moran served as chief of Moriarty's criminal gang and Holmes now considers Moran to be the most dangerous man in London. Moran has a distinguished Indian Army record and is 'the best heavy game shot that [the] Eastern Empire has ever produced'.[176] He is also the author of *Heavy Game of the Western Himalayas* (1881) and *Three Months in the Jungle* (1884) and is a heavy gambler who cheats at cards. None of these characteristics recall Wilde, nor do Moran's physical features. He is 'elderly . . . with a thin projecting nose, a high, bald forehead, and a huge grizzled moustache . . . His face [is] gaunt and swarthy, scored with deep, savage lines'.[177] However, there are many echoes of Wilde and his writings in the story of Moran and his attempted assassination of Holmes. These correspondences will be highlighted here, particularly those that suggest that the fallen Wilde, who formerly provided many engaging qualities for Doyle's heroic Holmes, now lent his villainous image to one of Doyle's most famous criminals.

The most extensive reading of Wilde's influence on 'The Empty House' has been made by Samuel Rosenberg, in his book *Naked Is the*

Best Disguise: The Death and Resurrection of Sherlock Holmes (1975).[178] As mentioned in Part 1, Rosenberg argues that there are several historical and legendary figures to be found in Doyle's fictional works. Rosenberg postulates that Doyle 'patterned the biography of Sebastian Moran on some facts in the life of Wilde'.[179] He sees the first clue in the story as being Watson's reference to their hunt for the '*wild* beast [my italics]' Moran.[180] (Holmes also states that he has not alerted the police to the threat from Moran as he believes they would view it as a '*wild* suspicion [my italics]'.[181]) Rosenberg provides the following list of similarities between Wilde and Moran as supporting evidence for his reading:

1. Both share the same initials: S.M. [Rosenberg refers here to Wilde's post-prison alias of 'Sebastian Melmoth'.]
2. Both are Irish . . .
3. Both are sons of Irish noblemen: Wilde was the son of Sir William Wilde. Sebastian Moran was the son of Sir Augustus Moran.
4. Both . . . are graduates of Oxford University.
5. Wilde was born in Dublin but spent the last half of his life in London. Moran's Irish family came to London, where Sebastian was born . . .
6. . . . both [were] authors . . .
7. Both Sebastians were outcasts from society.
8. Both lived underground criminal lives.
9. Both were imprisoned as a result of their involvement in a scandal arising from a relationship with a nobleman's son . . . Sebastian Moran killed Robert Adair, son of the Earl of Maynooth, because Adair threatened to ruin him for cheating at cards.[182]

In addition to these resemblances, Rosenberg points to the parallels between the wax figure of Holmes used as a decoy in 'The Empty House' and the picture of Dorian Gray in Wilde's novel, noting that both of these represent 'surrogate artistic targets which accept the murderous attacks intended for the man they portray . . . In both stories the attack upon the surrogate portrait fails and boomerangs upon the attacker [Rosenberg's italics removed]'.[183] Rosenberg also observes that the waxen image was sculpted by the French artist *Oscar* Meunier, noting that France was Wilde's last country of residence. Although Rosenberg's assertions sometimes rest upon rather tenuous connections—Wilde scholar Karl Beckson has called Rosenberg 'too ingenious for words'—the evidence he provides in this case is cumulatively persuasive.[184] Moreover, there is further supporting material in 'The Empty House', unnoted by Rosenberg, to bear out his claims. The following description of Moran's face also suggests a Wildean influence:

> With the brow of a philosopher and the jaw of a sensualist below, the man must have started with great capacities for good or for evil. But one could not look upon his cruel blue eyes, with their drooping, cynical lids, or upon the fierce, aggressive nose and the threatening, deep-lined brow, without reading Nature's plainest danger-signals.[185]

If this description had been the only one provided by Doyle, Moran would perhaps be more often identified as a fictional portrait of Wilde. As stated earlier in this study, Wilde's upper face was often described as noble and refined, whereas lower facial features were seen as gross and sensual. Moran's blue eyes with drooping, 'cynical' lids are also Wilde's. Doyle's reading of a threat in Moran's features, which he connects with '[n]ature's plainest danger-signals', may also reflect Doyle's posttrial knowledge of Wilde's homosexuality and the discomfort this knowledge inspired in the aggressively masculine author, who had previously been an admirer of Wilde's work and 'gentlemanly instincts'. Doyle is adamant in his 1924 memoir that, when he first knew Wilde, he observed no trace of arrogance or 'coarseness of thought'—that is, 'danger signals'—in the latter. Moreover, Doyle publicly attributed Wilde's 'dangerous' sexuality to innate, inherited traits.[186] Holmes offers essentially the same explanation for Moran's early promise and later descent into a life of crime:

> 'There are some trees, Watson, which grow to a certain height and then suddenly develop some unsightly eccentricity. You will see it often in humans. I have a theory that the individual represents in his development the whole procession of his ancestors, and that such a sudden turn to good or evil stands for some strong influence which came into the line of his pedigree—'[187]

Sexual impropriety was certainly known to be a feature of Wilde's family history. Wilde's father William Wilde sired at least three illegitimate children by different women before his marriage to Wilde's mother, and after his marriage was involved in a scandalous court case arising from an alleged sexual relationship with a young female patient, Mary Travers.[188] The idea that Doyle believed Wilde was inherently predisposed to perverse behavior is confirmed by the following statement, which Doyle made in 1930:

> I thought [in the 1890s], and still think, that the monstrous development which ruined him was pathological, and that a hospital rather than a police court was the place for its consideration.[189]

In conclusion, when one considers that 'The Empty House' was written less than a decade after Wilde's sensational trials, it is hardly surprising that Doyle (consciously or unconsciously) transferred distinctly Wildean characteristics from the largely sympathetic character of Holmes to the very 'shady' Colonel Moran.[190]

'The Empty House' was the last of Doyle's fictions to contain a character with so many Wildean overtones, but it was not to be Doyle's last written word on his infamous contemporary.[191] In the 1920s, Doyle, a committed student of the occult, became convinced that Wilde's spirit had communicated with the medium Hester Travers Smith; Smith published her account of these 'transmissions' in *Psychic Messages from Oscar Wilde* (1924). Doyle reviewed the book favorably in the London *Daily News* of April 16, 1924. He was fascinated by Smith's account and his genuine belief in her story is evinced by his request of her: '[i]f you are in contact [with Wilde again] you might mention me to him . . . and tell him that if he would honour me by coming through my wife who is an excellent automatic writer, there are some things which I should wish to say'.[192] As the dead Wilde does not appear to have taken Doyle up on this offer, we can only speculate as to what those things might have been.

John Davidson
Baptist Lake (1894)

Another contemporary author who was clearly intrigued by Wilde was John Davidson (1857–1909), the Scottish poet, playwright, novelist, translator, essayist, and author of *Baptist Lake*. Davidson had worked as a Scottish schoolmaster until 1889, when he left for London to try to make a living by his pen. In London he fell in with the Rhymers' Club, and through the Rhymers came into contact with Wilde.[193] While Davidson had produced a fictional farce on aestheticism nearly ten years before *Baptist Lake*—his first published work, *The North Wall* (1885)—*Baptist Lake* was his first work to contain a distinctly Wildean aesthete.

Davidson enjoyed a degree of success as a poet and novelist in the 1890s and was a regular contributor to the *Yellow Book* and other journals and newspapers. His work had an impact on such notables as T. S. Eliot, D. H. Lawrence, Ezra Pound, and Hugh MacDiarmid.[194] Davidson was not involved in the decadent movement; rather, he can be characterized by his adverse reaction to it. J. Lewis May has observed that in 'highly artificial states of society, it is natural to find at least some men giving utterance to a yearning for simpler mode of life'.[195] Davidson was such a man. Like many of his conservative contemporaries, he saw the aesthetes, with their affectations, ennui, and worship of beauty as an unnatural, unmanly lot. He believed that his own philosophical concerns with science and religion were far more appropriate masculine pursuits.[196] In light of these traits it is remarkable that Davidson was so closely associated with the Rhymers, which included the undeniably decadent Ernest Dowson, Richard Le Gallienne, Lionel Johnson, and Arthur Symons among its members. Another club member, W. B. Yeats, commented upon this incongruity in his *Autobiographies*:

> He saw in delicate, laborious, discriminating taste an effeminate pedantry, and would, when that mood was on him, delight in all that seemed healthy, popular, and bustling. Once when I had praised Herbert Horne for his knowledge and his taste, he burst out, 'if a man must be a connoisseur, let him be a connoisseur in women'! He, indeed, was accustomed, in the most characteristic phrase of his type, to describe the Rhymers as lacking in 'blood and guts', and very nearly brought us to an end by attempting to supply the deficiency by the addition of four Scotsmen.[197]

Davidson's writing often reflects his 'blood and guts' approach to life; Albert C. Baugh notes that while Davidson's poetry can be crude, it also contains a compelling vitality.[198] Some have seen Davidson's 'vitality' as its own type of affectation; May avers that Davidson was a 'shy, self-conscious, sensitive little schoolmaster, pathetically trying to play the strong man . . . [his] defiance was a symptom of a terrible inferiority complex'.[199] Norman Alford describes Davidson as 'emotionally off-balance perhaps as a result of his unhappy upbringing'.[200] Indeed, it is likely that Davidson's distaste for the trappings of decadence owed something to his early exposure to radical Calvinist ideology. His father was a minister in the Evangelical Union, and Davidson's rebellion against that strain of Christianity also resulted in a revolt against all systematized doctrines and reforming movements. However, Davidson's rebellion itself often assumed an evangelical bent.[201]

One can only wonder at the nature of a conversation between two men like Davidson and Wilde. Davidson was introduced to Wilde by

John Barlas, a handsome Scottish poet and revolutionary and associate of the Rhymers. Davidson was reportedly impressed when Wilde stood guarantor for Barlas after he was remanded in custody for discharging a revolver in Parliament.[202] Davidson was also an occasional member of Wilde's party at the Café Royal.[203] Two of Davidson's works, inscribed to Wilde, are extant. They are *Smith: A Tragedy* (1888) and *In a Music Hall and Other Poems* (1891). The inscription in the latter reads 'King Oscar from J. D. 7 Jan '92', the date of Barlas's arraignment for the shooting incident.[204] Whether Davidson was moved by Wilde's rescue of his countryman, or whether there was some other reason for his friendliness toward a man who was most definitely not of the 'blood and guts' type, remains a mystery. We can, however, partially gage Davidson's reaction to Wilde by examining his 1894 fictional portrait of the latter in *Baptist Lake*.

The eponymous Lake is immediately recognizable as Wilde; he is an extravagant, impudent, yet charismatic conversationalist and wit who takes a childish delight in his surroundings, is hopelessly inept at managing his money, and 'seldom [rises] before five o'clock in the evening'.[205] Like Wilde he is a little over six foot tall and is always perfectly dressed. He wears his hair longer than the fashion, carries a gold-headed cane like Wilde's, and is always looking into mirrors. Lake does not know why his titled father hates him but it is eventually revealed that Lake is the progeny of his mother's affair with a Frenchman. (As mentioned above, Wilde's aesthetic style was closely associated with French decadent culture.)

Lake tries to tempt the respectable Scotsman John Inglis into taking a mistress—a female friend of Lake's in financial need—and almost succeeds in this before Inglis is brought back to his senses by his love for his wife. As this plot development suggests, Davidson's is a roguish, trouble-making version of Wilde. There is also the suggestion that Lake has a less than proper relationship with Inglis's adolescent son, Islay. Soon after their first meeting Lake takes the young Islay across his knee and gives him 'a sound whipping'; he later invites Islay to do the same to him. This appears to win the younger man's affection and soon Lake's approbation becomes 'almost a necessity' to him. Lake responds by flattering Islay with his attention and tells the latter, 'you have [my heart]'.[206] Islay's reaction to Lake encapsulates Wilde's appeal to his younger acolytes: 'Islay was intoxicated with delight. To have impressed such a wonderful man as Baptist, was to him [one of the greatest triumphs] of his life'.[207]

Davidson's Lake is certainly not a flattering portrait of Wilde: he is revealed to be 'a mere farceur, very pleasant, but on a level with a hired entertainer'.[208] Like many of the authors already discussed, Davidson's fascination with Wilde's personality is evinced by his attempt to deconstruct the personal magnetism of the Wildean aesthete in fiction. Lake is humbled by the novel's denouement—he loses his cherished looks when his father disfigures his face with a knife—however, he is not condemned to an entirely bleak future; he ends by marrying the woman he tried to get Inglis to take as a mistress. Like Marie Corelli, Davidson seems to be of the opinion that Wilde's admirable qualities might prevail over his negative traits if he could be rid of his excessive self-esteem.

Some time before he marries, Lake flippantly expounds his theory about the inevitability of infidelity in marriage and his likely mistreatment of a future wife in a distinctly Wildean manner:

'Laws are made to be broken . . . It is only then that life becomes entertaining to the spectator. Ordinary law-breakers suffer and are not entertained. I have the extraordinary gift of being spectator and actor at once . . . it really is a miracle; it is genius'.[209]

Lake's musings on this subject, and his thoughts on appearing in the Divorce Court, are curiously prophetic and ironic in light of Wilde's trials the following year:

'there is nothing more entertaining than a *cause célèbre* in the Divorce Court, absolutely nothing that so stirs curiosity and imagination. Consider the perfectly ravishing pleasure of being the centre of the talk and speculation of high and low, rich and poor; of suffering *with* yourself and enjoying the acute interest of the world *in* [emphasis in the original] yourself . . . I shudder at the anticipation of such dreadful delight—'[210]

These reflections by Lake are particularly interesting in light of Wilde's remark to his friend Edward Sullivan, made while still a school boy, that 'there was nothing he would like better in after life than to be the hero of . . . a *cause célèbre* and to go down in posterity as the defendant in such a case as "Regina versus Wilde"'.[211] Wilde repeated this sentiment at Oxford, where he told his friend 'Bouncer' Ward that '[s]omehow or other, I'll be famous, and if not famous, notorious'.[212] It is possible that Davidson heard the mature Wilde express a similar sentiment.

In a satirical swipe at Wilde along the same 'topsy-turvy' lines as those taken by Beerbohm and Doyle, Davidson makes Lake an associate of the 'Middle-class Club', whose members have given up mimicking the aristocracy as Wilde did and now aim to make middle-class manners 'the perfection of style' and middle-class manners 'the essence of speech'.[213]

Davidson also parodies Wilde's famous rivalry with Whistler in depicting Lake's relationship with rival Hector Almond. John Inglis unwittingly invites both Lake and Almond to the same dinner, and is later warned by a friend that this could spell disaster:

> 'Baptist Lake was for a year the *ame damnée* of Hector Almond, and is now his imitator and traducer . . . Baptist's imitation is very good; but there's this difference. Hector's brains are the nimblest, the most working, the best supplied with blood, I've ever encountered; whereas Baptist invents before and commits to memory his sayings and stories, and prepares one or two Latin quotations to serve him for the week—'[214]

While the self-conscious Almond at first appears to be a fictional representation of Whistler, he also displays many more Wildean traits: he has a 'soft, rich voice' and 'musical' intonation, aspires to be 'a nineteenth-century Beau Brummel' and has 'the most wonderful temperament . . . He feels and can express without troubling his head the true inwardness of everything'.[215] It is also Almond, and not Lake, who plays the Wildean part in their rivalry. Baptist Lake, like Whistler apropos of Wilde, was established as a wit before Almond, and gives the latter his start in society. It is Almond's star that rises above Lake's and Lake who, Whistler-like, takes to 'maligning and avoiding his more fortunate rival'.[216] Davidson, like Ella Hepworth Dixon, appears to have appropriated elements of Wilde's personality for more than one character in the same novel.

We can only conjecture about what Wilde thought of *Baptist Lake*. A clue to his opinion of Davidson's poetry can be found in a post-prison letter to his publisher Leonard Smithers dated December 28, 1898: 'The *chef* here [in Napoule] is a much purer poet than John Davidson is'.[217] It is possible that Wilde's comment was inspired by his low opinion of Davidson's less-than-flattering novel.

After the publication of *Baptist Lake*, Davidson became increasingly preoccupied with philosophical questions relating to Darwinist philosophies and human perfectibility (the themes of his later aesthetic satire, *Earl Lavendar* [1895]). As Bruce K. Martin has noted, 'after 1900 [Davidson] seemed desperate to deal with cosmic issues, at the neglect of literary principles'.[218] As time went by, Davidson became bitterly disappointed and depressed as a result of personal problems, lack of recognition, and financial hardship, despite the patronage of people like Edmund Gosse and George Bernard Shaw and being awarded a Civil List pension. He felt that his was an unappreciated major talent, and critics have noted a marked bitterness and morbidity in his later work.[219] Davidson drowned off the Cornish coast in 1909. It is generally thought that he committed suicide.[220]

G. S. STREET

The Autobiography of a Boy: Passages Selected by His Friend, G. S. Street (1894)

Another Wilde-based fiction published in 1894 was *The Autobiography of a Boy: Passages Selected by His Friend, G. S. Street*, which was indeed written by G. S. (George Slythe) Street (1867– 1936). A journalist and author of many books and several plays that satirized his age, Street, like Richard Le Gallienne, also worked as a reader for the Bodley Head. Street was a true 1890s decadent. He was elegant and urbane and had a dandy's taste for fashion; he was also friendly with Wilde's cohorts Max Beerbohm, Ada Leverson, and the artist William Rothenstein. Street was particularly close to Beerbohm, who shared Street's underlying conservative outlook, admired and promoted Street's work, parodied his style in 1912's *A Christmas Garland* and drew more than twenty-five caricatures of him.[221] Beerbohm wrote Street's obituary, which appeared in the London *Times* of November 2, 1936, lauding the writer's kindness, wit, and personal charm.[222]

In light of their mutual friends and interests it is not surprising that Wilde and Street appear to have been acquainted. Wilde was interested enough in Street for Robert Ross to keep him appraised of Street's burgeoning career as a drama critic while Wilde was in jail.[223] However, little is known about the nature of their relationship.

While we have no evidence of Wilde's opinion of Street, the latter's *The Autobiography of a Boy* contains much commentary of a satirical nature on Wilde. Street's second and most famous work, *The Autobiography* was published in June 1894; most of it had already appeared in serial form in the *National Observer* by that time. The book proved to be popular, reaching a sixth edition by 1897. Street's narrative takes the form of an autobiography of an aesthete known only as 'Tubby', ostensibly edited by his friend Street. In a preface entitled 'The Editor's Apology', Street explains that he has made extensive cuts to his friend's manuscript and expresses the opinion that the reader could have 'borne no more' than he has allowed to remain.

Richard Le Gallienne, in reviewing the work of his fellow Bodley Head reader, explicitly stated that 'the book suggests a self-portrayal of Mr. Oscar Wilde as a young man', and indeed there are many indicators to point to Wilde as the principal model for Tubby.[224] The 'editor' explains in the preface that the excerpts from Tubby's reflections begin during his time at Oxford, where

> [he was sent] down in his third year . . . He was thought eccentric there . . . a certain amount of general popularity was secured to him by the disfavour of the powers, his reputation for wickedness, and the supposed magnificence of his debts. His theory of life also compelled him to be sometimes drunk. In his first year he was a severe ritualist, in his second an anarchist and an atheist, in his third wearily indifferent to all things, in which attitude he remained in the two years since he left the University until now when he is gone from us [to Canada].[225]

This is a canny summation of Wilde's Oxford years. Of course, the mention of a trip to Canada shortly after leaving Oxford is also telling, as Wilde lectured extensively there in the early 1880s. Tubby's manner and turn of phrase are also distinctly Wildean:

> it struck me that my new rug matched ill with my smoking suit. The better to test it I had sat down on the floor, when the door was flung violently open, and a needlessly loud voice proclaimed a typical barbarian. 'Hello, Tubby, as bad as all that?' It was not the meaningless nickname that distressed me: I permit it for its obvious affection. But my nerves are not what they were, and I felt helpless as I watched him hang his hat on my little *Ganymede*, and pull—so irrationally—the chair I call my Lady's Chair from the spot where long thought had placed it, and fill the room with the smoke of his cigar: I had denied myself a cigarette for my roses' sake—[226]

Tubby—a name that undoubtedly pokes fun at Wilde's increasing bulk—has Wilde's half-closed eyelids and many of the personality traits that were alienating his contemporaries in 1894. He is intensely vain, frequently pompous, and inordinately egoistic. He suffers the 'philistines' who surround him with 'smiling tolerance', seemingly oblivious to the antipathy he evokes among them and his peers.[227] Tubby writes poems and stories considered 'indecent', designs aesthetic clothing, routinely spends more than he earns, and dislikes middle-class conventionality and philanthropy.[228] Tubby also tries his hand at reviewing books, but he can only say that they are bad; clearly a dig at Wilde's often acrid reviewing style.

The allusions to Wilde proliferate. Tubby's worshipping of Juliet in the chapter entitled 'Alas' has many resonances of Wilde's early infatuation with Lillie Langtry and the speculation that surrounded their relationship. As was reportedly the case with Wilde, Tubby is horrified when the object of his devotion begins to respond to his persistent suit: 'I knew that my nature could never have supported a mutual passion for long'.[229] Wilde's growing arrogance is reflected in the chapter entitled 'The Old Generation', when Tubby expresses his belief that he has surpassed his old college professors in his appreciation of the 'Greek spirit' and blithely insults one of them with his disdainful condescension.[230] In 'Against Stupidity', Tubby's thoughts on religion certainly resemble Wilde's. He avers, 'From a purely aesthetic point of view, there is much that is acceptable in the Church's ritual and surroundings. Why trouble about the import of her teachings? I never listen to them'.[231] Moreover, Tubby wants to 'forget the world and its conventions [and aspires to] be joyous and free [like] Greeks of old', regards a concern with truth as indicative of a 'want of imagination' and, Wilde-like, is 'always the slave of the passing emotion'.[232] In an echo of Wilde's essay 'The Soul of Man Under Socialism', Tubby declares his belief in the great potential of the 'criminal class . . . those who have taken no taint of respectability at their births'.[233] Wilde's suggestive poetry and ambiguous sexuality is also alluded to with Tubby's 'Ballad of Shameful Kisses'.

Although J. Lewis May has described *The Autobiography of a Boy* as a 'genial' satire, and Holbrook Jackson has called Tubby a 'delightful', 'unforgettably comic exaggeration', the humor of Street's portrait is often cutting, particularly in its inference that Tubby is all affectation with no talent or intelligence.[234] Indeed, Tubby is the only person who is convinced of his genius, and his claims to special consideration are painted as delusions of grandeur at best, the disingenuous protestations of a freeloader at worst.

The Autobiography of a Boy received glowing reviews and secured Street a place among the London literati. The London *Bookman* of July 1894 commended Street's picture of the 'Cad Aesthetic', calling his portrait 'timely, happy, and humorously wise'. On September 15, 1894, the *Athenaeum* declared, 'here is a new vein of wit and satire, of literary tact and dexterity'. The *Athenaeum* critic compared Street's satire with that of Jonathan Swift and predicted that 'from Mr. Street we should have something big in fiction'.[235] However, while Street went on to write many more books, none were to equal the success of *The Autobiography*, and his growing interest in the theater after the turn of the century resulted in a marked decrease in his literary output.[236]

There can be no doubt that, like *Baptist Lake*, *The Autobiography* did Wilde's public image little good. Street's contribution to anti-Wilde feeling may have been uppermost in his mind when, as the Lord Chamberlain's reader in March 1918, he recommended that Wilde's controversial play *Salomé* be given a license (on the condition that John the Baptist's severed head should not be seen by the audience). As Beerbohm and another friend R. Ellis Roberts recalled, Street was essentially a kind man; he may have regretted his satiric derision of the talented Wilde whom he knew to be essentially good-hearted. Philip Hoare has observed that it is 'remarkable . . . how few objections the sensible Street had [to *Salomé*], considering the proscriptive nature of his office'.[237] Douglas Goldring's anecdote about Street at a party hosted by Violet Hunt, related in *South Lodge* (1943), supports the idea that Street may have experienced some regret about his cutting portrait of Wilde in *The Autobiography*:

> When we were alone and I had passed him the port, Street began talking about Oscar Wilde . . . Before we went upstairs Street suddenly turned on me . . . and said, with evident emotion: 'You know, what most people don't seem to realise is that Oscar was *such a dear* [emphasis in the original]!'[238]

Robert Hichens
The Green Carnation (1894)

Any damage to Wilde's career done by *The Autobiography of a Boy* or earlier fictions pales in comparison to that brought about by another work published anonymously on September 15, 1894; Robert Hichens's *The Green Carnation*. Of all the contemporary satires and *romans à clef* featuring Wilde, *The Green Carnation*, with its clever mimicry of the talk and idiosyncrasies of Wilde and his circle, proved to be the most popular and the most devastating. Despite occasional references in the novel to 'Oscar Wilde' and his writings, Hichens (1864–1950) left no room for doubt that the central characters Esmé Amarinth and Lord Reggie Hastings were portraits of Wilde and his constant companion, Lord Alfred Douglas. Indeed, in the American edition of *The Green Carnation*, there was a page identifying Wilde and Douglas as such.[239] Hichens's novel is set at the country house of a Mrs Windsor in Chenecote, where a small party has gathered for a holiday. Amarinth and Hastings are among Mrs Windsor's guests, and during his stay the Douglas-based Hastings half-heartedly toys with the idea of marrying the wealthy provincial widow Lady Locke, a cousin of their hostess.

The title of Hichens's book was inspired by the fashion among Wilde's circle of wearing artificially colored green carnations, first made popular by Wilde at the premiere of *Lady Windermere's Fan* in 1892. By that stage the flower appears to have become a symbol of homosexuality in Paris and among a select group in London.[240] In *The Green Carnation*, the flower is worn as a badge, identifying disciples of Amarinth and his philosophy. Lady Locke observes,

> 'all the men who wore [green carnations] looked the same. They had the same walk, or rather waggle, the same coyly conscious expression, the same wavy motion of the head. When they spoke to each other, they called each other by Christian names. Is it a badge of some club or society, and is Mr. Amarinth their high priest? They all spoke to him, and seemed to revolve round him like satellites around the sun'.[241]

In depicting Amarinth, Hichens greatly exaggerates and twists Wilde's talk and philosophies, but his facetious portrait was taken by many to be true to life—Richard Ellmann has noted that the book reads 'more like a documentary' than a parody—and it had a disastrous effect on Wilde's already tarnished public image.[242]

In the early 1890s Hichens was a working journalist, contributing regularly to the *Evening Standard*, the *Pall Mall Magazine*, and the *Globe*.[243] While recuperating from a bout of illness in Egypt during the winter of 1893–1894, Hichens made the acquaintance of Lord Alfred Douglas, E. F. (Edward Frederick) Benson, and Reggie Turner.[244] These three were Hichens's companions for some weeks in Luxor and on a Nile boat trip to Aswan. During this time the group regaled Hichens with amusing tales of Wilde and the 'smart set' in London. Benson had recently published a successful novel, *Dodo*, based on the life of Margot Tennant (later Mrs Asquith, wife of the prime minister). Benson's success and the stories told by his companions soon inspired Hichens to try to capture Wilde in fiction.

At this point, Hichens and Wilde had not met, although the former relates in his autobiography *Yesterday* that he had attended the first nights of all Wilde's plays and had heard him lecture some years before. (It must be said, however, that Hichens's autobiography cannot always be relied upon as an entirely truthful account of events.[245]) Upon returning to London from Egypt, Alfred Douglas arranged for Hichens and Wilde to meet. Hichens recalls that

> [t]he idea of meeting the most witty and sought after man in London thrilled me. But I was slightly alarmed at it too. Could I possibly hope to be up to Mr. Wilde's mark—if he had a mark? I am quite sure

I wasn't, but I found him the least alarming and least exigent of men, full of cordiality, humour, and what seemed to me to be exuberant good nature.[246]

Hichens and Wilde struck up an easy rapport at this first meeting (Hichens did not inform Wilde of his work in progress) and the two men saw each other several times that year; on two occasions Wilde visited Hichens at his home. Hichens later recalled that all his meetings with Wilde were happy ones:

> He was cordial in manner, good-natured, often deliberately absurd, and not at all insufferably vain . . . I have never heard him say a coarse thing. There was nothing Rabelaisian about him. He never showed himself to me as a man of sentiment . . . He was kind, but I don't know whether he was ready to put himself out in the way of kindness. He was always largely sure of himself . . . When he relapsed—one must call it that—into seriousness he was very interesting and at moments even profound. He was, I should say, an eminently likeable man.[247]

However, these recollections of Wilde, which are echoed in Hichens's introduction to a new edition of the novel in 1949,[248] bear little resemblance to Hichens's portrait of him in *The Green Carnation*. In many ways, Amarinth is true to his original; he has a 'large and sleek body', a 'carefully crimped head', 'a closely shaved, clever face, and rather rippling brown hair'. He also has Wilde's famous 'gently elaborate voice'.[249] Amarinth's occupation, celebrity status, manner, and conversational themes are all Wilde's; he is a married father of two boys (Wilde's two sons were born in 1885 and 1886), has one 'uncouth' brother (redolent of Willie Wilde), and revels in the art of 'preposterous conversation'.[250] He considers nature 'middle-class' and declares, 'There is nothing in the world worth having except youth, youth with its perfect sins'.[251] Amarinth has written a scandalous novel; Wilde's *The Picture of Dorian Gray* becomes Amarinth's *The Soul of Bertie Brown*.[252] Amaranth also demonstrates Wilde's flair for self-publicity and lack of concern with accusations of plagiarism:

> Whenever the public interest in him showed signs of flagging he wrote an improper story, or published an epigram in one volume, on hand-made paper, with immense margins, or produced a play full of other people's wit, or said something scandalous about the North Pole.[253]

The name of Hichens's Wildean protagonist is cleverly chosen; the plant genus *Amaranthus* typically produces ostentatious flowers and foliage. Amaranth is also a shade of purple, one of Wilde's favorite colors, and 'purple' is a word that was often used to describe Wilde's prose. However, Amarinth is far from being 'profound' and 'eminently likeable' as Hichens professed to find Wilde. In what Holbrook Jackson has called a 'cold, satirical echo' of the true Wilde, Hichens's fictional version is a pompous and foppish fool, who '[misunderstands] the drift of leading [newspaper] articles' and who is dangerously deluded.[254] Hichens embellishes and distorts Wilde's sagacious pronouncements on art and life so as to render them crude and absurd. Amarinth continually uses the word 'artistic' as a justification for all manner of nonsense and perversity, and there is the clear suggestion that something sinister underlies his aesthetic posturings. The fact that the author professed to be a friend and admirer of his subject makes this portrait a remarkable one.

It is true that Wilde frequently walked a thin line with his flippant rejections of middle-class Victorian values, but he was always circumspect in tempering his criticism and infusing it with good-natured humor. Hichens's Amarinth, however, despite politely enduring 'philistines' like Lady Locke and the local curate, flatly denounces all that is near and dear to the late Victorians and plainly declares his desire to undermine the foundations of their world. In an episode that must surely have struck fear into the hearts of God-fearing middle-class Victorian parents, Amarinth lectures some local children on the 'art of folly': 'To know how to be disobedient is to know how to live'.[255] Hichens takes Wilde's fascination with the concept of sin, evinced in *Dorian Gray*, a step further to transform it into an alarming doctrine; Amarinth's lecture to the local children is Wilde gone wild:

'There is nothing good and nothing evil. There is only art. Despise the normal, and flee from the seven deadly virtues. Cling to the abnormal. Shrink from the cold and freezing touch of nature . . . forget your Catechism—'[256]

As if indoctrinating the nation's impressionable youth in this fashion was not bad enough, Amarinth also derides the sacrosanct Victorian ideal of female purity:

'I love what are called warped minds, and deformed natures, just as I love the long necks of Burne-Jones' women, and the faded rose-leaf beauty of Walter Pater's unnatural prose. Nature is generally purely vulgar, just as many women are vulgarly pure'.[257]

Although Amarinth speaks disparagingly of women in general, Mrs Windsor—childless, cynical and worldly—is presented as an example of the 'unhealthy' type of femininity that Amarinth prefers. With light hair and dark brows, witty repartee, aesthetic taste in décor and a wealthy absent husband, Mrs Windsor is surely intended as a portrait of Wilde's friend Ada Leverson. Although Hichens's portrait of Leverson is not a flattering one—Mrs Windsor is painted as an unintelligent woman who tries very hard to appear clever—she and Hichens later became firm friends; they corresponded for many years into the twentieth century.[258]

Unsurprisingly, both Amarinth and Hastings show little respect for the revered Victorian institution of marriage, as demonstrated by the latter's thoughts of marrying Lady Locke:

> In modern days [marriage] is a contract of no importance, as Esmé Amarinth often said, and therefore a contract that can be entered into without searching of heart or loss of perfect liberty. To [Hastings] it simply meant that a good-natured woman, who liked to kiss him, would open an account for him at her banker's, and let him live with her when he felt so disposed.[259]

Amarinth relates, 'I married to be absurd; for marriage is one of the most brilliant absurdities ever invented by a prolific imagination'.[260] The particular absurdity inherent in Amarinth and Hastings taking wives, while never overtly stated by Hichens, is hinted at broadly enough to prompt Holbrook Jackson to comment, '[a]t times the book reads more like an indiscretion than a satire'.[261] Some readers may have been alerted to the suggestion of a homosexual subtext by the title of Hichens's book; as mentioned above the green carnation appears to have been worn in Paris at this time as a badge of homosexuality.[262] There are certainly many passages to confirm the hint in the title. Hastings is described as possessing 'an almost girlish beauty'. He also recalls '[trying] to be manly' in the company of an army officer and has not got 'the faintest idea how to woo *a woman* [my italics]'.[263] Hastings also refers to having 'the courage of one's desires', while Amarinth sings a song about an idyllic land where 'no voices ever call / Any passion-act, strange or unwise'.[264] When Lady Locke tells Hastings that he knows Amarinth 'far too well', Hastings looks at her 'rather curiously'.[265] To the unsuspecting Lady Locke, the young Hastings is 'strangely different from all the men and boys whom she had ever known, almost monstrously different'; 'a gentleman, and yet not a man at all'.[266] The worldly-wise Mrs Windsor does her best to educate Lady Locke: '[m]en may have women's minds, just as women may have the minds of men . . . it is quite common nowadays'.²⁶⁷ If there were any doubts remaining in the contemporary reader's mind about the import of these passages, the following speech from Amarinth, expressing his dislike of 'the natural', must surely have dispelled them:

> 'Certain things are classed as unnatural—for all the people born into the world. Individualism is not allowed to enter into the matter. A child is unnatural if it hates its mother. A mother is unnatural if she does not wish to have children. A man is unnatural if he never falls in love with a woman. A boy is unnatural if he prefers looking at pictures to playing cricket, or dreaming over the white naked beauty of a Greek statue to a game of football under Rugby rules'.²⁶⁸

If Amarinth's dangerously subversive doctrines and 'deviant' sexuality were not enough to set the Victorian public against his original, *The Green Carnation* contains a further implication that could not fail to alarm its readers. Undoubtedly the most sinister suggestion in Hichens's novel relates to Amarinth's and Hastings's influence over Lady Locke's son Tommy and a group of 'rosy' little choir boys from the local village, who come to Mrs Windsor's house to perform a piece composed by Lord Hastings. The two aesthetes have a prodigious effect on the impressionable boys. They 'were all hopelessly in love with Lord Reggie . . . but they gazed upon Amarinth with an awe that made their bosoms heave'.²⁶⁹ The awestruck children listen with wrapt attention to Amarinth's 'despise the normal' lecture described above. It is the interest of the two men in the children, however, which seems particularly designed to disturb. Amarinth's Wilde-like remark, 'There is nothing in the world worth having except youth',²⁷⁰ delivered while casting his eye over the group of small boys, assumes a disturbing resonance when considered in light of the conclusion of his lecture:

> 'remember only that you are young, and that some day, in the long-delayed fullness of time, you will be no longer innocent. He uttered the last words in a tone so soft and so seductive that it was like honey and the honeycomb, and then stood with his eyes fixed dreamily upon the children—'²⁷¹

Other incidents in the novel also invite the reader's conjecture on this subject: Amarinth encourages the head choir boy, Jimmy Sands, to '[whisper] confidences' to him and when Tommy Locke sits next to

Lord Hastings playing the organ, it is emphasized that they are entirely obscured by a curtain.[272] The power of Amarinth and Hastings over the children appears to be concentrated in the green carnation that they both wear; Jimmy Sands is mesmerized by it and Lady Locke realizes that she must keep her young son away from Hastings when she overhears the latter offering the boy the flower, in a manner that could be read as sexually suggestive.[273] Although she concludes that it is Hastings's 'pose' that is dangerous to her son, the reader's misgivings remain. Clearly, as Eric Susser has noted, the book's 'implications are really accusations reducing aestheticism to perversion and homosexuality'.[274] It is no wonder that publisher William Heinemann showed the book to his solicitor George Lewis before publishing it, to seek his advice about potential libel action.[275]

Why did Hichens include these sinister inferences in his satire? Did he share Lady Locke's concern about 'the influence that a mere pose may have upon others who are not posing', or does his fiction infer something far worse?[276] There is certainly something ominous about Amarinth's and Hastings's surreptitious whisperings and 'mesmerizing' of children. Amarinth's pronouncement, 'Our faces are really masks given to us to conceal our minds with'—a twisting of Wilde's many comments on faces and masks—reinforces the reader's misgivings.[277] Did Hichens believe that Wilde's 'unnatural' sexuality extended to a pedophilic impulse? It is a common sexual myth that homosexuality can be equated with pedophilia. However, it is widely accepted among biographers and scholars that Wilde's homosexual activity was confined to young adult males, who had attained physical maturity.[278]

Charles Burkhart and Dennis Denisoff have contended that Hichens's portrait does not completely annihilate Wilde or his aestheticism, arguing that it only 'superficially wounds'; Denisoff believes this can be attributed to Hichens's 'own investment in aestheticism's tenets'.[279] Hichens himself referred to the book as merely 'impudent'. However, in light of the passages discussed above, these conclusions are difficult to accept. Even allowing for the usual criticisms and barbs of satire, Hichens's book is unusually caustic. It is possible that Hichens's portrait of Wilde was negatively influenced by Douglas's reporting in Egypt; the relationship between Wilde and Douglas had cooled considerably before Douglas left London for the trip and Wilde had been avoiding him.[280] It is also possible that Hichens's rather menacing picture of Wilde was the result of the author's ambivalent feelings about his own sexuality. According to Richard Ellmann, Dennis Denisoff, and Gary Schmidgall, Hichens, like Raffalovich and James, shared Wilde's homosexual proclivities.[281] Richard Bleiler notes that Hichens possessed

> a hyperdeveloped sense of Edwardian morality, an attitude which makes his novels seem dated to present-day readers. In his moral universe those who disagree with the properly behaving representatives of established religion are invariably humbled.[282]

It could be that, like Raffalovich, Hichens (consciously or unconsciously) demonized Wilde for embracing a 'deviant' sexuality that sat uncomfortably in Hichens alongside his own 'hyperdeveloped' sense of morality. Denisoff contends that Hichens, despite his social position within the 1890s homosexual and decadent communities, did not agree with the 'isolationist elitism' of Wildean decadence.[283]

Whatever Hichens's motivation, his reading public were shocked by the novel and were not slow to react; *The Green Carnation* prompted an immediate *succès de scandale* upon its release. Wilde's friend Frank Harris reported, 'On all sides the book was referred to as confirming the worst suspicions'.[284] While Hichens was applauded for his imitation of Wilde and Douglas in some quarters, in others the book was condemned as being in poor taste. The reviewer from the *Academy* was typical in his condemnation of the book and Wilde:

> It is but a caricature of an affectation in life and literature, of an abnormality, a worship of abstract and scarlet sin, which must of its very nature pass away with the personality that first flaunted it before a wondering, half-attracted, half-revolted world. Was this worth caricaturing?[285]

Hichens also caused offense by having Amarinth and Hastings criticize many living people in the book, including Rhoda Broughton, Mrs Humphry Ward, and Eliza Lynn Linton, among others.[286] *Punch*, never slow to capitalize on an opportunity to satirize Wilde, responded on November 10 with a sketch entitled 'Two Decadent Guys: A Colour Study in Green Carnations', which replaced Esmé Amarinth and Lord Reggie Hastings with Sir Fustian Flitters and Lord Raggie Tattersall, as two of the traditional 'guys' burned on a bonfire during Guy Fawkes night. (See plates 6 and 7 for this caricature and a contemporary photograph of Wilde and Douglas.) Like Hichens's characters, Flitters and Tattersall are exaggerated copies of Wilde and Douglas, with magenta cauliflowers in their buttonholes instead of green carnations. They speak of their quest to imbue 'rose-coloured children' with some of their 'own lovely limpness', reinforcing the dark suggestion in Hichens's novel.

There can be little doubt that the escalating rumors about Wilde and Douglas, fueled by the success of *The Green Carnation*, fanned the ire of Douglas's father, the Marquess of Queensberry, who was to play such a pivotal role in Wilde's demise. The book played on Queensberry's worst fear; that Douglas had succumbed to Wilde's unhealthy and 'unnatural' influence. Moreover, and perhaps most disastrously, Queensberry appears thinly disguised in Hichens's book as Reggie's father, as does Douglas's famous insulting telegram, sent in reply to a particularly vehement ultimatum from his father: 'What a funny little man you are'.[287] Douglas probably fed this information to Hichens himself, never missing an opportunity to bait his belligerent parent. Like Lord Hastings, Douglas, 'far from fearing scandal... loved it'.[288] It was he who first revealed Hichens's authorship of *The Green Carnation* to journalists as he was dining with the author at the Café Royal.[289]

As publisher William Heinemann had foreseen, the anonymous authorship of *The Green Carnation* added considerably to the controversy surrounding the book (Hichens's name did not appear under the title until the book's fourth impression in 1895).[290] Before Hichens's authorship was revealed, a popular guess as to the identity of the author was Ada Leverson, Wilde's own first guess, who was friendly with both Hichens and Wilde and had previously parodied Wilde's works for *Punch* and the *Yellow Book* with Wilde's approval. On hearing of Hichens's authorship, Wilde sent a telegram to Leverson stating that he and Douglas were 'delighted to find that their Sphinx [was] not a minx after all'. He later apologized for wronging Leverson with his guess, but explained that there were 'many bits [of Hichens's book] not unworthy of your brilliant pen: and treachery is inseparable from faith'.[291] Marie Corelli and the poet Alfred Austin had also been considered likely suspects. Some had conjectured that Wilde himself wrote the book, prompting his letter to the *Pall Mall Gazette* on October 2, 1894:

> Kindly allow me to contradict, in the most emphatic manner, the suggestion, made in your issue of Thursday last, and since then copied into many other newspapers, that I am the author of *The Green Carnation*. I invented that magnificent flower. But with the middle-class and mediocre book that usurps its strangely beautiful name I have, I need hardly say, nothing whatsoever to do. The flower is a work of art. The book is not. I remain, sir, your obedient servant, Oscar Wilde.[292]

The 1895 sale catalogue of Wilde's Tite Street effects shows that he owned a copy of Hichens's novel. In conversation with friends, Wilde was characteristically philosophical about the book and granted that Hichens had talent. However, he also felt that he had been traduced rather than reproduced, and referred to Hichens as a 'doubting disciple who [had] written [a] false gospel'.[293] Wilde clearly resented the fact that Hichens had put their conversations and the anecdotes of his friends to such a use. To Frank Harris he remarked: 'I thought him rather pleasant, and saw a good deal of him. I had no idea that he was going to play reporter; it seems to me a breach of confidence—ignoble'.[294] To Hichens, however, he sent an (anonymous) amusing telegram contending that he had guessed at Hichens's authorship of the book. Despite this friendly gesture, Hichens and Wilde never saw each other again.[295] Wilde's reference to Hichens's play *The Daughters of Babylon*, then playing at the Lyric Theatre, in a letter to Reggie Turner dated August 3, 1897, suggests that the disgraced decadent felt a lingering resentment toward Hichens: '[t]he horizon of the English stage seems dark with Hichens. Do finish your play and stop him'.[296]

In public, however, and in accordance with his usual custom, Wilde adopted a pose of amused tolerance toward his latest fictional incarnation. His real concern about the impact of the book is demonstrated by his comments to the publisher of *Oscariana*, a book of his epigrams edited by his wife: 'After the *Green Carnation* . . . this book of "real Oscar Wilde" should be refined and distinguished'.[297] His final word on the book came the following year, in a line given to Lady Bracknell in the closing scene of the original four-act version of *The Importance of Being Earnest*: 'This treatise, *The Green Carnation* . . . seems to be a book about the culture of exotics . . . It seems a morbid and middle-class affair'.[298] While Alfred Douglas also maintained a show of indifference, sending Hichens a comic telegram in the same vein as Wilde's, he later remarked that *The Green Carnation* caused him 'a lot of harm' and was in reality 'a piece of perfidy'.[299]

Whether Hichens's novel was intended as an attack on Wilde, or whether it was merely imprudent, *The Green Carnation* did more than any other fiction to pillory him. For Hichens, however, the book's notoriety made his name. He succeeded Bernard Shaw in the latter's prestigious position as musical critic at the *World* and went on to write more than seventy books, several of which were best sellers.[300] According to his own report, Hichens showed some propriety in asking Heinemann to withdraw *The Green Carnation* from sale after Wilde was called to the dock in April 1895. When Hichens was later warned against writing a similar skit about Whistler, the author replied, 'Oh . . . don't be afraid. I'm no longer impudent. The years have chastened me. I don't say that I have learned wisdom, but I hope I have shed a certain amount of folly'.[301] The fact that several of Wilde's close friends, including Ada Leverson and Reggie Turner, stayed on friendly terms with Hichens after Wilde's disgrace and death also suggests that the author expressed some regret about the damage wrought by *The Green Carnation*. He was certainly reluctant to authorize a new edition of the book in 1943 until he had obtained the approval of Alfred Douglas, who was still living. (However, it must also be said that this gesture may have been prompted by Douglas's notorious reputation for litigiousness.) At Douglas's request, Hichens included 'a few friendly words' about him in the preface to the edition that was eventually published by the Unicorn Press in 1949, to soften what Douglas referred to as a 'vicious attack on me'.[302]

Robert Buchanan and Henry Murray
The Charlatan (1895)

Two far more favorable Wildean fictions were published before the Wilde scandal erupted in April 1895. The first of these was an adaptation of an 1894 drama featuring a younger, 'first phase' Wildean aesthete named Mervyn Darrell. The Scottish journalist, poet, novelist, and playwright Robert Williams Buchanan (1841–1901) was in the habit of incorporating real personalities into his works; 1882's *The Martyrdom of Madeline*, for example, contained portraits of Walter Pater, Edmund Yates, Henry Labouchere, and himself.[303] Buchanan created the epigram-spouting Oxford student Darrell for his 1894 play *The Charlatan*, the story of a fraudulent occultist and his cohort Madame Obnoskin, and their influence over an aristocratic English family. (Obnoskin is a satirical portrait of Madame Blavatsky, also fictionalized in Rosa Praed's *Affinities*, discussed in Part 1.) Herbert Beerbohm Tree, the actor-manager and half-brother of Max Beerbohm, commissioned the play for the Haymarket Theatre and played the charlatan of the title. The actor cast as Darrell in that production, Frederick Kerr, modeled his interpretation on Wilde.[304] The play enjoyed a modest success upon opening, and the story was soon serialized for newspaper publication before appearing as a novel in 1895, written in collaboration with Henry Murray. The novel version of *The Charlatan* was one of the many 'potboilers' Buchanan produced in the 1880s and 1890s in order to relieve his financial difficulties.³⁰⁵

Despite his premature baldness, Darrell is a throwback to the stereotypical Wildean aesthete of the 1880s. He is languid, supercilious, and indifferent to every subject save art, philosophy, and himself:

> Among the more frequent and favoured guests at Wanborough Castle was the Honourable Mr. Mervyn Darrell, a nephew of the Earl, a young gentleman blessed with a couple of thousands a year, perfect nerves and digestion, a more than moderate share of intelligence, and a colossal belief in himself. One of his few earthly troubles was that he had but very recently left his teens . . . the Honourable Mervyn's chief aspiration was to be superior to everything and everybody.³⁰⁶

Darrell studies at Oxford, where he is 'doing the honours' to a certain German professor of metaphysics, perhaps a deliberately suggestive phrase. Like Wilde, Darrell is derisive in speaking of Dickens, referring to him as a '[v]ulgar optimist'.³⁰⁷ Darrell's Wildean philosophy is encapsulated in the book he is reading—*The Sublimation of Personality, or the Quintessence of the Ego*—which he describes as

> 'an essay on the imperfections of human society. It shows, absolutely and conclusively, that everything is wrong except one's inner self— that Society, Morality, Duty, Respectability, and the other shibboleths, are only terms to express various phases of exploded bourgeois superstition'.³⁰⁸

Darrell's cousin Lottie, in speaking of Darrell's postuniversity career, provides a tongue-in-cheek description of Wilde's:

> 'At college you had the aesthetic scarlatina, and babbled about lilies, and sunflowers, and blue china. Then you became affected with Radicalism—went about disguised in corduroys, and lectured at Toynbee Hall. Then, after a few serious ailments, you caught the last epidemic, from which you are still suffering . . . Individualism *you* [emphasis in the original] call it, I believe; *I* call it the dumps'.³⁰⁹

Darrell is described as having a 'chubby, solid' face, redolent of the 1890s Wilde.³¹⁰ Darrell's appreciation of 'the aroma of social decay' for the purposes of artistic and intellectual inspiration may also be a reference to the contemporary Wilde.³¹¹ Wilde was keeping dubious company in the mid-1890s, particularly working-class 'renters'.

Indeed, 'intellectual and artistic inspiration' was the justification Wilde offered for forming these connections during his trials.

Although Buchanan's portrait of Darrell is less than complimentary, it is not entirely damning. Darrell chivalrously undertakes to locate the charlatan Phillip Woodville, who goes into hiding toward the end of the novel, for the sake of his cousin Lottie. Although Darrell is acquainted with the fraudulent Woodville, due to his interest in theosophy, they are not close friends. Darrell quickly perceives that Woodville is a 'humbug', although in true Wildean style he does not condemn him for this:

> 'I have always had the greatest respect for impostors. They are men of genius, who perceive by instinct the utter absurdity of human existence. They only do on a small scale what the spirit of the Universe does on a large scale—conceal the sublimely hideous reality with the amusing mask of Idealism'.[312]

It soon becomes apparent that, despite the surface evidence to the contrary, Darrell is a well-meaning man with a 'good heart'. Lottie remarks, 'You're a good fellow, Mervyn . . . when you aren't posing and pretending to be something you're not'.[313]

This would appear to be an accurate reflection of Buchanan's own opinion of Wilde. Buchanan might initially appear to be an unlikely ally of the arch-aesthete, particularly in light of his scathing 1872 attack on Pre-Raphaelite aestheticism entitled 'The Fleshly School of Poetry', a pamphlet that emphatically condemned the affectations and artistic 'immorality' of Dante Gabriel Rossetti and his circle.[314] Buchanan was a man whose outlook was heavily influenced by religious concerns; as his contemporary Archibald Stodart-Walker noted, 'to Mr. Buchanan life is a serious concern and poetry a serious mission'.[315]

However, despite their conflicting opinions on the relation of art to morality, Buchanan and Wilde had much in common. Both grew up in free-thinking households and both were socialists and humanitarians. Buchanan wrote passionately on such unpopular social topics as vivisection, censorship, religious hypocrisy, and the victimization of women, and no doubt appreciated Wilde's essays and fairy tales featuring humanitarian and utopian themes. Both men were also avid admirers of Walt Whitman and visited the poet in America: Wilde in 1882, Buchanan in 1884.

The history of Wilde's and Buchanan's relationship is a fascinating one. Wilde reviewed two of Buchanan's works in 1887: the novel

That Winter Night (in the *Pall Mall Gazette* of May 2) and the play *The Blue Bells of Scotland* (in the *Court and Society Review* of September 14). Wilde reviewed the former unfavorably (he declared the book 'quite unworthy of any man of letters'), and the latter favorably (finding in it 'a great deal of curious and interesting lore about queer and interesting people'). We know that Wilde and Buchanan occasionally moved in the same social circles; both were present at an 1889 luncheon party given by Mr and Mrs Skirrow, along with Marie Corelli, Robert Browning, Ellen Terry, and Sir Henry Irving.[316] We can also assume that Wilde saw other Buchanan plays after *The Blue Bells of Scotland*; his letters show that he planned to attend performances of *Dr Cupid* in 1889 and *Clarissa* in 1890.[317] Whether Wilde and Buchanan were first acquainted socially, or whether they met as a consequence of Wilde's patronage of Buchanan's plays (Wilde often wrote to authors to congratulate them on their work), is unclear. It is also possible that Buchanan was acquainted with Wilde's brother Willie, as he mentions knowing two brothers by the name of Wilde in a letter to the editor of the *Whitehall Review* c. 1890.[318]

We know that by 1891 the two authors had exchanged correspondence; a letter from Buchanan to Wilde dated August 5, 1891 reveals that Wilde sent Buchanan a presentation copy of *The Picture of Dorian Gray* soon after it was published in book form.[319] The letter also reveals that the two men acknowledged their often antithetical approaches to life and demonstrates that Buchanan admired Wilde regardless:

> My dear Oscar Wilde, I ought to have thanked you thus for your present of *Dorian Gray*, but I was hoping to return the compliment by sending you a work of my own: this I shall do in a very few days. You are quite right as to our divergence, which is temperamental. I cannot accept yours as a serious criticism of life. You seem to me like a holiday maker throwing pebbles into the sea, or viewing the great ocean from under the awning of a bathing machine. I quite see, however, that this is only your 'fun', and that your very indolence of gaiety is paradoxical, like your utterances. If I judged you by what you deny in print, I should fear that [you] were somewhat heartless. Having seen and spoken with you, I conceive that you are just as poor and self-tormenting a creature as any of the rest of us, and that you are simply joking at your own expense.
>
> Don't think me rude in saying that *Dorian Gray* is very very clever. It is more—it is suggestive and stimulating, and has (tho' you only outlined it) the anxiety of a human <u>Soul</u> in it. You care far less about <u>Art</u>

[emphasis in the original], or any other word spelt with a capital, than you are willing to admit, and [therein?] lies your salvation, as you will presently discover. Though here and there in your pages you parade the magnificence of the Disraeli waistcoat, that article of wardrobe fails to disguise you. One catches you constantly *in puris naturalibus*, and then the Man is worth observing. With thanks & all kind wishes, Yours truly, Robert Buchanan.[320]

Although this letter demonstrates that the two authors were on friendly terms in 1891, in 1893 Buchanan was unable to resist a rather sharp literary dig at Wilde and his 'divergent' temperament in his poem 'The Dismal Throng'. In this composition Buchanan denounces the 'literature of a sunless Decadence' and what he saw as its defining characteristics: 'gloom, ugliness, prurience, preachiness, and weedy flabbiness of style'.[321] Among the authors he derides for their 'dreary, dolent airs', devoid of 'Health . . . Mirth, and Song', are Zola, Verlaine, Tolstoy, Ibsen, Maupassant, George Moore, Mark Twain, George Meredith, and Wilde:

> And while they loom before our view,
> Dark'ning the air that should be sunny,
> Here's Oscar, growing dismal too,
> Our Oscar, who was once so funny!
> Blue China ceases to delight
> The dear curl'd darling of society,
> Changed are his breeches, once so bright,
> For foreign breaches of propriety![322]

Despite this jibe, Buchanan's relatively sympathetic portrait of Wilde in 1895's Mervyn Darrell suggests that he retained a degree of respect for the self-proclaimed leader of the decadents. This is also evinced by Buchanan's protest against Wilde's treatment in the press while awaiting trial in 1895. On April 15, 19, 22, and 23, 1895, Buchanan wrote to the editor of the *Star* newspaper pleading for mercy towards 'a brother artist'. The spirit of this correspondence is encapsulated in the following excerpt from his letter of April 15:

> I . . . wish to put on record my protest against the cowardice and cruelty of Englishmen towards one who was, until recently, recognised as a legitimate contributor to our amusement, and who is, when all is said and done, a scholar and a man of letters . . . His case still remains *sub judice* . . . Even if one granted for a moment that the man was guilty, would that be any reason for condemning work which we know in our hearts to be quite innocent? . . . Let us ask ourselves, moreover,

who are casting these stones, and whether they are those 'without in amongst us' or those 'who are notoriously corrupt'. Yours etc. Robert Buchanan.[323]

On April 22 Buchanan reiterated,

> no criminal prosecution whatever will be able to erase his name from the records of English literature. That I say advisedly, though we are far as the poles asunder in every artistic instinct of our lives, and though on more than one occasion I have ridiculed some of his opinions.[324]

Buchanan's courageous and compassionate words, which implied an abiding belief in Wilde's 'good heart' while society at large was baying for his blood, were long remembered by Wilde. In 1898 the outcast author sent Buchanan a copy of his poem *The Ballad of Reading Gaol* inscribed, 'Robert Buchanan, from the author, in admiration and gratitude. Paris '98'.[325]

ADA LEVERSON
'Suggestion' (1895)

Perhaps the closest person to Wilde to draw upon his personality for a work of fiction was Ada Leverson (1862–1933); one of her Wildean fictions was also the last to be published before Wilde's conviction for 'gross indecency' in May 1895. Like Buchanan's Mervyn Darrell, the narrator of Leverson's short stories 'Suggestion', first published in the *Yellow Book* in April 1895, and 'The Quest of Sorrow', which appeared in the *Yellow Book* of January 1896, possesses more than a passing resemblance to Wilde as a young man.

Leverson was the wife of a wealthy diamond merchant and by the early 1890s was the center of a lively literary salon. The publisher Grant Richard recalled in 1932,

> To the young man of the nineties one of the most important things that could happen was a meeting with Mrs. Ernest Leverson, Ada Leverson, the Egeria of the whole 'nineties movement, the woman whose wit provoked wit in others, whose intelligence helped so much to leaven the dullness of her period.[326]

Leverson and Wilde first met in 1892. Leverson had written an anonymous parody of *Dorian Gray* that had amused its author. As a result, he wrote to her to arrange a meeting and was reportedly astonished to discover that she was a woman.[327] The friendship that ensued is most often described as a type of 'mutual admiration society'; Wilde and Leverson shared the same incisive, epigrammatic wit and reveled in each other's company and correspondence. Wilde gave Leverson the nickname by which she became widely known—the Sphinx—after she satirized his poem of the same name in print.

Leverson often drew upon her experience of London's artistic set in her writings; in addition to Wilde, her friends included George Alexander, Aubrey Beardsley, Max Beerbohm, Herbert Beerbohm Tree, Charles Conder, John Gray, John Lane, André Raffalovich, Charles Ricketts, Robert Ross, Will Rothenstein, Walter Sickert, John Singer Sargent, Charles Shannon, G. S. Street, and Reggie Turner. By 1895, Leverson was no stranger to the art of Wildean parody; she wrote many good-humored satires of Wilde's work for *Punch*, which were published with his approval, including 'An Afternoon Party' (July 15, 1893), 'The Minx' (July 21, 1894), 'Overheard Fragment of a Dialogue' (January 12, 1895), and 'The Advisability of Not Being Brought up in a Handbag: A Trivial Tragedy for Wonderful People (March 2, 1895). She also wrote pastiches of works by Rudyard Kipling, and Max Beerbohm and satirized Beerbohm, Kipling, and George Moore. It appears that Wilde did not take umbrage at Leverson's parodies; on the contrary, he recommended that she collect her 'wonderful, witty, delightful [satirical] sketches—so slight, so suggestive, so full of *espirit* [emphasis in the original] and intellectual sympathy'.[328] Wilde perceived what Denis Denisoff has also observed; that although Leverson aimed to deflate aesthetic pomposity and misogyny with her satire, her writings essentially supported aestheticism, particularly its assertion of individuality and rejection of naturalized authority.[329]

Though Leverson did not meet Wilde until he was 38, the character of Cecil Carington in 'Suggestion', who deftly manipulates his widowed father's second marriage, is a harkening back to a younger Wilde. Carington is an aesthetically inclined 17-year-old, self-assured, effeminate, vain, and wholly conscious of his personal magnetism. His dearest wish is for an 'onyx-paved bath-room, with soft apricot-coloured light shimmering through the blue-lined green curtains in my chambers'.[330] Like Wilde, Carington physically resembles his mother and the women in his life revere him as an arbiter of taste. However, despite his arrogance, Carington also possesses Wilde's unique ability to poke fun at himself, thereby endearing himself to others. When his sister accuses him of laziness, Carington protests lightheartedly: 'Why, I've been swinging the censer in Laura's boudoir because she wants to encourage the religious temperament, and I've designed your dress for the Clive's fancy ball'.[331] Carington also shares Wilde's literary taste—he reads Pierre Loti—and makes frequent Wildean observations, such as his comment about the artist Adrian Grant: 'he is very popular and very much disliked', echoing Wilde's famous comment about George Bernard Shaw.[332] As Denisoff has noted, while Leverson pokes fun at Carington's elitism and egocentricism, he is also the only character in the story who acknowledges hypocritical behavior or 'demonstrates any notable degree of agency. His recognition of the artifice and subterfuge that is part of everybody's make-up allows him to effectively manage the actions of others'.[333] (Carington allows his new stepmother to cheat on his father, knowing that his father is about to commit adultery himself.)

Denisoff has also observed that, despite Charles Burkhart's assertion that Carington displays 'numerous classic homosexual traits, with his mother fixation, his narcissism, his antagonism to his father, his feminine slyness, his obsessive neurasthenia, and his love of posturing and posing', these things (excepting perhaps the mother fixation) do not necessarily mark Carington's sexuality but rather his aestheticism.[334]

Unlike many of those whom Wilde considered friends, Leverson's loyalty to Wilde never wavered after his reputation was lost. She never judged him for his divergent sexuality and bravely risked social ruin to provide a room for him between his trials in 1895. Leverson's reprisal of the character of Cecil Carington, for her story 'The Quest of Sorrow' (1896), is discussed in Part 3.

* * *

After April 1895 Wilde rapidly metamorphosed from eccentric literary personality to perverted fiend in the public eye. As Eric Haralson has noted, the trials that followed were to '*re*figure the "Oscar Wilde figure" forever'; he became the model for a stereotype of male homosexuality that still exists today.[335] Wilde's life in fiction was also dramatically refigured. With Wilde as a confirmed sexual 'deviant', authors had a license to imagine—and write—the worst, and many of them were not slow to use it.

3

Pariah 1896–1900

> Moral unconsciousness might be very well, but there was a way in things, and Horace, with his vices and mannerisms, went too far... there was danger not only in the companionship of Horace, but also in the band of casual inebriates whom, in his *tædium vitæ*, he had gathered round him.
>
> Frederic Carrel, *The Adventures of John Johns*

The events that led to Wilde's very public disgrace in 1895 were set in motion on February 18 by a calling card left for Wilde at his club, the Albemarle, by the Marquess of Queensberry. The vitriolic Queensberry had become increasingly incensed by the intimacy between Wilde and his son Lord Alfred Douglas, and the irate father had repeatedly threatened and insulted them both.[1] Queensberry's attempt to embarrass Wilde by delivering him a bouquet of vegetables at the opening night of *The Importance of Being Earnest* on February 14 had been thwarted, but four days later the Marquess left his card for Wilde at the Albemarle Club with the message 'To Oscar Wilde posing Somdomite [*sic*]'. Wilde, shocked by the direct and public nature of Queensberry's latest slur and goaded on by Douglas, swore out a warrant for Queensberry's arrest on the charge of libel.

The events of the three trials that followed, during which the scrutiny of the law shifted from Queensberry to Wilde after the former pleaded justification, have been well documented: Queensberry dug up enough evidence against Wilde to effect the latter's arrest for 'gross indecency' on April 5. Frank Harris described the public uproar that followed as 'an orgy of Philistine rancour', led by the puritan middle classes that Wilde had so frequently baited. Wilde was called upon by the prosecution to defend 'immoral' sections from his literary works, which he did admirably. However, when the focus moved from his literature to his private life, Wilde saw he was doomed. In late Victorian England, the spheres of law and morality almost entirely coincided; it was inevitable that once Wilde's 'immoral' lifestyle was exposed he would be punished to the full extent of the law. On May 25, Wilde was convicted under Section Eleven of the Criminal Law Amendment Act and sentenced to two years' imprisonment with hard labor.

Although there were some isolated attempts to stem the tide of 'philistine rancour' against Wilde, such as Robert Buchanan's letters to the *Star* mentioned in Part 2, the press was generally scathing in its denunciation of the fallen decadent. Wilde had become a perverted and depraved corrupter of innocent youth in the public eye; his aesthetic philosophies on art and life were quickly tarred with the same brush and the English flirtation with all things aesthetic was over. As Alan Sinfield has observed, Wilde became the personification of, and the scapegoat for, all the elements of English decadence that had antagonized the conservative man on the street: 'effeminacy, leisured idleness, immorality, luxury, insouciance, decadence and aestheticism'.[2] The following commentary in *The Daily Telegraph* of May 27, 1895 encapsulates the popular public response:

> the lesson of his life should not be passed over . . . Young men at the Universities, clever sixth form boys at public schools, silly women who lend an ear to any chatter which is petulant and vivacious, novelists who have sought to imitate the style of paradox and unreality, poets who have lisped the language of nerveless and effeminate libertinage—these are the persons who should ponder with themselves the doctrines and the career of the man who has now to undergo the righteous sentence of the law . . . his fugitive success served to dazzle and bewilder those who had neither experience nor knowledge of the principles which he travestied, or of that true temple of art of which he was so unworthy an acolyte. Let us hope that his removal will serve to clear the poisoned air, and make it cleaner for all healthy and unvitiated lungs.[3]

Punch was similarly vituperative, as evidenced by a poem that appeared on April 13:

> If such be 'Artists', then may Philistines
> Arise, plain sturdy Britons as of yore,
> And sweep them off and purge away the signs
> That England e'er such noxious offspring bore![4]

Many of Wilde's former friends renounced him. His publisher John Lane withdrew Wilde's books from circulation and stage producer

George Alexander removed Wilde's name from the play bills of *The Importance of Being Earnest*. Bailiffs took possession of Wilde's house and his books, papers, and effects were hurriedly sold for a fraction of their worth. His wife and two sons changed their surname (to Holland) and left the country. Wilde became a pariah; Thomas Beer relates that at least nine hundred sermons were preached against Wilde between 1895 and 1900.[5] While the Europeans, particularly the French, were rather more forgiving, it was clear that the playwright's reputation was utterly and ineffaceably ruined.

Robert Tanitch has observed that 'such was [the extent of] Wilde's disgrace and ostracism that it would be another forty years before he would be portrayed on stage, and then only for a private audience'.[6] One might also expect a parallel decline in fictional portraits. However, this did not occur; the figure of Wilde, now a sensational and diabolic one, continued to be appropriated and critiqued in fiction. Consequently, the 'Wildean' novels and short stories that appeared soon after Wilde's disgrace, whatever their own values, offer some fascinating insights into the impact of Wilde's downfall upon his literary contemporaries. Predictably, many of these works present a demonized version of Wilde; others, however, qualify Wilde's fiendish public image in diverse and surprising ways.

ADA LEVERSON

'The Quest of Sorrow' (1896)

As related in the previous section, Leverson reprised the character of Cecil Carington, who first appeared in 1895's 'Suggestion', for her story 'The Quest of Sorrow', published in the *Yellow Book* in January 1896. Here Carington recalls his eighteenth year, when he discovered that there was a void in his life; that he had 'missed [the] beautiful and wonderful experience' of sorrow.[7] Carington laments the fact that he has never suffered any pain on account of his appearance, his taste, his literary ability, his attractiveness to women, or his religious beliefs (although he is agnostic he is 'never . . . insensible to incense'). When an old school friend, Freddy, tells Carington that he has become engaged to Alice Sinclair, Carington promptly decides to fall in love with his friend's intended in order to enjoy the pain of a 'hopeless attachment'. (Here Leverson's story resembles G. S. Street's *Autobiography of a Boy* and its parody of Wilde's enthusiastic unrequited passion for Lillie Langtry.) However—much to Carington's dismay—Sinclair is soon won over by his 'imaginary' passion and breaks it off with Freddy. Carington quickly disengages himself from the situation and removes to a French resort, where he philosophically concludes, 'Grief [is] the one thing life [means] to deny me'.[8]

In light of the publication date of 'The Quest of Sorrow'—Wilde was languishing in Reading Gaol at the time—the story's playful satire on the aesthetic yearning for melancholy is difficult to fathom. As related in the previous section, Leverson stood by Wilde both during and after his trials; she and her husband Ernest also assisted Wilde financially after his disgrace and sent him books in prison. Leverson knew of Wilde's hardships in jail and was reportedly distraught at her friend's suffering. The irony of Leverson's tone and plot is even more pronounced when one considers *De Profundis*, written by Wilde in prison the following year. This work reveals Wilde's real struggle to transform his misery into enlightenment, to transform his debilitating sorrow into something beautiful.

The answer to the mystery of Leverson's seemingly cruel satire may well be that her story was submitted to the *Yellow Book* before Wilde's trials raised the likelihood of his very real future suffering. Despite Wilde's 'falling out' with Leverson's husband at one point over financial matters, she visited him in Paris after his release and the two friends stayed in touch until Wilde's death in 1900.

Aubrey Beardsley
The Story of Venus and Tannhäuser (1896)

Another associate of Wilde (and Leverson) who became a posttrial fictionalizer of Wilde was a young man better known as England's leading decadent artist of the 1890s: Aubrey Beardsley (1872–1898). Beardsley, who also had literary aspirations, had been acquainted with Wilde since 1891, but by 1896 had begun to resent the older man. In light of his grievances, which are outlined below, the fact that Beardsley included two less-than-flattering versions of Wilde in his unfinished erotic fantasy novel, *The Story of Venus and Tannhäuser*, is not surprising. Among other real-life portraits in the story,[9] there are two Wildean protagonists: Priapusa, Venus's chief female attendant, and the male singer Spiridion, both of whom participate in orgiastic same-sex scenes.

Indeed, the unexpurgated *Venus and Tannhäuser*, published in full after Beardsley's death by pornography publisher Leonard Smithers in 1907, is a remarkable example of late nineteenth-century erotica.[10] Composed from 1895 in the wake of Wilde's downfall,

Venus and Tannhäuser depicts a startling range of sexual antics—heterosexual, homosexual, bisexual, orgiastic, bestial, coprophilic, and even statuophilic—in a distinctly decadent manner. Beardsley's prose is at times florid, flippant, mischievous, satirical, cynical, and self-parodical, and has been compared to Jules Laforgue's parodic *Moralités légendaires*[11]. Like his illustrations, which often combine the erotic and the grotesque, the licentious and voyeuristic nature of Beardsley's *Venus and Tannhäuser* is thought to reflect the author's frustrated sexuality, a result of his chronic ill health. Malcolm Easton believes Beardsley was 'latently homosexual, fetishist [and] transvestist'.[12] Stanley Weintraub has observed that Beardsley had 'most of the mannerisms of the homosexual without any of the substance', a fact that undoubtedly contributed to his ambivalent relationship with Wilde. Beardsley's Tannhäuser, who is often an observer of sexual acts, is usually read as a fictional projection of Beardsley himself; the knight was at one stage of writing called 'Abbé Aubrey'.

Before he succumbed to tuberculosis at the age of 25, Beardsley published two censored excerpts from *The Story of Venus and Tannhäuser* as 'Under the Hill' in the January and April 1896 issues of the *Savoy*. Though I have used these dates to chronologically position Beardsley's story (as the first Wildean character also appears in the expurgated version), I will not be focusing on the *Savoy* text, but on the more complete version published by Smithers in 1907, nine years after Beardsley's death.[13]

The ancient Germanic legend of Venus and Tannhäuser captured the imaginations of many nineteenth-century artists; versions by Charles Baudelaire, Walter Pater, William Morris, Algernon Swinburne, Richard Wagner, and others had appeared before Beardsley produced his erotic interpretation.[14] According to the legend, the Christian knight Tannhäuser stumbles upon Venusberg, the home of the mythical Goddess of Love, and after being seduced by her charms abandons himself to the sexual hedonism of her court. After several years Tannhäuser becomes penitent and travels to Rome to appeal to the Pope for absolution for his sins. The pope refuses and Tannhäuser returns to Venus. Although the Pontiff later changes his mind and tries to find the knight, Tannhäuser is never seen again.

The full title that Beardsley gave his story indicates that he intended to adhere to this basic plot.[15] While his idea of how the tale should be told appears to have changed many times (before settling on the story's risqué, 'rococo' style, Beardsley envisioned it as both a realistic work and a verse composition), he always intended that the book in its final form would 'astonish everybody'.[16] However, the ailing artist was only able to complete ten chapters of *Venus and Tannhäuser* before his death in 1898. These chapters describe Tannhäuser's first full day with Venus and include eight of Beardsley's famous black and white line drawings in eighteenth-century style.

Before examining the Wildean portraits in *Venus and Tannhäuser*, it is necessary to relate something of Beardsley's complex relationship with Wilde. It is thought that the aspiring artist first met Wilde at the home of Edward Burne-Jones on July 12, 1891; Beardsley pronounced 'the Oscar Wildes' 'charming people' after sharing their carriage home.[17] A friendship between the two men, who shared a fascination with neopaganism and a love of artifice, appears to have ensued. Although nothing seems to have come of the idea, Beardsley planned to join Wilde on a trip to Paris in April 1893, and at one point the artist kept an autographed photograph of Wilde on his mantelpiece.[18] However, tensions arose in relation to Beardsley's involvement with the English translation of Wilde's French play *Salomé*, published in February 1894. Wilde commissioned Beardsley to illustrate the English version, believing that the artist shared his vision of the biblical dancer. (Wilde had inscribed a copy of the French version to Beardsley in March 1893, describing the latter as 'the only artist who, besides myself, knows what the dance of the seven veils is, and can see that invisible dance'. Presumably Wilde had seen Beardsley's drawing of Salome, inspired by Wilde's French text, for the next month's *Studio*.[19]) However, although Wilde admired Beardsley's final drawings, he thought them too Japanese to suit his Byzantine play.[20] In addition, Wilde was reportedly displeased to discover that Beardsley had facetiously caricatured him in three of the *Salomé* illustrations: he appears as Herod in 'The Eyes of Herod', as a jester in 'Enter Herodias', and as 'The Woman in the Moon' in the drawing of the same name. Beardsley had previously caricatured Wilde with regard to *Salomé* in 1893; his sketch suggesting that the playwright borrowed heavily from works by Gautier, Swinburne and Flaubert to write the play. (The sketch also implies that *Salomé* is written in amateurish French.[21]) Many critics have observed that Beardsley's caricatures of Wilde typically contain complex classical, literary and homosexual allusions, and were produced by Beardsley with the intention of establishing himself as an *agent provocateur* among the artistic and intellectual elite.[22]

Wilde's response to Beardsley's *Salome* illustrations may have piqued the young artist; Wilde's occasional claim to have 'created' Beardsley certainly did. Beardsley may also have taken offense at Wilde's jocular references to his appearance (Wilde famously said that the artist had a 'face like a silver hatchet [and] grass-green hair') and the 'school-boy naughtiness' of his drawings.[23] Beardsley was disappointed when Wilde rejected his attempt at translating *Salomé* into English, after finding fault with Alfred Douglas's initial translation.[24] Malcolm Easton has speculated that Wilde's pose as a connoisseur of visual art may also have irritated Beardsley.[25] Whatever the cause of the rift that grew between them, by late 1893 the relationship had become strained. In a letter to mutual friend Robert Ross during this period, Beardsley refers to Wilde and Douglas as 'really very dreadful people', and when Beardsley was appointed as art editor of the *Yellow Book* in 1894, he conspired to exclude Wilde from ever contributing to that publication.[26] Nevertheless, perhaps due to their many mutual friends, such as Ross, Ada Leverson, Max Beerbohm, and William Rothenstein, a friendship of sorts between the two men endured.[27]

Events connected with Wilde's trials in 1895 gave Beardsley further cause for resentment. At the time of his arrest, journalists reported that Wilde was carrying a 'yellow book' under his arm; this was (mistakenly) assumed to be a copy of the Beardsley-illustrated periodical. It was this perceived connection between Wilde and Beardsley—in addition to their previous collaboration on *Salome*— that led to Beardsley's dismissal from the *Yellow Book*.[28] Beardsley's association with Wilde had not only cost him his cherished position on the *Yellow Book*, but had also tarred him with the same brush of disgrace. While Beardsley found a new position from January 1896 as illustrator for the newly founded *Savoy*, and also received the patronage of Leonard Smithers and André Raffalovich from this time, he was clearly vexed by what he saw as Wilde's destructive influence on his life. He did not visit or write to Wilde during his trials or subsequent imprisonment.

After his release from prison, Wilde, having assumed the name 'Sebastian Melmoth' ('Sebastian' from Wilde's favorite persecuted saint, 'Melmoth' from the wandering romantic hero of Charles Maturin's 1820 novel *Melmoth the Wanderer*), encountered Beardsley in the popular Normandy seaside resort town of Dieppe. The town had long been fashionable with the English as a summer holiday location and was also popular with the French. By the mid-1890s it had become a haven for artists and writers from both countries, and there were many salons where artists and the aristocracy congregated. Wilde had visited Dieppe in 1879 and 1884, and it was probably his memories of the town's fashionably artistic atmosphere that made him choose it as his first place of residence after being released from prison, arriving by boat on May 20, 1897.

At first, Dieppe appeared to be the perfect choice for the exiled Wilde. In addition to Beardsley, Charles Conder, Ernest Dowson, Robert Ross, William Rothenstein, Walter Sickert, Arthur Symons, Leonard Smithers, and Reggie Turner were all regular visitors. However, while some of Wilde's old friends welcomed his arrival, he soon realized that he could not count upon the liberality of Dieppe's artistic community to overlook his scandalous past. He was continually snubbed by former friends and English tourists, which he found very hard to bear. Wilde was also aware that he was being followed by a private detective, on the orders of the Marquess of Queensberry, who was determined that Wilde should not contact his son.[29] After about a week of this life Wilde decided to take a house in the nearby village of Berneval, occasionally visiting Dieppe's Café Suisse to meet those old friends who had not abandoned him.

Richard Ellmann records that Wilde and Beardsley attended the same dinner party in Dieppe on July 19, 1897. There was some further contact in August of that year; Wilde wrote to Reggie Turner, 'I have made Aubrey buy a hat more silver than silver: he is quite wonderful in it'.[30] However, Beardsley appears to have cut Wilde in Dieppe on at least one occasion and avoided him whenever possible.[31] On another occasion, when Wilde invited him to dinner, Beardsley failed to appear. Wilde, offended, remarked, 'a boy like that, whom I made! No, it was too *lâche* of Aubrey'.[32] Merlin Holland and Rupert Hart-Davis speculate that Beardsley may have been influenced in this action by his mother, who was staying with him at the Hôtel Sandwich in Dieppe and who disapproved of Wilde. Beardsley may also have been concerned about upsetting his 'mentor' Raffalovich— as related above an enemy of Wilde's—who was providing Beardsley with financial support.[33] (Beardsley wrote to Raffalovich that he was considering looking for accommodation outside of the Hôtel Sandwich because '[s]ome rather unpleasant people come here. For other reasons too I fear some undesirable complications may arise if I stay'.[34])

Laurence Housman, in his semifictional recollection of Wilde in *Echo de Paris* (1923), includes a comment made by Wilde that appears to refer to his relationship with Beardsley:

> The worst thing you can do for a person of genius is to help him: that way lies destruction . . . only once did I help a man who was also a genius. I have never forgiven myself . . . When we met afterwards he had so greatly changed that, though I recognised him, he failed to recognise me. He became a Roman Catholic, and died at the age of

twenty-three, a great artist—with half the critics and all the moralists still hating him. A charming person.[35]

Beardsley was careful to avoid any future professional association with Wilde. In September 1897, Leonard Smithers wrote to Wilde that the artist had promised to draw a frontispiece for *The Ballad of Reading Gaol* 'in a manner which immediately convinced me that he will never do it'.[36] In December of that year, Beardsley told Smithers that he would only act as editor and illustrator for a projected new journal, *The Peacock*, on the condition that Wilde did not contribute anything to the magazine '*anonymously, pseudonymously or otherwise* [emphasis in the original]'.[37]

Beardsley and Wilde do not appear to have met again after their brief Dieppe contact. Beardsley succumbed to the tuberculosis he contracted when he was seven and died two years before Wilde in 1898, leaving *The Story of Venus and Tannhäuser* unfinished. Wilde wrote to Smithers on March 18 of that year:

> I was greatly shocked to read of poor Aubrey's death. Superbly premature as the flowering of his genius was, still he had immense development, and had not sounded his last stop. There were great possibilities always in the cavern of his soul, and there is something macabre and tragic in the fact that one who added another terror to life should have died at the age of a flower.[38]

Having examined Beardsley's and Wilde's relationship, let us now turn to the characters of Priapusa and Spiridion in *Venus and Tannhäuser*, characters who provide some interesting clues as to Beardsley's opinion of the man he saw as his *bête noir*. Beardsley had previously highlighted Wilde's sexual ambiguity by caricaturing him as a woman in *Salome's* 'The Woman in the Moon' and possibly 'L'Education Sentimentale' (see n. 21). Priapusa, Venus's female, bisexual, aging 'fat manicure and fardeuse', who first appears in chapter 11 of *Venus and Tannhäuser*, has been identified by Ian Fletcher as a version of Wilde.[39] While Priapusa's initial description does not immediately suggest Wilde—she wears a gown of white silk and gold lace, a 'false vermilion' necklace,[40] a large chignon, and a pink floral hat—the androgynous Priapusa has some physical qualities that do invoke Wilde:

> Priapusa's voice was full of salacious unction; she had terrible little gestures with the hands, strange movements with the shoulders, a short respiration that made surprising wrinkles in her bodice, a corrupt skin,

large horny eyes, a parrot's nose, a small loose mouth, great flaccid cheeks, and chin after chin.⁴¹

Priapusa is also considered wise, is an excellent storyteller, and is much loved by Venus just as Wilde was cherished by his female friends.

A reading of Priapusa as Wilde is supported by Beardsley's illustration *The Toilet*, in which Priapusa appears seated as Venus's toilet is in progress (see plate 8). This portrait resembles an overweight Wilde in drag, reclining in a complacent fashion with his familiar cane in hand (a hand with Wilde's tapering fingers), possibly wearing a (green?) carnation. Beardsley also appears to be poking fun at Wilde with the many pet names that Venus gives to her favorite servant. As Fletcher has noted in his discussion of the expurgated 'Under the Hill' (in which the Priapusa character is called Mrs Marsuple), many of these names have risqué, 'underground' resonances:

> 'Buttons', a page, suggests ludicrously a transsexual role and 'Dick-Dock' stands for penis and penis amputated . . . 'Pretty Poll' alludes also to the nautical phrase for a prostitute; 'Little Nipper' bears large ironies.⁴²

Priapusa's other nicknames, 'Mrs. Manly' and 'Naughty-naughty', could also be suggestive of Wilde.⁴³ The name Priapusa itself is a feminized version of the mythical Priapus, the Greek god known for his lechery, obscenity, and homosexual behavior, symbolized by the phallus.⁴⁴ Indeed, Priapusa is lascivious in the extreme: in chapter 4 she interrupts the lovemaking of Venus and Tannhäuser to '[tickle them] by turns, and [slip] her tongue down their throats, [she] refused to be quiet at all until she had a mouthful of the Chevalier [Tannhäuser]'.⁴⁵ Later, she appears 'from somewhere or other' to prevent Venus and Tannhäuser overturning their carriage with their sexual antics; presumably she has been watching them all along: 'How the old lady's eye glistened as Tannhäuser withdrew his panting blade! In her sincere admiration for fine things [a comic allusion to Wilde's aestheticism?], she quite forgot and forgave the shock she had received from the falling of the [carriage]'.⁴⁶ The strange blend of lust and parental affection that Priapusa displays toward Venus and Tannhäuser is perhaps also intended to be Wilde-like; she refers to them as her 'children' while carrying them to bed.⁴⁷ This may reflect Wilde's 'fatherly' treatment of younger men like Beardsley ('a boy like that, whom I made!') or perhaps merely mocks Wilde's predilection for younger sexual partners.

The amalgamation of parental and sexual overtones in a Wildean character is also to be found in Spiridion who appears in chapter 10. In this chapter Tannhäuser visits a Casino redolent of the casino in Dieppe. Indeed, a large portion of *Venus and Tannhäuser* was reportedly written by Beardsley in the concert room of the Dieppe Casino, a room that was frequented by Wilde.

The knight Tannhäuser first encounters Spiridion—'that soft incomparable alto'—in the casino, singing the part of the Virgin in Rossini's *Stabat Mater*. Beardsley describes this piece of music as a 'delicious *demodé pièce de décadence*' with 'a subtle quality . . . like the unhealthy bloom upon wax fruit'. Spiridion's physical features and appearance suggest and caricature Wilde and his conspicuously artificial aetheticism:

> [Spiridion] dressed the rôle most effectively. His plump legs up to the feminine hips of him, were in very white stockings clocked with a false pink. He wore brown kid boots, buttoned to mid-calf, and his whorish thighs had thin scarlet garters round them. His jacket was cut like a jockey's, only the sleeves ended in manifold frills, and round the neck, and just upon the shoulders, there was a black cape. His hair, dyed green, was curled into ringlets, such as the smooth Madonnas of Morales are made lovely with, and fell over his high egg-shaped creamy forehead, and about his ears and cheeks and back. The alto's face was fearful and wonderful—a dream face. The eyes were full and black, with puffy blue rimmed hemispheres beneath them, the cheeks, inclining to fatness, were powdered and dimpled, the mouth was purple and curved painfully, the chin tiny, and exquisitely modelled, the expression cruel and womanish.[48]

Spiridion is notably androgynous; the narrator significantly refers to him as 'the thing'.[49] Ian Fletcher observes that Spiridion's heavy cosmetics recall Henri Mondor's description of Wilde at the Parisian residence of Mallarmé in 1892, as described in Mondor's *Vie de Mallarmé* (1941).[50] Linda Dowling has asserted that Spiridion's green hair 'suggest[s] the motive behind [Wilde's] later notorious green-carnation boutonnière'.[51] (The reader will recall that Wilde also described Beardsley as having 'green' hair.)

Apart from his physical resemblances to Wilde, Spiridion also exhibits Wilde's distinctive flair for performance, literally 'singing for his supper'; Wilde did this figuratively with the table talk that made him the most sought after dinner guest in London.

> Heavens! How splendid [Spiridion] looked and sounded. An exquisite piece of phrasing was accompanied with some curly gesture of the hand,

some delightful undulation of the stomach, some nervous movement of the thigh, or glorious rising of the bosom. The performance provoked enthusiasm—thunders of applause.[52]

Dowling suggests there is another Wildean resonance in 'the effeminate Spiridion's impersonation of an innocent Virgin grieving over the loss of her Son'; she believes this 'wickedly parallels Wilde's loss, after his trial and imprisonment, of Bosie and his other boys'. Ian Fletcher concurs that this is precisely 'the species of "in-joke" that Beardsley might well make'.[53]

After Spiridion delivers his song he is 'pelted' with roses, but the enthusiasm of his audience does not stop there:

> Claude and Clair . . . carried [Spiridion] off in triumph to the tables. His costume was declared ravishing. The men almost pulled him to bits, and mouthed at his great quivering bottom! . . . Sup, the penetrating, burst through his silk fleshings, and thrust in bravely up to the hilt, whilst the alto's legs were feasted upon by Pudex, Cyril, Anquetin, and some others. Ballice, Corvo, Quadra, Senillé, Mellefont, Theodore, le Vit, and Matta, all of the egoistic cult, stood and crouched round, saturating the lovers with warm douches.[54]

This remarkable passage, which Linda C. Dowling highlights as one of many episodes of artistic disguise and sexual disclosure in *Venus and Tannhäuser*,[55] clearly satirizes Wilde's relations with his adoring disciples, although it is unclear whether Spiridion is a willing participant in these proceedings. If Beardsley did intend to depict a rape scene, this might also reflect the betrayal of the rent boys who testified against Wilde. Dowling interprets this incident as reflective of the 'conflicting ambitions and evasions' of *fin-de-siècle* decadence, which she contends 'seemed to Beardsley to expose itself perversely— because invitingly—to the forces that would compromise and truly corrupt it'.[56]

Wilde probably never saw his likeness in Mrs Marsuple, later Priapusa, in 'Under the Hill' in 1896, as he spent that year in jail. The unexpurgated *Venus and Tannhäuser*, which included the character of Spiridion, was not published until seven years after Wilde's death. While we can only guess at what Wilde's reaction to these characters might have been, he certainly held no grudge against Beardsley for his caricatures in *Salome* and elsewhere. After Beardsley's death in 1898 Wilde continued to promote the artist's work, facilitating the sale of some Beardsley drawings to the Russian collector Sergei Diaghilev.[57]

Mabel Wotton
'The Fifth Edition' (1896)

Mabel Emily Wotton (1863–1927), unlike Beardsley and indeed unlike most of the writers considered thus far, appears to have had no relationship with Wilde. Her short story 'The Fifth Edition' is one of a collection of tales in *Day-Books*, published in the Bodley Head's Keynote Series and edited by John Lane. The Wildean character in Wotton's story is the excessively vain and egotistical author Franklyn Leyden. Wotton employs very little subterfuge in describing Leyden's physique; he is Wilde all over: 'a fair haired giant with china-blue eyes, and large hands which were extraordinarily white and mobile'.[58] Like Wilde, Leyden is a poet, dramatist, and journalist who has written one novel that was a great success. Leyden finds a solution to the problem of a subject for his next novel when he befriends a poverty-stricken aspiring author, Miss Suttaby; an excessively meek and tragic figure who worships Leyden. Leyden takes advantage of Suttaby's privation and trusting nature and—after offering to promote her writing career—steals her brilliant autobiographical novel for a song, revising and publishing it under his own name. (Leyden's first successful novel was also stolen without acknowledgment, from a dying man in Algiers.) Suttaby's novel brings Leyden great success and soon reaches a fifth edition. Suttaby, however, suffers through hard times—having received only a small portion of the promised payment from her 'friend'—and finally dies of starvation. Throughout his association with Suttaby, Leyden blithely regards himself as her generous benefactor; when she goes missing without a trace (he remains ignorant of her death) he is at first mortified by her ingratitude, then he promptly forgets her.[59]

Wotton's story is often read as an allegory of the New Woman writer and the competition she faced from her male contemporaries. However, it is clear that, in her portrait of Franklyn Leyden, Wotton is criticizing Wilde in particular.[60] In addition to the physical description given above, the reader is given many clues as to the identity of Leyden's original: he speaks in Wilde's 'dulcet tones', has Wilde's habit of looking through 'half-closed lids', and has Wilde's lips with the 'curves of weak good-nature'.[61] Leyden's habit of 'habitually fingering the lappet of his coat', while not a gesture commonly attributed to Wilde, is also interesting in light of the 1892 photograph of Wilde at plate 5.[62] Like Wilde, the indolent Leyden is strongly attracted to 'the class of ritual and ease and plenty', has 'an intense hatred of even a passing discomfort', and is 'depressed or elated with trifles too insignificant to weigh with other men'.⁶³ Leyden has also spent time in Algiers; Wilde's visit there in January 1895 was widely reported in the London press. Wotton's description of Leyden's literary career is also revealing, particularly when considered as a posttrial revision of the secret of Wilde's success:

> He had tried his 'prentice hand at some small plays preparatory to taking the dramatic world by storm . . . and he had turned out two books of verse . . . [which] sold well. His publisher, who had seen too many versifiers perhaps to be especially impressed by this one, always declared that the soft voice and the white gesticulating hands were more responsible for the success than were the lines themselves . . . Added to these slender pillars was the solid background of press work.⁶⁴

Leyden is also like Wilde in his adoption of the role of literary advisor for female writers of his acquaintance. As Margaret Stetz has noted,

> since the early 1880s Wilde had made himself an integral and indispensable part of the careers and personal histories of his female contemporaries. He often served as a source of literary commissions . . . through the exercise of influence with editors and publishers. He played the role, too, of an unpaid literary advisor. In 1886, for instance, when [Edith] Nesbit sent him *Lays and Legends*, her first volume of poetry, he wrote back to praise it and to say: 'Any advice I can give you is of course at your disposal.'

Stetz points out that Wilde was responding to the dilemma of the 'modern' woman author, that is, that men had

> greater access to and information about the world of books and letters, and thus, regardless of their feminist principles, women writers had to rely upon male contacts in pursuing careers. And many took up Wilde's offer of assistance. Indeed, few prominent men of the day did more than Wilde to encourage the ambitions of female artists—⁶⁵

The success of Leyden's first novel, *Wrecked*, takes him 'several rungs up the literary ladder'; the same is true of Wilde's *Dorian Gray*. However, Wotton stresses that Leyden has only a small talent and no capacity for originality; he '[can] not create. No one seemed to have discovered this as yet, for his critical powers [are] good, and his receptivity enormous'.⁶⁶ To further belittle Wilde's abilities, Wotton asserts that Leyden's seemingly profound observations on life are unintelligible even to himself; the author relies on the interpretations of others to imbue his remarks with significance. For example, after making a comment upon 'worshippers' at the 'altar of Art', a favorite topic of Wilde's, Leyden realizes that he

> was not quite sure what he meant, though he thought it sounded well. But he had often found that women made a beautiful translation from a very imperfect original, and he waited for [Miss Suttaby] to answer, knowing it would furnish the keynote to what she believed she had discovered in him.[67]

Wilde's genial, social nature is similarly undermined:

> Every man knows the satisfaction of telling a good story when he can confidently count upon an appreciative laugh; and this feeling . . . had been abnormally developed by Franklyn Leyden. It interested him if he were shut into a railway carriage with a complete stranger, to imagine what mirth . . . or of what anger the man were capable; and then he would back himself within a given time to test the aptness of his theorising . . . he had grown to look upon his fellow-beings as so many pegs on which to hang his own emotions through the skilful drawing out of theirs—[68]

In this manner Wotton depicts one of Wilde's most celebrated talents as evidence of a base and insensitive nature. Wilde's generosity and empathy are also evinced as a form of selfishness:

> Undoubtedly Franklyn Leyden made an admirable audience. Your good things might bore him, but your sad ones never, averred his friends, and in their whole-hearted enthusiasm they rarely noticed that all his kindnesses and all his consideration were called forth . . . by what affected him personally. His best friend might be dying, and he would give him a wide berth for fear of a heart-ache; but if he came upon a little child who had tripped in the street, it would be impossible for him to pass it without attempted consolation.[69]

Wilde's place in fashionable society is described in the same jaundiced fashion:

> [Leyden was] a person whom a certain set of aspiring nobodies used to point out to each other at first nights and other society functions, and whom the real somebodies tolerated in a good humoured fashion as a hanger-on who might speedily become one of themselves.[70]

Little is known about Wotton's life and there is no record of any relationship between Wotton and Wilde. However, Wilde did review a book edited by Wotton, a collection of descriptive profiles from various sources entitled *Word Portraits of Famous Writers*. Wilde's review of this book appeared in *The Woman's World* of March 1889. It may be that it was this project or Wilde's review of the book that inspired Wotton to attempt her own 'word portrait' of Wilde. Wilde's review of *Word Portraits* was light-hearted and largely approbatory:

> Miss Mabel Wotton has invented a new form of picture-gallery. Feeling that the visible aspect of men and women can be expressed in literature no less than through the medium of line and colour, she has collected a series of *Word Portraits of Famous Writers* extending from Geoffrey Chaucer to Mrs. Henry Wood—[71]

Wilde jokes that many of Wotton's famous writers, such as Godwin, Kingsley, Lamb, Pope, and Richardson 'seem to have been very ugly' and goes on to remark, 'We must console ourselves . . . with the pictures of those who had some comeliness, and grace, and charm', pointing to Spenser, Lovelace, Keats, Chatterton, and Byron as examples. Wilde makes an interesting comment toward the end of his review:

> Hazlitt once said that 'A man's life may be a lie to himself and others, and yet a picture painted of him by a great artist would probably stamp his character'.[72]

Did these words inspire Wotton's portrait of Franklyn Leyden? Wotton painted her picture of Wilde soon after his life had been proven 'a lie'. Did Wotton see herself as a 'great artist' destined to 'stamp' Wilde's character? It seems likely that Wotton held some grievance against Wilde. While there is seemingly nothing in Wilde's 1889 review of *Word Portraits* that would have provoked a counterattack from Wotton (on the contrary, Wilde compliments Wotton on her editorial skills), Carolyn Christensen Nelson has highlighted Wotton's unhappy relations with male writers and editors and Elaine Showalter has noted that Wotton, like Corelli, 'nursed a lingering bitterness throughout her life towards the world of books and bookmen' after her work received disparaging reviews.[73] Of course, it is also possible that Wotton was merely articulating the general view of the disgraced author—'The Fifth Edition' certainly encapsulates the strong anti-Wilde feeling that existed among most of his peers in the wake of his conviction.

Richard Le Gallienne
'Brown Roses' (1896)

In contrast to 'The Fifth Edition', there is little anti-Wilde feeling discernible in the fourth short story published in 1896, written by Wilde's former intimate Richard Le Gallienne. As related in Part 2, the poet Hyacinth Rondel, who first appeared in Le Gallienne's 'The Woman's Half-Profits' in *Prose Fancies* (1894), reappeared in the second series of *Prose Fancies* in 1896, in the story 'Brown Roses'. In this tale Rondel instructs his barber to cut his trademark long, brown hair, just as Wilde had done some years before. Rondel reflects that his hair had been 'worth five shillings a week to many a poor paragraph writer'.[74] Watching the falling locks Rondel compares them to '[b]rown roses scattered over the winding-sheet of one's youth', wistful words that perhaps reflect Le Gallienne's sadness at the lost reputation of his old friend.[75] Alternately, the story may have been written before Wilde's disgrace—perhaps soon after the author first cut his trademark long hair—as it is suggested that Rondel is making this sacrifice for his wife. (As related earlier in this book, Wilde cut his hair and adopted a more sophisticated image shortly after his marriage.)

Although Le Gallienne and Wilde do not appear to have seen much of each other after the early 1890s, Le Gallienne continued to proclaim Wilde's talents after his downfall and death and proved to be a canny critic of his writing. Le Gallienne wrote the introduction for an American edition of Wilde's works in 1907, praising his 'extraordinary individuality' and comparing him to Keats, Sheridan, and Beau Brummel.[76] Le Gallienne's enduring sympathy for the disgraced Wilde is also evinced in his poem 'On Some Recent Editions of Oscar Wilde', published in 1910 in an anthology of poetry entitled *New Poems*:

> These are the poems of that tragic one
> Who, loving beauty much, loved Life too well—
> Therefore, to-night he makes his bed in hell.
> Gone are the grace and glory, all is gone;
> Fallen the tower that so proudly shone
> In the sun's eye; and now the hucksters sell
> The sculptured stone, foul groping where it fell—
> O ruin fair for ghouls to batten on!
>
> Maggots in the decay of the divine,
> Ghouls of the printing press; ere yet he died,

You spat your little venom on his name,
You who now pick and pillage his fame,
Robbing the pockets of the crucified—
But the great silent talker makes no sign.[77]

Bram Stoker

Dracula (1897)

The year 1897 saw the appearance of a work with a plethora of Wildean connections that enjoys a phenomenal popularity to this day: Bram Stoker's *Dracula*. While this is not a novel that people usually associate with Wilde, the following critique will demonstrate how the fallen decadent and his trials significantly influenced Stoker's (1847–1912) most famous work. At the core of a Wildean reading of *Dracula* is the relationship between Wilde and Stoker, who were known to each other since their youth in Dublin. Stoker, like Wilde, attended Trinity College, where he distinguished himself in science and athletics, as well as serving a term as president of the Philosophical Society. It is not known when Stoker and Wilde first met, but this probably happened in the late 1860s or early 1870s, possibly at Trinity (although Stoker graduated in 1868, three years before Wilde commenced), or at one of the Wildes' regular literary 'at homes' in Dublin. With his love of literature and the theater Stoker was quickly welcomed into the Wildes' artistic set and soon won the respect of Oscar's parents, Sir William and Lady Jane.[78] Stoker nominated Oscar for the Trinity Philosophical Society, although Wilde was never particularly active, unlike his brother Willie.

In 1875 Stoker spent Christmas with the Wilde family, including Oscar, who had returned home for the holidays after his first year at Oxford. At this time, or shortly afterward, Wilde began courting a young woman named Florence Balcombe, the daughter of an English lieutenant-colonel who had served in India and the Crimea. The relations between Wilde, Balcombe, and Stoker are pivotal to a Wildean interpretation of *Dracula*.

In 1876, in a letter to his friend Reginald Harding, Wilde described Florence Balcombe as 'exquisitely pretty . . . just seventeen with the most perfectly beautiful face I ever saw and not a sixpence of money'.[79] The relationship between Wilde and Balcombe appears to have reached its romantic peak in late 1876; Wilde drew a portrait of Balcombe in August and in September he sent her a watercolor painting of Moytura House, the Wildes' holiday home. An undated letter from Balcombe to Wilde during this period suggests that Wilde was a welcome visitor in the Balcombe home. After thanking Wilde for sending her a copy of one of his poems and complimenting him on its 'sublime' perfection, Balcombe concludes, 'We want to hear you read it yourself to us. Do come out tomorrow evening'.[80] The Wilde/Balcombe relationship appears to have stalled sometime in 1877. It is possible that Wilde, still a student, was not in a position to marry his sweetheart. He alludes to his regret at their separation in a letter written to Balcombe in April 1878: 'if I had not a good memory of the past I would be very happy'.[81]

Whatever it was that put an end to their relationship, Wilde was clearly distressed to discover in mid-1878 that Balcombe had become engaged to Stoker, who lived next door to her family in Dublin, without informing him.[82] In a letter from Wilde to Balcombe written in September 1878, Wilde politely requests that Balcombe return a gold cross to him, a past Christmas present, which was engraved with his name. In the letter he thanks her for 'the sweetest of all the years of my youth' and wishes her happiness, despite his obviously injured pride. He also mildly rebukes her for not thinking it 'worth while' to let him know of her impending marriage. An exchange of letters followed regarding arrangements for the returning of the gold cross. Wilde believed etiquette dictated that this should happen at the home of Balcombe's parents (as opposed to the house of Stoker's brother); Balcombe seems to have interpreted this as a request for a clandestine meeting and resisted the idea. Wilde's final letter on the subject in October is curt; after explaining the innocent reasons for his request, he closes, 'after all, I find you know me very little'.[83] Richard Ellmann conjectures that Balcombe was responsible for the despondent tone of several of Wilde's poems written around this time.[84]

Balcombe and Stoker were married in December 1878 and promptly moved to London; Stoker gave up his position in the Irish civil service to become the business manager for Henry Irving's recently acquired Lyceum Theatre.[85] Wilde evidently overcame his feelings of hurt and rejection; he later visited the Stokers for dinners and 'at homes' at their fashionable London residence, no doubt enticed by the frequent presence of Irving and other members of London's artistic elite. However, a letter from Wilde to Ellen Terry, a close friend and member of Irving's company, written two years after Balcombe's marriage to Stoker, suggests that Wilde still had feelings for his old flame. In January 1881, Wilde asked Terry to give Balcombe a crown of flowers he had bought for the latter's stage debut in Lord Tennyson's *The Cup*. He asked Terry to tell Balcombe they were a gift from herself:

> I should like to think that she was wearing something of mine the first night she comes on the stage, that anything of mine should touch her. Of course if you think—but you won't think she will suspect? How could she? She thinks I never loved her, thinks I forget. My God how could I![86]

It appears that relations between Wilde and Balcombe became easier after Wilde's own marriage in 1884; the Bram Stokers and the Oscar Wildes appear to have been on very friendly terms.[87] As well as attending dinners and parties at the Lyceum, the Wildes also attended private functions at the Stokers' home in Chelsea. The Stokers in turn visited the Wildes and attended the premiere of *Lady Windermere's Fan* in February 1892. Wilde sent the Stokers copies of his books and plays as they were published and Stoker was rumored to be a member of the occult society attended by Constance Wilde: the Hermetic Order of the Golden Dawn.

One can only guess at Stoker's feelings about Wilde and the playwright's past involvement with his wife. Stoker and Wilde had much in common, apart from their interest in the same woman: nationality, education, early aestheticism, love of literature, and the theater and—in both Dublin and London—social circle. Both admired Henry Irving's acting and the poetry of Walt Whitman; both visited the latter in America. David J. Skal has observed that both men also wrote

> a masterwork of macabre fiction portraying archetypal title characters who remain supernaturally young by draining the life force from Victorian innocents [and both] were attracted to literary themes of doubles, masks, and boundaries in general.[88]

One might expect that these commonalities, combined with Wilde's and Stoker's mutual interest in Balcombe, would result in some competitiveness between the two men. This may have been the case, however, there is no evidence of any rivalry. Stoker often invited Wilde to the Lyceum's backstage 'Beefsteak Room' in his early London days and gossip columnists reported that Wilde and Stoker were seen shaking hands at the theater.[89] Unfortunately, there is no historical documentation that adequately describes their relationship, but what records there are do not indicate that the two men were close. This may have been attributable to Wilde's history with Balcombe, or to the two men's divergent personalities. Wilde was an irreverent questioner of conventional morality whereas Stoker habitually championed it; Stoker also personified the athletic 'manliness' that was noticeably absent in Wilde. Of course, it is possible that their relationship was more complex than the history books show; certainly the intertwining of their lives with Balcombe's would suggest this. Several critiques of Wilde's influence on *Dracula* explore this hypothesis.

The most comprehensive and compelling of the theories that examine the Wilde/Balcombe/Stoker triangle in *Dracula* has been offered by Talia Schaffer in her article "A Wilde Desire Took Me": The Homoerotic History of Dracula' (1994). As Schaffer's article constitutes something of a definitive Wildean reading of *Dracula* it will be discussed extensively here. Schaffer contends that Stoker's anxiety about his wife's relationship with Wilde is reflected in several incidents in the novel. For example, in one scene Count Dracula remarks, 'Your girls that you all love are mine already; and through them you and others shall yet be mine—my creatures, to do my bidding and to be my jackals when I want to feed'; in another, Dracula and Doctor Van Helsing's associates argue over the dead Lucy Westenra and to whom she really belonged in life.[90] Another possible reflection of Stoker's anxiety over the Wilde/Balcombe relationship is Van Helsing's brandishing of a small gold crucifix, similar to the one that Wilde gave Balcombe, when he discovers Mina Murray in bed with Dracula, submitting to the count's vampiric 'extramarital' sensuality. In such readings it is deemed significant that, despite many 'close calls', Stoker never allows Mina to fully succumb to Dracula's powerful charms.[91]

Of course, there have been many alternate interpretations about the influences operating in Stoker's famous story; anyone acquainted with the novel will appreciate that its strange, symbolic descriptions lend themselves to comprehensive analysis. It is well known that Stoker was knowledgeable about European history and folklore and that the character of Dracula is partially based on Vlad Tepes, Prince of Wallachia (1431–1476), called 'Vlad the Impaler' for the atrocities he committed against his enemies and his own subjects. Stoker had also read about a Hungarian noblewoman named Elizabeth Bathory (1560–1611), who reportedly murdered 650 young girls in order to drink their blood.[92] The author was undoubtedly influenced by Dr John Polidori's novel *The Vampyre* (1819) and Sheridan Le Fanu's *Carmilla* (1872), and probably by C. R. Maturin's *Melmoth the Wanderer* (1820), Robert Louis Stevenson's *Dr Jekyll and Mr Hyde* (1886), Wilkie Collins's *The Woman in White* (1860), and Wilde's own *The Picture of Dorian Gray* (1891).[93] Other influences that have been suggested are Henry Irving's performance of Mephistopheles in *Faust* and the 'Jack the Ripper' murders of 1888.[94] Stoker himself claimed that the inspiration for *Dracula* came after a nightmare induced by a meal of dressed crab![95]

Bad crab or no, *Dracula*'s phenomenal success is most commonly attributed to its evocation of some type of collective fantasy or repression. It has been interpreted as reflective of many political, social, scientific, and cultural concerns existing in *fin de siècle* Britain, including imperialism, Darwinism, and technological advances, and it continues to inspire much gender-based, psychoanalytic, new historicist, and deconstructionist criticism.[96] Of all the subtexts perceived in Stoker's story, it is the sexual symbolism that is the most obvious; the vampire's stock in trade involves secret, nocturnal bedroom visits, erotic physical aggression, and submission triggered by uncontrollable urges, and of course, the exchange of bodily fluids. Blood becomes a metaphor for semen and vampire teeth and stakes are unmistakable phallic symbols. There is also a healthy dose of voyeurism in the novel; Schaffer notes that '[a]ll the scenes of sexual release by staking depend on a spectator's pleasure'.[97] As many critics have noted, the masking symbolism of vampirism also allowed Stoker and his Victorian readers to enjoy the sexuality of the novel surreptitiously, perhaps unconsciously.[98] This aspect of *Dracula* certainly escaped comment by contemporary reviewers of the novel, who, while acknowledging the book to be sensational, found nothing morally objectionable in it.

In addition to this camouflaging effect, there is another aspect of vampirism that is particularly relevant here, namely the abnormality of the vampire's eroticism. It has been argued that the vampire's sexual perversity reflects the threat of the decadent and the New Woman to polarized gender and sexual mores; the merging of these during the late Victorian period was perceived as a sign of general cultural degeneration.[99] In Stoker's novel, virtuous women become sensuous she-devils feeding on men and young children, strong men become passive and submit to the sexual aggression of the female vampire. Stoker's vampires show no respect for life and are concerned only with their own appetites.[100]

Indeed, the sexuality in *Dracula* is dark, savage, and grotesque. Some critics interpret this as a consequence of Stoker's own sexual frustration, married to a woman who was reportedly cold and 'anti-sex'; others conjecture that this aspect of the novel reflects Stoker's contraction of syphilis from a prostitute.[101] Here we will explore the possibility that the threatening and perverse sexuality of the vampire reflects Stoker's suppressed homosexuality, which was inextricably linked with Wilde and his fate; so much so that Wilde himself can be glimpsed in Stoker's monstrous count.

There are many parallels between vampiric and homosexual practices: both require concealment due to society's censure of their 'unnatural' nature (homosexuals or 'inverts' in *fin de siècle* England were frequently classified by medical experts as the 'intermediate' sex, neither male nor female),[102] both possess the fascination of the forbidden and both are forms of eroticism operating outside of the sanctity of marriage.[103] *Dracula* certainly appears to contain a wealth of displaced homoerotic desire; Christopher Craft notes that 'the sexual threat [that *Dracula*] evokes, manipulates, sustains, but never finally represents is that Dracula will seduce, penetrate, drain another male'.[104] Craft also highlights protagonist Jonathan Harker's 'feminine' passivity in his readiness to be 'penetrated' by Count Dracula's female minions. Dracula's angry declaration on intervening during this scene in the novel—one of the first lines Stoker wrote for his story—has been read as particularly revealing: 'This man belongs to me'.[105] The close relationships between the band of men who attempt to thwart Dracula and the combined 'sexualized' blood transfusions they give Lucy have also been cited as symbolic of a homosexual alliance.[106]

Such readings assume a greater significance when considered in light of Stoker's ambiguous sexuality. The author's conspicuous adoration of, and devotion to, men like Irving, Walt Whitman, Lord Tennyson, and Sir Richard Burton, have led many critics to conclude that he had homosexual leanings.[107] Stoker's letters to Whitman in the 1870s are commonly cited as evidence for this supposition. Although Stoker's references to homosexuality are veiled in the letters to Whitman, who was well known for his homoerotic poetry, they are easily discernible. Stoker makes repeated references to their 'kind', his inability to write his true thoughts, and the fact that he reads Whitman's poetry 'with my door locked late at night'.[108] Marie Mulvey-Roberts convincingly argues that '[h]omosexual repression helps to explain why *Dracula* is such a "backlash text" through which Stoker sets out to restore the status quo with a vengeance'.[109]

Given the likelihood of Stoker's repressed sexuality and his long-standing relationship with Wilde, it is difficult not to read the homoerotic elements in *Dracula*, in part at least, as a response to Wilde's trials for 'gross indecency', which took place just a month before Stoker began writing his novel. (Ironically, *Dracula* was released in May 1897, the same month that Wilde was released from prison.) Maggie Kilgour refers to Wilde as Stoker's 'own Gothic double'; one who, unlike himself, did not abide by the rules.[110] Schaffer considers the effect of Wilde's trials on Stoker as 'an earthquake that destabilised the fragile, carefully elaborated mechanisms through which Stoker routed his desires'.[111] The conspicuous absence of all reference to Wilde in Stoker's recollections and correspondence after 1895 is notable here. In Stoker's *Personal Reminiscences of Henry Irving* (1906), Stoker deliberately precludes Wilde from a twelve-page list of his famous acquaintances. The concern with secrecy that Stoker had demonstrated in his letters to Whitman was compounded tenfold by Wilde's public disgrace, which brought the issues of 'deviant' sexuality and secret lives into the public domain. Stoker began to publicly denounce 'decadent' and 'indecent' writings in reactionary rhetoric. In 'The Censorship of Fiction' (1908), Stoker asserts that 'the only emotions which in the long run harm are those arising from sex impulses', and vehemently distances himself from '[v]ices so flagitious, so opposed to even the decencies of nature in its crudest and lowest forms, that the poignancy of moral disgust is lost in horror'.[112] In this article, Stoker stresses the criminality of authors of 'immoral' works and recommends that such writings be heavily censored.[113] By 1912, he was arguing for the imprisonment of homosexual authors.[114]

Immediately after Wilde's conviction, however, Stoker's reaction to 'vices' like Wilde's appears to have been tempered by anxiety about his own sexuality. There is an unsubstantiated report that Stoker, on hearing of Wilde's financial difficulties in 1900, traveled to Paris to give him money.[115] If this is true, Stoker demonstrated a remarkable empathy for the exiled homosexual, particularly in light of his later remarks on such individuals. Schaffer contends that *Dracula* represents an attempt by Stoker to come to terms with his sexuality, to work through the 'monster' image of the homosexual Wilde presented in the popular press and create a viable alternate model.[116] She argues that Count Dracula represents

> the complex of fears, desires, secrecies, repressions, and punishments that Wilde's name evoked in 1895. Dracula is Wilde-as-threat, a complex cultural construction . . . [he] represents the ghoulishly inflated version of Wilde produced by Wilde's prosecutors, the corrupting, evil, secretive, manipulative, magnetic devourer of innocent boys.[117]

Schaffer goes on to state that 'Stoker used the Wildean figure of Dracula to define homosexuality as simultaneously monstrous, dirty, threatening, alluring, buried, corrupting, contagious and indestructible', and indeed, the amount of textual evidence to support this claim is considerable.¹¹⁸ Perhaps the most convincing evidence is to be found in Jonathan Harker's description of the count, lying in his coffin after feeding, profoundly changed from his former slender, pale self:

> the cheeks were fuller . . . even the deep, burning eyes seemed set amongst swollen flesh, for the lids and pouches underneath were bloated . . . he lay like a filthy leech, exhausted with his repletion. I shuddered as I bent over to touch him, and every sense in me revolted at the contact.¹¹⁹

This physical description is undeniably redolent of Wilde's physique c. 1895; Schaffer points to Frank Harris's contemporary description of Wilde:

> There was something oily and fat about him that repelled me . . . his hands were flabby, greasy; his skin looked bilious and dirty . . . His appearance filled me with distaste. I lay stress on this physical repulsion, because I think most people felt it.¹²⁰

Schaffer goes on to reflect upon Harker's actions after seeing Dracula in this state:

> After Harker 'felt all over the body', he muses that Dracula might 'create a new and ever widening circle of semi-demons to batten on the helpless' . . . This image of monstrous progenitor amidst a horrible circle is precisely what dominated public rhetoric about Wilde during the trial.¹²¹

Schaffer raises another interesting point when she cites Eve Sedgwick's hypothesis that male competition for the love of a woman can provide an opportunity for the expression of homoerotic energy. She asserts, 'In 1878, Florence [Stoker] became the conduit through which Wilde's and Stoker's complex feelings for each other could flow'.¹²² This possibility is also raised by Barbara Belford, who conjectures that what 'made Stoker uncomfortable [about Wilde], perhaps, was not jealousy but the psychological impulse called troilism, in which homosexual desire for someone is expressed in wanting to share a partner'.¹²³ Of course, while such speculations are interesting, they are virtually impossible to corroborate.

Schaffer draws another comparison between Dracula and Wilde when she notes that 'the conditions of secrecy necessary for nineteenth-century homosexual life—nocturnal visits, shrouded windows, no servants—become ominous emblems of Count Dracula's evil'. She goes on to compare Dracula's castle with the aesthetic, airless rooms of Alfred Taylor, who procured male prostitutes for Wilde; both have windows that are never opened and rooms that are not regularly cleaned. An article in *The Evening News* on the day of Wilde's conviction refers to Wilde as a morally 'diseased' threat to 'healthy humanity': 'To him and such as him we owe the spread of moral degeneration amongst young men'.[124] Like Dracula's bite, Wilde's touch is infectious. Schaffer does not shy from another, rather sordid comparison:

> One of the worst pieces of evidence against Wilde was the presence of fecal stains on sheets in which Wilde had slept, adduced as evidence of anal sex . . . Dracula's bed is a pile on notably smelly dirt . . . when the Englishmen clean Dracula's coffins, they use the term that Ellen Terry, Willie Wilde, and the *Westminster Gazette* all employed to describe Wilde's punishment: 'purification'—[125]

The similarities proliferate: Nina Auerbach observes that Dracula is like Wilde in that he is 'hunted and immobilised by the "stalwart manliness" of normal citizens'.[126] Grigore Nandris compares the dancing of prostitutes upon Wilde's conviction with the regalement of the female vampires at Dracula's castle.[127] Schaffer draws attention to the fact that the novel's structure, with its emphasis on newspaper clippings and journalistic techniques such as shorthand, 'obliquely acknowledges its debt to the Wilde-saturated newspapers of April, May and June, 1895'. She also highlights another interesting correspondence:

> Oscar Wilde was convicted [on] May 24, 1895. The papers reported the event [on] May 25 . . . *Dracula*'s vital date is May 24 and 25. The first five chapters reconstruct what three different characters felt on May 24 and 25. On this pivotal date, we meet the characters and see the 'crimes' committed that the rest of the novel works to recompense.[128]

Alongside these reflections of Wilde in *Dracula*, there is evidence to suggest that Stoker identified with Wilde as a homosexual man, despite the anxiety the disgraced playwright inspired in him. Schaffer argues that, in addition to Dracula being a fictional projection of Wilde, the character of Jonathan Harker represents a fictional projection of Stoker. In addition to the similar sound of their surnames, Schaffer notes that both men are married solicitors who have never practiced law and both work for a revered older man; Stoker for Irving, Harker for the solicitor Peter Hawkins.[129] The wives of both men are also renowned for their beauty and intelligence.

If we allow that Harker is a projection of Stoker, the many correspondences between Harker and Dracula can be read as evidence of Stoker's identification with Wilde. Dracula initially appears to be radically different to the serious young solicitor, but many similarities soon become evident. Like Stoker and Wilde, they have similar physical proportions and share the same aptitudes and literary tastes. Both also possess the unnatural ability to crawl like a bat on the outside walls of the castle. Harker looks for Dracula's face when he peers into his own mirror; an interesting gesture in light of the fact that in 1895 Wilde became the public 'face' of homosexuality.[130] By the end of the novel Harker and Dracula have become even more alike in appearance—Harker's hair grows white like the count's—and behavior.

Schaffer highlights a very tangible example of Stoker's identification with Wilde in the section of the novel dealing with Harker's imprisonment in Dracula's castle. Stoker composed this section, which describes Harker's experiences as a prisoner, while Wilde was in Pentonville Gaol; the author was most likely reading of Wilde's prison experiences in *Reynolds's News* and other newspapers at the time.[131] Schaffer notes that the incarcerated Harker's experience resembles Wilde's in many respects: Harker cries often, his hair turns white, he has difficulty with personal grooming, and he can only write letters with permission.[132] Schaffer argues that, by imagining Harker suffering in this way, Stoker allowed himself to empathize with Wilde. In this regard, as with other works examined here, the appearance of the word 'wild' at crucial points in the text may be read as a hint as to Wilde's influence. The captive Harker recalls, 'When I found out that I was a prisoner a sort of *wild* feeling came over me [my italics]'. With regard to the key that could effect his escape, Harker relates, 'a *wild* desire took me to obtain that key at any risk [my italics]'.[133]

Stoker's empathy for Wilde could also explain his increasingly sympathetic portrayal of Dracula in the last third of the novel. In this section the reader is encouraged to see the vampire as a wretched slave to his 'unnatural' desires, who is hounded incessantly by righteous, 'normal' men. Schaffer contends that when Harker finally destroys Dracula, Stoker is effectively exorcising his own self-hatred by destroying the popular image of the grotesque homosexual. It is significant that after Dracula's death the Stoker-like Harker is established as a better, respectable version of the vampire count.[134] At the end of the novel Harker is free to assume the qualities he admired in Dracula, such as the latter's intellectual power, self-confidence, and resilience; the same qualities that his creator Stoker could salvage from the wreck of Wilde in revising his own homosexual model.[135] Schaffer argues that Harker's assumption of Dracula's identity at the end of the novel also represents a resolution of the Stoker/Florence/Wilde triangle for the author.[136]

Certainly, such theories offered by Schaffer and others are persuasive in their analysis of Wildean subtexts in *Dracula*. In light of their conclusions and the commentary above, it is difficult to deny that the figure of Wilde constitutes an intrinsic element of a character that has become one of our most enduring modern myths.

John Strange Winter (Henrietta Stannard)

A Seaside Flirt (1897)

As mentioned earlier, the release of Stoker's novel coincided with Wilde's release from prison in May 1897. Wilde's subsequent sojourn in Dieppe and the neighboring town of Berneval, already described in relation to Aubrey Beardsley, was fictionalized in a remarkably objective and sympathetic novel that also appeared that year: *A Seaside Flirt* by John Strange Winter, the pseudonym of Mrs Henrietta Eliza Vaughan Stannard (1856–1911). Like Ada Leverson, Stannard was one of the few female friends who steadfastly stood by Wilde after his disgrace.

By 1897, Stannard had established a reputation as a prolific and popular novelist.[137] Most of Stannard's novels and short stories draw upon her family's long association with the armed forces. Her works typically present a middle- or upper-class British soldier as a noble, humane character in a domestic setting. Her most popular work, 1885's *Bootle's Baby: A Story of the Scarlet Lancers*, is a tale about a compassionate cavalry officer who adopts a baby girl. John Ruskin described John Strange Winter as 'the author to whom we owe the most finished and faithful rendering ever yet given of the character of the British soldier'.[138] Indeed, before Stannards's true identity was revealed to the public in 1889, her readers had assumed she was a soldier. In fact, Stannard was a journalist, the first president of the Writers' Club (1892), the president of the Society of Women Journalists (1901–1903), and a Fellow of the Royal Society of Literature. A staunch campaigner for the disadvantaged who strongly protested against cruelty to animals, Stannard was known as a strong and capable woman with a kind heart. She also found time to forge a career as a successful socialite; the *Woman's Signal* newspaper reported on

January 30, 1896 that Stannard went 'a great deal into society', and that her parties were 'wonderful gatherings of all that is best in London literary and artistic society', tastefully set against aesthetic décor.[139] Wilde's comment about Stannard to a prison warder during his incarceration demonstrates his acquaintance with the author. The same warder who had quizzed him about Marie Corelli asked,

> 'John Strange Winter, sir: would you tell me what you think of him, sir?'
> 'A charming lady, he is a charming lady; but I would rather talk to her than read his books'.[140]

Wilde had reviewed Stannard's book *That Imp* in the *Saturday Review* of May 7, 1887. By his reference to 'Mr. Winter' in inverted commas in this review, we can assume that Wilde was aware of the author's identity at least two years before her reading public. In his critique of *That Imp*, Wilde refers to *Bootle's Baby* as a masterpiece and Winter's other works as 'amusing and audacious' with 'brilliant description[s]' of army life. However, Wilde also expresses the hope that Stannard will move on to new topics: 'It would be sad if such a clever and observant writer became merely the garrison hack of literature'.[141]

Stannard and her civil engineer husband Arthur established a home in Dieppe in 1896, in the hope of improving Arthur's health. As already mentioned, by the late 1890s the French resort town had become a 'home away from home' for many English writers and artists. After Wilde moved there in 1897, Stannard was furious to observe the rebuffs he frequently received in the town, especially the slights from his former friends. A letter from Wilde to Stannard dated May 28, 1897 shows that the latter had extended the hand of friendship to Wilde just a week after his arrival in Dieppe; it also reveals that Stannard was on friendly terms with Wilde's mother:

> Your kind husband gave me a very sympathetic and touching message from you yesterday, for which pray accept my most sincere thanks: he also asked me from you to call, a privilege of which I hope to avail myself tomorrow afternoon . . . I am conscious that I was leading a life quite unworthy of a son of my dear mother whose nobility of soul and intellect you always appreciated, and who was herself always one of your warmest and most enthusiastic admirers . . . Accept these few flowers as a slight token of my gratitude—[142]

Wilde did visit the Stannards, and they were often seen with Wilde about town. They also invited him to dine at their home and on at least one occasion Wilde had the couple to tea at his house in Berneval. Clearly, the postprison Wilde did not see Stannard's production of populist, military fiction as an impediment to their friendship, although he certainly retained his aversion to it. In a letter to Robert Ross of May 31, 1897, Wilde gently mocks Stannard's *Bootle's Baby* in his own inimitable fashion:

> I breakfast tomorrow with the Stannards: what a great passionate splendid writer John Strange Winter is! How little people understand her work! *Bootle's Baby* is une œuvre symboliste: it is really only the style and the subject that are wrong. Pray never speak lightly of *Bootle's Baby*—indeed, pray never speak of it at all; I never do.[143]

A clue to Wilde's friendship with Stannard may be contained in a request he makes of Ross in the same letter; Wilde asks Ross to send Stannard a copy of an article he had recently published in the *London Chronicle*, calling for more humane prison conditions. Both writers had a strong humanitarian streak, and this may well have been the common ground on which they based their friendship.

While Stannard's recorded kindnesses to Wilde in Dieppe constitute the only historical record we have of her opinion of him, her fictional portrait of the Irish wit Vivian Dermott in *A Seaside Flirt* provides many further clues to the nature of their friendship. Stannard's novel was completed in July 1897, just two months after Wilde and Stannard had renewed their acquaintance in Dieppe. The novel takes the form of a series of diary-style commentaries written by Cynthia Wilmot, the flirt of the title. Wilmot, like Stannard, has a 'weakness for society' and has come to Dieppe with her husband and young child. In chapter 4, 'A Society Flâneur', set in the Dieppe casino, Wilmot is informed by her friend Billy Raymond that the notorious Vivian Dermott is in Dieppe and that the town is 'all agog':

> To tell the truth, strictly between you and me, dear reader, it has long been one of the ambitions of my life to know Vivian Dermott, with his great reputation for brilliancy, his unparalleled audacity, and his picturesque, forcible, nonchalant appearance.[144]

Raymond tells Wilmot that he knows Dermott and refers to him as a 'wonderfully clever chap—what those French Johnnies call adroit. Never at a loss, always got a sharp answer ready'.[145] No sooner has Raymond imparted this information than Dermott appears, towering above the crowd and looking slightly bored; an impression created partly by his Wildean habit of looking through half-closed eyes.

Dermott also displays Wilde's propensity to gossip about society personalities, previously highlighted by Ella Hepworth Dixon and other writers: 'How mercilessly and cruelly [Dermott] was able to sum up people, who probably fancied that he took them precisely at their own valuation!'[146] In 'deliberate, rather affected tones' he greets Raymond and enquires after the identity of Wilmot, whose turquoise eyes have attracted his attention.

Another of Wilmot's companions, the Russian prince Pellnikoff, is impressed that Wilmot has been 'spotted' by Dermott, who, like Wilde, 'can make any woman the fashion if he chooses'. However, he warns Wilmot that 'in a sense, [Dermott] is a dangerous person to know'.[147] It soon becomes apparent that the prince is irritated by Dermott's presence; he admits to feeling generally 'awkward and lumbering' in the face of Dermott's quick-witted repartee and he is clearly jealous of Wilmot's interest in him. However, Stannard suggests that something else has provoked the prince's animosity toward Dermott. When Wilmot questions the prince's warning, the vexed prince responds, 'I can't make you understand . . . that's all'.[148] Dermott is well aware of Pellnikoff's antipathy toward him but feigns ignorance of it; this trait of Dermott's is most likely drawn from Stannard's observation of Wilde in Dieppe.

Wilmot and Dermott are soon introduced, and Wilmot is quickly won over by Dermott's compliments and intelligence. It is not long before Dermott's attentions have made Wilmot the most fashionable woman in Dieppe. However, Wilmot relates that she is under no misapprehension about Dermott's interest in her; she realizes that 'a woman whom he can make the world talk about is a necessity to him, an essential part of his curious and peculiar position':

> I cannot help laughing at the idea of my being Vivian Dermott's latest. Never was a shot that hit wider of the mark . . . I never knew a man who was less in love with me. By the *wildest* stretch of the imagination I could not flatter myself that I am more to him than the mere gratification of an artistic instinct [my italics].[149]

John Stokes sees Dermott as 'a kind of heterosexual Wilde', although he contends that Stannard's picture of Dermott as a solely 'artistic' admirer of Wilmot may be a 'delicate tribute' to Wilde's sexuality.[150] The present writer would go further to suggest that Stannard's many textual hints point quite clearly to Dermott's 'deviant' sexuality. When Wilmot voices her assumption that many women must be in love with the charismatic Dermott, Prince

Pellnikoff vehemently replies, 'Oh no; you wrong your sex. Believe me, you do . . . I don't think that in all the world such a noxious beast as Vivian Dermott has his equal!'[151] When Dermott first tells Wilmot that he is her admirer in a purely artistic sense, her reaction also implies that something is amiss: 'I don't know that in all my life I had ever felt such a strange sensation go through my heart as there did at that moment'.[152]

Despite Wilmot's awareness that Dermott's interest in her is purely aesthetic, and despite his avowal that to be a flâneur is his métier ('but there I stop . . . I have a regard for the welfare and the reputation of the women I like'), Wilmot is consumed with jealousy when he spends time in the company of other women.[153] When she does regain Dermott's attention and he asks her to dance, Wilmot's relief is palpable:

> I was conscious only that I was dancing with a man who interested me more at that moment than any other man in the world; that, I was the most remarkable woman in the room; that, having got Vivian Dermott's distinct approbation, nothing else mattered.[154]

Wilmot later admits that she thinks herself in love with Dermott, but her infatuation proves to be short-lived. Wilmot is reminded of her deeper love for her husband when the latter proposes to defend her honor in a duel with Pellnikoff (who engineers Wilmot into a compromising position), and the marriage is strengthened by the couple's mutual jealousy. Wilmot later reflects that she misinterpreted her feelings for Dermott. Her thoughts on the subject contain some interesting clues to Wilde's relationship with Stannard and his popularity with women in general:

> I had been in some curious, strange manner glamoured by—by—by what? Upon my word, I hardly knew. By the cadence of a voice, by a trick of gesture, by a felicity of expression, by a certain social cachet—[155]

Despite these realizations, Wilmot continues to value Dermott's genuine friendship and wise counsel, particularly after Dermott accompanies her on the train to Brussels to stop the impending duel: 'How good that man was to me . . . so gentle, so considerate! . . . he made me eat . . . He talked brilliantly . . . He made me try to sleep . . . How amusing and interesting he was!'[156] However, the novel's ambivalent closing lines suggest that Wilmot's feelings for Dermott will always be something other than platonic—perhaps as

Stannard's also were for her remarkable friend. These lines may also cast some light on Stannard's opinion of Wilde's acquiescent wife, Constance, already discussed in relation to Rosa Praed's *Affinities* in Part 1:

> Yesterday [Dermott] came to tell me that he is engaged . . . I congratulated him. She is very rich, and she is not bad looking, and she idolizes him with a devotion which is absolutely pathetic. He tells her how to look, what to say, what to wear, and he orders her about in a way which I should not stand for five minutes. He will always be my good friend, he says . . . [Stannard's ellipsis][157]

Perhaps these final words echoed Wilde's parting words to Stannard; by September 1897 Wilde had grown weary of his life in Berneval and Dieppe. Tired of being isolated and shunned, he decided to leave Normandy for Paris, then headed to Italy to defy his wife and all his friends by living with Alfred Douglas.

FREDERIC CARREL

The Adventures of John Johns (1897)

February 1897 saw a brief but notable appearance by Wilde in Frederic Carrel's popular novel *The Adventures of John Johns*.[158] Carrel (1869–1928) was an American journalist and novelist who worked in England and contributed to such journals as the *Nineteenth Century*, *Scientific Progress*, and the *Fortnightly Review*, the last while it was being edited by Wilde's friend Frank Harris during 1893 and 1894.[159] Carrel's association with the *Fortnightly Review* is significant. Despite the author's remarks to the contrary in the preface to *John Johns*, its eponymous central character is clearly based on Frank Harris, and the popularity of the novel can be largely attributed to the transparency of Carrel's fictional sketch of the editor and others.[160] Carrel offers an interpretation of the friendship between Harris and Wilde in describing the friendship between Johns and his poet friend Horace.

The Adventures of John Johns, first published anonymously, is a biting satire on the rise of Harris—a brash, roguish womanizer—through the ranks of London's journalistic set. While Harris was aggressively and unashamedly ambitious, Carrel's scathing portrait of an unscrupulous schemer who uses whatever means necessary to succeed—particularly the manipulation of women—is generally held to be a shallow and inaccurate one.[161] While we know little about Carrel or the nature of his relationship with Harris, at the time of writing *Johns Johns* the author was clearly familiar with him, as he includes many of Harris's distinctive characteristics in the novel. Carrel appears to have intensely disliked his editor, and he incorporates many unfounded speculations into his portrait in order to paint Harris in the most unfavorable light. Unfortunately, in the absence of contradictory information, the novel cemented a negative picture of Harris in the public mind and Harris's reputation suffered as a result, just as Wilde's suffered after the publication of Hichens's *The Green Carnation* in 1894.[162] Interestingly, Carrel's own depiction of Wilde, two years after the latter's disgrace, is nowhere near as damning as Hichens's earlier portrait. While there is no record of an acquaintance between Carrel and Wilde, we can reasonably assume that—as Carrel's knowledge of Harris appears to extend beyond a purely business knowledge—Carrel probably met Wilde while socializing with Harris.[163]

Another intriguing connection is evidenced by an undated letter, written in French, from Carrel to Wilde's friend Ada Leverson, which indicates that Carrel and Leverson were known to each other, and that there may have been some 'falling out' between the two authors:

> Dear Madam, I sent you a word to Broadstairs at the beginning of the week but I am not certain that you received it. In any case your silence remains inexplicable to me. Could it be a prejudice? I understand it even less on re-reading your last letter in which you announced to me the next installment of your article, in which I find nothing which might have foretold this sudden unwillingness to talk. I don't want to believe you capable of ending a friendship which seemed to me very sincere, with a brusqueness which would hurt me very much. Silence neither explains nor illuminates anything. Self-respect, which is sometimes a law, prevents me from saying anything further.[164]

This is the only extant record of any relationship between Leverson and Carrel. Though it is possible, in light of Carrel's mention of Leverson's article, that theirs was a purely literary association, it is also possible that the two had a more intimate relationship. It is well known that the married Leverson had several lovers and Carrel's tone appears unduly despondent. In any case, the connection between Leverson and Carrel suggests that the latter had more than one possible point of entry into Wilde's inner circle.

Certainly, if the character of Horace in *John Johns* is anything to go by, Carrel had the opportunity to observe Wilde closely. Horace is a tall, 'erotic' poet with long curled hair, a shaven face, and 'large fleshy hands', whose mind is 'a strange mixture of wit and incoherence, and who [has] attracted the attention of the public by his eccentricities'.[165] Horace appears in only one scene in the novel, walking affectionately arm-in-arm with Johns after leaving a restaurant on the Embankment; both men indulging in some inebriated rhetoric. In disagreeing with Johns on the merit of realism in art, Horace discourses on one of Wilde's favorite themes:

> 'John, dear John, reality does not exist. Reality is one of those chimeras which are forged by the middle classes to account for elephantine dulness. Reality, dear John, is like that obelisk, an ugly thing, a thing inimical to art. Do you think Praxiteles or any of the divine Greeks descended to the real? No, dear John, they worshipped at the perennial font of fantasy. Ah, no! ah, no! In this land of groverdom it is not substance we must cultivate, but artifice. We are surfeited with realism. Our lives in this city of brute commerce are made burdensome with the hideousness of trade; we are submerged in a repugnant sea of barter. Our sense of beauty is ever lacerated. Look at the lovely flower which for a brief day is living with me in my button-hole! Do not its tender petals, so reposeful in their pallor, seem to shrink from the crude brutality of yonder land of ugliness? Is it not so perfect that it deserves the praise of being called unreal'?[166]

Carrel, in his description of Johns's reaction to Horace's elaborate oratory, illuminates the nature of the Harris/Wilde friendship:

> Johns had listened to [Horace's] panegyric patiently. He knew, like everybody, the nature of the man; that he had a band of followers who worshipped him, a woman here and there in London whose thoughts and feelings he had utterly capsized, and for some reason which no one had ever clearly understood, he professed to think him a great genius, and supported him in his habitual arraignment of the middle classes, at whom he had, himself, so often tilted.[167]

On their walk, the pair encounter Johns's ascetic newspaper friend Tarte, who proceeds to denounce their drunkenness and sybaritism. Horace affably delivers a witty reply, but Tarte, unphased, goes on to deliver a prophetic warning:

> 'I say to you that if you let art take too much room in life, you will fall victims to it. When the tree of culture has been climbed until the top is reached, a fall is imminent, and that fall is often into the pond of incoherence. Sometimes the road of the cultured hedonist leads to Bedlam, sometimes it leads to Newgate, and in neither of those places are the muses wooed, my friends. If either of you take one or the other of those

roads, you'll be worse off than I, the Philistine, whose days are destined to be ended in a select establishment of paupers.'[168]

Johns is struck by the sense in the old man's warning and resolves to curb his hedonism and 'practice respectability'. He recognizes the inherent danger of 'getting soft in leading this emollient life of pleasure'.[169] What 'getting soft' might entail is broadly hinted at in Carrel's description of Horace's nature and social circle:

> Horace was very well in his own way, but he wasn't a man to be seen with often, for though he had the thoughts and bearing of a genius, and though he (Johns) had pronounced him to be one, there was an instability about the man which made him a person to be frequented with caution. Moral unconsciousness might be very well, but there was a way in things, and Horace, with his vices and mannerisms, went too far. In short, he recognized there was danger not only in the companionship of Horace, but also in the band of casual inebriates whom, in his *tædium vitæ*, he had gathered round him.[170]

Carrel's story significantly deviates from fact here. Harris did not avoid Wilde's 'dangerous' company; he corresponded and associated with Wilde after his imprisonment when the playwright's reputation was at its very lowest.

By abstaining from an 'emollient life of pleasure' in public, Johns manages to maintain his position of power and privilege (he continues to lead an extraordinarily caddish life in private). In contrast, Horace, Wilde-like, dismisses Tarte's warning with flippant arrogance: '[Tarte] is an example . . . of the infirmity of sense-perception which afflicts some men who have never known the higher things. I shall write a poem on his singular perversity'.[171] Horace is not glimpsed again for the remainder of the novel; the Victorian reader familiar with Wilde's demise would have had little trouble imagining Horace's fate.

Curiously, Wilde commented on Harris's caricature in *John Johns*, but he was conspicuously silent on his own. In a letter to Robert Ross dated July 20, 1897, Wilde wrote, 'The sketch of Frank Harris in *John Johns* is superb. Who wrote the book? It is a wonderful indictment'.[172] Certainly, Wilde was in a position to judge Carrel's portrait, being familiar with Harris's somewhat abrasive personality and wayward behavior. While Harris was in many ways a good friend to Wilde, supporting him emotionally and financially during his times of greatest need, Harris's forceful personality led to several conflicts with the playwright during their friendship. In attempting to resolve one such disagreement, Wilde wrote to Harris on June 13, 1897:

> You are a man of dominant personality; your intellect is exigent, more so than of any man I ever knew; your demands on life are enormous; you require response, or you annihilate. The pleasure of being with you is in the clash of personality, the intellectual battle, the war of ideas. To survive you one must have a strong brain, an assertive ego, a dynamic character. In your luncheon-parties, in the old days, the remains of the guests were taken away with the *débris* of the feast. I have often lunched with you [at your home] in Park Lane and found myself the only survivor.[173]

It is tempting to conjecture that Carrel was present on one such occasion, and was one of those unfortunates who did not 'survive' the experience. Perhaps the amiable 'intellectual battle' between Johns and Horace reflects an actual encounter between Harris and Wilde, as witnessed by one of the disgruntled casualties of Harris's dominant personality. This would certainly account for the bitter edge to Carrel's portrait. However Carrel was inspired to translate the Harris/Wilde relationship into fiction, he proved unable to repeat the success of *The Adventures of John Johns*. His subsequent quirky expositions on ethical, eugenicist, and scientific themes were not commercial successes and have long since faded into obscurity.

Grant Allen

Linnet: A Romance (1898)

Linnet: A Romance, by the prolific author, philosopher, Darwinist, and popularizer of science, C. G. B. (Grant) Allen (1848–1899), appeared the year after Carrel's *John Johns* in 1898.[174] Wilde returned to publishing and the public consciousness in February of that year with *The Ballad of Reading Gaol*, the long poem inspired by his incarceration, which denounces the inhumanity of the English prison system.[175] Reviews of *The Ballad* were mixed; although some critics lauded the poem's humanitarianism and literary merit, others such as W. E. Henley, who reviewed *The Ballad* in the *Outlook* of March 5, 1898, dismissed it as 'sentimental slush'.

Wilde's disgrace was too recent for many of his contemporaries to revise their opinion of the man or his work. Grant Allen appears to have been a case in point. Allen's writings were an unusual combination of atheism, humanism, rationalism, and moralism, and his prolific output of novels, short stories, and essays on a wide range of topics won him much renown among his contemporaries. Allen's first love was science; he was a talented naturalist, anthropologist, and physicist who was fascinated by theories of evolution and energy; Charles Darwin and Herbert Spencer were among his friends and mentors. Allen also published various reflections on philosophy, geography, history, and art and held radical views on religion and morality. In his two 1895 novels *The British Barbarians: A Hill-Top Novel* and *The Woman Who Did*, Allen incited much controversy with his ardent attacks on contemporary sexual *mores*. The year 1898's *Linnet*, however, falls squarely into the 'pot-boiler' category. Allen wrote many works of this type, which were far more remunerative than his scientific or scholarly writings. However, Allen usually managed to incorporate 'serious' themes into his popular fiction, including many criticisms of established Victorian conventions; *Linnet* is no exception in this regard.

The melodrama of *Linnet* commences in the Tyrol. Wildean critic Florian Wood is holidaying in Austria alongside the hero of the story, Will Deverill, an operatic composer and poet. They encounter Lina Telser, a beautiful Catholic peasant girl who is a gifted singer; the 'Linnet' of the title. Deverill quickly falls in love with Linnet and she with him, but the composer is persuaded out of proposing marriage by Wood, who is resentful of Linnet's preference for Deverill. Instead, Linnet marries a cold and opportunistic Austrian innkeeper, who is also physically abusive and unfaithful. The action of the plot moves to London and Monte Carlo as Linnet's husband, greedy for money and reflected glory, promotes her singing career. In a short time Linnet becomes the darling of the European opera scene. After much authorial criticism of social values pertaining to sex and Catholic views on divorce, a jealous admirer conveniently murders Linnet's abusive husband. Despite a nefarious attempt by Wood to take advantage of the vulnerable Linnet in order to have her for himself, she and Deverill are eventually united with the aid of a papal dispensation.

Allen often included portraits of contemporary personalities in his fiction and the 'intensely modern' Florian Wood is clearly based on Wilde.[176] An aesthetic arbiter of taste and a brilliant conversationalist, Wood occupies Wilde's unique former position in fashionable society. Wood's diminutive physical stature does little to blind the reader to his original; his 'smooth and girlish cheek' and plump hands are more accurate indicators. Wood's foibles are Wilde's worst: he is vain, affected, lazy, and cynical. Wood clearly reflects the demonized image of Wilde that prevailed after the latter's trials. He is an insincere flatterer, a mercenary, a pretender, and—as is ultimately revealed by his treatment of Linnet—he is immoral and unscrupulous. He is in every way inferior to Deverill, who is depicted as a true gentleman of the arts. Wood makes many Wildean quips about women and marriage and is only prepared to take a wife if he is financially compensated. He also shows an affinity for the fraudulent psychic Joaquin Holmes.

However, Wood also possesses Wilde's undeniably attractive qualities: his good humor, tolerance, and worldly outlook, his 'exquisitely modulated' voice, and his ability to speak authoritatively on almost any subject. Wood, like Wilde, prides himself (not always justifiably) on being a discoverer and supporter of up-and-coming artists like Linnet; he also acts as a social sponsor for attractive and charismatic women like the pretty American widow Rue Palmer. Wood's attendance at a dinner party is a virtual guarantee of success; his conversation is 'richly worded' and 'sparkles'.[177] Wood's popularity in fashionable circles is that formerly experienced by Wilde: he is 'the spoiled child of society . . . Clubs [hang] on his clear voice; women [pet] and [make] much of him'. For Wood, as for Wilde, the necessities of life are the luxuries: 'stalls at the opera and hansoms *ad libitum*'.[178]

The correspondences between Wilde and Wood proliferate: Wood is widely known by his distinctive first name and he has Wilde's manner of suggesting how nature can be improved upon. Wood's distinctive aestheticism is also Wilde's; he shares Wilde's obsession with ancient Greek culture and 'drinks things in with sensuous delight'.[179] Wood also owns a first edition of Andrew Lang's book of poetry *Ballades in Blue China* (1880); blue china being one of Wilde's most famous early enthusiasms. Moreover, though Wood is not aggressively masculine, he '[isn't] exactly the sort of man to be bullied' either, as many of Wilde's contemporaries were surprised to discover.[180] If the reader is left in any doubt of the inspiration for Allen's epicurean philosopher, it should be allayed by Wood's pronouncement that '[c]onsistency is the virtue of the Philistine intellect'.[181] This remark clearly echoes Wilde's own aphorisms on the subject. In 'The Relation of Dress to Art' in the *Pall Mall Gazette* of February 28, 1885, Wilde writes, 'consistency is the last resort of the unimaginative'. In *Dorian Gray*, Lord Henry Wotton remarks that '[f]aithfulness is to the emotional life what consistency is to the life of the intellect—simply a confession of failure'.[182]

Allen's convincing portrait of Wilde in *Linnet* would suggest that the two men were acquainted at some point. This is also likely in light of a *Times* reviewer's observation that 'Mr. Grant Allen is most at home on the artistic fringes of fashionable society'.[183] Allen and Wilde shared several mutual acquaintances, including Richard Le Gallienne, Frank Harris, and Bernard Shaw (Allen and Shaw were both members of the Fabian Society), and a publisher, John Lane. While Allen and Wilde differed in many respects, the two men had much in common: both were fascinated by aesthetics, particularly by color and flowers. Allen wrote several books on these subjects, including *Physiological Aesthetics* (1877) and *The Colour Sense: Its Origin and Development; An Essay in Comparative Psychology* (1879). Both men revered their Celtic heritage, actively encouraged young writers and artists, and were unorthodox socialists and vocal nonconformists. Moreover, in Allen's controversial essay 'The New Hedonism' of March 1894, he echoed and expanded upon Wilde's comments on the subject in *Dorian Gray* (1891), arguing for aestheticism over asceticism and advocating that intellectual '[s]elf-development is greater than self-sacrifice'.[184] In the same essay Allen praised Wilde's poetic hero, the 'great soul . . . Walt Whitman', for speaking out against puritanism.[185] Both Allen and Wilde also wrote fictional works inspired by Vera Zassoulich, a Russian revolutionary whose story appeared in the popular press in 1878. Wilde wrote a play entitled *Vera: or, The Nihilists* (1883) and Allen published a novel entitled *For Maimie's Sake: A Tale of Love and Dynamite* (1886).

We know that Allen admired Wilde sufficiently in 1891 to laud him in his essay 'The Celt in English Art', which appeared in the *Fortnightly Review* in February of that year. In this article, Allen—who was of Irish, Scottish, and French-Canadian descent—argues that 'the great and victorious aesthetic movement . . . is a direct result . . . of the Celtic reflux on Teutonic Britain', and writes, 'Mr. Oscar Wilde, whom only fools ever mistook for a mere charlatan, and whom wise men know for a man of rare insight and strong common-sense, is an Irishman to the core'.[186] As it happened, Wilde's essay 'The Soul of Man Under Socialism' appeared in the same issue of the *Fortnightly*, and Allen wrote to Wilde to congratulate him on it on February 6, 1891:

> Dear Mr. Wilde, Will you allow me to thank you most heartily for your noble and beautiful essay in this month's *Fortnightly*? I would have written every line of it myself—if only I had known how. There is hardly a word or a clause in it with which I don't agree most cordially. It comes home to me all the more because I am one of those poor devils who work for daily bread, and have therefore never been able to do any artistic realisation of my own individuality. But apart from particular persons altogether, the large and wise utterance of your article has

pleased me so much that I can't refrain from expressing to you the greatness of my pleasure. It is years since I've read anything so important or so interesting in an English review. Excuse writing from a hand worn out with the production of shilling shockers to order, and believe me to remain, with very genuine admiration, Sincerely yours, Grant Allen.

A letter from Wilde to Allen may have crossed this one in the post, as it does not acknowledge receipt of Allen's note. Wilde's letter, dated c. February 7, 1891, reads,

> Dear Mr. Grant Allen, I beg you will allow me to express to you my real delight in your article in the *Fortnightly*, with its superb assertion of that Celtic spirit in Art that Arnold divined, but did not demonstrate, at any rate in the sense of scientific demonstration, such as yours is. I was dining at the House of Commons on Thursday, and proposed to some Scotch and Welsh members, who had read your article with pride and pleasure, that as to break bread and drink wine together is, as Christ saw, the simplest and most natural symbol of comradeship, *all* of us who are Celts, Welsh, Scots, and Irish, should inaugurate a Celtic Dinner, and assert ourselves, and show these tedious Angles or Teutons what a race we are, and how proud we are to belong to that race. You are, of course, a Celt. You must be. What do you think of the idea? It is the outcome of your article, so I want you to join in getting our gorgeous banquet up. Think it over. In any case, we all owe you a debt. My mother is fascinated and delighted by your article, and begs me to tell you so. Truly yours, Oscar Wilde.[187]

Josephine Guy and Ian Small contend that Wilde's reconciliation of Socialism and Individualism in 'The Soul of Man' (by combining a socialist approach to private property with an individualistic antistatism) had already been put forward more effectively by Allen in his essay 'Individualism and Socialism', which appeared in the *Contemporary Review* of May 1889. Guy and Small aver there 'may have been something a little arch' in Allen's 'I would have written every line of it myself—if only I had known how', because 'in a sense, he *had* [emphasis in the original] written some of Wilde's essay'. Guy and Small conclude that 'the effusiveness of Wilde's praise [for Allen] may have hidden an element of embarrassment and defensiveness' as a result of this.[188] Of course, it is also possible that Wilde's enthusiasm was sincere.

Whatever the case, there is no record of Wilde's proposed 'Celtic Dinner' ever taking place. Such an event may have occurred, or the two men may have met to discuss Wilde's suggestion. It is tempting to read Allen's description of Wood's conversation in *Linnet* as the result of a conversation between Allen and Wilde, discoursing at length on their favorite subjects at a fashionable London restaurant. Allen writes of Wood, 'He played with science as he played with everything else; and he could talk of the environment by the hour with the best of them, in his airy style'.[189]

Allen's characterization of Wood suggests that the author's high opinion of Wilde—clearly evident in 'The Celt in English Art'—did not endure. Florian Wood, although charismatic, is an unscrupulous cad. Moreover, while he can wax lyrical on any subject, Wood's knowledge and wisdom are repeatedly undermined and called into question, in a manner redolent of Mabel Wotton's 'The Fifth Edition', discussed above:

> though in his capacity as man of culture, the philosopher of taste was prepared to give a critical opinion offhand at any moment, on Goethe or Heine, the Minnesänger, or the Nibelungenlied, he was innocent of even the faintest acquaintance with the German language.[190]

Allen paints Wilde's famed ability to speak authoritatively on any subject as a foible rather than a strength: 'He couldn't bear to have it thought he was ignorant of anything, from mathematics or music to esoteric Buddhism'.[191] These observations may reflect a 'rivalry of raconteurs' between Allen and Wilde. Richard Le Gallienne described Allen as 'an amazing talker', remarking that '[n]o more brilliant generaliser can ever have lived'—impressive testimony from a man who was well acquainted with Oscar Wilde.[192] It is also possible that at some point Allen bested Wilde in conversation: the narrator of *Linnet* remarks that it 'was a way of Florian's to be bland when he saw he was getting the worst of an argument'.[193]

A further possibility relates to Robert Hichens's popular satire *The Green Carnation* (1894), discussed in the previous section. In Hichens's book the Wildean character Esmé Amarinth remarks,

> [England's] artists, as they call themselves, are like Mr. Grant Allen: they say that all their failures are 'pot-boilers'. They love that word. It covers so many sins of commission. They set down their incompetence as an assumption, which makes it almost graceful, and stick up the struggle for life as a Moloch requiring the sacrifice of genius. And then people believe in the travesty. Mr. Grant Allen could have been Darwin, no doubt; but Darwin could never have been Mr. Grant Allen.[194]

It is possible that Allen took these sentiments to be reflective of Wilde's; Amarinth's original was immediately recognized by the

British public and, as related in Part 2, there were many who thought the (originally anonymous) book had been written by Wilde himself. Allen must have been particularly sensitive to being judged by his popular fiction in this manner, as he saw these works as a means to a more serious end. The disparaging comparison with Charles Darwin, Allen's friend and mentor, would also have displeased Allen.

Of course, while these are all conceivable reasons for a change in Allen's opinion of Wilde, the most likely cause would be the revelations that ensued from the latter's 1895 trials. Although Allen's views on sexuality were liberal and progressive in many ways, as mentioned above, his was a strange blend of liberalism and moralism. In his essay 'The New Hedonism', Allen stridently denounces puritanism about sexuality and argues that the enlightened hedonist recognizes that 'the sex-instinct is the origin and basis of all that is best and highest within us'.[195] The latter part of this statement, however, encapsulates an essential difference in the two men's conception of the New Hedonism, and contains the key to Allen's likely condemnation of Wilde, as does the following passage in Allen's essay:

> [The hedonist's] object will always be so to use these [sexual] functions as not to abuse them . . . by acquiescence in a hateful *régime* of vice [and] disease . . . He knows that . . . chastity means a profound disinclination to give the body where the heart is not given in unison.[196]

There can be little doubt that Allen's liberal views about sexual relations did not extend to homosexuality. In his introduction to *The British Barbarians: A Hill-Top Novel*, a futuristic dystopian satire published soon after Wilde's conviction in 1895, he observed that 'of late we have been flooded with stories of evil tendencies'.[197] Allen was also vocal on the evils of prostitution and would have taken a dim view of Wilde's infamous associations with 'rent boys'. In *The British Barbarians*, Allen announces the inauguration of a new type of 'Hilltop Novel', the purpose of which is to '[raise] a protest in favour of purity' in opposition to the state of contemporary London, which 'stagnates and ferments, polluted with the diseases and vices of centuries . . . strange decadent sins and morbid pleasures'.[198] In 'The New Hedonism', Allen had averred that

> the poets, the painters, the composers, the singers [who 'make most of' the sexual passions] are the salt of the earth . . . They are the most gifted, the most imaginative, the most beautiful-minded, the most dainty-souled.[199]

Allen paints a very different picture of the arts in his introduction to *The British Barbarians*:

> the theatre and the music-hall spread their garish gas-lamps . . . O decadents of the town, we have seen your sham idols, your tinsel Arcadias. We have tired of their stuffy atmosphere, their dazzling jets, their weary ways . . . Your studied dalliance with your venal muses is little to our taste—[200]

Three years later in *Linnet*, Allen is still referring to the artistic and theatrical worlds as places 'where morals and religion are all topsy-turvy'.[201]

Although we can detect a faint glimmer of Allen's former admiration for Wilde in his portrayal of Florian Wood ('[t]o give Florian his due, he bubbled and sparkled'; '[he] was really a good natured fellow in a lazy sort of way'[202]), the reader is left in no doubt as to the narrator's low opinion of the decadent critic. After Wood's attempt to take advantage of the vulnerable Linnet, the heroic Will Deverill finally refuses to speak to him. Just as Wilde had beaten a hasty retreat from England after his release from prison, the disgraced Wood 'slinks' out of Deverill's house, and Allen's novel, for good.[203]

Joseph Conrad
'The Return' (1898)

Joseph Conrad's 'The Return' was published in the same year as Allen's *Linnet*, appearing in Conrad's first volume of short stories entitled *Tales of Unrest* (1898). The Polish-born Conrad (born Joseph Korzeniowski, 1857–1924), a retired sailor, settled in London in 1894 and began to pursue a literary career; his 1895 romantic adventure *Almayer's Folly* proved a great success. Further tales of adventure soon followed: *An Outcast of the Islands* (1896) and *The Children of the Sea: A Tale of the Forecastle* (1898). The subject of Conrad's 'The Return' is marital conflict in a contemporary middle-class London household. While this subject represents a significant departure from his previous works, the story's themes of infidelity and the constraints of civilized society frequently appear in Conrad's wider *œuvre*.

In 'The Return' the conservative businessman Alvan Hervey comes home to discover a note from his (unnamed) wife, in which the latter explains that she has left him for another man—a revelation that demolishes Hervey's pompous self-assurance. The exact contents of the letter are not disclosed. As the story unfolds it becomes clear that the couple do not love each other and are primarily concerned with maintaining their respectable image. It is this concern that appears to prompt Hervey's wife to return to her husband before anyone is the wiser, but Hervey decides that he cannot continue in a loveless and faithless union and he leaves his wife. The Wildean character in the story is the (unnamed) literary man who has tempted Mrs Hervey away from her husband. He is the aesthetic editor of Hervey's 'moribund . . . semi-political, and wholly scandalous' paper, which Hervey considers respectable because of its 'excessive dulness . . . [utter faithlessness, lack of] new thought . . . wit, satire or indignation'.[204] While the editor is a frequent visitor to the Hervey house, the narrator relates that Hervey thinks his editor

> rather an ass because he had such big front teeth (the proper thing is to have small, even teeth) and wore his hair a trifle longer than most men do. However, some dukes wear their hair long, and the fellow indubitably knew his business. The worst was that his gravity, though perfectly portentous, could not be trusted. He sat, elegant and bulky, in the drawing room, the head of his stick hovering in front of his big teeth, and talked for hours with a thick-lipped smile (he said nothing that could be considered objectionable and not quite the thing) talked in an unusual manner—not obviously—irritatingly. His forehead was too lofty—unusually so—and under it there was a straight nose, lost between the hairless cheeks, that in a smooth curve ran into a chin shaped like the end of a snow-shoe. And in this face that resembled the face of a fat and fiendishly knowing baby there glittered a pair of clever, peering, unbelieving black eyes. He wrote verses too. Rather an ass. But the band of men who trailed at the skirts of his monumental frock-coat seemed to perceive wonderful things in what he said. Alvan Hervey put it down to affectation. Those artist chaps, upon the whole, were affected. Still, all this was highly proper—very useful to him—and his wife seemed to like it—as if she also had derived some distinct and secret advantage from this intellectual connection.[205]

The Wildean characteristics described in this passage are obvious: the bulky elegance, high forehead, thick lips and disguised teeth, as well as the marked affectation, brilliant conversation, distinctive manner of speech, and admiring band of disciples; it is also revealed that the editor has Wilde's 'fat, white hand[s]'.[206] Of course, the editor's profession recalls Wilde's editorship of *Woman's World* from 1887 to 1889 and his long hair harks back to Wilde's early days in London, as does his reputation as a poet. These Wildean resonances are perhaps not surprising in light of the fact that Wilde was released from prison in the same month that Conrad began writing 'The Return' (May 1897).

Many of the editor's similarities to Wilde have been noted by Paul Kirschner in his 1993 article 'Wilde's Shadow in Conrad's "The Return"'. Kirschner also draws parallels between Conrad's story and Wilde's play *Lady Windermere's Fan*—primarily with regard to their themes of 'the artificiality of fashionable society and the broadening of moral vision in one of its members'.[207] Kirschner points to the appearance of two objects in both plots—a fan and a farewell note—and highlights certain Wildean echoes in Conrad's story:

> Lady Windermere's reflection, 'Actions are the first tragedy in life, words are the second. Words are perhaps the worst. Words are merciless . . . ' is echoed in the Herveys' fear of speaking because 'words are more terrible than facts' . . . The satirical wit in 'The Return' also may partly be modelled on Wilde's: the incongruous associations Mrs. Hervey awakens of 'an elephant, a giraffe, a gazelle; of a gothic tower— of an overgrown angel'; Hervey's belief that 'the proper thing is to have small, even teeth, his wistful reflection on discovering his wife's disgrace, 'Now—if she had only died!' and his 'envy of respectable bereavement'—

Kirschner also highlights the editor's Wildean quips: 'men do not weep. Foreigners do' and 'deception should begin at home'.[208] While these correspondences are persuasive, Kirschner's conclusion that the 'reminders of Wilde [in 'The Return'] . . . do not seem polemical so much as a covert salute to a brilliant contemporary achievement on the same ground [i.e., *Lady Windermere's Fan*]', does not ring true to the present writer.[209] There are certain Wildean echoes not discussed by Kirschner, including allusions to Wilde's poetry, which do appear to be polemical; these are mainly to be found in Conrad's portrayal of the editor's relationship with Mrs Hervey.

Let us first consider Conrad's allusion to Wilde's poetry. A book of the editor's verse in the Hervey house, with its 'contorted gold letters sprawling [over the cover] in an intricate maze', recalls Wilde's well-known predilection for artistically bound editions of his works.[210] Moreover, the title of the volume, *Thorns and Arabesques*, contains an echo of a memorable passage from one of Wilde's best-known poems, 'The Harlot's House', first printed in the *Dramatic Review* of April 11, 1885. In Wilde's poem a couple standing outside a prostitute's house observe the dancing figures inside:

> Like strange mechanical grotesques,
> Making fantastic arabesques,
> The shadows raced across the blind.[211]

The theme of Wilde's poem, in which the narrator's lover leaves him to enter 'the house of lust', may well have had some bearing on Conrad's choice of this particular Wildean resonance, as might the irony in the fact that Wilde's harlot dances to a tune called 'Treues Liebes Herz' ('Faithful, Dear Heart'). The 'thorns' in *Thorns and Arabesques* conceivably allude to Wilde's fairy tale 'The Nightingale and the Rose'. In this story, a nightingale impales itself on a rose thorn in order to produce the red rose desired by a young man for the object of his affection, a girl who callously rejects both flower and lover for another suitor. These echoes of sexual capriciousness and infidelity in Wilde's works, paralleled by Conrad in his depiction of Mrs Hervey and her Wilde-like lover, may be coincidental but certainly add to the cumulative impression of a Wildean influence.

The nature of the relationship between the editor and Hervey's wife is not the central focus of Conrad's narrative—that being the emotional turmoil experienced by Hervey in response to his wife's actions—however, this aspect of the story does present some controversial possibilities regarding the Wildean influence in 'The Return'. Although Mrs Hervey appears to confirm her husband's assumption that the editor knew of her plans to leave her marriage, her communications on this subject are far from categorical:

> 'What made you come back?'
> 'I didn't know myself', she murmured . . .
> 'Did he expect this? Was he waiting for you'? he asked.
> She answered him by an *almost imperceptible* nod [my italics], and he continued to look at her for a good while without making a sound.
> Then, at last—
> 'And I suppose he is waiting yet?' he asked quickly.
> Again she *seemed* to nod at him [my italics].[212]

While the common interpretation of the tale—that the wife returns to her husband because of her fear of flouting social convention—is a wholly plausible one, Mrs Hervey's reluctance to confirm that the editor expects her and continues to wait suggests to the present writer an alternate interpretation. Namely, that she has misinterpreted the editor's intentions, has offered herself to him and has been rejected.

As discussed in the preceding sections, it appears that Wilde's flattering attentions toward women were often misinterpreted; fictional illustrations of this have already been highlighted in Stannard's *A Seaside Flirt* (1897) and Carrel's *The Adventures of John Johns* (1897). Conrad's Hervey recalls his wife's 'rapt expression' while listening to the editor discourse for long periods on her beautiful 'soul'.²¹³ The fact that the editor, like Wilde, manages to turn women's heads is hardly surprising in light of Conrad's description of Hervey's regular set: they '[fear] emotion, enthusiasm, or failure, more than fire, war, or mortal disease; [tolerate] only the commonest formulas of commonest thoughts, and [recognize] only profitable facts'.²¹⁴ However, while Wilde professed undying love for women like Ellen Terry and Lillie Langtry, it seems that he never translated these romantic sentiments into action. One reading of 'The Return' is that Conrad's editor also demonstrated a reluctance in this regard.

Wilde's 'deviant' sexuality also seems to be reflected in the suggestion that Mrs Hervey has discovered something unspeakable about the editor; something that precludes a relationship with him and possibly something that her husband had suspected previously. (Hervey sees the editor at various times as 'fiendishly knowing', 'effeminate', and 'unhealthy'.²¹⁵) It appears significant that the reason for Mrs Hervey's return is never articulated but only ambiguously referred to between husband and wife. She says,

> 'You know why I came back . . . You know that I could not'
>
> It was impossible, of course! He knew it. She knew it. She confessed it . . . That man knew it too—as well as anyone; couldn't help knowing it.
>
> 'I am ready to go,' she said very low. 'I have forfeited everything . . . to learn . . . to learn . . . '. Her chin fell on her breast; her voice died out in a sigh.²¹⁶

Mrs Hervey also relates that her letter constituted the 'beginning and the end' of her romantic relationship with the editor, and refers to the episode as 'an honest mistake'; the narrator refers to her 'self-deception'. Moreover, Mrs Hervey experiences feelings of 'bitter resentment' and 'hate' toward the editor. While Alvan Hervey later reflects that his wife did not have the 'faith, the love, the courage' to go to the editor, the suggestion that the editor has let down Mrs Hervey in some way is never eliminated.²¹⁷

Several passages in 'The Return' appear to reflect a degree of empathy with the recently released Wilde. There are certainly overtones of Wilde's situation in the bleak future Alvan Hervey envisions for himself after his marriage collapses; he reflects,

> [there] are in life events, contacts, glimpses, that seem brutally to bring all the past to a close. There is a shock and a crash, as of a gate flung to behind one by the perfidious hand of fate . . . a trail of invincible

sadness, a sense of loss and bitter solitude . . . For a moment he ceased to be a member of society with a position, a career, and a name attached to all this . . . He stood alone, naked and afraid, like the first man on the first day of evil . . . There is a moment of dumb dismay, and the wanderings must begin again—[218]

Conrad had experienced several expatriations himself and he shared Wilde's 'outsider' status as a non-English native; Kingsley Widmer notes that Conrad appears to have experienced a deep sense of loss and alienation as a result of his itinerant early life.[219] It is possible that the pathos of Wilde's plight, brought to the public's attention by the popular press, inspired Conrad to conquer his distaste for the aesthete. By all accounts Conrad did not appreciate Wilde's studied 'amorality'. Jeffrey Meyers writes,

> Joseph Retinger . . . emphasised [Conrad's] conventional morality, calling him 'a man of stern principles and straight lines in his private life, [who] despised weakness of character . . . and the display of immorality. [Conrad] disliked consequently the works of Oscar Wilde, because he had a profound contempt for his way of living'.[220]

However, it has also been observed that despite Conrad's 'conventional morality',

> the adventurous and artistic side of Conrad had an interest in, a tolerance of and perhaps even a vicarious pleasure in the extremely irregular and immoral sexual lives of his intimate friends . . . Many of Conrad's friends were homosexuals [some of whom were] recklessly indiscreet.[221]

While the present writer has been unable to locate evidence of any acquaintance between Wilde and Conrad, they did have several mutual associates including William Rothenstein, Leonard Smithers, literary agent James Pinker, and (the recklessly indiscreet) André Gide. While Conrad could not be classed as part of the 1890s decadent set, he was certainly influenced by the decade's aesthetic *Zeitgeist*. As Kingsley Widmer notes, Conrad was 'from a proud gentry background, was rather snobbish, and in appearance and manner rather a dandy'.[222] Conrad contributed to Arthur Symons's decadent journal *The Savoy* and first thought of the *Yellow Book* for publishing 'The Return'. In the wake of the Wilde scandal Conrad told Edward Noble that he considered *Yellow Book* contributors 'very aest[h]etic very advanced . . . all certainly writers of talent'.[223] Conrad's choice of the *Yellow Book* as a potential publisher for 'The Return' may have been motivated by the presence of the Wildean character in his story; although Wilde never contributed to the journal, its ostentatiously decadent flavor meant that he was inevitably associated with it in the public eye. Conrad expressed a concern that the 'right people' should read his story; *Yellow Book* readers would certainly be more likely to recognize Conrad's allusions to Wilde and his work.[224]

Conrad's unflattering portrait of Alvan Hervey also demonstrates his dislike for the 'philistine', conformist mentality that was so loathsome to Wilde and his set; Conrad aimed to ridicule 'the gospel of the beastly bourgeois' with his story.[225] Consequently, it is likely that Conrad sympathized with Wilde at some level as a target of the braying middle classes. Indeed, this may explain Conrad's conspicuous silence on the sensational Wilde trials in his letters from the period. Conrad once averred that all people were either idiots or convicts, in a manner that suggests that he would have been reluctant to join the multitude of 'idiots' attacking the convict Wilde:

> One must drag the ball and chain of one's selfhood to the end. It is the price one pays for the devilish and divine privilege of thought; so that in this life it is only the elect who are convicts—a glorious band which comprehends and groans but which treads the earth amidst a multitude of phantoms with maniacal gestures, with idiotic grimaces. Which would you be: idiot or convict?[226]

Conrad's ambivalence regarding Wilde may explain some of the difficulty the author experienced in writing 'The Return'. Conrad often referred to the enormous mental strain involved in composing it and the resulting deficiencies of the story. Indeed, many critics concur with Conrad's assessment, pointing to the story's excessive length (over 20,000 words), laborious style, tedious characters, unconvincing dialogue, and incongruous shifts in point of view.[227] While Conrad first thought the story good, with an admirable 'moral effect', the criticism of his trusted touchstone, editor Edward Garnett, alerted Conrad to the story's faults and he soon came to despair of it: 'what I've written seems to me too contemptible for words. Not in conception perhaps, but in execution'.[228] Conrad's correspondence from this period reflects the intensity of his dissatisfaction with the story. He wrote to Garnett on September 27, 1897:

> The work is vile—or else good. I don't know. I can't know. But I swear to you that I won't alter a line—a word—not a comma—for you. There! And this for the reason that I have a physical horror of that

story. I simply won't look at it any more. It has embittered five months of my life. I hate it.²²⁹

And on October 11:

> [I wrote the 'The Return'] with a constant, haunting fear of being lost in the midst of thickening untruth. I felt all the time there was *something* [emphasis in the original] wrong with that story. I feel it now more than ever.²³⁰

Conrad said that his frustration with the story stemmed largely from his inadequate portrayal of the Alvan Hervey character and his failure to effectively satirize the 'beastly bourgeois'. In light of the commentary above, however, it is tempting to speculate that Conrad's conflicting thoughts on Wilde may also have contributed to the anxiety provoked by 'The Return'.²³¹ Conrad later commented that despite the 'dismal wonder' he felt rereading the story, there were doubtless good psychological reasons for his writing it.²³² Perhaps one of those reasons was the author's subconscious desire to revisit, and reconcile himself to, the ex-prisoner Wilde.

Mrs (Rosa) Campbell Praed

The Scourge-Stick (1898)

Rosa Praed's second fictional depiction of Wilde, after her 1885 portrait in *Affinities*, appeared in 1898's *The Scourge-Stick*. As mentioned in Part 1, Wilde did not appear to harbor any resentment about his demonic depiction in Praed's earlier novel and the subsequent friendly relations between the two authors seem to have continued unabated. In 1888 Wilde wrote a genial note to Praed in his capacity as editor of *The Woman's World*:

> Your article on America is so delightful that I hope you will contribute to a monthly magazine to which I have been asked to become literary adviser. I am anxious to make it the organ through which women of culture and position will express their views . . . I have a long list already of contributors and hope you will allow me to add your name.
> Could you write me a short article on Royat, where I hear you are going?'²³³

'At Royat' by Praed duly appeared in *The Woman's World* in 1888. Praed and Wilde still appeared to be on good terms in 1892, when

Praed attended the first night of *Lady Windermere's Fan* in February.²³⁴ It is possible that Praed became closer to Wilde as time passed; her second fictional version of him is much kinder than her first, which is remarkable considering that it was published just three years after the event of his ignominious disgrace.

The protagonist in *The Scourge-Stick* is Esther Vassal, a sensitive girl who, faced with poverty, marries a wealthy older man whose cruel nature she quickly grows to hate. After turning to writing to relieve her depression, Esther's pseudonymous first novel becomes a great success. Starved for affection, she enters into an affair with her publisher's reader, a married man who she later discovers is her husband's nephew and heir. Esther becomes pregnant and is forced to give up her lover for the sake of her son; they are never reunited. The tone of Praed's highly melodramatic novel, which is largely in the form of diary-style entries by Vassal, is often desperate and bleak. Patricia Clarke and other commentators have noted that this heightened intensity can be attributed to the novel's largely autobiographical content: Vassal—a novelist, like Praed—is hopelessly trapped in a loveless marriage much like Praed's own.²³⁵ Clarke also highlights Praed's 'aversion to heterosexual relations'; the author later separated from her husband and lived with a woman she called her 'twin soul', Nancy Harward.²³⁶

In addition to the reflections of Praed's troubled home life in the novel, *The Scourge-Stick*, like *Affinities*, often borrows from the author's experience of London's literary and theatrical worlds. In particular, Praed directly transposed many of the letters she received from publishers, readers, and critics in documenting Esther's Vassal's early writing career.²³⁷ She also reproduced actual conversations (which she was in the habit of recording) and appropriated several of her real-life associates for the novel, including the dramatic critic Joe Knight, who appears as Frank Leete, and Oscar Wilde, who is unmistakable as the Oxford don, writer, and critic Cosmo Paravel. Paravel is one of the members of the London 'bohemian contingent'—many of whom have been satirized by *Punch*—who attend Mr Vassal's parties. Esther Vassal writes,

> Mione says of [the 'medieval-looking' Paravel with his 'stained glass face'] that he ought to carry a halo under his arm when he goes out to a party, instead of an opera hat. He is . . . a man of grave thinkings which are often hidden under a show of aesthetic fantasy; a writer on art subjects, his chosen period the Renaissance, so that sometimes his talk is as an echo of the troubadours, or a waft from the Rose of Chivalry. He interests me in a fashion. Just now he is meditating a new work, of which he has told me the gist—²³⁸

Like Wilde, Paravel is remarkably genial in the face of hostile criticism and is on excellent terms with members of the female aristocracy, most notably the waggish Lady Diana Cleeve. (An ex-minister in the Vassal party observes that 'Lady Diana . . . divides humanity into four classes . . . men, women, politicians, and—Paravel'.[239]) The drama critic Leete identifies Paravel as being responsible for one of English literature's 'running sores . . . the little host of doctrinaires . . . who write biographies and lay down the law about everything'.[240] Paravel's doctrines are undeniably Wildean; he declares himself inordinately fond of superstition ('Alas! The Reformation killed our superstition, and at the same time it killed our art'),[241] and discourses eloquently in his 'deep', 'poetic', and 'musical' voice on the Wildean subjects of temperament and individuality:

> 'Shall I tell you what it is that absolutely rules the world? It is temperament . . . I speak of "temperament" in its English sense . . . not in its usual French adaptation . . . [temperament is] . . . an imponderable quantity—a mist, an atmosphere, which permeates, surrounds, qualifies, and binds together an individuality—an unknown something, no more to be analysed than you can analyse animal magnetism or spiritual affinity. A link between body and soul; of the substance of both, and yet neither. Briefly, the very essence of personality'.[242]

Though intrigued by Paravel's musings on such subjects, Esther Vassal, is puzzled as to her husband's interest in him:

> I have been wondering what his attraction can be to [my husband] that he has been invited to join this yachting party. Yet I have sometimes fancied that Mr. Vassal's tendency towards psychological analysis is stronger than I had imagined.[243]

Indeed, the aesthetic and sensitive Paravel does seem a curious cohort for Esther's brash and unsympathetic husband, a man who abhors sentimentality and refers to poetry as 'drivel'.[244] The mention of Paravel's psychological interest probably reflects the recent revelations regarding Wilde's sexuality. Mr Vassal is unusually confident that Paravel's attentions to his wife do not present a romantic threat, as evidenced by the following conversation with Lady Cleeve:

> 'Mr. Vassal, I've come to tell you that Cosmo Paravel is quoting Dante to your wife, and that you'd better go and look after her.'
>   'Thank you . . . But I'm not afraid of Dante.'
>   'Nor of Mr. Paravel?'
>   'Nor of Paravel.'[245]

Mr Vassal's interest in Paravel's psychological makeup may also derive from his interest in the 'darker' side of life, although Paravel is more harmlessly aesthetic than dangerously decadent.

Vassal, after 'scour[ing] the Arabian town of] Mandour in search . . . of a sensation', arranges for his friends to watch 'a meeting of religious madmen', who swallow live snakes and practice ritual sacrifice. Paravel, however, is the least interested in this spectacle and the first to leave.[246]

Reviews of *The Scourge-Stick* were mixed; although several critics complimented the book's 'atmosphere' and character development, most found fault with Praed's style, technique, and narrative construction. The distinctiveness of Praed's sketch of Paravel—referred to by one critic as 'the last thing in dilettanti dons'—was noted,[247] but her dismal picture of marriage did not prove popular with reviewers or the public, and the book was never reprinted after the second edition.[248]

Given the year that Praed's story was published, it is curious that it is Vassal who is fascinated by the darker side of decadence and not the Wildean Paravel. It is possible that Praed wrote the Paravel sections before Wilde's downfall; she began work on *The Scourge-Stick* at the beginning of the decade. However, we know that Praed did not tie the threads of her novel together until 1897, over two years after Wilde's disgrace.[249] In light of this fact, Praed's decision not to demonize the Wilde character would appear to reflect a degree of sympathy with a long-standing associate.

Cyril Arthur Edward Ranger Gull

The Hypocrite (1898)

Miss Malevolent (1899)

The fourth Wildean fiction to appear in 1898, *The Hypocrite*, was published anonymously in November and reached a fifth edition in less than a year. The author was Cyril Arthur Edward Ranger Gull (1876–1923), a Fleet Street journalist who published a prolific amount of fiction under his own name and the pseudonym 'Guy Thorne'.[250] Gull was educated at Oxford and embarked upon a career as a journalist in London from the late 1890s.[251] He spent a great deal of time on the Strand, which he later recalled as home to '[m]any of the writers and artists of the [d]ecadence'.[252] Some of these were Wilde's associates; Gull was particularly friendly with Wilde's publisher in later years, Leonard Smithers. The publisher Grant Richards remembered Gull as 'an odd, attractive, and rather unprincipled little chap'.[253] Gull fictionalized Wilde in *The Hypocrite* and another little-known novel, *Miss Malevolent*, published the following year. In addition, it is not generally known that Gull published two biographical works on Wilde in the early years of the twentieth century, under the name of Leonard Cresswell Ingleby. While Wilde scholars have largely dismissed the biographical works as highly partial, however, they present a fascinating adjunct to Gull's earlier fictions.[254]

In 1898, Gull's publishers promoted the 22-year-old's *Hypocrite* as 'a powerful realistic story of modern life in Oxford and London'. The central character in both of these settings is Caradoc Yardly Gobion, a perpetually inebriated aesthete and swindler who 'talks nonsense very pleasantly'. Gobion draws upon his assets of 'felicity and facility of expression, more or less wide reading, and [his] power of intuition and knowledge of the public mind' to take advantage of every situation.[255] Gull's depiction of Gobion demonizes Wilde to an inordinate degree; *The Hypocrite* is a tendentious diatribe on egotism, artifice, and depravity in the wake of Wilde's disgrace. The cover features a man in evening dress with features sufficiently ambiguous to suggest Wilde's; he has a menacing expression and is holding a smiling mask.

In the novel, Gobion is first seen as a student at Oxford, arrogantly describing his influence over his gullible contemporaries to two caddish friends, Union President Mordaunt Sturtevant and Merton churchman Condamine:

> 'owing to my youthful appearance and earnest eyes, I have an admiring circle of people who worship me as their god—good, healthy, red people, who like moonlight in the quad, and read leading articles ... It is very amusing. I wear a great mass of hair, and look at them with far-away eyes instinct with intellectual pain; and sometimes when we get very solemn, the tears rise slowly, and I talk in clear tones of effort, of will—the toil, the struggle, the Glorious Reward! They absolutely love me, and I live on them, borrow their allowances, drink their whiskey—in short, rook them largely all round'.[256]

Gull, who would have heard something of Wilde's undergraduate career as an orator while at Oxford, goes on to describe Gobion's success at the Oxford Wadham debate and its intoxicating effect on the egotistical aesthete:

> he spoke well and brilliantly, and [afterward he] lit his cigarette with a pleasing sense of strength and nerve running through him. The

sunshine of applause seemed to warm his impressionable brain, to make it expand with the power of receiving and mentally recording more vivid impressions. He had a pleasing consciousness of being very young and very interesting . . . He felt instinctively how all his carefully-studied tricks of manner and personal eccentricities told. The big football-playing, warm-hearted undergraduates admired him for his soft felt hat, his terra-cotta tie, his way of arranging his hands when he sat down, and his epigrams.[257]

Gobion's epigrams contain many echoes of, and plays on, Wildean aphorisms. Where Wilde stated '[s]cience is the record of dead religions', Gobion declares 'the sham of yesterday takes an alias and calls itself the religion of the future'.[258] Wilde's famous comment that the 'aim of the critic is to see the object as . . . it really is not', is transformed into Gobion's observation that the 'cynic only sees things as they really are'.[259] Gobion also resembles Wilde in his ability to argue a point from both sides. However, rather than suggesting a complex personality that embraced diversity, Gull asserts that Gobion's philosophical flexibility is a tool used to cultivate the good will and financial benevolence of others, a tactic that is almost invariably successful.

Someone who *is* immune to Gobion's charms, however, is his father, who disowns his son when the full extent of Gobion's misbehavior becomes apparent. The Oxford student's dissolute life of drinking, debt, and dalliances with 'low' women constitute an exaggerated version of Wilde's undergraduate shenanigans as imagined by Gull some twenty years after the event. Curiously, Gull adds a dismal academic record to Gobion's list of failings. (As outlined in Part 1, Wilde, while often lax in his adherence to university rules, had an enviable academic reputation.) Wilde's attraction to Roman Catholicism while at Oxford is also reduced in Gobion to a sly means of procuring money from a sympathetic priest.[260] It is after Gobion's father cuts off his allowance that the reader first sees the cold, heartless Gobion behind the 'mask':

> The feeling of ruin was already passing away, and his face lost its sweetness and youth, while a sharp keen look took its place—the look that he wore when at night he was alone and plotting, a haggard, old look which no one ever saw but Condamine or Sturtevant.[261]

Alongside such passages, which present Gobion as almost a caricature of evil, Gull devotes a significant amount of space to character analysis—albeit intensely moralistic—of Gobion/Wilde. In the following lines

Gull imagines a past to account for the strange depravity of his egoist:

> [Gobion] saw himself a boy of fifteen, keenly sensitive and inordinately vain. He remembered how his eager hunger for admiration had lead him to pose even to his father and mother; how, when he found out he was clever, he used to lie carefully to conceal his misdoings from them. Gradually and slowly he had grown more evil and more bitter at the narrowness which misunderstood him. When love had gone the deterioration was more marked, and he threw himself into grossness. His imagination was too quick and vivid to let him live in vice wholly without remorse, and every now and again he wildly and passionately confessed his sins and turned his back on them . . . Then after a week or two the emotional fervour of repentance would wear off, and he would plunge more deeply into vice, and lead a jolly, wicked life.[262]

Homosexual activity is never directly identified as one of Gobion's transgressions, but Gull frequently alludes to it. Gobion's life is described as 'unnatural' and he frequents a mysterious 'Grecian' bar in London. Gull goes beyond a green carnation to signal Gobion's homosexuality, giving his wicked protagonist an entire green suit.[263] Gobion's unsavory companions are also implicated in this lifestyle; Sturtevant frequents the same Grecian bar and he, Gobion, and Condamine are described as being 'bound together by many an orgie [*sic*] [and] shady intrigue'. However, Gull's Gobion, like Wilde, is also popular with women, and females feature in Gobion's memories of 'hot kisses . . . suppers and patchouli-scented rooms' in Oxford and London.[264] The aesthete indulges in these trysts despite his 'one pure affection' for country girl Marjorie Lovering, a 17-year-old clergyman's daughter. When Gobion feels no remorse after Marjorie severs her ties to him, he realizes with some regret that his soul has finally 'passed into the twilight'. Gobion ascribes his predilection for 'shady pleasures' to the bad behavior of his father, a 'repentant rake' who paid scant attention to his children. As discussed in Part 2, the philandering of Wilde's father had previously been alluded to by Arthur Conan Doyle as a likely cause of Wilde's sexual 'aberrations'.[265]

Gull also implies that Wilde has a 'sinister influence' on impressionable young men with his portrayal of the relationship between Gobion and the curiously named Bravery Reginald Scott. Scott is 'a good young man, rather commonplace in intellect, but of a blameless life', who has been seduced by Gobion's fantastic talk and 'nobleness of ideal and breadth of thought'.[266] Gobion shamelessly constructs an image of purity and unworldliness for Scott in order to extract money from him; at one point he even paints dark circles under his eyes in order to stir the young man's pity. A more serious manipulation is also suggested; the observant reader cannot fail to note the implied nature of Gobion and Scott's relationship. They are seen together in Oxford walking arm in arm in the moonlight and many years later Scott tells Gobion, 'Don't you know you've *always* [emphasis in the original] got me? Don't you remember how once for a joke in those Ship Street rooms you made me put my hands between yours and swear to be your man? Well, it wasn't a joke—to me'.[267]

Apart from Gobion's relationship with Scott, there is also mention of a 'disgraceful affair' with an Anglican canon's son which required much 'hush[ing] up'. The reader is told that 'the poor boy, dazzled by being in the society of men of whom he heard everyone talking, made a fool of himself and came to utter grief, much to the pecuniary benefit of Condamine, Sturtevant, and Gobion'.[268] Indeed, there is little distinction made between the proclivity to commit sexual 'misdemeanors' and the proclivity to commit blackmail and other crimes in Gull's novel. Gull's amalgamation of these tendencies in Gobion probably reflects the wide publicity given to blackmailing 'renters' during Wilde's trials three years before.

After Gobion's enforced departure from Oxford (due to financial hardship), his new career as a journalist in London affords Gull further opportunity to deride Wilde. Just as Wilde made a living by writing clever, flippant reviews after leaving Oxford, Gobion writes for *The Pilgrim*, a distinctly decadent publication read by 'all the young men and women who considered themselves clever, and who, under the comprehensive shield of "soul", sucked poison from strange flowers'.[269]

In light of Gull's comparison of Gobion with his fellow *Pilgrim* journalists, it must be granted that the author is capable of providing an astute appraisal of Wilde's personality:

> Although Gobion was of a somewhat finer nature than most [journalists working on the *Pilgrim*], he recognized the type instantly. Cheap cynicism was the keynote of most of the conversation, and his lighter side revelled in it. Most complex of all men, he could suck pleasure from every shade of feeling. Lord Tennyson's beautiful line: 'A glorious devil large in heart and brain', fitted him exactly. With his intellect he might have been saint, instead of which he was sublime in nothing whatever. With the face of an angel, he loved goodness for its beauty, and sin for its excitement.[270]

Once again, however, Gull quickly moves on from such insights to further vilify his subject. While Wilde's career in journalism was curtailed by his success as a novelist and dramatist, Gobion's sojourn on

Fleet Street comes to an end after his treacherous denouncement of the *Pilgrim*'s editor in a rival newspaper; after this incident Gobion is blacklisted by every paper in London. Undeterred, he joins forces with Sturtevant to swindle a rich young lord for £1,000. However, Sturtevant turns the tables on Gobion by leaving the country with all the money, leaving Gobion a wry note and just £10 of the profits.

Gull, perhaps inspired by stories of Wilde's postprison life in Paris, transports his now disgraced and destitute Gobion to a squalid London boarding house, worlds away from his former life of pleasure and excess. At first reveling in the new sensations of poverty, Gobion soon wearies of a life without luxury and determines to take his own life. Even this most traumatic of experiences, however, leaves Gobion strangely nonplussed. Insincerity has become so much a part of his nature that he is no longer capable of evoking any real feeling, even in contemplating his own suicide.

The 'just deserts' that the reader has long been expecting soon follow. After the most unappealing of last meals in a Houndsditch public house, the former lord of language is at a loss for words as well as feeling; the suicide note he leaves for Scott simply reads 'Goodbye'.[271] His death by chloroform is similarly prosaic, apart from the dying visions he has of his mother, which leave him whimpering in horror in a corner.[272] Although Wilde died of natural causes in Paris two years after publication of *The Hypocrite*, Gull's image of an impoverished fallen literary idol dying ignominiously in a run-down hotel room is notably prophetic.

Unsurprisingly, Gobion's death serves to demonstrate to the reader the price to be paid for leading a dissolute life. His sole mourner is Scott, who has become a priest and who romanticizes Gobion in a novel and in his sermons. Gobion's other intimates remember him as an ungrateful fool who was 'rather poor fun' despite his 'considerable personal charm'.[273] Gull, in his description of young man-about-town Bradley Bere in the closing chapter, set twenty years after Gobion's death, suggests that Wilde's was not a unique personality:

> Mr. Bradley Bere was . . . a youth apparently of seventeen, but of a great name; the rich uncleanness of his life almost rivalling his stories, and both being given undue prominence by his friends in the weekly press . . . [Bere said] that poetry was the pursuit of the unattainable by the unbearable, hoping [it would be repeated] as having come from him.[274]

The allusion in this passage is to Wilde's *A Woman of No Importance* (1893) and Lord Illingsworth's reference to the 'English country gentleman galloping after a fox' as 'the unspeakable in full pursuit of the uneatable'.[275] Gull implies that Wilde is just one of a long line of sensationalists, and that only his clever words, not his memory, will endure.

Clearly, Gull firmly positioned himself on the moral high ground in the wake of Wilde's disgrace. If we are to take Gull at his word, there was no significant relationship between himself and Wilde; in his later 'Ingleby' books, Gull states that he only heard Wilde speak on two (unspecified) occasions.[276] It is possible that Gull's more insightful descriptions of Wilde's personality reflect detailed information provided by one or more mutual acquaintances. As stated above Gull was on friendly terms with Wilde's publisher Leonard Smithers, and through that connection would have had the opportunity to meet More Adey, Aubrey Beardsley, Charles Conder, Ernest Dowson, Robert Sherard, Vincent O'Sullivan, Rennell Rodd, and Will Rothenstein.

Gull's preface to the third edition of *The Hypocrite* may throw some light on his motivation for writing the novel. In this preface he defends the book from the charges of immorality that had been directed at it from several quarters:

> Here I have taken an idea, the idea of a fine-brained scamp. I have endeavoured to show, by a history of his career, the awful and inevitable end of a life which is devoted to pleasure of the body and pleasure of the mind, without any sense of duty. *Circumstance threw me into a kind of life which was evil in its conception and unhappy in its execution. From that I made my book* [my italics] . . . it seems to me that in these dark times, *in the light of the life I have known and seen* [my italics], no words can be too tipped with fire, no expression of experience can be too strong, to make clear the results of folly and sin. I commit myself to a moral view of life rather than an artistic view of life. I hope to be thought sincere.[277]

These comments suggest some interesting possibilities. Gull may have been closely involved with Wilde, or someone in Wilde's decadent circle. It could be that there is an autobiographical element to the young Scott's earnest devotion to Gobion, and the latter's careless dismissal of his young disciple. If Gull, the son of a Church of England minister, really did believe that he had experienced a narrow escape from decadent 'folly and sin', it would certainly account for his fervid moralism on the subject of Wilde.

Of course, it is also possible that Gull implied a personal connection to Wilde in his preface to promote interest in his book; the novel's anonymous publication may also have been intended to encourage this assumption and boost sales. Contemporary reports like Grant Richards's suggest that Gull was not averse to bending the truth in order to succeed. If Gull intended to promote conjecture with his book he certainly did succeed; like *The Silver Domino* and *The Green Carnation*, the novel inspired much speculation regarding its authorship. The suspicion that the book was written by a member of Wilde's circle may have been the reason that the Mudie Library refused to circulate it, although in his *Hypocrite* preface Gull attributed this to a misguided belief that the book's subject was 'improper'.[278]

Whatever Gull's reasons for his prefatory statements and anonymous authorship of *The Hypocrite*, it is clear from the fervid moral tone of his novel that he meant to record his disapproval of Wilde's 'artistic view of life', perhaps with a view to capitalizing on the wholesale condemnation of Wilde that was occurring at the time.[279] Indeed, Gull's censorious approach proved highly successful with the 'philistine' public; the book sold well and the popular press lauded the novel as a forceful sermon against immorality. The *Echo* compared its brilliance with *The Green Carnation*, *Lloyds* applauded the 'vividly drawn' caricatures of actual persons, and the *London Morning* commended the book's 'brutally frank analysis of the temperament of a man with brain and mind hopelessly diseased'.[280]

Gull published an anonymous 'companion volume' to *The Hypocrite* the following year. Entitled *Miss Malevolent* (1899), Gull's second novel tells the story of Kitty Nugent, a mean-spirited and unscrupulous flirt who conducts a vendetta against the married artist Gilbert Russhe, who has spurned her advances. Interestingly, one of the dedicatees ('in friendship') of this book is Richard Le Gallienne, who, as mentioned in Part 2, was a close friend and fictionalizer of Wilde. Perhaps it was in deference to Le Gallienne that Gull made his portrait of Wilde in *Miss Malevolent* a much kinder one; the renowned poet and journalist Guy Waye, friend to both Nugent and Russhe, is a far more sympathetic character than his fictional predecessor in *The Hypocrite*. Waye is also more carefully disguised than Gobion, perhaps as a result of the Mudie Library's objection to Gull's previous Wildean novel. In his preface to *Miss Malevolent*, Gull asserts,

> When my last book, 'The Hypocrite', appeared, it was said in various quarters that some of the characters in it were faithful portraits of well-known living people. In order to prevent another such misconception, I beg to say that 'Miss Malevolent' contains no portraits whatever, so no one need be offended.[281]

However, the reader soon perceives that Gull is dissembling here; Guy Waye is surely based on Wilde. His 'light badinage and flow of talk' ('Paradox is only truth standing on its head to attract attention'), the 'refined delicacy' of his writing style, his heightened appreciation of beautiful objects, his love of physical ease and his appetite for delicacies like *fois gras* and hothouse gooseberries, are all indicators of his original.[282] Further hints are contained in his 'dreamy' moods and discourses on Shakespeare, which he delivers 'in a pretty but rather affected way' with 'a deep, mellow voice [which resounds] with conscious periods . . . every dactyl had its full significance'. The casual observer quickly deduces that Waye is 'no mere dilettante . . . an indefinable air of manner and pose told you instinctively that he was successful and a man who had "arrived"'. Waye's aesthetic dress, long hair, 'deep grey eyes' and 'long thin face in which sensuality struggled with intellect', are also clearly Wilde's.[283] Waye's style and slender physique suggest a younger Wilde, and indeed Waye's age is specified as 30.

Further allusions to the 'first phase' Wilde are made with Waye's fondness for writing 'prose poems' and observation: 'I am a great temperament, a sort of stringed instrument upon which the sorrows of others strike, and their pain gives music to the world'.[284] Here Gull refers to Wilde's 1881 poem 'Hélas!':

> To drift with every passion till my soul
> Is a stringed lute on which all winds can play
>
> Is it for this that I have given away
> Mine ancient wisdom, and austere control?[285]

Gull adds several blinds to counter these obvious allusions to Wilde, including Waye's 'middle height', small lips, moustache, lack of university education, and accent. Waye's accent is a curious mix of 'north-country' and American resonances; perhaps an allusion to Wilde's Irish heritage and lecture tour of America. However, these cursory screens cannot disguise Waye's derivation, particularly in light of the following passage:

> [Waye] was a well-known figure in modern literature, and in many cases a well-hated figure also . . . he had succeeded in publishing some fourteen or fifteen books of verse and essays, no single one of which had failed. There is an idea that success in literature makes enemies; but even if the idea is true, it was not merely his success that had made many important people enemies of this man. He had offended certain sections of society by his extreme outspokenness on questions of sex,

which he spoke of and wrote of in an open and possibly sometimes in an inopportune manner.[286]

In addition to Waye's Wildean propensity for such transgressions, he also demonstrates Wilde's familiar fusion of masculine and feminine traits. He is roundly mocked for his 'feminine sympathies', has 'a girlish way', is 'too soft and caressing' with women, and revels in the admiration of his female fans. With men, however, he can drop his '*[a]ir des femmes*' to reveal a manly strength, drink beer, smoke a pipe, and have his 'cold tub in the morning like everyone else'.[287]

Gull's comments on Waye's aesthetic circle clearly reflect his opinion of Wilde's coterie, as previously recorded in *The Hypocrite*:

> These men always said and did whatever occurred to them, and their every night was more unhealthy and sapping to the brain than inexpressible orgies [*sic*]; for they were like those Parisian looking-glasses you can buy in the toy shops, distorting all they reflect in quaint and fantastic parodies of the truth ... they were immoral and had no sense of duty ... All they wrote, acted, painted, played had an astonishingly bad effect upon a far larger circle than their achievements ever warranted.[288]

Despite Gull's clear disapproval of the decadents, and his former disparaging fictional portrait of Wilde in Gobion, *Miss Malevolent* offers a far more attractive version of Wilde. While Waye is ensconced among the aesthetic set, his strength of character and 'finer side' also set him apart from them. He is 'a sweet-natured, decent-tongued man', who is shocked at Nugent's cold-hearted malevolence.[289] It is Waye who warns Russhe about Nugent's base nature and devises a plan to save his friend from her wicked machinations. Waye also encourages Reginald, one of his disillusioned decadent associates, to break from the group and retire to the country, recognizing the ill-effects of their lifestyle on his weaker personality. Waye, like Wilde, is consistently charming and kind, and the narrator implies that, as a result of 'his qualities of brain, his knowledge, his cleverness, and his achievements', he should not be judged by the standards applied to ordinary people.[290]

Clearly, in the period between the publication of *The Hypocrite* in 1898 and *Miss Malevolent* in 1899, Gull had substantially revised his opinion of Wilde. Was this the result of Le Gallienne's or another's influence? It is possible that, just as Alfred Douglas insisted that the editor of *The Ephemeral* meet Wilde in person after publishing a derogatory portrait of him (see Part 2), one of Wilde's friends arranged a meeting for Gull with a similar intention? Whatever the case, Gull's twentieth-century, nonfictional writings on Wilde under the Ingleby pseudonym, *Oscar Wilde* (1907) and *Oscar Wilde: Some Reminiscences* (1912),[291] demonstrate that Gull continued to waver between approbation of Wilde and his work and condemnation of the decadence he represented. The 1907 book, in which Gull intersperses commentary on Wilde's nature with (somewhat impercipient) descriptions of his writings, presents an extraordinary combination of praise and censure. The author includes quotations from the popular press, Henry Labouchere, and Max Nordau to demonstrate the diversity of responses to Wilde in the wake of his disgrace.

Gull's *Oscar Wilde* is most significant for our purposes in demonstrating that, while Gull was obviously reluctant to praise Wilde or his work soon after the scandal, he continued to exhibit a degree of sympathy for the fallen decadent. While Gull questions the wisdom of *De Profundis*, an expurgated version of which had been published two years before ('a brilliant piece of literature and an amazing tissue of misrepresentations'),[292] he argues that Wilde's 'social downfall' can be attributed to 'a certain kind of elliptiform insanity' and that this unfortunate state of affairs should not lessen the public's appreciation of the genius displayed in Wilde's work.[293] Gull concludes that Wilde was 'one of the strangest, saddest, most artistic and powerful brains of modern times'.[294] The possibility that Gull's revised view of Wilde was the result of a personal encounter with the latter is also suggested by his recollection that '[o]n the two occasions when I myself heard Oscar Wilde talking, I realised how unprecedented his talent for conversation was, and wished that I could hear him at times when he attempted his highest flights'.[295]

Every acknowledgment of Wilde's good nature and genius in Gull's *Oscar Wilde*, however, is tempered with a corresponding qualification that recalls the author's previous tone in *The Hypocrite*:

> Generous-hearted, free with all material things, kind to the unfortunate, gentle to the weak—Oscar Wilde was all these things. Yet, at the same time, he committed the most dreadful crimes against the social well-being; without a thought of those his influence led into terrible paths, without a thought of those nearest and dearest to him, he deliberately imposed upon them a horror and a shame with an extraordinary and almost unparalleled callousness and hardness of heart.[296]

Such curiously mitigated praise occurs repeatedly in *Oscar Wilde*: Gull commends Wilde's poetry, then highlights passages where the latter has been overly imitative. He praises Wilde's society plays and calls his 'Poems in Prose' 'blasphemous and horrible'.[297] It appears that, despite the sympathetic leanings toward Wilde that were first discernible in *Miss Malevolent*, Gull was either conflicted about his opinion of Wilde or was afraid of appearing to be a Wilde sympathizer.

Gull's second biographical work, *Oscar Wilde: Some Reminiscences*, a 'book of personalia' published five years later, rehashes much of his first biography and adds some quotations from Wilde and further reflections on Wilde's personality by those who knew him. Probably as a result of the general public's renewed interest in, and sympathy for Wilde at this time, Gull's second book is far less trenchant than its predecessor. As Gull observes in *Reminiscences*, '[t]o-day the name of Oscar Wilde is no longer identified solely with disaster and shame. It is a name the world recognises as standing for the work of a powerful, if bizarre, genius without parallel in our time'.[298] Gull no longer depicts Wilde as tragically insane, but as an 'unhappy genius'. Wilde's 'dreadful crimes against the social well-being' become '[t]hings he had done, or was supposed to have done, things for which he suffered very grievously'.[299]

Whether Gull's fictional and nonfictional depictions of Wilde reflect a genuine endeavor to come to terms with an infamous contemporary, or an attempt to profit by a fleeting brush with infamy, we are unlikely to discover at this chronological distance. What is clear from Gull's writing on Wilde is the powerful fascination that the latter's personality exercised on one of his contemporaries. Interestingly, if Richard Aldington's memory is to be relied upon, Gull grew rather Wildean himself with age. Aldington remembered the older Gull as being a worldly and portly '*bon vivant*', who 'never refused a double whisky' and 'thought very highly of his abilities'.[300]

Curtis Yorke (Susan Richmond Lee)

Valentine: A Story of Ideals (1899)

The poet Fabian Wade, in *Valentine: A Story of Ideals* by Curtis Yorke (the pseudonym of Susan Richmond Lee) (1854?–1930), was to be Wilde's final fictional incarnation of the nineteenth century. Little is known about Richmond Lee; she was born in Glasgow as Susan Rowley Long, married a mining engineer, lived in North Kensington, contributed to various magazines, and wrote more than fifty romance novels, many of which ran to several editions.[301] *Valentine* is typically lightweight 'Curtis Yorke' fare; the novel documents the romantic trials and tribulations of 16-year-old *ingénue* Valentine Glynn during her first London season. The fifth edition cites *The Speaker*'s judgment that '[i]t would . . . be hard to find a brighter, cheerier book'.

Glynn first encounters the Wildean Wade soon after her arrival in London, at an afternoon party thrown by her aunt. The affected 30-year-old aesthete is known primarily as a risqué poet, as Wilde was at the same age. Wade is referred to as 'a *wild*-looking creature [my italics]', and indeed he has the young Wilde's pale, 'cameo-like' face, 'dreamy, half-shut eyes' and long hair that 'wave[s] over his ears and collar, and [hangs] heavily upon his white forehead'.[302] Wade's overornamented conversation consists mainly of effusive reflections on youth, the 'true artist', the soul, and floral subjects ('I never could bear orchids. They are so fatiguing'). He also delivers Wildean witticisms, such as '[women] only find their hearts to lose them' and '[s]ecurity always brings satiety. It is in uncertainty that we find rapture'.[303] (The last remark recalls Wilde's aphorism in *Dorian Gray*: 'A cigarette is the perfect type of a perfect pleasure. It is exquisite and it leaves one unsatisfied'.[304])

While Wade's attributes and dialogue are clearly intended to suggest Wilde, there is much in Richmond Lee's portrait to indicate that—while she may have met Wade's original—her acquaintance with him was slight. In this regard, Fabian Wade resembles Broughton's Francis Chaloner in *Second Thoughts*, examined in Part 1. Wade is not a sympathetic character and like Chaloner is fragile, melancholic, and essentially humorless, all un-Wildean characteristics that were often assumed to be typical of the young aesthete in the 1870s and 1880s. Several of Wade's other qualities also suggest that Wilde was not well known to Richmond Lee; his 'monotonous' voice is mentioned several times, whereas Wilde was known for the rich and varied tone of his speech. Wade avoids Greek philosophy, one of Wilde's favorite subjects, and his observations are usually nonsensical and rarely 'hit home' like Wilde's. Wade is also a believer in 'the supremacy and superiority of man', whereas Wilde, as mentioned earlier in this study, demonstrated progressive views on 'the woman question' and was friendly with many 'New Woman' authors. Perhaps the most un-Wildean of Wade's quirks is his abstemiousness; he does not smoke, hardly eats, and does not drink alcohol, tea, or coffee but prefers to drink milk and water 'with the aid of a tea-spoon'! (The brassy Gilberte Fanshawe asks, 'Is tea too strong for you? Or are you too weak for tea'?[305]) Richmond Lee's portrait suggests unfamiliarity rather than deliberate satire, and as with Broughton's novel, a reliance on early aesthetic stereotypes.

Although the *ingénue* Glynn is at first drawn to the eccentric poet, his pretensions, selfishness, and egotism soon begin to 'jar upon her'.[306] Like many of the portraits examined here, the negativity of Richmond Lee's portrait may reflect some ill feeling toward Wilde. As discussed above in relation to Dixon, Stannard, and Carrel, many of

Wilde's female contemporaries appear to have felt slighted after experiencing his flattering but fleeting attentions. It is perhaps significant that, while Glynn is pleased that Wade speaks to her 'as if her intellect were on a par with his own', the reader is told that

> [Wade] talked to most young girls in this strain . . . his dreamy utterances were all, to a certain extent, formulas, subject to various alterations . . . he possessed, in a marked degree, the faculty of seeming absorbed in his companion of the moment.[307]

Richmond Lee appears to think little of Wilde's poetic talents, if Wade's are anything to go by. After Wade composes a spontaneous and rather extravagant ode to Glynn, Gilberte Fanshawe mocks his effort by producing her own verse composition in fifteen minutes, poking fun at Wade's vanity and pretentiousness:

> TO A POET—CURLING HIS HAIR.
>
> To thee, whom I see, at day's dawn,
> Thy garment the finest of lawn,
>
> With the tongs poised aloft, like a bird,
> As thou curlest a second and third
>
> Tuft of lank-falling hair, can one dream,
> When uncurled, how queer thou must seem!
>
> No longer a wonder, one can
> Only find thee a common young man.
>
> O poets, who reason in rhyme,
> Get your hair cut, it's just about time![308]

Richmond Lee also makes much of Wade's 'lady-like' manner: 'Certainly there was a certain effeminacy in the gentle poet's mien'.[309] However, as with several of the fictions discussed in this study, *Valentine* simultaneously casts its Wildean character as a womanizer; one character attributes this trait to Wade's poetic profession.[310] Wade gazes amorously at Glynn and other women in the novel. Fanshawe determines to make a fool of the poet and shamelessly flatters him until, dazzled, he proposes. Fanshawe promptly refuses him, saying 'I could never marry a man who wore his hair like a woman'.[311]

Wade's exit from the novel and Glynn's life occurs exactly as he had predicted. Captivated by Glynn at their first meeting—'[t]he very young, the very fresh, always interest me'—Wade tells her at the outset that '[w]hen you have gone through a few London seasons, my interest in you will fade'.[312] Sure enough, when he observes that the death of Glynn's uncle has 'withdrawn the charm of [her] unspoilt naïveté', Wade's interest in Glynn abruptly ceases:

> 'you have discovered, perchance, that you have a heart. From that point femininity becomes interesting to the man of the world. But to the artist—to the poet—the bloom has gone. Gone—irrevocably. Farewell—we may not meet again'.³¹³

* * *

On November 30, 1900, the year after Richmond Lee's *Valentine* was published, Wilde died in his room at the Hôtel d'Alsace in Paris, of cerebral meningitis. After spending three and a half years as an itinerant social pariah, occasionally managing to travel the continent with friends, but always financially embarrassed, Wilde's indignities were finally at an end.³¹⁴ His faithful friend Robert Ross, who was with him when he died, related that Wilde jested during his final days that he could not outlive the century as 'the English people would not stand it'.³¹⁵ Ross wrote to Adela Schuster that Wilde's passing was for the best, as '[t]wo things were absolutely necessary for him, contact with comely things . . . and social position'. As Ross observed, while the postprison Wilde could usually manage the former, the latter was lost to him.³¹⁶ To another friend Ross confided, 'He was very unhappy, and would have become more unhappy as time went on'.³¹⁷ Wilde's obituary in *The Times* on December 1, which referred only obliquely to 'the revelations of the criminal trial in 1895', was predictably condescending:

> Death has ended what must have been a life of wretchedness and unavailing regret . . . Even before he left the University in 1878 Wilde had become known as one of the most affected of the professors of the aesthetic craze and for several years it was as the typical aesthete that he kept himself before the notice of the public. At the same time he was a man of far greater originality and power of mind than many of the apostles of aestheticism. As his Oxford career showed, he had undoubted talents in many directions, talents which might have been brought to fruition had it not been for his craving after notoriety . . . [his plays all had] a paradoxical humour and a perverted outlook on life—³¹⁸

Despite all appearances, however, Wilde's reputation was not irrevocably destroyed, and he would have been pleased to know that in death, as in life, 'Art' did not forget him. The twentieth century was to see the emergence of many fictional Wildes from beyond the grave. Just as nineteenth-century fiction had reflected Wilde's symbolic relation to his own world, so were twentieth-century works to chart his continuing relation to a new era.

Conclusion

'Let me at any rate have some sort of sketch of you, as a kind of feather from the angel's wing, or a photograph of the ghost, to prove to me in the future that you were once a solid, sociable fact, that I didn't utterly fabricate you.'

Nick Dormer to Gabriel Nash,
in Henry James, *The Tragic Muse*

This quotation from *The Tragic Muse*, examined in Part 1, is a particularly fitting one to revisit at the conclusion of this study. One suspects that Nick Dormer's motivation in sketching the Wildean Gabriel Nash was shared not only by Henry James, but also by many of the other authors examined here. While, like Dormer's portrait, the works discussed above are ultimately unable to reduce the enigmatic Wilde to a simple, 'solid' fact, *en masse* they do successfully depict the social reality of a major Victorian writer and one of the most intriguing personalities of the late nineteenth century. Just as Dormer's painting of Nash slowly fades, so many of these fictions have faded into obscurity with the passing of time. However, this study demonstrates that while these 'photographs of the ghost' may have faded they still have much to teach us about their fascinating subject and his milieu.

In the Introduction it was demonstrated that Wilde lived his life in such a way as to promote artistic interpretation of his personality, an approach that resulted in the appearance of a remarkable number of fictional portraits of the author in his own lifetime. It was argued that these 'hybrid' works, artistic fusions of fact and fiction, are a particularly appropriate means for reading Wilde, who reveled in blurring the lines between these modes. It was also asserted that the medium of fiction allowed Wilde's contemporaries a rare freedom to make personal, authentic observations of the author, which serve to clarify his Victorian context. The need for this clarification was demonstrated by an overview of the plethora of twentieth-century and later interpretations of Wilde, and the contextual deficiencies inherent in these.

Part 1's analysis of Wilde's early fictional career, from his first forays into public life to the eve of his greatest success, demonstrated how his egotism, audacity, and flamboyance invited parodic and satirical fictional portraits from the first. Several of these early characterizations were shown to be superficial, stereotypical aesthetic satires that reflect Wilde's status as an 'unknown quantity' during this period; Besant's and Rice's *Monks of Thelema*, A. T. D's 'O'Flighty', and Rhoda Broughton's *Second Thoughts* are all cases in point. It was also revealed that alongside these 'light-weight' works more comprehensive character studies appeared, often written by authors who had the opportunity to observe Wilde at close quarters and were clearly intrigued by him; writers such as George Bernard Shaw (*Immaturity*), Rosa Praed (*Affinities*), and Henry James (*The Tragic Muse*).

In Part 2 it was revealed that, as Wilde became increasingly arrogant and brazen after his literary reputation was won, parodic and satirical portraits of him became more scathing. This development reflected not only the antagonism inspired by his arrogance, but also the growing suspicion of something 'immoral' or 'unwholesome' prompted by Wilde's suggestive writings and reckless behavior. These sentiments are clearly discernible in Marie Corelli's *Silver Domino*, John Davidson's *Baptist Lake*, and G. S. Street's *Autobiography of a Boy*. The increasing severity of satirical depictions culminated in the vicious parody of Robert Hichens's *The Green Carnation*, the success of which undoubtedly hastened Wilde's downfall. Alongside these works, however, more balanced fictions continued to be written by those less prejudiced observers who remained sympathetic to Wilde, such as Richard Le Gallienne ('The Woman's Half-Profits'), Arthur Conan Doyle ('The Greek Interpreter' and 'The Empty House'), and Robert Buchanan (*The Charlatan*).

Part 3 chronicled Wilde's surprisingly numerous fictional appearances during the short years between his disgrace and death. Many of these works vilify Wilde to an inordinate degree: in Aubrey Beardsley's *Venus and Tannhäuser* and Bram Stoker's *Dracula*, Wilde becomes a sexual monstrosity, in Mabel Wotton's 'Fifth Edition' he is a heartless plagiarist, in Grant Allen's *Linnet* an unscrupulous pretender, and in C. A. E. Ranger Gull's *The Hypocrite* a cold, calculating swindler. Some fictions, such as *Linnet* and *The Hypocrite*, mollified their unsympathetic depictions with minor concessions to the complexity of Wilde's unique personality, but only a handful of authors, such as Henrietta Stannard (*A Seaside Flirt*), Richard Le Gallienne ('Brown Roses'), and Mrs (Rosa) Campbell Praed (*The Scourge-Stick*), were courageous enough to offer largely sympathetic portraits of Wilde in the midst of this chorus of censure.

The London *Echo* declared on April 6, 1895, 'The best thing for everybody now is to forget all about Oscar Wilde'.[1] However, neither Wilde's disgrace in 1895 nor his death in 1900 stemmed the tide of public interest in the author. Fictional depictions of Wilde continued to appear, with the first posthumous portrait being published just three years after Wilde's death (Haldane Macfall's *The Masterfolk* in 1903). In fact, Wilde's premature death in exile effectively reconstituted his celebrity and enhanced his previously demonstrated ability to be all things to all people. In the Appendix to this book there is a bibliography of over eighty novels and short stories detailing the remarkably diverse series of portraits of Wilde that have appeared between 1900 and the present day. This catalogue of fictions demonstrates how Wilde's symbolic relation to the world has changed as the world has changed, a development that—one feels safe in saying—would surely have pleased him. It also reflects Wilde's phoenix-like rise from the ashes of ruin and disgrace over the course of the last century.

While the passing of time, the relaxing of moral codes, and the revival and resurgence in popularity of Wilde's plays could all be said to have contributed to Wilde's reconstituted reputation, this turnaround can largely be accounted for by two factors. The first was the publication in 1905 of a heavily expurgated version of Wilde's prison letter, *De Profundis* (often translated as *Out of the Depths*).[2] All references to Lord Alfred Douglas, to whom the letter was addressed, were initially omitted by Wilde's literary executor Robert Ross, and Wilde's remaining philosophical reflections on his downfall and life in prison revived interest in the author and evoked much sympathy among contemporary readers.[3] In his epic letter (the original was closely handwritten over eighty pages), Wilde meditates on his literary and cultural significance and blames himself for behaving in a manner unworthy of an artist. The central themes of the letter are the significance of sorrow, suffering, and humility; Wilde's observations on these subjects lead to an extensive discussion of Christ. Wilde wrote *De Profundis* for a larger audience than Douglas; he had copies of the manuscript made on his release from prison and his dying wish was that Ross publish it for him, in the hope that it would to some degree resurrect his reputation, which it undoubtedly did.[4]

The second key factor that fostered sympathy for the fallen Wilde was public access to the previously unpublished parts of *De Profundis*, which highlighted the destructive role played by Alfred Douglas in

Wilde's demise. When Douglas sued Wilde's biographer Arthur Ransome for libel in April 1913, Wilde's literary executor Ross was obliged to disclose the (often damning) Douglas-related references in Wilde's letter in open court.[5] The previously suppressed excerpts were widely quoted in press reports of the trial. As a result, Wilde's corrupting, Svengali-like image transferred to Douglas and Wilde emerged as an unfortunate genius, whose generosity had been abused by a selfish young aristocrat.

These shifts in public opinion of Wilde are reflected in the contemporary literature of the day. In addition to fictionalizations of Wilde's life, recollections published by Wilde's friends and acquaintances began to appear more frequently and by 1920 a memoir or biography of Wilde was virtually assured publication, regardless of the quality or reliability of the work.[6] Wilde's society plays were soon playing to packed houses around the world and, with the exception of *De Profundis*, his complete works have not been out of print since Ross's first collected edition in 1908. Today, over one hundred years after his death, the pioneering Victorian self-fashioner still serves as a model for the modern media celebrity. Moreover, Wilde's cultural permanence is evinced by his enduring popularity with people from every class, country, and walk of life and the multitude of literary, dramatic, and filmic versions of his life that continue to appear. He has indeed transcended disgrace and death to achieve a kind of immortality in art.

Wilde also lived on in legend: stories contending that he was alive and well were still circulating in 1930 and myths surrounding the gruesome nature of his death (some reports allege a horrific 'explosion') and the state of his body when transferred from Bagneux cemetery to Père Lachaise cemetery in 1909 (it was reportedly unnaturally preserved) continue to fascinate and intrigue.[7]

Clearly, Wilde was too captivating a character for many writers to say goodbye to; as he faded from living memory, many authors felt compelled to negotiate their relation to Wilde and did this by recreating him in fiction. Attempting to breathe life into the legend, they abandoned the genres of satire, parody, and caricature and the moralistic tone of their predecessors and adopted new approaches in crime, thriller, historical, and queer fiction.[8] Wilde has also had fictional turns in vampiric, time travel, and other paranormal fictions. Such works constitute a rich resource for future study, particularly in light of Wilde's own interest in the supernatural and the occult.

As with the Victorian fictions examined here, later representations offer an eclectic mix of Oscar Wildes. In Mary Elizabeth Braddon's *The Rose of Life* (1905) the author is a kind-hearted financial fraudster, in old flame Violet Hunt's *Their Lives* (1916) he is a half-hearted lover, in Laurence Housman's *Echo de Paris* (1923) he is a brilliant raconteur in exile, and in Ronald Firbank's *Concerning the Eccentricities of Cardinal Pirelli* (1926) he is a corrupt epicurean clergyman with a passion for chasing altar boys! Other notable Wildean appearances include stints as a Dublin tavern-keeper in James Joyce's *Finnegans Wake* (1939), a female reincarnation in Eve Langley's *Wild Australia* and *The White Topee* (1953–1954), a diligent diarist in Paris in Peter Ackroyd's *The Last Testament of Oscar Wilde* (1983), and a crime-solver in colonial America in Walter Satterthwait's *Wilde West* (1992); not to mention his regular appearances in Jack the Ripper and Sherlock Holmes pastiches.

In considering the more recent works it is clear that, in the wake of poststructuralist theories undermining traditional conceptions of truth and knowledge from the mid-1970s, Wilde's fictionalizers generally take far greater liberties with their subject than their Victorian counterparts. In the poststructuralist view (and Wilde's own, as outlined in the Introduction), 'truth' and 'history' are merely human constructs, which cannot be objectively represented. Consequently, the lines between fact and fiction in all literatures have become blurred and Wilde has made several appearances in the controversial new genres of 'alternate history' and historiographic metafiction.

Many critical questions about Wilde's later appearances in fiction are yet to be answered; it is hoped that the Victorian works discussed here will provide a useful reference point for the scholar of Wilde's posthumous fictional life. For example, do Wilde's later fictionalizers, at a substantial historical distance from their subject, rely more than their Victorian predecessors on stereotypical notions of Wilde? Or are their poststructuralist portraits more personal?; do the later works represent a more significant merging of author and subject? Peter Ackroyd, perhaps encouraged by his philosophical affinities with Wilde, does not shy from writing in Wilde's voice in an autobiographical framework. Do Wilde's modern fictionalizers write about him because they feel that he belongs to them in some way, that philosophical sympathy equals ownership? Does Harold Bloom's 1963 theory of 'the anxiety of influence' come into play here, particularly when an author has—consciously or unconsciously—appropriated Wilde's writing style, form, or subject matter? Australian writer Eve Langley professed to be a reincarnation of Wilde and actually changed her name to 'Oscar Wilde' by deed poll. Does the act of 'writing Wilde' in itself constitute a literary alliance with him? Indeed, by writing a convincing fictional representation of Wilde, authors will henceforth be associated with him in literary criticism, as they are here.

In many instances Wilde's modern fictional appearances seem tantamount to wish fulfillment, a fantastical indulgence, an imagined 'meeting' and 'knowing' of a literary great and one of the most charismatic personalities of recent history. Certainly, the realm of the imagination is the only one that remains available to us in order to 'meet' Wilde, if one discounts supernatural encounters, such as those reportedly experienced by Hester Travers in the 1920s. Some authors, such as J. M. Stuart-Young, Neil Bartlett, and C. Robert Holloway, have gone so far as to enter into their own fictions in order to engage with Wilde. Stuart-Young, who never met Wilde, included forged letters and signed photographs from Wilde to himself in his book *Osrac, the Self-Sufficient and Other Poems with a Memoir of the Late Oscar Wilde* (1905).

As Ian Fletcher has noted, many modern homosexual authors have felt the need to 'make their peace with Wilde',[9] like Henry James, André Raffalovich, and Robert Hichens before them. In *Who Was that Man?: A Present for Mr Oscar Wilde* (1988), Neil Bartlett defines himself as a gay man in the 1980s by revisiting Wilde's own life, writing him letters, and imagining himself as Wilde's lover. C. Robert Holloway strikes up a supernatural postal correspondence with the dead Wilde in *The Unauthorised Letters of Oscar Wilde* (1997), serving as a touchstone for the Victorian author to discuss twentieth-century homosexual issues. The psychological complexities of these works present some fascinating material for future Wilde studies.

Another intriguing avenue for investigation by modern scholars is the impact of Wilde's fictional career on biographical literature and artistic representations of Wilde's life in drama and film. Andrew Shelley has asserted that any rewriting of Wilde's life is in a sense a retrial: a reviewing and responding to the man and to past reactions and judgments of him.[10] How have judgments and reactions in past fictions influenced our perception of Wilde? The 1960 film biography *The Trials of Oscar Wilde*, featuring Peter Finch as Wilde, was partially based on a 1955 work of fiction, *The Stringed Lute*, by John Furnell. The popular Finch film has certainly influenced twentieth-century views of the writer.

Clearly, there are many potential future directions for academic studies of Wilde in fiction. However, the importance of the early fictions examined here must not be underestimated. Apart from revealing the astonishing degree of Wilde's success in inspiring the imagination of his century, these Victorian works also demonstrate the central role of contemporary societal mores and anxieties in transmuting complex characters like Wilde's into fiction. It is hoped that this study will serve as a timely reminder that our own interpretations of Wilde say as much about ourselves and our historical position as the works discussed here. We must resist the modern tendency to read Wilde with blinkered critical eyes, focusing solely on particular elements of his persona—his Irishness, his socialism, his feminism, his homosexuality—in order to establish and argue for his primary motivation. Wilde was not a single-minded man but a man who contained multitudes and this is reflected in the fiction of those who knew him best, his friends and contemporaries. While each one of these authors saw Wilde differently, each portrait contains its own 'truth'. As Merlin Holland has argued, the correct way to view Wilde is as 'a multicoloured kaleidoscope of apparent contradictions in need not of resolution but of appreciation'.[11] The fiction of Wilde's contemporaries widens that kaleidoscope, allowing us to appreciate not only Wilde's many colors and forms, but also how the colors and forms around him merged with his own to create the fascinating images we see through our latter-day lens.

Appendix: Oscar Wilde as a Character in Fiction, 1900–2007

The Masterfolk. London: William Heinemann, 1903.
Haldane Macfall
A *roman à clef* of decadent and literary life in London and Paris in the 1890s. The poet 'Aubrey' is a version of the young, aesthetic Wilde. The writer Quilliam Myre—known as 'Quogge' Myre or 'The Brixton Celt'—resembles the older, decadent Wilde.

'The Empty House'. *The Strand Magazine*, 1903.
Arthur Conan Doyle
Colonel Sebastian Moran, the one-time friend and associate of Sherlock Holmes's most famous adversary, Professor Moriarty, exhibits shades of Wilde in this short story.

'The World's Slow Stain', in *One Doubtful Hour and Other Side-Lights on the Feminine Temperament*. London: Grant Richards, 1904.
Ella Hepworth Dixon
Gilbert Vincent, the malicious friend of London socialite and New Woman Adela Buller, is Dixon's fifth and final fictional portrait of Wilde.

The Rose of Life. London: Hutchinson, 1905.
Mary Elizabeth Braddon
Braddon's poet and witty sensualist Daniel Lester is clearly based on Wilde, but instead of being denounced for homosexual activity, Lester commits financial fraud.

Passion's Peril: A Romance. London: Hermes Press, 1906.
John Moray Stuart-Young
Stuart-Young, a notorious forger of letters from Wilde, offers a fictional portrait of the author in the character of Selwyn Waring.

The Sphinx's Lawyer. London: William Heinemann, 1906.
Frank Danby (Julia Frankau)

The disgraced poet and hedonist Algernon Heseltine is a blatant portrait of Wilde.

House of the Vampire. New York: Moffat, Yard & Company, 1907.
George S. Viereck

The Wildean New Yorker Reginald Clarke, master of literature, style, and conversation seduces young authors with his charismatic personality and then plagiarizes their unwritten works by supernatural means.

'In Memoriam', in *The Antinomian: An Elegiac Poem also A Prose Trifle in Memory of 'Sebastian'.* London: Hermes Press, 1909.
John Moray Stuart-Young

Stuart-Young offers some further fictional insights into the 'Friend' who spent time in Reading Gaol.

The Street of Adventure. London: William Heinemann, 1909.
Philip Gibbs

The cynical journalist 'Codrington' is a portrait of Wilde.

The Reluctant Lover. London: Herbert Jenkins, 1912.
Stephen McKenna

Society novel of the early 1900s, set in Oxford. Cynical but charming idler and arbiter of taste, Cyril Fitzroy is based on Wilde.

Shadows of Flames. London: Hurst and Blackett, 1915
Amélie Rives (Princess Troubetzkoy)

Melodrama that includes a brief fictional treatment of Wilde in the shape of the 'truly vile' Oswald Tyne.

Their Lives. London: Stanley Paul, 1916.
Violet Hunt

Largely autobiographical family saga. The relationship between Christina Radmall and Philip Wynyard reflects Hunt's early romance with Wilde.

The Fortune: A Romance of Friendship. Dublin: Maunsel, 1917.
Douglas Goldring

Society novel set in London.

Echo de Paris: A Study from Life. London: Jonathan Cape, 1923.
Laurence Housman

Housman draws upon his memories of the postprison Wilde to recreate their conversations in Paris.

Concerning the Eccentricities of Cardinal Pirelli. London: Duckworth, 1926.
Ronald Firbank

The corrupt epicurean cardinal of the title has a distinctly Wildean quality. Firbank's biographer Brigid Brophy has suggested he is a composite of Wilde and Firbank himself. Wilde is also caricatured by Firbank as Lord Orkish, who lives in exile in Firbank's play *The Princess Zoubaroff* (1920).

Ryder. New York: Horace Liverwright, 1928.
Djuna Barnes

Wilde is briefly glimpsed in Barnes's first novel, a largely autobiographical family saga. Barnes's grandmother Zadel was a friend of Wilde's mother, and held regular 'at homes' that Wilde attended.

'A Real Phantasy', *Oscar Wilde: A Study.* London: Braithwaite and Miller, 1930.
Patrick Braybrooke

Brief prose piece with Wilde's Happy Prince and the dead Wilde observing the annual dinner of the 'Happy Prince Club'.

Co-Stars: Cecil Spooner and Oscar Wilde: A Mere Little Comedy about More or Less Legitimate Actors on Two Sunday Mornings and One Sunday Night. Orrtanna, PA: White Squaw Press, 1930.
Will W. Whalen

Farcical story of an American theater company. The Wildean character is the fickle and heartless Oscar Windermere, poet and playwright of such works as *Margaret Erlynne's Bracelet* and *Woman Without a Name.* Windermere neglects his young family for his literary work and his flirtations with a leading actress.

The Madonna of Montmartre: A Story Oscar Wilde Never Told. Liverpool, E. A. Bryant, 1930.
G. W. Mathews

Privately printed.

Conversations with Oscar Wilde. London: Phillip Allan, 1931.
Arthur Henry Cooper-Pritchard

Features various scenes depicting Wilde with the author, who paints himself as an intimate friend of Wilde's. Scenarios include 'Oscar Wilde in Politics: A Conversation with Walt Whitman', 'Oscar Wilde at the Royal Military Tournament', and 'Oscar Wilde at a Dog Show'.

'Oscar Wilde by the Styx', *The Bookman* (New York) LXXV, no. 2, 1932.
Hugh Kingsmill

Hugh Kingsmill visits Wilde in the underworld, where he asks for and receives the latter's opinions on writers who succeeded him in the public favor, including George Bernard Shaw, H. G. Wells, John Galsworthy, G. K. Chesterton, James Joyce, Lytton Strachey, and D. H. Lawrence.

Oscar Wilde: Recollections. London: Nonesuch Press, 1932.
J. P. Raymond and Charles Ricketts

A prefatory note by Thomas Lowinsky states that 'Ricketts wrote and in 1929 privately issued "Beyond the Threshold", which he pretended was his translation from the original French of Jean Paul Raymond. He again introduces this imaginary author into his own recollections of Oscar Wilde . . . [drawn from] the diaries and letters that he kept [which communicate his] passionate indignation at the fate of his friend'.

Finnegan's Wake. London: Faber & Faber, 1939.
James Joyce

Joyce's Dublin tavern-keeper, Humphrey Chimpden Earwicker, connected with the theme of the fall in *Finnegan's Wake*, has been read as a portrait of Wilde.

The Sensualist: A Novel of the Life and Times of Oscar Wilde. New York: Jonathan Swift, 1942.
Clement Wood

A moralistic anti-Wilde, antihomosexuality novel set in London. Wilde is depicted as a demonic seducer of youth.

All Past Years: A Novel. London: Robert Hale, 1948.
Vicky Lancaster (Laura Conway)

A novel of 1870s Dublin society. The young Wilde attempts to elope with Lalla, a tubercular girl with boyish good looks who dresses as a man for Wilde.

Wild Australia (Unpublished, Mitchell Library MSS 3269/135, State Library of New South Wales), 1953–1954.
Eve Langley

A sequel to Langley's *The Pea Pickers*. With her depiction of the androgynous Eve/Steve, Langley undermines and parodies popular conceptions of identity, gender, sex, space, and time. Langley, variously regarded as brilliantly eccentric or mentally unstable, changed her name to 'Oscar Wilde' by deed poll in 1954.

The White Topee. Sydney: Angus and Robertson, 1954.
Eve Langley

Langley's androgynous Eve/Steve is revealed to be a reincarnation of Oscar Wilde.

Beyond His Means: A Novel Based on the Life of Oscar Wilde. London: Peter Davies, 1955.
Sewell Stokes

Fictional moralistic biography.

The Stringed Lute: An Evocation in Dialogue of Oscar Wilde. London: Rider, 1955.
John Furnell

Includes an introduction by G. Wilson Knight. Wilde's life flashes before his 'ghost' and a later inhabitant of his London residence. Furnell's novel, with H. Montgomery Hyde's *The Trials of Oscar Wilde* [1948], served as a source for the 1960 film *The Trials of Oscar Wilde*.

I Give You Oscar Wilde: A Biographical Novel. New York: New American Library, 1965.
Desmond Hall

'Recollections' of the American Lawrence Young, who befriends Wilde on the boat to America in 1881 and who, after sporadic correspondence, reprises the friendship a few months before Wilde's death in Paris.

The Exile of Capri. London: Panther, 1969.
Roger Peyrefitte

English translation of *L'Exile de Capri* [1959], translator Edward Hyams, foreword by Jean Cocteau. Peyrefitte's novel is based on the life of Baron Jacques d'Adelsward-Fersen [1880–1923]. Wilde appears in a fictional account of his visit to Capri in 1897.

'Diana Raffles and Oscar Wilde', *Raffles of the Albany: Footprints of a Famous Gentleman Crook in the Times of a Great Detective.* London: Hamilton, 1976.
Barry Perowne

Pastiche of the Raffles stories by E. W. Hornung. Raffles visits his niece in Paris, sees Wilde in a café and steps in to save him from danger.

Moriarty. London: Pan, 1976.
John Gardner

Sherlock Holmes pastiche in which Moriarty tracks down Jack the Ripper. Published as 'The Return of Moriarty' in the United states.

The West End Horror: A Posthumous Memoir of John H. Watson, MD, as Edited (i.e. Written) by Nicholas Meyer. London: Hodder & Stoughton, 1976.

Sherlock Holmes pastiche. In chapter 5, Holmes and Watson question Wilde, who has just instituted proceedings for libel against the Marquess of

Queensberry, about his meeting with a man who was recently murdered. The dead man had been attempting to blackmail Wilde.

The Blackheath Poisonings: A Victorian Murder Mystery. London: Collins, 1978.
Julian Symons

Murder mystery set in 1890s London. The central characters attend a performance of *Lady Windermere's Fan*, after which Wilde appears to make a short speech.

Chelsea. New York: Doubleday, 1979.
Nancy Fitzgerald

Romance set in the salons and studios of late nineteenth-century Chelsea, London. Wilde expounds on art and life to the artist Devin and his model Cecily.

The Detling Murders. London: Macmillan, 1980.
Julian Symons

Later published as *The Detling Secret*. Wilde appears briefly at a society soirée. He is surrounded by 'an efflorescence of geniality' and leaves 'an impression of conceited dandyism among those who had not spoken to him, and of warmth and generosity in those who had'.

'The Truth about Oscar', *The Bulletin Literary Supplement*, December 22/29, 1981.
Yvonne Rousseau

A young female scientist disguises herself as a late Victorian man and time travels to 1895 to warn Wilde of the consequences of prosecuting the Marquess of Queensberry for libel.

Dracula's Diary. New York: Beaufort, 1982.
Michael Geare and Michael Corby

Wilde appears briefly in this Sherlock Holmes and *Dracula* pastiche, in which Count Dracula encounters Holmes and Watson during their Jack the Ripper investigation.

The Private World of St John Terrapin: A Novel of the Cafe Royal. London: Sidgwick and Jackson, 1982.
Chapman Pincher

Diary of a deaf lip-reader who 'eavesdrops' on Wilde and others at the Café Royal.

The Last Testament of Oscar Wilde. London: Hamish Hamilton, 1983.
Peter Ackroyd

Wilde keeps a journal in Paris in the months before his death.

W. G. Grace's Last Case: or, The War of the Worlds Part Two. London: Methuen, 1984.
William Rushton

Farcical novel lampooning many historical and fictional characters. English cricketer W. G. Grace and Dr Watson of Sherlock Holmes fame encounter Wilde during his last days in Paris. Wilde accompanies the two men to the Moulin Rouge.

'Jack the Ripper', *I'm Sorry I'll Read That Again.* Poole: Javelin, 1985.
Graeme Garden and Bill Oddie

Wilde features briefly in this Jack the Ripper send-up.

The Adventures of Inspector Lestrade. London: Macmillan, 1985.
M. J. Trow

Sherlock Holmes pastiche. Inspector Lestrade questions Wilde at the Cadogan Hotel regarding the murder of Philip Faye, a London pimp who Wilde calls 'a dear friend'.

The God of Mirrors. Boston: Atlantic Monthly, 1986.
Robert Reilly

Fictional biography covering the period from Wilde's first meeting with Robert Ross to his death in Paris.

Skullduggery. New York: Carroll and Graf, 1987.
Peter Marks

Includes a fictional rendering of Wilde's meeting with Arthur Conan Doyle at the Langford Hotel in 1888. In Marks's novel, Wilde accompanies the unwitting Doyle to a male brothel after this meeting.

Druid's Blood. London: Headline, 1988.
Esther M. Friesner

Sherlock Holmes pastiche. The Dr Watson character, Dr John H. Weston, gets into a fist fight with Wilde's companion 'Alfred' at the Café Royal; a full-scale brawl ensues.

Sherlock Holmes and the Mysterious Friend of Oscar Wilde. New York: St. Martin's Press, 1988.
Russell Brown

Sherlock Holmes joins forces with Wilde in 1895 to solve two mysteries. Holmes and Watson declare a strong dislike of the overtly homosexual Wilde, although it occasionally appears that the two friends 'protest too much'. Wilde eventually wins their respect with his superior intellect.

N for Narcissus. London: GMP, 1990.
Chris Hunt

An aristocratic acquaintance of Wilde's succumbs to his homosexuality at the time of Wilde's trials. Wilde features briefly.

Good Night, Mr Holmes. New York: Tor, 1990.
Carole Nelson Douglas

Sherlock Holmes pastiche. American opera singer Irene Adler bests Holmes in the 'Scandal in Bohemia' case, and also assists Wilde with a delicate matter of the heart.

The Coward Does It With a Kiss. London: GMP, 1990.
Rohase Piercy

In an epic epistle to her disgraced husband, Constance Wilde 'recounts' pivotal episodes from their marriage.

The Dracula Caper. London: Headline, 1990.
Simon Hawke

Sherlock Holmes pastiche. Dracula uses new technology to genetically engineer vampires and werewolves.

Anno-Dracula. New York: Pocket Books, 1992.
Kim Newman

Outlandish sequel to *Dracula* featuring Jack the Ripper plot and the British royal family, in which 'London is awash with parvenu vampires'. Newman's Wilde embraces the new vampire state with enthusiasm.

Wilde West. London: Crime Club, 1992.
Walter Satterthwait

Wilde plays detective in a murder case during his 1882 American tour.

Farrier's Lane. New York: Fawcett-Columbine, 1993.
Anne Perry

Inspector Thomas Pitt and his wife Charlotte investigate an opium poisoning with some help from Wilde.

The Confessions of Aubrey Beardsley. London: Bantam, 1993.
Donald S. Olsen

Aubrey Beardsley's life from infancy to death at age 25, as narrated by Beardsley in confessional letters to a French priest. Beardsley comments upon his strained relationship with Wilde.

The Eye in the Door. London: Viking, 1993.
Pat Barker

The middle book of Barker's World War I trilogy refers to Wilde's trials.

The Whitechapel Horrors. New York: Carroll and Graf, 1993.
Edward B. Hanna
Sherlock Holmes pastiche about Jack the Ripper.

Without Sanction. Boston: Alyson, 1993.
J. M. Roberts
A story of homosexual love set in Victorian London and New York. The central character, handsome actor Kit St. Denys, meets a fawning Wilde at a 'gentlemen-only' party and takes an instant dislike to him. Wilde later makes a fumbling pass at St. Denys and is rebuffed.

Dan Leno and the Limehouse Golem. London: Sinclair-Stevenson, 1994.
Peter Ackroyd
Wilde is fleetingly glimpsed at the British Library in Ackroyd's story of George Gissing's involvement in Jack the Ripper–type murders.

The Strange Adventures of Charlotte Holmes. London: Constable, 1994.
Hilary Bailey
Documents the adventures of Sherlock Holmes's sister Charlotte, who is also a skilled detective. Wilde attends a large breakfast party hosted by Charlotte. Wilde, along with George Bernard Shaw, is campaigning for the release of a man convicted in relation to a Fenian bomb planted in Baker Street.

The Curse of the Imperial Paperweights. Santa Cruz: Paperweight, 1995.
George N. Kulles
Thriller. Three crystal paperweights are commissioned by Princess Eugenie of France in 1864 to commemorate the rule of Maximilian and Carlotta, emperor and empress of Mexico. Unknown to Eugenie, the paperweights carry a curse, and as they pass from person to person wreak havoc on their owners' lives. Wilde is given one of the paperweights by Eugenie; his downfall soon follows.

Vanitas: Escape from Vampire Junction. New York: Tor, 1995.
S. P. Somtow
Vampire rock star Timmy Valentine reflects in flashback on his past associations with Wilde and other historical personages including Marlowe and Shakespeare.

Supping with Panthers. London: Little, Brown, 1996.
Tom Holland
Vampire/Jack the Ripper fantasy. A vampiric Lord Byron discusses eternal youth with Wilde at a dinner party hosted by Bram Stoker. U.S. title: *Slave of My Thirst.*

The Hunger and Ecstasy of Vampires: A Novel. Shingletown, CA: Mark V. Ziesing, 1996.
Brian Stableford

Science fiction vampire story. Victorian anthropologist Edward Copplestone discovers a drug that enables him to travel into the future, where he learns that vampires have conquered the human race. Wilde is one of the select intellectual group Copplestone chooses to let in on the secret.

'A Letter to Posterity from John H. Watson, M.D.', *The Secret Cases of Sherlock Holmes.* London: Macmillan, 1997.
Donald Thomas

Sherlock Holmes pastiche. Dr Watson briefly describes a meeting between Sherlock Holmes and Wilde, when the former reprimanded the latter about his egotism.

Billy Gashade: An American Epic. New York: Tom Doherty Associates, 1997.
Loren Estleman

The eponymous Gashade, a wandering musician, has a drink and a conversation with Wilde in a bar in an American boomtown.

Dorian: A Sequel to The Picture of Dorian Gray. London: Peter Owen, 1997.
Jeremy Reed and Oscar Wilde

Dorian Gray survives the slashing of his portrait and seeks to escape his murderer's guilt by immersing himself in drugs, sex, sadomasochism, and the occult. Dorian meets the recently released prisoner Wilde in Paris.

'Exit Centre Stage', *Crime Through Time.* New York: Berkeley, 1997.
M. J. Trow

Sherlock Holmes pastiche.

'Parris Green', *First Cases Volume Two: First Appearances of Classic Amateur Detectives.* New York: Signet, 1997.
Carole Nelson Douglas

Sherlock Holmes pastiche.

'The Black Blood of the Dead'. *Interzone,* January and February 1997.
Brian Stableford

Sequel to Stableford's *The Hunger and Ecstasy of Vampires* [1996]; see above. During his last days in Paris, Wilde narrates the story of his meeting with 'Sherrinford' [Sherlock] Holmes, who like himself, was previously told by anthropologist Edward Copplestone about his discovery of a time-travel drug. Holmes has used Copplestone's drug to travel to the future; as the story closes Holmes surreptitiously injects the dying Wilde with the formula.

The Unauthorised Letters of Oscar Wilde: A Novel. Princeton, NJ: Xlibris, 1997.
C. Robert Holloway
Wilde enters into a racy posthumous postal correspondence with late twentieth-century author C. Robert Holloway.

The Untouchable. London: Picador, 1997.
John Banville
Homosexual Irish spy Victor Maskell exhibits shades of Wilde.

Wilde: A Novel. London: Orion, 1997.
Stefan Rudnicki
Based on the screenplay of the film *Wilde* [1997] by Julian Mitchell.

'A Hamster of No Importance', *Midnight Louie's Pet Detectives.* New York: Tor/Forge, 1998.
Wilde and some members of his circle discover the identity of an infamous London jewelry thief, with the assistance of Wilde's namesake, a pet hamster.)

'The Adventure of the Old Russian Woman', *The Confidential Casebook of Sherlock Holmes.* New York: St. Martin's Press, 1998.
H. Paul Jeffers
Sherlock Holmes pastiche.

'A Roman of No Importance', *Cat Crimes Through Time.* New York: Carroll & Graf, 1999.
Elizabeth Foxwell
Wilde meets an invalid called Bunbury at a play rehearsal for *The Passion of Cleopatra.* During the rehearsal one of the cast members is mysteriously poisoned. Bunbury solves the mystery and inspires Wilde to write a play.

Flashman and the Tiger: And Other Extracts From The Flashman Papers. London: HarperCollins, 1999.
George Fraser
Wilde is briefly glimpsed by Flashman at the theater in the company of Colonel Moran, the assassin and card-sharp who features in the Sherlock Holmes story 'The Adventure of the Empty House'. In this story Flashman

encounters Holmes and Watson in the middle of their 'Empty House' adventure.

Manly Pursuits. New York: Bloomsbury, 1999.
Ann Harries

Oxford ornithologist Francis Wills visits Cecil Rhodes in Africa and recalls his previous associations with such Victorian notables as Wilde, Kipling, and Ruskin.

Pilgrim. Toronto: HarperFlamingo, 1999.
Timothy Findley

Documents the adventures of a man called Pilgrim who cannot die. In one of his past lives Pilgrim was a friend of Wilde's.

'The Adventure of the Christmas Bear', *More Holmes for the Holidays.* New York: Berkley Prime Crime, 1999.
Bill Crider

Sherlock Holmes pastiche.

Architects of Emortality. New York: Tor, 2000.
Brian Stableford

Another Stableford science fiction featuring Wilde. Oscar Wilde is an ostentatious genetic engineer of specialty flowers in this murder mystery set 300 years in the future. Originally a novella entitled *Les Fleurs du Mal* (1994).

Half Moon Street. London: Headline, 2000.
Anne Perry

Wilde again assists Inspector Pitt, as he did in Perry's *Farrier's Lane* (1993). This time the crime is the murder of a society photographer.

The Case of the Pederast's Wife: A Novel. Chester Springs, PA: Dufour, 2000.
Blossom Elfman

Sympathetic but homophobic doctor Martin Frame dabbles in psychotherapy with Wilde's wife Constance in the wake of Wilde's disgrace. Frame eventually comes face to face with the dying Wilde in Paris and questions him in an attempt to understand Wilde's complex relation to his family.

The Man Who Was Dorian Gray. Houndmills: Palgrave, 2000.
Jerusha McCormack

Wilde's relationship with the poet John Gray is imagined in McCormack's semifictional biography of Gray, which includes extensive academic footnotes.

The Problem of the Evil Editor: A Charles Dodgson/Arthur Conan Doyle Mystery. New York: Minotaur, 2000.
Roberta Rogow
Wilde is a suspect in the murder of a disreputable children's magazine editor.

Sherlock Holmes and the Apocalypse Murders. Florida: Second Opinion, 2001.
Barry Day
Sherlock Holmes pastiche. Wilde assists Holmes and Watson in their investigation of a Jack the Ripper–style murder.

'The Specter of Tullyfane Abbey', *Villains Victorious*. New York: Daw, 2001.
Peter Tremayne
Sherlock Holmes pastiche. Dr Watson reveals that Sherlock Holmes was a friend of Wilde's, and that they attended Trinity College, Dublin and Oxford University together.

'The Two Failures of Sherlock Holmes', *Sherlock Holmes and the Running Noose*. London: Macmillan, 2001.
Donald Thomas
Sherlock Holmes pastiche. Dr Watson relates how Wilde visited Baker Street in February 1895 to ask Holmes for some informal advice on his libel action against the Marquess of Queensberry. Holmes, who despises Wilde's vanity and posturing, easily deduces the latter's 'guilt' and advises him to drop the case. Canadian title: *Sherlock Holmes and the Voice from the Crypt: And Other Tales*.

Sense and Sensuality: Jesus Talks to Oscar Wilde on the Pursuit of Pleasure (Great Conversations Series). Sisters, OR: Multnomah, 2002.
Ravi Zacharias
A fictional discussion between Wilde and Jesus Christ on the nature of pleasure, beauty, freedom, responsibility, and love.

Oscar Wilde Discovers America. New York: Scribner, 2003
Louis Edwards
Wilde's 1882 American tour as seen through the eyes of his African American valet.

The Witches of Chiswick. London: Gollancz, 2003.
Robert Rankin

Wilde has a walk-on part as a notorious womanizer in this quirky time-travel story.

Arthur and George. New York: Alfred A. Knopf, 2006.
Julian Barnes

Arthur Conan Doyle tells the story of his two meetings with Oscar Wilde and describes the changes he observed in Wilde over time.

Notes

Introduction

1. Oscar Wilde, Epigrams and Aphorisms, ms., William Andrews Clark Memorial Library Archives, University of California, Los Angeles. For an examination of Wilde's life in performative terms, see, Francesca Coppa, 'Performance Theory and Performativity', in *Palgrave Advances in Oscar Wilde Studies*, ed. Frederick S. Roden (New York: Palgrave Macmillan, 2004), pp. 72–95.
2. André Gide, *Oscar Wilde*, trans. Bernard Frechtman (New York: Philosophical Library, 1949), p. 16.
3. Ian Fletcher notes that Wilde 'exploited and [was] exploited by the new means of communication: the "new journalism" originating in the United States in the earlier 1880s. As a consequence of the acts enforcing compulsory education in England in 1870 and 1874, the new literate masses were let loose on the printed word, and newspapers and magazines were furnished for them, vowed to instant news, instant controversy, instant polarization, and the routine coarsening of issues into personalities'. Ian Fletcher, *Aubrey Beardsley*, Twayne's English Authors Series, ed. Herbert Sussman (Boston: Twayne, 1987), p. iv.
4. Terry Eagleton, 'The Doubleness of Oscar Wilde', *The Wildean* 19 (2001), p. 7.
5. Oscar Wilde, *The Complete Letters of Oscar Wilde*, ed. Merlin Holland and Rupert Hart-Davis (London: Fourth Estate, 2000), p. 729.
6. Some of the scholarly studies that have appeared include Oscar Cargill, 'Mr. James's Aesthetic Mr. Nash', *Nineteenth Century Fiction* 12.1 (1957); J. H. Miller, 'Oscar in *The Tragic Muse*', Paper presented at *The Importance of Being Misunderstood: Homage to Oscar Wilde* (Parma: 2000); Tanya Olson, '"I Would Be Master Still": *Dracula* as the Aftermath of the Wilde Trials and Irish Land League Policies', *Thirdspace* 2.1 (2002); Lyall Powers, 'Mr. James's Aesthetic Mr. Nash—Again', *Nineteenth Century Fiction* 13.1 (1959); Shelley Salamensky, *Difference in a Desert: Julia Constance Fletcher and the Mirage of Oscar Wilde*, May 23, 1999, Harvard University, available www.english.upenn.edu/conferences/Travel99/Abstract/Salamensky.html, last accessed July 16, 2007; Talia Schaffer, '"A Wilde Desire Took Me": The Homoerotic History of Dracula', *ELH* 61.2 (1994); Eric Susser, 'Unnatural Flower: *The Green Carnation* and the Threat of Wilde's Influence', *In-Between: Essays and Studies in Literary Criticism* 10.2 (2001); Stanley Weintraub, 'Narcissus Exposed: Oscar Wilde and *The Green Carnation*', *The Green Carnation* (Lincoln: University of Nebraska Press, 1970). A short review of some of Wilde's early fictional incarnations can be found in Michael Seeney, 'The Fictional Career of Oscar Wilde', *The Wildean* 9 (1996).
7. John Stokes, *Oscar Wilde: Myths, Miracles, and Imitations* (Cambridge, UK: Cambridge University Press, 1996), p. 187; Robert Tanitch, *Oscar Wilde on Stage and Screen* (London: Methuen, 1999).

8. Seeney, 'The Fictional Career of Oscar Wilde', pp. 46–47.
9. Robert Ross, 'A Note of Explanation', *Letters to the Sphinx from Oscar Wilde with Reminiscences of the Author* (London: Duckworth, 1930), p. 15.
10. William Amos, *The Originals: Who's Really Who in Fiction* (London: Jonathan Cape, 1985); Alan Bold and Robert Giddings, *True Characters: Real People in Fiction*, Longman Pocket Companion Series (Harlow, Essex: Longman, 1984); David Pringle, *Imaginary People: A Who's Who of Fictional Characters from the Eighteenth Century to the Present Day*, 2nd edn. (Aldershot, Hampshire: Scolar, 1996); M. C. Rintoul, *Dictionary of Real People and Places in Fiction* (London: Routledge, 1993).
11. Bold and Giddings, *True Characters*, p. i.
12. Amos, *The Originals,* pp. xix, xviii.
13. Ibid., pp. xiii, xix.
14. Anonymous, 'Three Novels (Book Reviews)', *Saturday Review*, April 4, 1885.
15. Merlin Holland, 'Biography and the Art of Lying', in *The Cambridge Companion to Oscar Wilde*, ed. Peter Raby (Cambridge, UK: Cambridge University Press, 1997), p. 10.
16. Jonathan Freedman notes that 'Roland Barthes . . . for example, may be read as a deeply Wildean critic, one who both constructed and interpreted himself under the sign of textual desire. Wildean as well are the arguments of American critics Harold Bloom and Geoffrey Hartman for the creative aspects of the critical act. And Wilde's work anticipates, as Joel Fineman brilliantly suggests, many of the central tenets of *both* [emphasis in the original] deconstruction and analytic philosophy'. Jonathan Freedman, 'Introduction: On Oscar Wildes', in *Oscar Wilde: A Collection of Critical Essays*, ed. Jonathan Freedman (Upper Saddle River, NJ: Prentice Hall, 1998), p. 6.
17. Michael Bronski, 'The Oscar Wilde Fad', 1998, *Z Magazine*, available www.zmag.org/zmag/articles/dec98bronski.htm, last accessed July 16, 2007.
18. Matthew Sweet, *Inventing the Victorians* (London: Faber and Faber, 2001), p. 227.
19. Holland cited in Stephen Moss, 'The Importance of Being Merlin', *The Guardian*, November 24, 2000.
20. Richard Ellmann, *Oscar Wilde* (London: Penguin, 1987), p. 553.
21. Alan Sinfield, *The Wilde Century: Effeminacy, Oscar Wilde and the Queer Movement* (London: Cassell, 1994), p. vii.
22. Matthew Sturgis, *Aubrey Beardsley: A Biography* (London: HarperCollins, 1998), p. 216.
23. While the word 'homosexual' appears throughout this book, it is used with reference to same-sex desire, as opposed to suggesting a homosexual identity or community in the twentieth-century sense.
24. For recent examples of many of these approaches, see Roden, ed., *Palgrave Advances*.
25. Ibid., pp. xiii, xv.
26. Ibid., pp. xi, xiii.
27. Ian Small, *Oscar Wilde Revalued: An Essay on New Materials and Methods of Research*, 1880–1920 British Authors Series (Greenboro: ELT Press, 1993), pp. 2, 174.
28. Melissa Knox, *Oscar Wilde in the 1990s: The Critic as Creator*, Studies in English and American Literature, Linguistics and Culture: Literary Criticism in Perspective, ed. James Hardin (Rochester: Camden House, 2001), p. xix.

29. James C. Simmons, *The Novelist as Historian: Essays on the Victorian Historical Novel* (The Hague: Mouton, 1973), p. 33.
30. K. Jenkins, *Re-Thinking History* (London: Routledge, 1991), p. 5.
31. Neil Sammells, *Wilde Style: The Plays and Prose of Oscar Wilde* (Harlow: Longman, 2000), p. 123.
32. Wilde, *Collins Complete Works of Oscar Wilde* (Glasgow: Harpercollins, 1999), p. 1081.
33. Thomas Wright, ed., *Table Talk: Oscar Wilde* (London: Cassell, 2000), p. 110.
34. Wilde cited in Jacques Daurelle, 'An English Poet in Paris', in *Oscar Wilde: Interviews and Recollections*, vol. 1, ed. E. H. Mikhail (London: Macmillan, 1979), p. 171.
35. Wilde, *Collins Complete Works of Oscar Wilde*, p. 1080.
36. Thomas Wright, 'The Poet in Hell', *The Wildean* 20 (2002), p. 31.
37. In a letter to T. H. S. Escott in 1885, Wilde said that he would like to write on a subject that he had been 'for some time studying, Impressionism in Literature'. Wilde, *The Complete Letters of Oscar Wilde*, p. 253.
38. Wilde, *Collins Complete Works of Oscar Wilde*, pp. 91, 128, 1073.
39. Hesketh Pearson, *The Life of Oscar Wilde* (London: Methuen, 1946), p. 65.
40. Denisoff, *Aestheticism and Sexual Parody 1840–1940*. Cambridge studies in Nineteenth-Century Literature and Culture. Ed. Gillian Beer. vol. 31 (Cambridge, UK: Cambridge University Press, 2001), p. 2.
41. Oscar Wilde, *Reviews*, The First Collected Edition of the Works of Oscar Wilde, vol. 12, 15 vols ed. Robert Ross, (London: Dawsons, 1969), p. 447.

1 Aesthete (1877–1890)

1. Walter Pater, *The Renaissance: Studies in Art and Poetry* (London: Macmillan, 1904), p. 236.
2. Notable exceptions include Walter Hamlin in *Miss Brown: A Novel*, 3 vols. (Edinburgh and London: William Blackwood and Sons, 1884), Marmaduke White in Robert Buchanan's *The Martyrdom of Madeline*, 3 vols (London: Chatto & Windus, 1882) and Lewis Seymour in George Moore's *A Modern Lover* (London: Tinsley, 1883).
3. *The Nile Novel* was republished as *Kismet* in 1877.
4. W. W. Ward, 'Oscar Wilde: An Oxford Reminiscence', in *Son of Oscar Wilde*, ed. Vyvyan Holland (Oxford: Oxford University Press, 1988), p. 255.
5. Julia Constance Fletcher, *Mirage* (Boston: Roberts Brothers, 1878), p. 153.
6. Ibid., pp. 238–9.
7. Ellmann, *Oscar Wilde*, p. 72; Wilde, *Collins Complete Works of Oscar Wilde*, p. 755.
8. Wilde, *The Complete Letters of Oscar Wilde*, p. 58.
9. Ellmann, *Oscar Wilde*, p. 72.
10. Fletcher, *Mirage*, pp. 86, 292.
11. Ibid., p. 203.
12. Ibid., p. 292.
13. Ibid., p. 154.
14. Ibid., p. 204.
15. Ibid., p. 287.
16. Ibid., p. 297.
17. Ibid., p. 190.
18. Ibid., p. 238.

19. Ibid., p. 246.
20. Ibid., p. 247.
21. Salamensky, *Difference in a Desert: Julia Constance Fletcher and the Mirage of Oscar Wilde*.
22. Fletcher, *Mirage*, p. 246
23. See Angela Kingston, 'Homoeroticism and the Child in Wilde's Fairy Tales', *The Wildean* 19 (2001).
24. Henry James, *Mirage (Book Review)*, 1877, University of Virginia Library, May 18, 2001.
25. Wilde, *The Complete Letters of Oscar Wilde*, pp. 60–1.
26. Vyvyan Holland, *Son of Oscar Wilde* (Oxford: Oxford University Press, 1988), p. 253.
27. Possibly Frank (later Sir Frank) Benson, who knew Wilde at Oxford.
28. Julia Constance Fletcher, letter to Oscar Wilde, June 12, 1878 (Clark).
29. Wilde also introduced Fletcher and her stepfather to the Reverend Archibald Henry Sayce, a fellow of Queen's College and a family friend. See Wilde, *The Complete Letters of Oscar Wilde*, p. 68.
30. Peter Vernier, 'A "Mental Photograph" of Oscar Wilde', *The Wildean* 13 (1998), pp. 47–8; Holland, *Son of Oscar Wilde*, p. 253.
31. John Sutherland, *The Stanford Companion to Victorian Fiction* (Stanford, CA: Stanford University Press, 1989), p. 59.
32. Walter Besant and James Rice, *The Monks of Thelema* (London: Chatto and Windus, 1892), p. 220.
33. Ibid., p. 24.
34. Ibid., pp. 24, 300.
35. Ibid., p. 31. S. Squire Sprigge records that Besant had a particular aversion to people with 'vain pretension[s]' to 'powers of discrimination or criticism of higher and more delicate character than those granted to ordinary mortals'. Walter Besant, *Autobiography of Sir Walter Besant* (Michigan: Scholarly Press, 1971), p. xii.
36. Wilde, *Collins Complete Works of Oscar Wilde*, p. 376.
37. E. H. Mikhail, ed., *Oscar Wilde: Interviews and Recollections*, 2 vols (London: Macmillan, 1979), p. 57; Wilde, *The Complete Letters of Oscar Wilde*, p. 318.
38. Mikhail, ed., *Oscar Wilde, Interviews and Recollections*, p. 306.
39. Wilde, *The Complete Letters of Oscar Wilde*, p. 356.
40. As Jonathon Fryer has noted, this was common practice for opponents to a candidate's membership as well as his supporters; it is possible that Besant was in the former category. Jonathan Fryer, 'Oscar and the Savilians', *The Wildean* 18 (2001), p. 44. Unanimous support for the proposed candidate was required and Wilde was never elected to the club.
41. Wilde, *Collins Complete Works of Oscar Wilde*, p. 1151.
42. Wilde, *The Complete Letters of Oscar Wilde*, p. 488.
43. Ibid., p.1177.
44. Jopling cited in Ellmann, *Oscar Wilde*, p. 104.
45. Ibid., p. 112.
46. Arthur H. Nethercot, 'Oscar Wilde and the Devil's Advocate', *Publications of the Modern Language Association of America* 59.3 (1944), p. 843.
47. After initially refusing to see *Where's the Cat?*, Wilde later changed his mind and attended a performance of the play with Ellen Terry. However, he was

reportedly disappointed with the production's low quality. Michael Sadleir, *Things Past* (London: Constable, 1944), p. 116.
48. Lloyd Lewis and Henry Justin Smith, *Oscar Wilde Discovers America [1882]* (New York: Benjamin Blom, 1967), p. 46.
49. Leonée Ormond, *George Du Maurier* (London: Routledge, 1969). Various other *Punch* writers and illustrators satirized Wilde with references to 'Ossian Wilderness', 'Oscuro Wilde-Goose', and 'Mr. Wilde Hoskar'.
50. Anonymous (A. T. D.), 'O'Flighty', *The Oxford and Cambridge Undergraduate's Journal*, February 27, 1879. After examining contemporary university and British Census listings, Oxford scholar Peter Vernier has speculated in a letter to the present writer that Arthur Thomas Davies, a graduate of Jesus College Oxford, may have written 'O'Flighty'.
51. Anonymous (A. T. D.), 'O'Flighty'.
52. Ibid.
53. Ibid.
54. Shaw wrote five novels between 1879 and 1883. Richard Dietrich has described these as an ambitious blend of 'avant-garde realism with comic fantasy, social satire of the Dickens or Thackeray sort, parody of the popular novel, and a modernized, antisentimental version of the chivalric romance of Scott'. Richard Farr Dietrich, *Bernard Shaw's Novels: Portraits of the Artist as Man and Superman* (Gainesville: University Press of Florida, 1996), p. xiii.
55. George Bernard Shaw, 'Preface', *Immaturity*, vol. 1, The Works of Bernard Shaw (London: Constable, 1930), p. xlii.
56. Margaret Crosland, in 'Ada Leverson', in *Late-Victorian and Edwardian British Novelists: First Series*, vol. 153, Dictionary of Literary Biography ed. George M. Johnson, (Detroit: Gale Research, 1995), p. 133.
57. Nicholas Grene, 'The Maturing of *Immaturity*: Shaw's First Novel', *Irish University Review* (Autumn 1990), pp. 37, 235.
58 Shaw, *Immaturity*, p. 109.
59. Ibid., pp. 113–14.
60. Shaw, *Immaturity*, p. 158.
61. Ibid., pp. 71, 159, 230, 314. In a letter to George Macmillan of March 22, 1879, Wilde proposes to edit two plays by Euripides for the publisher. Wilde, *The Complete Letters of Oscar Wilde*, p. 78.
62. Ibid., pp. 226–7.
63. Ibid., pp. 298, 303.
64. Ibid., p. 413.
65. Ibid., p. 379.
66. Shaw, in consultation with Alfred Douglas, revised Harris's biography for its second edition in 1938.
67. Shaw recalled seeing the Wildes at a concert in Dublin and remembered that Oscar's father, the ophthalmologist Sir William, operated on Shaw's father to correct a squint.
68. See Oscar Wilde, Reading Room application, March 1, 1879, ms. Additional 48341, British Library, London. In the 1930 preface to *Immaturity*, Shaw relates that the character of Agatha Wylie, who appeared in his novel *An Unsocial Socialist* (1887), was wholly inspired by a young female novelist he noticed in the British Museum Reading Room. Shaw, 'Preface', pp. xliii–xliv.
69. George Bernard Shaw, 'My Memories of Oscar Wilde', in *Oscar Wilde*, ed. Frank Harris (New York: Dorset, 1989), p. 330; Stanley Weintraub, '"The

Hibernian School'": Oscar Wilde and Bernard Shaw', *Shaw: The Annual of Bernard Shaw Studies* 13 (1993).
70. Shaw, 'My Memories of Oscar Wilde', pp. 330–1. Shaw also told Hesketh Pearson that he and Wilde treated one another 'with [such] elaborate courtesy . . . that we never got on familiar terms'. Pearson, *The Life of Oscar Wilde*, p. 156.
71. Shaw, *Immaturity*, p. 346.
72. Dan H. Laurence, ed., *Bernard Shaw: Collected Letters 1874–1897*, vol. 1, 4 vols (London: Max Reinhardt, 1965), p. 210.
73. Karl Beckson, *The Oscar Wilde Encyclopedia* (New York: AMS, 1998), p. 337; Weintraub, '"The Hibernian School"', p. 33.
74. See David J. Gordon, 'Shavian Comedy and the Shadow of Wilde', in *The Cambridge Companion to George Bernard Shaw*, ed. Christopher Innes (Cambridge, UK: Cambridge University Press, 1998), p. 124, and Gary Schmidgall, *The Stranger Wilde: Interpreting Oscar* (New York: Dutton, 1994), p. 353.
75. Shaw, 'My Memories of Oscar Wilde', p. 329.
76. Shaw, *Immaturity*, p. 295.
77. Ibid., pp. 11, 218, 300.
78. Shaw, 'My Memories of Oscar Wilde', p. 334.
79. Shaw, *Immaturity*, p. 228.
80. Shaw, 'My Memories of Oscar Wilde', p. 336.
81. Ibid., p. 303.
82. Mary Hyde, ed., *Bernard Shaw and Alfred Douglas: A Correspondence* (London: John Murray, 1982), p. 124.
83. R. F. Dietrich, *Portrait of the Artist as a Young Superman: A Study of Shaw's Novels* (Gainesville: University of Florida Press, 1969), p. 75.
84. Dietrich, *Bernard Shaw's Novels: Portraits of the Artist as Man and Superman*, p. 57.
85. Holroyd mistakenly refers to Hawkshaw as 'Hawksmith', reflecting the common reading of Smith as Shaw's self-portrait. Michael Holroyd, *Bernard Shaw: The Search for Love 1856–1898*, vol. 1, 4 vols (New York: Random House, 1988), p. 75.
86. Dietrich, *Bernard Shaw's Novels*, p. 57.
87. Shaw, *Immaturity*, pp. 14, 90, 226, 311.
88. See Grene, 'The Maturing of *Immaturity*: Shaw's First Novel', pp. 28, 225, 227.
89. George Bernard Shaw, 'Immaturity', ms. 847, National Library of Ireland, Dublin, pp. 396–404.
90. Ibid., p. 396.
91. Ibid., pp. 397–8.
92. Ibid., pp. 400–1.
93. Ibid., pp. 402–3.
94. Ibid., pp. 403–4.
95. For Shaw's handwritten amendments to the original version of *Immaturity*, see Shaw, *Immaturity*, ts. Additional 50651–50653 (BL). This is the 1921–2 typescript of the 1879–81 version of *Immaturity* that Shaw had made up in order to make his revisions.
96. Shaw, *Immaturity*, pp. 266–7.
97. Shaw, 'Preface', p. xliv.

98. Grene, 'The Maturing of *Immaturity*: Shaw's First Novel', p. 228.
99. Shaw, *Immaturity*, p. xliv.
100. Shaw, 'My Memories of Oscar Wilde', p. 334.
101. Ibid., pp. 331–2.
102. Ibid., p. 334.
103. Ibid., p. 333.
104. Stanley Weintraub argues that Shaw 'fail[ed] to realize that [*The Importance of Being Earnest*] satirized the late-Victorian veneer of earnestness'. Weintraub, '"The Hibernian School"', p. 39.
105. Shaw, 'My Memories of Oscar Wilde', pp. 336–7.
106. Crosland, 'Ada Leverson', p. 338.
107. Wilde, *The Complete Letters of Oscar Wilde*, p. 554.
108. Dan H. Laurence, ed., *Bernard Shaw Theatrics* (Toronto: University of Toronto Press, 1995), pp. 8–9.
109. Wilde, *The Complete Letters of Oscar Wilde*, pp. 563–4.
110. Shaw often repeated this remark and admitted the truth of it to Ellen Terry in a letter of September 25, 1896, saying it was 'quite true; they don't like me; but they are my friends, and some of them love me'. Karl Beckson, 'Oscar Wilde's Celebrated Remark on Bernard Shaw', *Notes and Queries* 239.3 (1994), p. 361.
111. Frank Harris, *Oscar Wilde* (New York: Dorset, 1989), p. 279.
112. See Sherard's *Oscar Wilde 'Drunkard and Swindler': A Reply to George Bernard Shaw, Dr G. J. Renier, Frank Harris etc.* (Calvi, France: Vindex, 1933) and his *Bernard Shaw, Frank Harris and Oscar Wilde* (New York: Greystone Press, 1937).
113. Shaw, 'My Memories of Oscar Wilde', pp. 341–2. Shaw also said, 'Oscar was an overgrown man, with something not quite normal about his bigness . . . I have always maintained that Oscar was a giant in the pathological sense, and this explains a good deal of his weakness'. Shaw cited in Beckson, *The Oscar Wilde Encyclopedia*, p. 337.
114. Beckson, *The Oscar Wilde Encyclopedia*, p. 339.
115. Shaw thought that *De Profundis* contained 'pain . . . inconvenience, annoyance, but no real tragedy, all comedy'. Shaw cited in H. Montgomery Hyde, *Oscar Wilde: The Aftermath* (London: Methuen, 1963), p. 191.
116. Shaw cited in Schmidgall, *The Stranger Wilde: Interpreting Oscar*, p. 359.
117. Hyde, ed., *Bernard Shaw and Alfred Douglas: A Correspondence*, p. 117. Shaw and Douglas became regular correspondents during the 1930s and early 1940s.
118. George Woodcock, 'Books and Comment: Wilde?—The Reality Behind the Legend', *New Republic*, December 6 (1954), p. 22.
119. Schmidgall, *The Stranger Wilde: Interpreting Oscar*, pp. 368–74. Wilde's influence has also been detected in Shaw's plays *You Never Can Tell* (1897), *Candida* (1897), *Major Barbara* (1905), and *Man and Superman* (1905). See Beckson, *The Oscar Wilde Encyclopedia*, pp. 339–41; Harold Bloom, ed., *Modern Critical Views: George Bernard Shaw* (New York: Chelsea House, 1987), p. 10; Gordon, 'Shavian Comedy and the Shadow of Wilde'; David Rose, 'Shavings', *The Oscholars* 3:6, June (2003), available: www.irishdiaspora. net, December 3, 2006, last accessed in July 17, 2007; Weintraub, '"The Hibernian School", pp. 43–6; Nicola Nixon, 'The Reading Gaol of Henry James's *In the Cage*', *ELH* 66.1 (1999).

120. Ian Fletcher defines the 'New Woman' as 'active in politics, art, music, and literature, reacting against the double standard of morality, experimental in her celebration of sexuality, whether heterosexual or Sapphic'. Fletcher, *Aubrey Beardsley*, p. vi.
121. Sadleir, *Things Past*, p. 116. Oxford don C. L. Dodgson (Lewis Carroll) reportedly refused to attend a social gathering where Broughton was also expected to be present. Paul Schlueter and June Schlueter, ed *An Encyclopedia of British Women Writers: Revised and Expanded Edition* (New Brunswick, NJ: Rutgers University Press, 1998), p. 98.
122. Marilyn Wood, *Rhoda Broughton (1840–1920): Profile of a Novelist* (Stamford, UK: Paul Watkins, 1993), p. 54. Frustratingly, this is the first reference Wood makes to any prior invitation from Wilde to Broughton.
123. Margaret L. Woods, 'Oxford in the "Seventies"', *Fortnightly* 150 (1941), p. 281.
124. R. C. Terry 'Rhoda Broughton', in *Victorian Novelists After 1885*, vol. 18 ed. Ira B. Nadel (Detroit: Gale Research, 1983), p. 17; Ethel M. Arnold, 'Rhoda Broughton as I Knew Her', *Fortnightly Review* 114 (1920), p. 276; Sadleir, *Things Past*, pp. 84, 85, 89–91, 94, 101.
125. Arnold, 'Rhoda Broughton as I Knew Her', p. 267; Sadleir, *Things Past*, p. 90.
126. Woods wrote in 1941: 'If Ruskin created the aesthetic movement, Oscar Wilde destroyed it by making it ridiculous . . . I was frequently at his tea-parties . . . The truth was I did not really like Oscar. What his morals at that time were I did not then and do not now know, but I felt for him that instinctive repugnance which quite innocent and ignorant girls sometimes feel for immoral men'. Woods, 'Oxford in the "Seventies"', pp. 281–2.
127. Rhoda Broughton, *Second Thoughts*, vol. 1, 2 vols (London: Richard Bentley & Son, 1880), p. 18.
128. Ibid., vol. 1, pp. 9–10, 17, 18 and vol. 2, pp. 48, 55.
129. Ibid., vol. 2, p. 9.
130. Ibid., vol. 1, pp. 16.
131. Broughton, *Second Thoughts*, vol. 2, pp. 2, 56–7, 60. Marilyn Wood observes the similarity of these pictures to Dante Gabriel Rossetti's paintings of Elizabeth Siddal. Wood, *Rhoda Broughton (1840–1920)*, p. 56.
132. Ellmann, *Oscar Wilde*, pp. 84–5.
133. Broughton, *Second Thoughts*, vol. 2, p. 8.
134. Laurence, ed., *Bernard Shaw: Collected Letters 1874–1897*, p. 223.
135. Wilde, *Reviews*, pp. 99–100.
136. Ibid., p. 100.
137. Woods, 'Oxford in the "Seventies"', p. 281.
138. Anonymous cited in Tanitch, *Oscar Wilde on Stage and Screen*, pp. 16–17. Wilde 'got his own back' on Burnand in his essay 'The Decay of Lying', averring that a dinner party without a 'cultured and fascinating liar' was as dull as 'a lecture at the Royal Society, or a debate at the Incorporated Authors, or one of Mr. Burnand's farcical comedies'. Wilde, *Collins Complete Works of Oscar Wilde*, p. 1081.
139. William Schwenck Gilbert and Arthur Sullivan No 6: Recit. &Song (Bunthorne) in *Patience*, 1881, Opera, Gilbert and Sullivan Archive, http://math-cs.boisestate.edu/gas/patience/webop/pat06.html, last accessed on July 17, 2007.
140. Ibid., p. 123.
141. Anonymous, *Ye Soul Agonies in Ye Life of Oscar Wilde* (New York: Privately printed, 1882), p. 3.

142. Ibid., p. 8.
143. Ibid., p. 9.
144. G. T. Atkinson, 'Oscar Wilde at Oxford', *Cornhill Magazine* 66 (1929), p. 564.
145. Anonymous, *Ye Soul Agonies in Ye Life of Oscar Wilde*, p. 10.
146. Ellmann, *Oscar Wilde*, pp. 509–10.
147. Anonymous, *Ye Soul Agonies in Ye Life of Oscar Wilde*, p. 11.
148. William Gaunt, *The Aesthetic Adventure* (London: Jonathan Cape, 1945), p. 188.
149. Patricia Clarke, 'Rosa Praed (Mrs. Campbell Praed)', in *Australian Literature 1788–1914*, vol. 230, Dictionary of Literary Biography, ed. Selina Samuels (Detroit: Gale Research, 2001), p. 302.
150. Praed cowrote three political novels in the 1880s with her friend the Irish MP Justin McCarthy, who was also known to Wilde. After McCarthy's death, Praed edited his letters to her and published them as *Our Book of Memories: Letters of Justin McCarthy to Mrs Campbell Praed*. (London: Chatto and Windus, 1912).
151. Clarke, 'Rosa Praed (Mrs. Campbell Praed)', p. 309.
152. See G. A. Cevasco, ed., *The 1890s: An Encyclopedia of British Literature, Art, and Culture* (New York: Garland, 1993), p. 482; Clarke, 'Rosa Praed (Mrs. Campbell Praed)', p. 308; Sandra Kemp, Charlotte Mitchell, and David Trotter, *Edwardian Fiction: An Oxford Companion* (Oxford: Oxford University Press, 1997), p. 319.
153. Another fictional portrait of Madame Blavatsky appears in Robert Buchanan's and Henry Murray's *The Charlatan* (1895), discussed in Part 2.
154. Patricia Clarke, *Rosa! Rosa! A Life of Rosa Praed, Novelist and Spiritualist* (Melbourne: Melbourne University Press, 1999), p. 83; Clarke, 'Rosa Praed (Mrs. Campbell Praed)', p. 306.
155. Mrs Campbell Praed, *Affinities: A Romance of To-Day* (London: George Routledge & Sons, 1886), p. 217.
156. Colin Roderick, *In Mortal Bondage: The Strange Life of Rosa Praed* (Sydney: Angus and Robertson, 1948), p. 107.
157. Clarke, *Rosa!, Rosa!*, pp. 85, 100.
158. Praed, *Affinities*, p. 24.
159. Ibid., p. 189.
160. Praed, *Affinities*, pp. 30–1, 34, 50, 56, 86, 109, 221.
161. Ibid., p. 188.
162. Ibid., p. 187.
163. Ibid., pp. 156–7.
164. Ibid., pp. 69, 131–2.
165. Ibid., pp. 21, 76, 88, 110.
166. Ibid., p. 173.
167. Gabrielle Maupin Bielenstein, 'Affinities for Henry James?' *Meanjin*, June (1957), p. 196.
168. Anonymous, 'Three Novels (Book Reviews)', p. 451. See also Anonymous, 'New Novels (Book Reviews)', the *Academy*, March 21, 1885, p. 202.
169. Bentley cited in Roderick, *In Mortal Bondage*, pp. 106–7.
170. Praed, *Affinities*, pp. 26–7, 35.
171. Barbara Belford, *Bram Stoker: A Biography of the Author of Dracula* (New York: Alfred A. Knopf, 1996), p. 216.
172. Praed, *Affinities*, p. 172.
173. Ibid., p. 203.

174. Anne Clark Amor, *Mrs Oscar Wilde: A Woman of Some Importance* (London: Sidgwick and Jackson, 1983), p. 40.
175. Praed, *Affinities*, p. 224.
176. Lowndes cited in Amor, *Mrs Oscar Wilde*, p. 60.
177. *Affinities: A Drama in Three Acts Adapted from Mrs. Campbell Praed's Novel 'Affinities'* (London: Bentley, 1885). Patricia Clarke relates that the dramatic version 'gave much more prominence to the clash of personality between Esmé Colquhoun and Madame Tamvaco'. Clarke, *Rosa! Rosa!*, p. 85.
178. Jopling cited in Mikhail, ed., *Oscar Wilde: Interviews and Recollections*, p. 204.
179. Ibid.
180. Ibid., p. 206.
181. Ibid.
182. Praed, *Affinities*, p. 146.
183. Ibid., pp. 94–5.
184. For Wilde's previously recorded observations on Australia, see John Willis, *Oscar Wilde and the Antipodes*, 2nd edn. (Fairfield: Privately printed, 2002).
185. Praed, *Affinities*, pp. 188–9.
186. Reeves cited in Clarke, *Rosa! Rosa!*, p. 84.
187. Ibid., pp. 85, 200.
188. Cevasco, ed., *The 1890s*, p. 657.
189. Gisela Argyle, 'Mary Augusta Arnold Ward (Mrs Humphry Ward) (1851–1920)', in *Nineteenth-Century British Women Writers: A Bio-Bibliographical Critical Sourcebook*, ed. Abigail Burnham Bloom and Emmanuel S. Nelson (Westport, CT.: Greenwood, 2000), pp. 396–7.
190. William S. Peterson, *Victorian Heretic: Mrs Humphry Ward's Robert Elsmere* (Leicester, UK: Leicester University Press, 1976), p. 133.
191. Ibid., p. 134.
192. Mrs Humphry Ward, *Robert Elsmere*, 24th edn. (London: Smith, Elder, 1889), pp. 395–6.
193. Besant and Rice, *The Monks of Thelema*, p. 25.
194. Horst Schroeder, 'A Quotation in *Dorian Gray*', *Notes and Queries* 38.3 (1991), p. 328.
195. Ward, *Robert Elsmere*, pp. 430–2.
196. Ellmann, *Oscar Wilde*, p. 50.
197. Peterson, *Victorian Heretic*, p. 99.
198. Both Ward and Broughton were also friends of the eminently conservative Henry James.
199. Anonymous, 'Grand Fancy Ball at Headington Hill', *Oxford and Cambridge Undergraduate's Journal*, May 2, 1878.
200. Mrs Humphry Ward, *A Writer's Recollections* (London: W. Collins Sons, 1918), pp. 119–20.
201. Pearson, *The Life of Oscar Wilde*, p. 97.
202. John Sutherland, *Mrs Humphry Ward: Eminent Victorian Pre-Eminent Edwardian* (Oxford: Clarendon, 1990), p. 93.
203. Haldane Macfall, *Aubrey Beardsley: The Man and His Work* (London: John Lane The Bodley Head, 1928), p. 63; Sutherland, *Mrs Humphry Ward*, p. 191; Jean Moorcroft Wilson, *I Was an English Poet: A Critical Biography of Sir William Watson (1858–1936)* (London: Cecil Woolf, 1981), pp. 125–6.
204. Harris, *Oscar Wilde*, p. 279.
205. Wilde, *Collins Complete Works of Oscar Wilde*, pp. 107–5.

206. Ibid., p. 1076.
207. Schroeder, 'A Quotation in *Dorian Gray*', p. 328.
208. Aldington cited in William A. Cohen, 'Willie and Wilde: Reading *The Portrait of Mr. W. H.*', *The South Atlantic Quarterly* 88.1 (1989), p. 243.
209. Quentin Anderson sees Gabriel Nash as James's celebration and criticism of his recently deceased father. Cargill, 'Mr. James's Aesthetic Mr. Nash', p. 177. Lyall Powers, like Leon Edel before him, argues that Nash was an amalgamation of Herbert Pratt and James himself. Powers, 'Mr. James's Aesthetic Mr. Nash—Again', pp. 344–5. Jonathan Freedman notes that 'physically, [Nash is] an amalgam of Oscar Wilde and Henry James'. Freedman, *Professions of Taste: Henry James, British Aestheticism and Commodity Culture* (Stanford, CA: Stanford University Press, 1990), p. 183. Freedman's observation is interesting in light of the fact that Nash's name combines the names of two famous Elizabethan literary adversaries: Gabriel Harvey and Thomas Nashe. Lyall Powers also argues that Nash derives in some part from a female character in one of James's earlier stories 'Gabrielle de Bergerac' (1869). Powers, 'Mr. James's Aesthetic Mr. Nash—Again', p. 347.
210. Kevin J. Hayes, ed., *Henry James: The Contemporary Reviews* (Cambridge, UK: Cambridge University Press, 1996), pp. 227–8.
211. Ibid., p. 238.
212. Roger Gard, ed., *Henry James: The Critical Heritage* (London: Routledge & Kegan Paul, 1968), p. 209.
213. Henry James, *The Tragic Muse*, The Laurel Henry James (New York: Dell, 1961), p. 70.
214. Ibid., p. 39.
215. Ibid., p. 61.
216. Ibid., p. 59.
217. Ibid., p. 31.
218. Ian Fletcher and John Stokes have concluded, and the present writer agrees, that Osmond is a general aesthetic portrait, not specifically Wilde. Ian Fletcher and John Stokes, 'Oscar Wilde', in *Recent Research on Anglo-Irish Writers: A Supplement to Anglo-Irish Literature: A Review of Research*, ed. Richard J. Finneran (New York: The Modern Language Association of America, 1983), p. 45.
219. For James's relation to the aesthetic movement, see Jonathan Freedman's *Professions of Taste* (Stanford, CA: Stanford University Press, 1990) and Richard Ellmann, 'James Amongst the Aesthetes', in *Henry James and Homo-Erotic Desire*, ed. John R. Bradley (London: Macmillan, 1999).
220. George Monteiro, 'A Contemporary View of Henry James and Oscar Wilde', *American Literature* 35 (1964), p. 530.
221. Henry James, in *Henry James: A Life in Letters*, ed. Philip Horne (London: Penguin, 1999), p. 135.
222. Ellmann, *Oscar Wilde*, p. 171; Schroeder, *Additions and Corrections to Richard Ellmann's Oscar Wilde*, p. 61.
223. Ellmann, *Oscar Wilde*, p. 170.
224. Freedman observes that 'where for Wilde [Paterian] intensity must be sought through the senses, for James, it is discovered through the mobilization of the quickened, multiplied consciousness'. Freedman, *Professions of Taste*, p. 199.
225. Ibid., pp. 169–70. The failure of James's play *Guy Domville* made a stark contrast to the success of Wilde's *An Ideal Husband*, which was playing at the

same time; James felt this keenly. To add insult to injury James's play was replaced after a month by Wilde's *The Importance of Being Earnest*.
226. Sheldon M. Novick, 'Introduction', in *Henry James and Homo-Erotic Desire*, ed. John R. Bradley (London: Macmillan, 1999), p. 10. For further discussion of James's sexuality, see Eve Kosofsky Sedgwick, 'The Beast in the Closet: James and the Writing of Homosexual Panic', *Epistemology of the Closet* (London: Penguin, 1994).
227. Eric Haralson, 'The Elusive Queerness of Henry James's "Queer Comrade": Reading Gabriel Nash of *The Tragic Muse*', in *Victorian Sexual Dissidence*, ed. Richard Dellamora (Chicago: University of Chicago Press, 1999), p. 197.
228. Freedman, *Professions of Taste*, p. 171.
229. Ellmann, *Oscar Wilde*, pp. 87, 171.
230. James, *Henry James*, pp. 279–80.
231. Ellmann, *Oscar Wilde*, p. 463. For a discussion of the relation of James's novella *In the Cage* (1898) to Wilde's *The Ballad of Reading Gaol* (1898), see Nicola Nixon, 'The Reading Gaol'.
232. Wilde, *Reviews*, p. 261.
233. Ibid., pp. 261–2.
234. Wilde, *Collins Complete Works of Oscar Wilde*, p. 1074.
235. Laurence Housman, *Echo de Paris: A Study from Life* (London: Jonathan Cape, 1923), p. 9.
236. Richard Ellmann, 'James Amongst the Aesthetes', p. 37.
237. Wilde, *The Complete Letters of Oscar Wilde,* p. 1118. It has been suggested that James's 'The Turn of the Screw', particularly in its expression of sexuality through fear, was heavily influenced by Wilde's trials. See Neill Matheson, 'Talking Horrors: James, Euphemism, and the Specter of Wilde', *American Literature* 71.4 (1999).
238. Hayes, ed., *Henry James: The Contemporary Reviews*, p. 225.
239. Cargill, 'Mr. James's Aesthetic Mr. Nash', p. 186; Freedman, *Professions of Taste*, p. 192.
240. John Carlos Rowe, in *The Other Henry James*, New Americanists, ed. Donald E. Pease (Durham, NC: Duke University Press, 1998), pp. 93–4; Regenia Gagnier, *Idylls of the Marketplace: Oscar Wilde and the Victorian Public* (Aldershot: Scolar, 1986), p. 222.
241. Powers, 'Mr. James's Aesthetic Mr. Nash—Again', pp. 344–5.
242. James, *The Tragic Muse*, pp. 421–2.
243. Ellmann, *Oscar Wilde*, p. 353. James particularly liked Wilde's comment that 'London is all sad people and fogs. I don't know whether fogs produce the sad people, or the sad people produce the fogs'. Beckson, *The Oscar Wilde Encyclopedia*, p. 170.
244. Ellmann, 'James Amongst the Aesthetes', pp. 39–41; Sammells, *Wilde Style*, p. 55.
245. James, *Henry James*, pp. 279–80.
246. Ibid., p. 288.
247. James, *The Tragic Muse*, pp. 289, 375.
248. Ibid., p. 292.
249. Ibid., pp. 161, 290.
250. Ibid., p. 72.
251. Ibid., p. 134.
252. Ibid., p. 140.
253. Ibid., p. 135.

254. Ibid., p. 310.
255. Ibid., pp. 63, 374–6.
256. Ibid., p. 376.
257. Haralson, 'The Elusive Queerness of Henry James's "Queer Comrade"', p. 204.
258. Rowe, *The Other Henry James*, p. 96.
259. James, *The Tragic Muse*, p. 549.
260. Ibid., p. 399.
261. Ibid., p. 407.
262. Miller, 'Oscar in *The Tragic Muse*'.
263. James, *The Tragic Muse*, p. 143.
264. Ibid., p. 550; Haralson, 'The Elusive Queerness of Henry James's "Queer Comrade"', p. 192.
265. James, *The Tragic Muse*, p. 549.
266. Ibid., p. 560.
267. Ibid., pp. 49, 55, 551.
268. Powers, 'Mr. James's Aesthetic Mr. Nash—Again', p. 346.
269. James, *The Tragic Muse*, p. 553.
270. Ibid., p. 554.
271. James, *The Tragic Muse*, pp. 554–5.
272. Wilde, *Collins Complete Works of Oscar Wilde*, pp. 1075–6.
273. James, *The Tragic Muse*, p. 556.
274. Rowe, *The Other Henry James*, p. 98.
275. Haralson, 'The Elusive Queerness of Henry James's "Queer Comrade"', p. 205.
276. Ibid., p. 204.
277. Ellmann, *Oscar Wilde*, p. 293.
278. Freedman, *Professions of Taste*, p. 191.
279. Christopher Lane, 'The Impossibility of Seduction in James's *Roderick Hudson* and *The Tragic Muse*', *American Literature* 68.4 (1996). See also Christopher Lane, 'Framing Fears, Reading Designs: The Homosexual Art of Painting in James, Wilde and Beerbohm', *ELH* 61.4 (1994).
280. Cargill, 'Mr. James's Aesthetic Mr. Nash', pp. 183–5.
281. Ibid., p. 186.
282. Ibid., pp. 178–9; James, *The Tragic Muse*, pp. 35–6.
283. Freedman, *Professions of Taste*, pp. 93, 168.
284. Kerry Powell, 'Tom, Dick and Dorian Gray: Magic-Picture Mania in Late Victorian Fiction', *Philological Quarterly* 62, Spring (1983).
285. James cited in Powers, 'Mr. James's Aesthetic Mr. Nash—Again', p. 349.
286. Wilde cited in Ellmann, *Oscar Wilde*, (p. 414).
287. Raffalovich has been described by Brocard Sewell as 'congenitally homosexual by temperament'. Sewell cited in Linda C. Dowling, '*Venus and Tannhäuser*: Beardsley's Satire of Decadence', *The Journal of Narrative Technique* 8.1 (1978), p. 33.
288. Ellmann, *Oscar Wilde*, p. 266; Schroeder, *Additions and Corrections to Richard Ellmann's Oscar Wilde*, p. 95.
289. André Raffalovich, 'Oscar Wilde', in *Footnote to the Nineties: A Memoir of John Gray and André Raffalovich*, ed. Brocard Sewell (London: Cecil and Amelia Woolf, 1927), p. 110.
290. Matthew Sturgis has asserted that Raffalovich was exclusively homosexual in the 1880s. Sturgis, *Aubrey Beardsle*, p. 244.
291. Raffalovich, 'Oscar Wilde', p. 111.

292. Ibid., p. 108.
293. Wilde, *Reviews*, pp. 12–13.
294. Ellmann, *Oscar Wilde*, p. 248.
295. Raffalovich, 'Oscar Wilde', p. 111.
296. Ibid., p. 112.
297. Rupert Croft-Cooke, *Feasting with Panthers: A New Consideration of Some Late Victorian Writers* (New York: Holt, Rinehart & Winston, 1967), pp. 215–18.
298. Ian Fletcher, ed., *The Poems of John Gray* (Greensboro, NC: ELT, 1988), p. 8.
299. Raffalovich cited in Ellmann, *Oscar Wilde*, p. 266; Schroeder, *Additions and Corrections to Richard Ellmann's Oscar Wilde*, p. 95.
300. Brocard Sewell, *Footnote to the Nineties: A Memoir of John Gray and André Raffalovich* (London: Cecil and Amelia Woolf, 1968), p. 29.
301. Raffalovich cited in ibid., p. 28.
302. Raffalovich cited in Ellmann, *Oscar Wilde*, p. 267.
303. Raffalovich cited in Sewell, *Footnote to the Nineties*, p. 29.
304. Ibid., p. 30.
305. Ibid., p. 42.
306. Raffalovich, 'Oscar Wilde', p. 111; Schroeder, *Additions and Corrections to Richard Ellmann's Oscar Wilde*, pp. 151–2.
307. Wilde also used this quip about the fictional Lady Brandon in *The Picture of Dorian Gray*. Wilde, *Collins Complete Works of Oscar Wilde*, p. 22.
308. Croft-Cooke, *Feasting with Panthers*, p. 215.
309. Raffalovich, 'Oscar Wilde', p. 112.
310. For a discussion of Raffalovich's sublimation of his own sexuality, see Sturgis, *Aubrey Beardsley*, p. 244.
311. Sewell, *Footnote to the Nineties*, pp. 36–7.
312. Joseph Pearce, *The Unmasking of Oscar Wilde* (London: HarperCollins, 2000), p. 244.
313. Croft-Cooke, *Feasting with Panthers*, pp. 23, 221.
314. Arthur Conan Doyle, *Memories and Adventures* (London: John Murray, 1930), pp. 94–5.
315. Paul Barolsky, 'The Case of the Domesticated Aesthete', *Virginia Quarterly Review* 60 (1984), p. 444; Owen Dudley Edwards, ed., *A Study in Scarlet* (Oxford: Oxford University Press, 1993), p. 171; John A. Hodgson, 'An Allusion to Arthur Conan Doyle's *A Study in Scarlet* in *The Picture of Dorian Gray*', *English Language Notes* 34.2 (1997), p. 42.
316. Hodgson, 'An Allusion to Arthur Conan Doyle's *A Study in Scarlet* in *The Picture of Dorian Gray*', pp. 43–4. Hodgson does not consider Edwards's point that 'scarlet thread' also appears in the Song of Solomon 4:3: 'thy lips are like a thread of scarlet, and thy speech is comely'. Edwards, ed., *A Study in Scarlet*, p. 171.
317. Doyle, *Memories and Adventures*, p. 95.
318. Samuel Rosenberg, *Naked Is the Best Disguise: The Death and Resurrection of Sherlock Holmes* (London: Arlington, 1975), p. 2.
319. Arthur Conan Doyle, 'The Sign of Four', *The Celebrated Cases of Sherlock Holmes*, Treasury of World Masterpieces (London: Octopus, 1981), pp. 36, 632. Rosenberg has noted the echo here of Wilde's epigram delivered during his American lecture tour in 1882: 'The American Woman? She is *a charming oasis in the bewildering desert* of commonsense [Rosenberg's italics]'. Rosenberg, *Naked is the Best Disguise*, p. 133.

320. Doyle, 'The Sign of Four', pp. 636–7.
321. Ibid., p. 638. Rosenberg overreads Sholto's 'weakness' for art as a reference to Wilde's 'weak' sexuality. He makes the astonishing interpretation of the mention of Bouguereau, the painter of a picture owned by Sholto, as being suggestive of the phrase 'bugger-oh'! Rosenberg also sees Sholto's admiration of the 'French school' of painting as a reference to fellatio! Rosenberg, *Naked is the Best Disguise*, p. 134. Here is a clear example of Wilde's sensational life impeding objective critical analysis.
322. Ibid., p. 641.
323. Wilde wrote letters from prison in 1896 and 1897 attempting to ascertain if this coat could be saved for him. The coat was pawned by his brother Willie and this upset Wilde greatly. Wilde, *The Complete Letters of Oscar Wilde*, p. 807.
324. Doyle, 'The Sign of Four', p. 641.
325. Ibid., p. 638.
326. Ibid., p. 639.
327. Doyle, *Memories and Adventures*, pp. 318, 450.
328. Randy Roberts controversially concludes that the most likely explanation for Doyle's allusion to Queensberry is that the plethora of Wilde and Douglas biographers have misdated the pair's first meeting. Roberts contends that the two men could have met as early as 1889. Randy Roberts, 'Oscar Wilde and Sherlock Holmes: A Literary Mystery', *Clues* 1.1 (1980).
329. Doyle, 'The Sign of Four', p. 633.
330. Arthur Conan Doyle, 'A Study in Scarlet', *The Celebrated Cases of Sherlock Holmes*, Treasury of World Masterpieces (London: Octopus, 1981), p. 559.
331. Doyle, 'The Sign of Four', pp. 33, 627.
332. Ibid., p. 672.
333. Ian Ousby, *Bloodhounds of Heaven: The Detective in English Fiction from Godwin to Doyle* (Cambridge, MA Harvard University Press, 1976), pp. 157–8.
334. H. R. F. Keating, *Sherlock Holmes: The Man and His World* (New York: Charles Scribner's Sons, 1979), p. 112.
335. Owen Dudley Edwards, *The Quest for Sherlock Holmes: A Biographical Study of Arthur Conan Doyle* (Edinburgh: Mainstream, 1983) p. 25; Doyle, 'The Sign of Four', pp. 88, 626.
336. Barolsky, 'The Case of the Domesticated Aesthete', p. 439. Barolsky also sees the influence of Walter Pater and Bernard Berensen in Doyle's detective.
337. Martin Priestman, *Detective Fiction and Literature* (London: Macmillan, 1990), p. 106.
338. Arthur Conan Doyle, 'The Greek Interpreter', *The Celebrated Cases of Sherlock Holmes*, Treasury of World Masterpieces (London: Octopus, 1981), p. 302.
339. Beckson, *The Oscar Wilde Encyclopedia*, p. 175.
340. Doyle, 'The Sign of Four', p. 47.
341. Arthur Conan Doyle, 'The Noble Bachelor', *The Celebrated Cases of Sherlock Holmes*, Treasury of World Masterpieces (London: Octopus, 1981), p. 150.
342. It is interesting that the American conception of Holmes, significantly influenced by actor William Gillette—who adapted Holmes for the stage—is distinctly Wilde-like. Pierre Nordon notes that Gillette emphasized the detective's 'dandyism and somewhat sinister charm . . . also his "disappointment with the Atlantic"', borrowing from Wilde's famous statement upon

2 Decadent (1891–1895)

1. Cohen, 'Willie and Wilde', n. 27, p. 243.
2. Ellmann, *Oscar Wilde*, pp. 288–9.
3. Guy Deghy and Keith Waterhouse, *Café Royal: Ninety Years of Bohemia* (London: Hutchinson, 1955), pp. 58–59.
4. Gaunt, *The Aesthetic Adventure*, p. 136.
5. Corelli perpetrated many fantastic inventions about herself and her history. She told George Bentley that her father was a native Venetian and she could trace her Venetian ancestry back to the musician Arcangelo Corelli. (Corelli was the daughter of Scottish balladeer and journalist Charles Mackay.) Corelli reportedly believed herself to be a reincarnation of Shakespeare. *Who Was Who 1897–1915: A Companion to Who's Who Containing the Biographies of Those who Died during the Period 1897–1915*, 6th edn (London: A & C Black, 1988), p. 132; Sutherland, *The Stanford Companion to Victorian Fiction*, p. 149.
6. John Lucas, 'Marie Corelli', in *Novelists and Prose Writers*, ed. James Vinson and D. L. Kirkpatrick, Great Writers of the English Language (London: Macmillan, 1979), p. 283.
7. S. Boswin, *The Writings of Marie Corelli* (Bombay: Examiner Press, 1907), p. 34.
8. Sutherland, *The Stanford Companion to Victorian Fiction*, p. 149.
9. Margaret B. McDowell, 'Marie Corelli', in *British Novelists, 1890–1929: Traditionalists*, vol. 34, ed. Thomas F. Staley, Dictionary of Literary Biography (Detroit: Gale Research Company, 1985), pp. 86, 88.
10. Brian Masters, *Now Barabbas Was a Rotter: The Extraordinary Life of Marie Corelli* (London: Hamish Hamilton, 1978), pp. 114–15.
11. See ibid., pp. 115–16.
12. Bertha Vyver, *Memoirs of Marie Corelli* (London: Alston Rivers, 1930), p. 119.
13. Masters, *Now Barabbas Was a Rotter*, p. 117.
14. Ibid.
15. William Stuart Scott, *Marie Corelli: The Story of a Friendship* (London: Hutchinson, 1955), p. 81.
16. Anonymous (Marie Corelli), *The Silver Domino or Side Whispers, Social and Literary*, 22nd edn. (London: Lamley and Company, 1894), p. 166.
17. Ibid., p. 171.
18. Ibid., p. 172.
19. Ibid., p. 169.
20. Vyver, *Memoirs of Marie Corelli*, pp. 91–2.
21. Anonymous (Marie Corelli), *The Silver Domino or Side Whispers*, pp. 166–7.
22. Ibid., pp, 171–2; Ellmann, *Oscar Wilde*, p. 185.
23. Anonymous (Marie Corelli), *The Silver Domino or Side Whispers*, pp. 174–5.
24. Ibid.
25. Ibid., p. 178.
26. Ibid.
27. Shaw wrote to *New Review* editor Tighe Hopkins in 1889 that '[w]hen I used to review for the *Pall Mall* . . . an *Auto da fe* took place once a month or

arriving in America in 1882. Pierre Nordon, *Conan Doyle*, trans. Frances Partridge (London: John Murray, 1966), p. 204.

so . . . the executioner being sometimes Oscar Wilde, sometimes William Archer, sometimes myself . . . there was no saying, in the absence of signatures, which was the real torturer on these occasions; and to this day there are men who hate me for inhumanities perpetrated by Archer and Wilde'. Laurence, ed., *Bernard Shaw: Collected Letters 1874–1897* pp. 222–3.
28. Anonymous (Marie Corelli), *The Silver Domino or Side Whispers*, pp. 73, 167.
29. Ibid., p. 179.
30. Ibid., p. 260.
31. Ibid., pp. 345–6.
32. Ibid., p. 170.
33. McDowell, 'Marie Corelli', p. 84; Joy Melville, *Mother of Oscar: The Life of Jane Francesca Wilde* (London: John Murray, 1994), p. 158.
34. Masters, *Now Barabbas Was a Rotter*, pp. 60, 89.
35. Boswin, *The Writings of Marie Corelli*, p. 23.
36. Vyver, *Memoirs of Marie Corelli*, pp. 91–2.
37. Masters, *Now Barabbas Was a Rotter*, p. 74.
38. Vyver, *Memoirs of Marie Corelli*, p. 87; Wilde, *The Complete Letters of Oscar Wilde*, p. 382.
39. Anonymous (Marie Corelli), *The Silver Domino or Side Whispers*, p. 171.
40. Annette R. Federico states that Corelli's 'mission was to rescue England from commercialism, religious indifference, and political corruption'. *Who Was Who 1897–1915*, p. 133; Sutherland, *The Stanford Companion to Victorian Fiction*, p. 149.
41. Eileen Bigland, *Marie Corelli: The Woman and the Legend* (London: Jarrolds, 1953), p. 164.
42. Pearson, *The Life of Oscar Wilde*, p. 324.
43. Wilde, *The Complete Letters of Oscar Wilde*, p. 1011.
44. Philip Hoare, 'Wilde's Last Stand', *The Wildean* 11 (1997), pp. 1, 17; Philip Hoare, *Wilde's Last Stand: Decadence, Conspiracy and the First World War* (London: Duckworth, 1997), p. 90.
45. McDowell, 'Marie Corelli', p. 88.
46. At one point Corelli changed her story to aver that she had only contributed some of the less offensive parts of *The Silver Domino*. Masters, *Now Barabbas Was a Rotter*, pp. 118–20.
47. Ella Hepworth Dixon, *As I Knew Them: Sketches of People I Have Met on the Way* (London: Hutchinson, 1930), p. 35.
48. Ibid.
49. Ibid. pp. 34–5.
50. Ibid., p. 35.
51. Ibid.
52. Ibid. Bernard Partridge knew Wilde and caricatured him in *Punch*, most notably with his 'Fancy Portrait' on March 5, 1892 and 'The Decadent Guys' on November 10, 1894 (see discussion of Robert Hichens's *The Green Carnation* and plate 6). Partridge also illustrated Wilde's poetic 'Fantaisies Décoratives. I. Le Panneau. II. Les Ballons' in the 1887 Christmas number of the *Lady's Pictorial* (reprinted in *Poems*, 1908) and Wilde's story 'The Young King' in the 1888 Christmas *Lady's Pictorial*.
53. Margaret Wynman (Ella Hepworth Dixon), *My Flirtations*, 1893, Victorian Women Writers Project, available www.indiana.edu/~letrs/vwwp/dixon/myflirt.html, April 4, 2000, last accessed on July17, 2007.

54. Ibid.
55. Ibid.
56. Ibid.
57. Ibid.
58. Margaret Diane Stetz, 'The Bi-Social Oscar Wilde and "Modern" Women', *Nineteenth-Century Literature* 55.4 (2001), pp. 60–1, 535. On January 21, 1893, *Punch* observed that 'anyone in the London world could easily label' the originals of Wynman's fictional portraits 'were he not baffled by the art of the skilful writer, and by the equally skilful illustrator . . . [who have] combined to throw the reader off the right scent'. Donald Mead, ed., '*Punch* and the New Woman and *My Flirtations*', *Intentions*, no. 33 (London: Privately printed, 2004), p. 21.
59. Wynman (Ella Hepworth Dixon), *My Flirtations*.
60. Ibid.
61. Ibid.
62. Dixon, *As I Knew Them*, p. 35.
63. Stetz, 'The Bi-Social Oscar Wilde and "Modern" Women', pp. 535–6.
64. Wynman (Ella Hepworth Dixon), *My Flirtations*, pp. 64–5.
65. Ibid.
66. Dixon, *As I Knew Them*, p. 136.
67. Stetz, 'The Bi-Social Oscar Wilde and "Modern" Women', p. 517.
68. Ella Hepworth Dixon, *The Story of a Modern Woman*, 1894, Novel, Victorian Women Writers Project, available www.indiana.edu/~letrs/vwwp/dixon/storymod.htm, April 4, 2000, last accessed on July 17, 2007.
69. Mikhail, ed., *Oscar Wilde: Interviews and Recollections*, p. 152.
70. Dixon, *The Story of a Modern Woman*, p. 79.
71. Ibid.
72. Ibid.
73. Ibid. These resemblances lead me to believe that Ann Heilmann is mistaken in her identification of Beaufort as Wilde. Ann Heilmann, 'Wilde's New Women: The New Woman on Wilde', in *The Importance of Reinventing Oscar: Versions of Wilde during the Last 100 Years*, ed. Uwe Böker, Richard Corballis, and Julie A Hibbard (Amsterdam, Netherlands: Rodopi, 2002), p. 136.
74. Ibid.
75. Ibid.
76. Ibid.
77. Ibid.
78. Margaret Diane Stetz, 'Ella Hepworth Dixon', in *Late Victorian and Edwardian British Novelists: Second Series*, vol. 197, Dictionary of Literary Biography, ed. George M. Johnson (Detroit: Gale Research, 1999), pp. 100, 104.
79. Stetz, 'The Bi-Social Oscar Wilde and "Modern" Women', p. 525.
80. Mikhail, ed., *Oscar Wilde: Interviews and Recollections*, pp. 152–3.
81. Ella Hepworth Dixon, 'The World's Slow Stain', *Turn-of-the-Century Women* 1.2 (1984), p. 10.
82. Ibid., p. 220.
83. Ibid., pp. 3–4.
84. Ibid., pp. 4, 8, 9.
85. Ibid., p. 3.
86. Ibid., pp. 3, 6.

87. Ibid., p. 5.
88. Ibid., p. 8.
89. This sympathy is perhaps most evident in Mary Elizabeth Braddon's *The Rose of Life* (London: Hutchinson, 1905).
90. Wilde had a friend named Adela Schuster. She was the daughter of a wealthy Frankfurt banker, who gave Wilde money during his trials and after he was released from prison; she also sent a wreath to his funeral. Mikhail, ed., *Oscar Wilde: Interviews and Recollections* pp. 340–1n; Ellmann, *Oscar Wilde*, p. 549. Unfortunately, there is not enough extant information on Schuster to draw a comparison with Dixon's Adela Buller.
91. Dixon, 'The World's Slow Stain', pp. 3, 5.
92. Ibid., pp. 4, 6–7.
93. The same can be said of Frank Danby's (Julia Frankau's) novel *The Sphinx's Lawyer* (London: William Heinemann, 1906).
94. Dixon, *As I Knew Them*, pp. 35–6.
95. Ibid., p. 281.
96. Charles Hallam Elton Brookfield, *The Poet and the Puppets* in The Lord Chamberlain's Plays and Day-Books, 1851–1899, ms. Additional 52929–53701 (BL).
97. Harold Munro, Press cuttings relating to Oscar Wilde, mostly 1879–1895, ms. Additional 57767 passim, vol. 34 (ff. 98), no. 30 (BL). Wilde's often derivative style of writing occasionally prompted accusations of plagiarism, but this is the first reference the present writer has seen to Wilde being 'tight' with money.
98. Ellmann, *Oscar Wilde*, pp. 349–50.
99. Merlin Holland, *Irish Peacock and Scarlet Marquess: The Real Trial of Oscar Wilde* (London: Fourth Estate, 2003), p. xxiv. Tanitch, *Oscar Wilde on Stage and Screen*, pp. 1–19. The reason for Brookfield's antipathy toward Wilde is something of a mystery; Wilde is not mentioned in Brookfield's memoirs (*Random Reminiscences*, 1911). Vincent O'Sullivan believed that Brookfield resented Wilde's insistence that the cast of *An Ideal Husband* met on Christmas Day. Ellmann, *Oscar Wilde*, p. 404. Max Beerbohm recalled that Brookfield felt 'snubbed' by Wilde in some way. S. N. Behrman, *Conversation with Max* (London: Hamish Hamilton, 1960), p. 68. Richard Ellmann thought 'the fact that Brookfield may have been Thackeray's illegitimate son made him particularly sensitive to immorality'. Ellmann, *Oscar Wilde*, p. 349. Karl Beckson speculates that 'Wilde's brilliant success apparently provoked [Brookfield] to jealousy'. Beckson, *The Oscar Wilde Encyclopedia*, p. 36. Herbert Beerbohm Tree reported that Wilde could be an 'infernal nuisance' during rehearsals of his plays, often interrupting with objections and suggestions. Holland, *Son of Oscar Wilde*, p. 192. It is possible that Brookfield took exception to Wilde's frequent gibes about the acting profession and his reference to actors as 'puppets'; indeed that was the inspiration for the title of Brookfield's burlesque. Michael Seeney provides an overview of interpretations of Brookfield's dislike of Wilde in Michael Seeney, 'Charles Brookfield', *The Wildean* 21 (2002).
100. Arthur Cunliffe and Arthur Hamilton Grant, *The Ephemeral*, May 18, 1893.
101. A. Hamilton Grant, '"The Ephemeral": Some Memories of Oxford in the Nineties', *Cornhill Magazine* 71.426 (1931), p. 647.
102. Arthur Cunliffe, 'Ossian Savage's New Play', *The Ephemeral*, May 18, 1893, p. 3.

103. Ibid., p. 4.
104. Ibid.
105. Ibid.
106. Ibid., p. 3.
107. Alfred Douglas, 'To the Editor of "The Ephemeral"', May 20.
108. Anonymous (Arthur Cunliffe), 'Re Ossian Savage's New Play', The Ephemeral, May 22.
109. Alfred Douglas, 'To the Editor of "The Ephemeral"', The Ephemeral, May 24, p. 47.
110. Grant, '"The Ephemeral".
111. Ibid., pp. 645–6.
112. Ibid., p. 648.
113. Ibid., p. 650.
114. Anonymous, 'Grant, Sir (Alfred) Hamilton', *Who Was Who 1929–1940*, 6th edn (London: Adam and Charles Black, 1941); Grant, '"The Ephemeral"', p. 641.
115. Although Beerbohm praises Wilde as an 'incomparable wit' in this essay, he also highlights the latter's indolence and vanity. The overall picture of Wilde is one of an eccentric genius, in possession of 'a spirit which makes him a perfect type and a personality without flaw'. Beerbohm cited in Beckson, *The Oscar Wilde Encyclopedia*, p. 25.
116. Ellmann, *Oscar Wilde*, pp. 291–2.
117. J. G. Riewald, *Sir Max Beerbohm, Man and Writer: A Critical Analysis with a Brief Life and a Bibliography* (The Hague: Martinus Nijhoff, 1953), p. 129.
118. Max Beerbohm, *Letters to Reggie Turner* (London: Rupert Hart-Davis, 1964), p. 35.
119. Behrman, *Conversation with Max*, p. 67; Beerbohm, *Letters to Reggie Turner*, p. 95; Mikhail, ed., *Oscar Wilde: Interviews and Recollections*, p. 273.
120. Beerbohm, *Letters to Reggie Turner*, p. 37.
121. Besant and Rice, *The Monks of Thelema*, p. 25.
122. Seeney, 'The Fictional Career of Oscar Wilde', p. 46.
123. In a letter to Reggie Turner on September 29, 1893, Beerbohm wrote, 'Bobbie [Robert Ross] has offended Oscar most *fearfully* [emphasis in the original] by telling him that . . . he is a gentleman of the old school. Isn't it exquisitely funny? There *is* something rather Georgian in Oscar's deportment'. Beerbohm, *Letters to Reggie Turner*, p.72.
124. Max Beerbohm, *A Peep into the Past and Other Prose Pieces* (London: Heinemann, 1972), pp. 3–8.
125. Ibid., p. 6.
126. Ibid., p. 4.
127. Ibid., p. 6.
128. Ibid., p. 5.
129. Notes from Beerbohm's private character book reveal his close observation of Wilde's appearance and mannerisms, which Beerbohm translated into caricature:

> Luxury-gold-tipped matches-hair curled-Assyrian-wax statue-huge rings-fat white hands-not soigné-feather bed-pointed fingers-ample scarf-Louis Quinze cane-vast malmaison-cat-like tread-heavy shoulders-enormous dowager-or schoolboy-way of laughing with hand over mouth-stroking chin-looking up sideways-jollity overdone—But

real vitality . . . Effeminate, but vitality of twenty men. Magnetism-authority-Deeper than repute or wit-Hypnotic. David Cecil, *Max: A Biography* (London: Constable, 1964), p. 71.
130. Behrman, *Conversation with Max*, p. 69.
131. Ibid., p. 66.
132. Cecil, *Max: A Biography*, p. 73.
133. Beckson, *The Oscar Wilde Encyclopedia*, p. 26.
134. Wilde, *The Complete Letters of Oscar Wilde*, p. 856.
135. Max Beerbohm, 'Charterhouse and Oxford: 1890–1895', *Max in Verse; Rhymes and Parodies by Max Beerbohm*, ed. J. G. Riewald (London: Heinemann, 1964), p. 7.
136. Max Beerbohm, '1880', *The Works of Max Beerbohm* (London: John Lane, The Bodley Head, 1921), p. 46.
137. Cecil, *Max: A Biography*, p. 73.
138. Beckson, *The Oscar Wilde Encyclopedia*, p. 24.
139. Wilde, *The Complete Letters of Oscar Wilde*, p. 962.
140. Behrman, *Conversation with Max*, p. 68.
141. Beerbohm, *Letters to Reggie Turner*, p. 53.
142. Beckson, *The Oscar Wilde Encyclopedia*, p. 25.
143. Beerbohm attended Wilde's trials to lend his support. Richard Ellmann is incorrect in his statement that Beerbohm wrote 'cruelly in April–May 1895 to Mrs Leverson [at the time of Wilde's trials], "I look forward eagerly to the first act of Oscar's new Tragedy. But surely the title *Douglas* must have been used before."' This was actually written to Leverson by Aubrey Beardsley, not Beerbohm. Aubrey Beardsley, *The Letters of Aubrey Beardsley*, ed. Henry Maas, J. L. Duncan, and W. G. Good (London: Cassell, 1970), p. 82; Ellmann, *Oscar Wilde*, p. 400; Schroeder, *Additions and Corrections to Richard Ellmann's Oscar Wilde*, p. 151.
144. Beerbohm took part in a deputation that attempted to alleviate Wilde's suffering in prison.
145. Beerbohm sent Wilde a selection of books after his release from prison; Wilde responded by sending Beerbohm a copy of *The Ballad of Reading Gaol*.
146. Cecil, *Max: A Biography*, p. 121.
147. Beerbohm, *Letters to Reggie Turner*, pp. 102, 20.
148. Ibid., pp. 136–7.
149. Beerbohm was one of the few people to have seen the unexpurgated version of *De Profundis* before it was published in its entirety in 1962. Ibid., p. 122.
150. Beerbohm saw Wilde's profession of humility in the letter as an attitude struck for the sake of art, and alleged that Wilde experienced 'an artist's joy' in his own tragedy. Beerbohm, *A Peep into the Past and Other Prose Pieces*, pp. 37–40.
151. Max Beerbohm, *Letters of Max Beerbohm: 1892–1956* (London: John Murray, 1988), p. 118; Beckson, *The Oscar Wilde Encyclopedia*, p. 27.
152. Beerbohm, *A Peep into the Past and Other Prose Pieces*, p. 41.
153. L. Amery, F. W. Hirst, and H. A. A. Cruso, *Aristophanes at Oxford* (Hamilton: Kent, 1894).
154. Ibid., p. 64.
155. Wilde, *The Complete Letters of Oscar Wilde*, p. 457.
156. Richard Le Gallienne, review of Oscar Wilde's *Intentions*, ts. (Clark).
157. Richard Le Gallienne, 'The Décadent to His Soul', *English Poems* (London: The Bodley Head, 1895).

158. Beckson, *The Oscar Wilde Encyclopedia*, p. 194.
159. Richard Le Gallienne, *Prose Fancies* (London: Elkin Mathews and John Lane, 1894), pp. 35–6, 45.
160. Mikhail, ed., *Oscar Wilde: Interviews and Recollections*, p. 396.
161. Charles Higham, *The Adventures of Conan Doyle: The Life of the Creator of Sherlock Holmes* (London: Hamish Hamilton, 1976), p. 103.
162. William S. Baring-Gould, ed., *The Annotated Sherlock Holmes*, 2 vols (London: John Murray, 1968), p. 591; Ronald Burt De Waal, *The World Bibliography of Sherlock Holmes and Dr. Watson: A Classified and Annotated List of Materials Relating to Their Lives and Adventures* (Boston: New York Graphic Society, 1974), pp. 220–1.
163. Doyle, *Memories and Adventures*, p. 95.
164. Doyle, 'The Greek Interpreter', p. 302.
165. Ibid.
166. Mycroft's comment in the later story, 'The Bruce-Partington Plans': 'to run here and there, to cross-question . . . and lie on my face with a lens to my eye—it is not my *métier* is an interesting echo of Henry James's Gabriel Nash in *The Tragic Muse*: 'I've no *état civil* . . . Merely to be is such a *métier*'.
167. Doyle, 'The Greek Interpreter', p. 304.
168. Robert Ross and Jean-Joseph Renaud said Wilde's eyes were blue, Ada Leverson said they were blue-gray, Max Beerbohm said they were gray, and Alfred Douglas thought they were green. Jeremy Reed recently asserted they were brown. Frances Turner, 'Jeremy Reed and the Colour of Oscar Wilde's Eyes', *The Wildean* 9 (1996).
169. Arthur Conan Doyle, 'The Bruce-Partington Plans', *The Complete Sherlock Holmes* (London: Secker and Warburg, 1981), p. 916.
170. Doyle, 'The Greek Interpreter', p. 303.
171. Ibid.
172. It has also been argued that the Diogenes Club was modeled after the Athenaeum and the Travellers' Clubs in Pall Mall. C. O. Merriman, 'In Clubland', *Sherlock Holmes Journal* 7 (1964); S. Tupper Bigelow, 'Identifying the Diogenes Club: An Armchair Exercise', *Baker Street Journal* 18.2 (1968).
173. Doyle, 'The Bruce-Partington Plans', p. 914.
174. Ibid.
175. Wilde's mother encouraged him to use his rhetorical powers to enter British politics. See Ellmann, *Oscar Wilde*, p. 234.
176. Arthur Conan Doyle, 'The Empty House', *The Celebrated Cases of Sherlock Holmes*, Treasury of World Masterpieces (London: Octopus, 1981), pp. 358, 361.
177. Ibid., pp. 359–60.
178. Rosenberg, *Naked Is the Best Disguise*.
179. Ibid., p. 140. Rosenberg also postulates that Moran's appearance is partially derived from that of Friedrich Wilhelm Nietzsche.
180. Doyle, 'The Empty House', p. 357.
181. Ibid., p. 363.
182. Rosenberg, *Naked is the Best Disguise*, pp. 140–1.
183. Ibid., p. 139.
184. Beckson, *The Oscar Wilde Encyclopedia*, p. 83.
185. Doyle, 'The Empty House', p. 360.
186. Doyle, *Memories and Adventures*, p. 95.

187. Doyle, 'The Empty House', p. 363.
188. Coincidentally, during Oscar's 1895 trials he was the same age as his father was at the time of the Travers case.
189. Doyle, *Memories and Adventures*, p. 95.
190. Moran's fame as a hunter of dangerous animals, particularly tigers, might also carry a Wildean resonance. After his release from prison, Wilde often referred to life as a tiger, particularly in relation to the time of his greatest success, when he admitted that he had recklessly 'played with that tiger life'. Wilde, *The Complete Letters of Oscar Wilde*, p. 1123.
191. An interesting adjunct to 'The Empty House' is the 1999 short story 'Flashman and the Tiger' by George MacDonald Fraser, part of Fraser's 'Flashman' series that imagines the adult adventures of Harry Flashman, the notorious bully from *Tom Brown's Schooldays* (1857) by Thomas Hughes. For 'Flashman and the Tiger', Fraser appropriates Doyle's Sherlock Holmes, Dr Watson, Lestrade, and 'Tiger' Moran (the last is revealed to be an old enemy of Flashman's) when Flashman unwittingly stumbles into the denouement of the 'The Empty House'. Interestingly, in Fraser's story, Wilde is briefly glimpsed by Flashman in the company of Moran at the theater. Flashman is scathing in his description of Wilde, whom he refers to as an insolent, mincing posturer, surrounded by 'toadies' with the appearance of 'an overfed trout in a toupé'. George MacDonald Fraser, *Flashman and the Tiger and Other Extracts from the Flashman Papers* (London: HarperCollins, 2000), pp. 290–1.
192. Karl Beckson, 'Psychic Messages from Oscar Wilde: Some New A. Conan Doyle Letters', *English Language Notes* 17 (1979), p. 41. Doyle attended séances as early as 1879 and became an investigator for the Society for Psychical Research in 1894. Beckson, 'Psychic Messages from Oscar Wilde', pp. 39–40.
193. Norman Alford, *The Rhymers' Club* (London: Macmillan, 1997), p. 5.
194. Cevasco, ed., *The 1890s*, pp. 44, 142.
195. J. Lewis May, *John Lane and the Nineties* (London: John Lane The Bodley Head, 1936), p. 98.
196. Carroll V. Peterson, in *John Davidson*, '"Art for man"' Twayne's English Authors Series, ed. Sylvia E. Bowman (New York: Twayne, 1972), pp. 143–4.
197. W. B. Yeats cited in Robert Duncan Macleod, *John Davidson: A Study in Personality* (Glasgow: Holmes, 1957), p. 15.
198. Albert C. Baugh, ed., *A Literary History of England* (London: Routledge and Kegan Paul, 1967), p. 1545.
199. May, *John Lane and the Nineties*, p. 101.
200. Alford, *The Rhymers' Club*, p. 129.
201. Baugh, ed., *A Literary History of England*, p. 1544, Alford, *The Rhymers' Club*, p. 128. Lionel Johnson said of Davidson:
> *Powerful* is the word: fervour, ardour, energy, rapid imagination and passion, sometimes heated and turbulent—a dash of . . . sobriety would improve him. Intensely interested in *life* and its questions . . . has tried so many ways and done so much . . . Has not quite 'found himself' in literature or in life. Alford, *The Rhymers' Club*, pp. 129–30; emphasis in the original.
202. Wilde, *The Complete Letters of Oscar Wilde*, p. 1114n. According to the pianist Frank Liebich, he met Wilde at a private dinner party at a Soho restaurant in the company of John Davidson, John Barlas, and John Gray. Liebich cited in

Neil McKenna, *The Secret Life of Oscar Wilde* (New York: Basic Books, 2005), p. 121. Barlas wrote an article on Wilde and his work for the *Novel Review*. John Barlas, letter to Oscar Wilde, March 2, 1892 (Clark). Barlas's son recalled that his father was 'a great admirer of Wilde as a man of letters'. C. Douglas Barlas, letter to A. J. A. Symons, December 20, 1925 (Clark). Mark Samuels Lasner has advised the present writer that Davidson praised Wilde's efforts on behalf of Barlas in a letter to W. S. McCormick.
203. Deghy and Waterhouse, *Café Royal*.
204. Wilde, *The Complete Letters of Oscar Wilde*, p. 1114n.
205. John Davidson, *Baptist Lake* (London: Ward and Downey, 1894), p. 142.
206. Ibid., pp. 71–6.
207. Ibid., p. 88.
208. Ibid., pp. 285–6.
209. Ibid., p. 131.
210. Ibid., pp. 131–2.
211. Harris, *Oscar Wilde*, p. 15.
212. Ellmann, *Oscar Wilde*, p. 45.
213. Ibid., p. 137.
214. Davidson, *Baptist Lake*, pp. 266–7.
215. Ibid., pp. 72–3, 279.
216. Ibid., pp. 271–6.
217. Wilde, *The Complete Letters of Oscar Wilde*, p. 1114.
218. Cevasco, ed., *The 1890s*, p. 143.
219. May, *John Lane and the Nineties*, p. 102; Baugh, ed., *A Literary History of England*, p. 1545.
220. Cevasco, ed., *The 1890s*, p. 143.
221. Beerbohm's *A Christmas Garland* also parodies the style of two other authors considered in this study: George Bernard Shaw and Henry James. Linda Anne Julian, 'G. S. Street', in *Dictionary of Literary Biography*, vol. 135, ed. William B. Thesing (Detroit: Gale Research, 1994), p. 349.
222. Ibid.
223. Wilde, *The Complete Letters of Oscar Wilde*, pp. 725–6.
224. Richard Le Gallienne, *Retrospective Reviews: A Literary Log* (London: John Lane: The Bodley Head, 1896), p. 22.
225. George Slythe Street, 'The Editor's Apology' *The Autobiography of a Boy*, The Decadent Consciousness: A Hidden Archive of Late Victorian Literature, ed. Ian Fletcher and John Stokes (New York: Garland, 1977), pp. ix–x.
226. Ibid., p. 46.
227. Ibid., p. xii.
228. Ibid., pp. 14, xiii.
229. Ibid., pp. 4–5.
230. Ibid., pp. 12–13.
231. Ibid., p. 55.
232. Ibid., pp. 64, 73, 101.
233. Ibid., p. 77.
234. Holbrook Jackson, *The Eighteen Nineties*, vol. 17 The Life and Letters Series, (London: Jonathan Cape, 1934), p. 68.
235. Julian, 'G. S. Street', p. 350.
236. Street's best-known later literary work is *The Ghosts of Piccadilly* (1907), a nostalgic collection of essays on the famous London street.

237. Street succeeded Charles Brookfield as examiner of plays in the Lord Chamberlain's Department from 1913. Hoare observes that Street's recorded observations on *Salomé* represent a valuable insight into how Wilde's contemporaries saw the work, as well as providing a relatively unbiased view of its moral implications. Hoare, *Wilde's Last Stand*, p. 62.
238. Douglas Goldring, *South Lodge* (London: Constable, 1943), p. 187.
239. Richard Bleiler, 'Robert S. Hichens', *Late-Victorian and Edwardian British Novelists: First Series*, vol. 153, Dictionary of Literary Biography, ed. George M. Johnson (Detroit: Gale Research, 1995), p. 108.
240. Beckson, *The Oscar Wilde Encyclopedia*, p. 122. In his essay 'Pen, Pencil and Poison', Wilde wrote that a love of the color green 'in individuals is always the sign of a subtle artistic temperament . . . in nations [it] is said to denote a laxity, if not a decadence, of morals'. For a detailed discussion of the emergence of the green carnation as a symbol of homosexuality, see Denisoff, *Aestheticism and Sexual Parody 1840–1940*, pp. 110–11.
241. Robert Hichens, *The Green Carnation*, ed. Stanley Weintraub (Lincoln: University of Nebraska Press, 1970), p. 17.
242. Ellmann, *Oscar Wilde*, p. 400.
243. St. John Adcock, *The Glory that Was Grub Street: Impressions of Contemporary Authors* (London: Sampson Low, 1928), p. 110.
244. E. F. Benson later wrote an essay on Wilde's *De Profundis*, which defended Wilde's and Robert Ross's management of the text. A copy of this piece is held in the William Andrews Clark Memorial Library Archives, Los Angeles.
245. Richard Bleiler notes many internal contradictions in *Yesterday* and observes that several passages from that work appear verbatim in Hichens's fictional works. Bleiler, 'Robert S. Hichens', p. 108.
246. Robert Hichens, *Yesterday: The Autobiography of Robert Hichens* (London: Cassell, 1947), pp. 65–6.
247. Ibid., pp. 66, 69.
248. Robert Hichens, 'Introduction', *The Green Carnation* (London: Unicorn, 1949). This was the first English edition to be printed since the novel was withdrawn from circulation during the Wilde scandal in 1895.
249. Hichens, *The Green Carnation*, pp. 6, 131.
250. Ibid., p. 196.
251. Ibid., pp. 29, 122.
252. Ibid., pp. 42, 198.
253. Ibid., p. 165.
254. Ibid., p. 173; Jackson, *The Eighteen Nineties*, p. 68.
255. Hichens, *The Green Carnation*, pp. 93, 191.
256. Ibid., p. 199.
257. Ibid., p. 126.
258. Julie Speedie, *Wonderful Sphinx* (London: Virago, 1993), p. 49.
259. Hichens, *The Green Carnation*, p. 140.
260. Ibid., p. 198.
261. Jackson, *The Eighteen Nineties*, p. 67.
262. Bleiler, 'Robert S. Hichens', p. 112.
263. Hichens, *The Green Carnation*, pp. 12, 143.
264. Ibid., pp. 75, 109.
265. Ibid., p. 169.
266. Ibid., pp. 36, 69.

267. Ibid., p. 18.
268. Ibid., p. 125.
269. Ibid., p. 132.
270. Ibid., p. 122.
271. Ibid., p. 201.
272. Ibid., pp. 65, 131.
273. See Denisoff, *Aestheticism and Sexual Parody 1840–1940*, pp. 117–18.
274. Susser, 'Unnatural Flower', p. 187.
275. Hichens, *Yesterday: The Autobiography of Robert Hichens*, p. 70.
276. Hichens, *The Green Carnation*, pp. 184–5.
277. Ibid., p. 66.
278. For further discussion on this subject, see Kingston, 'Homoeroticism and the Child in Wilde's Fairy Tales'.
279. Charles Burkhart, *Ada Leverson* (New York: Twayne, 1973), p. 22; Denisoff, *Aestheticism and Sexual Parody 1840–1940*, pp. 14, 112.
280. Wilde, *The Complete Letters of Oscar Wilde*, p. 577; Ellmann, *Oscar Wilde*, p. 383. For a fictional elaboration on this possibility, see Clement Wood, *The Sensualist: A Novel of the Life and Times of Oscar Wilde* (New York: Jonathan Swift, 1942), p. 269.
281. Ellmann, *Oscar Wilde*, p. 401, Denisoff, *Aestheticism and Sexual Parody 1840–1940*, pp. 15, 111; Schmidgall, *The Stranger Wilde: Interpreting Oscar*, p. 441.
282. Bleiler, 'Robert S. Hichens', p. 110.
283. Denisoff, *Aestheticism and Sexual Parody 1840–1940*, p. 10.
284. Harris, *Oscar Wilde*, p. 107.
285. Weintraub, 'Narcissus Exposed', p. xxiii.
286. Denisoff reads *The Green Carnation* as a reaction to Mrs Humphry Ward's aesthetic Mr Wood in *Robert Elsmere*. Denisoff, *Aestheticism and Sexual Parody 1840–1940*, pp. 113–14. Eliza Lynn Linton responded to *The Green Carnation* by attacking Hichens in a London newspaper in an article entitled 'Young Dogs'. Hichens, *Yesterday: The Autobiography of Robert Hichens*, pp. 55, 74.
287. Hichens, *The Green Carnation*, p. 4.
288. Ibid., p. 5.
289. Hichens, *Yesterday: The Autobiography of Robert Hichens*, p. 72.
290. Hichens, 'Introduction', p. xi.
291. Speedie, *Wonderful Sphinx*, pp. 48–9.
292. Weintraub, 'Narcissus Exposed', p. vii. Despite Wilde's published denial, *Punch* published a sketch a few weeks later entitled 'The Blue Gardenia', which operated on the assumption that Wilde had written *The Green Carnation*. See Schmidgall, *The Stranger Wilde: Interpreting Oscar*, p. 206.
293. Wilde, *Collins Complete Works of Oscar Wilde*, p. 615; Weintraub, 'Narcissus Exposed', p. viii.
294. Harris, *Oscar Wilde*, pp. 106–7; Wilde, *Collins Complete Works of Oscar Wilde*, p. 615. Hichens read passages of *The Green Carnation* to Reggie Turner and Max Beerbohm, both mutual friends of Hichens and Wilde; in 1949 Hichens could not recall what they thought of it. Hichens, 'Introduction', p. xi. Beerbohm, *Letters of Max Beerbohm: 1892–1956*, p. 5; Weintraub, 'Narcissus Exposed', p. xii.
295. Hichens, *Yesterday: The Autobiography of Robert Hichens*, p. 69; Weintraub, 'Narcissus Exposed', pp. viii–ix.

296. Wilde, *The Complete Letters of Oscar Wilde*, p. 921.
297. Weintraub, 'Narcissus Exposed', p. xxvi.
298. Wilde, *Collins Complete Works of Oscar Wilde*, p. 418. In her essay 'Sexuality, the Public, and the Art World', Regenia Gagnier refers to the first part of this quotation to argue that Wilde approved of *The Green Carnation* and was 'advertising' it in *Earnest*. However, Gagnier does not include the final reference to the book being 'morbid and middle-class', which would seem to indicate Wilde's disapproval. Regenia Gagnier, 'Sexuality, the Public, and the Art World', in *Critical Essays on Oscar Wilde*, ed. Regenia Gagnier (New York: G. K. Hall, 1991), p. 38.
299. Weintraub, 'Narcissus Exposed', pp. viii–ix, xiii.
300. Bleiler, 'Robert S. Hichens', p. 107.
301. Hichens, *Yesterday: The Autobiography of Robert Hichens*, pp. 72, 216–17; Hichens, 'Introduction', p. xv.
302. See Alfred Douglas, letter to Adrian Earle, May 25, 1943 (Clark) and Hichens, 'Introduction', p. xiii.
303. Christopher D. Murray, 'Robert Buchanan', in *Victorian Novelists After 1885*, vol. 18, Dictionary of Literary Biography, ed. Ira B. Nadel and William E. Fredeman (Detroit: Gale Research, 1983), p. 21.
304. Tanitch, *Oscar Wilde on Stage and Screen*, p. 18. Kerr was doubtless coached by Tree, a friend of Wilde's who had previously performed Wildean roles in Albery's *Where's the Cat?* and Burnand's *The Colonel* in the 1880s.
305. Andrew Nash, *Buchanan, Robert Williams*, The Literary Encyclopedia, available www.litencyc.com/php/speople.php?rec=true&UID=627>, last accessed on July 17, 2007. May 1, 2002.
306. Robert Buchanan and Henry Murray, *The Charlatan* (London: Chatto and Windus, 1896), p. 15.
307. Ibid., pp. 21, 211.
308. Ibid., p. 19.
309. Ibid., p. 18.
310. Ibid., p. 88.
311. Ibid., p. 21.
312. Ibid., p. 154.
313. Ibid., pp. 19, 216.
314. Buchanan later regretted his attack on Rossetti, which earned him a reputation for insensitivity, hostility, and cowardice. In 1881 he symbolically dedicated a novel about the futility of hatred—*God and the Man*—to 'The Old Enemy'. Nash, *Buchanan, Robert Williams*. Dennis Denisoff has noted that Buchanan later 'refashioned himself as a critic who could appreciate these writers, even though his role in the cultivation of their fame had been based on disparagement'. Denisoff, *Aestheticism and Sexual Parody 1840–1940*, p. 27.
315. Archibald Stodart-Walker, *Robert Buchanan: The Poet of Modern Revolt* (London: Grant Richards, 1901), p. 305.
316. Vyver, *Memoirs of Marie Corelli*, pp. 91–2.
317. Wilde, *The Complete Letters of Oscar Wilde*, pp. 390, 422.
318. Robert Buchanan, letter to E. C. K. Wilde, February 21, (c. 1890), Mark Samuels Lasner Collection, Delaware.
319. Ian Small offers an explanation for Wilde sending Buchanan *Dorian Gray*, a book whose themes were most unlikely to appeal to the latter: 'Wilde, ever the

opportunist, was simply attempting to enlist an ally, or at the very least attempting to forestall overt criticism from a potential opponent'. Small, *Oscar Wilde Revalued: An Essay on New Materials and Methods of Research*. (Greenboro: ELT Press, 1993), p. 71, number eight in the 1880–1920 British Authors Series.
320. Ibid., p. 81.
321. Robert Buchanan, 'The Dismal Throng', *The Idler* (1893), p. 612.
322. Ibid., p. 610. It is not certain which 'foreign breaches of propriety' Buchanan refers to here; perhaps he is referring to Wilde's recently published controversial play *Salomé*, written in French. Wilde's latest overseas trip had been for a 'rest cure' in Bad Homberg in 1892, accompanied by Lord Alfred Douglas. However, Wilde's biographers make no mention of any controversy or remarkable incident on that excursion.
323. Wilde, *The Complete Letters of Oscar Wilde*, pp. 710–11n.
324. Jonathan Goodman, *The Oscar Wilde File* (W. H. Allen, 1988), p. 98.
325. Ellmann, *Oscar Wilde*, p. 526.
326. Grant Richards, *Memories of a Misspent Youth: 1872–1896* (London: William Heinemann, 1932), p. 300.
327. Osbert Sitwell, 'Ada Leverson, Wilde and Max', *The National and English Review* 135.811 (1950), pp. 286–7.
328. Wilde, *The Complete Letters of Oscar Wilde*, p. 569.
329. Denisoff, *Aestheticism and Sexual Parody 1840–1940*, pp. 10, 105.
330. Ada Leverson, 'Suggestion', in *Daughters of Decadence: Women Writers of the Fin-de-Siècle*, ed. Elaine Showalter (London: Virago, 1993), p. 43.
331. Ibid., p. 42.
332. Ibid., p. 43.
333. Denisoff, *Aestheticism and Sexual Parody 1840–1940*, p. 106.
334. Burkhart cited in ibid., p. 105.
335. Haralson, 'The Elusive Queerness of Henry James's "Queer Comrade" ' p. 191. Alan Sinfield has observed,
    After [Wilde's] trials, everyone knew what the queer man was like... People had begun to talk about homosexuality. Sexologists were theorising it (Ulrichs, Ellis, Freud); parliamentarians were criminalising it (Labouchere); activists were promoting it (Carpenter, Symonds). But with the trials, a distinctive possibility cohered, far more clearly and for far more people. The unspoken had gained a name. Alan Sinfield, 'The Wilde Way of Setting Up Camp', *Irish Times* November 21, 2000.

3 Pariah (1896–1900)

1. Queensberry's irritation at the Wilde Douglas's relationship was undoubtedly exacerbated by two events in 1894: the controversy surrounding Robert Hichens's *The Green Carnation*, published in September, and the death of his eldest son, Viscount Drumlanrig, in October. Drumlanrig's death, ostensibly the result of a shooting accident, was widely suspected to be a suicide triggered by his homosexual relationship with the British foreign minister, Lord Rosebery.
2. Sinfield, *The Wilde Century: Effeminacy, Oscar Wilde and the Queer Movement*, p. 118.

3. Goodman, *The Oscar Wilde File*, p. 133.
4. Schmidgall, *The Stranger Wilde*, p. 209.
5. Thomas Beer, *The Mauve Decade: American Life at the End of the Nineteenth Century* (New York: A. A. Knopf, 1926), p. 129.
6. Tanitch, *Oscar Wilde on Stage and Screen*, pp. 18–19.
7. Ada Leverson, 'The Quest of Sorrow', *The Yellow Book* 8, January (1896), p. 325.
8. Ibid., p. 335.
9. The artist De La Pine closely resembles Charles Conder. Cardinal Guido Poldo Pezzoli, to whom the story is dedicated, has been read as suggestive of Beardsley's patron André Raffalovich. The character of Sporion has been interpreted as both Herbert Percy Horne and Beardsley himself. Dowling, '*Venus and Tannhäuser*: Beardsley's Satire of Decadence', pp. 32–3; Ian Fletcher, 'Inventions for the Left Hand: Beardsley in Verse and Prose', *Reconsidering Aubrey Beardsley*, ed. Robert Langenfeld (Ann Arbor: UMI Research, 1989), p. 238.
10. Beardsley sent Smithers sections of the text at various intervals during composition. In 1907 Smithers printed 300 copies, without illustrations, from the original manuscript. James G. Nelson, *Publisher to the Decadents: Leonard Smithers in the Careers of Beardsley, Wilde, Dowson* (University Park, PA: Pennsylvania State University Press, 2000), pp. 276, 408.
11. Susan Owens, 'The Satirical Agenda of Aubrey Beardsley's "Enter Herodias"', *Visual Culture in Britain* 3.2 (2002), p. 97.
12. Malcolm Easton, *Aubrey and the Dying Lady: A Beardsley Riddle* (London: Secker and Warburg, 1972), p. 153.
13. A parody of the first instalment of 'Under the Hill' called 'Dickens Up to Date' by Ada Leverson, a friend to Beardsley as well as Wilde, appeared in *Punch*, January 25, 1896.
14. For a detailed history of the legend and its various nineteenth-century versions, see Fletcher, 'Inventions for the Left Hand', pp. 229–32.
15. Beardsley's full title reads *The Story of Venus and Tannhäuser, in which is Set Forth an Exact Account of the Manner of State Held by Madam Venus, Goddess and Meretrix, Under the Famous Hörselberg, and Containing the Adventures of Tannhäuser in that Place, his Repentance, his Journeying to Rome, and Returning to the Loving Mountain.*
16. Sturgis, *Aubrey Beardsley: A Biography*, p. 210.
17. Beardsley, *The Letters of Aubrey Beardsley*, p. 22. Horst Schroeder supports Matthew Sturgis's recent claim that this remark could refer to Beardsley meeting only Constance Wilde and the two Wilde children at the Burne-Jones reception. Schroeder, *Additions and Corrections to Richard Ellmann's Oscar Wilde*, p. 103.
18. Beckson, *The Oscar Wilde Encyclopedia*, p. 22; Easton, *Aubrey and the Dying Lady*, p. 31; Beardsley, *The Letters of Aubrey Beardsley*, p. 47.
19. Wilde, *The Complete Letters of Oscar Wilde*, p. 578n.
20. William Rothenstein, *Men and Memories: A History of the Arts 1872–1922 Being the Recollections of William Rothenstein*, vol. 1, 2 vols (New York: Tudor, 1937), p. 184; Wilde, *The Complete Letters of Oscar Wilde*, p. 587.
21. Caricatures of Wilde have also been identified in Beardsley's frontispiece for John Davidson's *Plays* (1889) and in his drawings 'L'Education Sentimentale' for the *Yellow Book* of April 1894 (which features a female character resembling Wilde) and 'Lucian's Strange Creatures' for C. E. Lucian's *Lucian's True History* (1894). Fletcher, *Aubrey Beardsley*, p. 131; Linda Gertner Zatlin, *Aubrey Beardsley and Victorian Sexual Politics* (Oxford: Clarendon, 1990), pp. 6n, 32.

22. Michael Cadden and Mary Ann Jensen, *Oscar Wilde: A Writer for the Nineties* (Princeton, NJ: Princeton University Library, 1995), p. 43; Owens, 'The Satirical Agenda of Aubrey Beardsley's "Enter Herodias"'. For further analysis of Beardsley's drawings of Wilde, see Fletcher, *Aubrey Beardsley*, pp. ii, 12, 26–7, 57, 66, 77–8, 82–90, 131; Lorraine Janzen Kooistra, *The Artist as Critic: Bitextuality in Fin-de-Siècle Illustrated Books* (Aldershot: Scolar, 1995); Brian Reade, *Beardsley* (London: Studio Vista, 1967); Chris Snodgrass, 'Beardsley's Oscillating Spaces: Play, Paradox and the Grotesque', *Reconsidering Aubrey Beardsley*, ed. Robert Langenfeld and Nicholas A. Salerno (London: U.M.I. Research, 1989); Zatlin, *Aubrey Beardsley and Victorian Sexual Politics*, pp. 32–4
23. Ellmann, *Oscar Wilde*, pp. 290, 355; Weintraub, *Beardsley: A Biography*, pp. 57–8.
24. Ellmann, *Oscar Wilde*, p. 380; Frances Winwar, *Oscar Wilde and the Yellow Nineties* (New York: Harper & Brothers, 1940), p. 212.
25. Easton, *Aubrey and the Dying Lady*, pp. 53–4.
26. Beardsley, *The Letters of Aubrey Beardsley*, p. 58; Fletcher, *Aubrey Beardsley*, p. 12.
27. Beckson, *The Oscar Wilde Encyclopedia*, pp. 22–3, Fletcher, *Aubrey Beardsley*, p. 12.
28. Matthew Sturgis contends that Beardsley's assumed connection with Wilde was also fostered by a passage in Robert Hichens's *The Green Carnation*, discussed in chapter 2:

    Mr Amarinth [decides] to stay at home and read the latest issue of the '*Yellow Disaster*'; 'I want to see', he declares, 'Mr Aubrey Beardsley's idea of the Archbishop of Canterbury. He has drawn him sitting in a wheelbarrow in the garden of Lambeth Palace, with . . . the motto *J'y suis, j'y reste*. I believe he has on a black mask. Perhaps it is to conceal the likeness'. Hichens cited in Sturgis, *Aubrey Beardsley: A Biography*, pp. 215–16.

    As mentioned above, one of the most vocal advocates for Beardsley's dismissal from the *Yellow Book* was Mrs Humphry Ward, author of *Robert Elsmere*, discussed in chapter 1.
29. Ellmann, *Oscar Wilde*, p. 505.
30. Wilde, *The Complete Letters of Oscar Wilde*, p. 921.
31. Schroeder, *Additions and Corrections to Richard Ellmann's Oscar Wilde*, p. 193.
32. Ellmann, *Oscar Wilde*, p. 504.
33. Wilde, *The Complete Letters of Oscar Wilde*, p. 919. Beardsley spoke to Vincent O'Sullivan of the difficulty of staying on friendly terms with Wilde in light of Raffalovich's antagonism toward him. Sturgis, *Aubrey Beardsley: A Biography*, p. 334.
34. Schroeder, *Additions and Corrections to Richard Ellmann's Oscar Wilde*, pp. 193–4.
35. Housman, *Echo de Paris*, pp. 39–40.
36. Wilde, *The Complete Letters of Oscar Wilde*, p. 931n.
37. Beardsley, *The Letters of Aubrey Beardsley*, p. 409.
38. Wilde, *The Complete Letters of Oscar Wilde*, p. 1040.
39. Fletcher, 'Inventions for the Left Hand: Beardsley in Verse and Prose', pp. 40–1, 234.
40. In his collection of Wilde's spoken stories, Thomas Wright observes that Wilde particularly enjoyed the rhythm and sound of the word 'vermilion'. Wright, ed., *Table Talk: Oscar Wilde*, p. 18.

41. Aubrey Beardsley, *The Story of Venus and Tannhäuser* (New York: Universal, 1967), p. 70.
42. Fletcher, 'Inventions for the Left Hand: Beardsley in Verse and Prose', p. 235.
43. Beardsley, *The Story of Venus and Tannhäuser*, pp. 70–1.
44. Ivor H. Evans, ed., *The Wordsworth Dictionary of Phrase and Fable* (Ware: Wordsworth Editions, 1993), p. 861.
45. Beardsley, *The Story of Venus and Tannhäuser*, p. 96.
46. Ibid., p. 143.
47. Ibid., p. 118.
48. Beardsley, *The Story of Venus and Tannhäuser*, pp. 151–3.
49. Ibid., p. 153.
50. Fletcher, 'Inventions for the Left Hand', p. 244.
51. Dowling, '*Venus and Tannhäuser*', p. 30.
52. Beardsley, *The Story of Venus and Tannhäuser*, p. 153.
53. Dowling, '*Venus and Tannhäuser*', p. 30; Fletcher, 'Inventions for the Left Hand', p. 243.
54. Beardsley, *The Story of Venus and Tannhäuser*, p. 153.
55. Dowling, '*Venus and Tannhäuser*', p. 30.
56. Ibid., p. 29.
57. Wilde, *The Complete Letters of Oscar Wilde*, p. 1060.
58. Mabel Emily Wotton, 'The Fifth Edition', in *Daughters of Decadence: Women Writers of the Fin-de-Siècle*, ed. Elaine Showalter (London: Virago, 1993), p. 142.
59. This element of Wotton's story has curious overtones of Wilde's fairy tale 'The Devoted Friend' (1888), in which a kind-hearted gardener named Hans is taken advantage of by an unfeeling and selfish Miller. Hans's dearest wish, a secondhand wheelbarrow for his garden, is just as pathetic as Miss Suttaby's, who merely desires to buy a headstone for her dead stepbrother. Both the Wilde's Miller and Wotton's Leyden are in a position to easily fulfill these simple wishes, but are too selfish to do so, electing instead to exploit their admiring, less fortunate companions. Both also congratulate themselves on being the epitome of generosity, long after their selfishness has driven their 'friends' to the grave.
60. For a New Woman reading of 'The Fifth Edition', see Elaine Showalter, ed., 'Introduction', in *Daughters of Decadence: Women Writers of the Fin-de-Siècle* (London: Virago, 1993), pp. xiv–xv.
61. Mabel Emily Wotton, 'The Fifth Edition', pp. 40, 42, 47, 141.
62. Ibid., p. 142.
63. Ibid., pp. 39, 40, 149.
64. Wotton, 'The Fifth Edition', pp. 145–6.
65. Stetz, 'The Bi-Social Oscar Wilde and "Modern" Women', pp. 518–19.
66. Wotton, 'The Fifth Edition', p. 146.
67. Ibid., p. 151.
68. Ibid., pp. 148–9.
69. Ibid., p. 143.
70. Ibid., p. 146.
71. Wilde, *Reviews*, p. 444.
72. Ibid., pp. 446–7.
73. Carolyn Christensen Nelson, *British Women Fiction Writers of the 1890s*, Twayne's English Authors Series, ed. Herbert Sussman (New York: Twayne, 1996), p. 35; Showalter, 'Introduction', pp. xiv–xv.

74. Richard Le Gallienne, *Prose Fancies (Second Series)* (London: John Lane, 1896), p. 110.
75. Ibid.
76. Beckson, *The Oscar Wilde Encyclopedia*, p. 348.
77. Richard Le Gallienne, 'On Some Recent Editions of Oscar Wilde', *New Poems* (London: The Bodley Head, 1910).
78. Lady Wilde wrote to Oscar of Stoker: 'He never gets into debt, and his character is excellent.' Belford, *Bram Stoker*, p. 86. Stoker drew upon Sir William Wilde's accounts of his archeological expeditions to Egypt when he wrote *The Jewel of Seven Stars* in 1903. Daniel Farson, *The Man Who Wrote Dracula* (London: Michael Joseph, 1975), p. 39.
79. Wilde, *The Complete Letters of Oscar Wilde*, p. 29. Balcombe was considered one of the most beautiful women in England; see Wilde, *The Complete Letters of Oscar Wilde*, p. 47n; David J. Skal, *Hollywood Gothic: The Tangled Web of Dracula from Novel to Stage to Screen* (New York: W. W. Norton, 1991), p. 31.
80. Florence Balcombe, letter to Oscar Wilde, n.d. (Clark).
81. Wilde, *The Complete Letters of Oscar Wilde*, p. 66.
82. Barbara Belford believes that Balcombe was appealing to Wilde and Stoker because her chaste image posed no threat to their ideal of womanhood. Barbara Belford, *Oscar Wilde: A Certain Genius* (New York: Random House, 2000), p. 62.
83. Wilde, *The Complete Letters of Oscar Wilde*, pp. 71–3.
84. Ellmann, *Oscar Wilde*, pp. 99–100.
85. By all reports Balcombe, intelligent and flirtatious with aspirations to act, was very happy with her new position in London society. A little too happy for some members of the Stoker family, who referred to her as 'a cold woman', more interested in society than her husband and son Noel. Farson, *The Man Who Wrote Dracula*, pp. 50, 213. Others thought it fortuitous that Balcombe was resourceful enough to become a successful society figure, as much of her husband's leisure time was spent with Irving, a man he admired intensely. Stoker served Irving faithfully as his business manager for twenty-seven years. In 1906, a year after the actor's death, Stoker published his *Personal Reminiscences of Henry Irving*.
86. Wilde, *The Complete Letters of Oscar Wilde*, p. 107. In *The Man Who Wrote Dracula*, Daniel Farson writes: 'When I first saw this letter, in [Stoker's son's collection], it was placed in an envelope with a covering letter from Ellen Terry to Florence. This was written towards the end of her life . . . [Terry] explained she had been tearing up old letters all that evening and thought that "by rights this belongs to you"'. Farson, *The Man Who Wrote Dracula*, p. 61.
87. There are two short, friendly letters extant from Wilde to Bram Stoker, arranging social meetings, thought to be written in 1889 and 1894, respectively. Wilde, *The Complete Letters of Oscar Wilde*, p. 394. Oscar Wilde, letter to Bram Stoker (1894?) (Clark). An 1893 letter from Balcombe to Constance Wilde includes news of her son and enquires after the well-being of the Wilde children, as well requesting that Wilde visit Balcombe's mother while she was in London. Florence Stoker, letter to Constance Wilde, December 24, 1893 (Clark).
88. Skal, *Hollywood Gothic*, pp. 34–5.
89. Belford, *Bram Stoker*, p. 127.
90. Bram Stoker, *Bram Stoker, Dracula: Complete, Authoritative Text with Biographical, Historical, and Cultural Contexts, Critical History, and Essays from*

Contemporary Critical Perspectives, Case Studies in Contemporary Criticism, ed. John Paul Riquelme (Boston: Bedford/St. Martin's, 2002), p. 304.

91. If Stoker was anxious about his wife's residual feelings for Wilde, it is possible that his fears were not entirely unfounded. Barbara Belford notes that after Stoker's death his wife 'surrounded herself with artifacts from the Wilde period, directing visitors' attention to the Moytura watercolor "poor O. painted for me"'. Belford quotes a letter from Florence Stoker to Phillipa Knott that describes her disappointment when a proposed meeting with Wilde's son Vyvyan fell through in 1937: '"I wanted him to come & see me, being so fond of his father," she wrote, "but he never turned up"'. She also took a keen interest in biographies of Wilde. Belford, *Bram Stoker*, p. 325.
92. Cevasco, ed., *The 1890s*, p. 176.
93. David J. Skal comments upon the similarity of *Dracula* to *The Picture of Dorian Gray*. David J. Skal, *V is for Vampire* (London: Robson, 1996), pp. 220–1.
94. Cevasco, ed., *The 1890s*, p. 176; Farson, *The Man Who Wrote Dracula*, p. 152.
95. Daniel Farson and Philip B. Dematteis, 'Bram Stoker', in *British Novelists, 1890–1929: Modernists*, vol. 36, Dictionary of Literary Biography, ed. Thomas F. Staley(Detroit: Gale Research, 1985), p. 251.
96. Maggie Kilgour, 'Vampiric Arts: Bram Stoker's Defence of Poetry', in *Bram Stoker: History, Psychoanalysis and the Gothic*, ed. William Hughes and Andrew Amith (London: Macmillan, 1998), p. 47. See also Stoker, *Bram Stoker, Dracula*.
97. Schaffer, '"A Wilde Desire Took Me"', p. 416.
98. See Ted Bain, 'Oscar Wilde: Myths, Miracles, and Imitations (Book Review)', *Modern Drama* 41.3 (1998), p. 106 and Christopher Bentley, 'The Monster in the Bedroom: Sexual Symbolism in Bram Stoker's *Dracula*', *in Dracula: The Vampire and the Critics*, Studies in Speculative Fiction ed. Margaret L. Carter, (London: UMI Research, 1988), pp. 25–6.
99. Ann Heilmann, 'Wilde's New Women', p. 135.
100. Richard Dyer, 'Children of the Night: Vampirism as Homosexuality, Homosexuality as Vampirism', in *Sweet Dreams: Sexuality, Gender and Popular Fiction*, ed. Susannah Radstone (London: Lawrence and Wishart, 1988), p. 59.
101. Farson and Dematteis, 'Bram Stoker', p. 259.
102. See Symonds's *A Problem in Greek Ethics* (1883) and Havelock Ellis's *Sexual Inversion* (1897) for contemporary discussion on homosexuality. Stoker even refers to two of the principal commentators on the subject, Cesare Lombroso and Max Nordau, in *Dracula*: 'The Count is a criminal, and of criminal type. Nordau and Lombroso would so classify him'. Stoker, *Bram Stoker, Dracula*, p. 336. Nordau's *Degeneration* (1892) specifically mentions Wilde as an example of the degenerate, self-absorbed artist.
103. Richard Dyer notes that decadent homosexuals who aspired to the aristocracy like Wilde share something of the same 'refined paleness' of the classical vampire, who is usually aristocratic. Dyer, 'Children of the Night', pp. 53, 60.
104. Christopher Craft, '"Kiss Me with Those Red Lips": Gender and Inversion in Bram Stoker's *Dracula*', in *Dracula: The Vampire and the Critics*, Studies in Speculative Fiction ed. Margaret L. Carter, (London: UMI Research, 1988), p. 170.
105. Schaffer, '"A Wilde Desire Took Me"', p. 404; Stoker, *Bram Stoker, Dracula*, p. 62.

106. Craft, '"Kiss Me with Those Red Lips"', p. 189.
107. Kilgour, 'Vampiric Arts', p. 51; Schaffer, '"A Wilde Desire Took Me"', pp. 381–90.
108. Schaffer, '"A Wilde Desire Took Me"', pp. 383–4.
109. Marie Mulvey-Roberts, '*Dracula* and the Doctors: Bad Blood, Menstrual Taboo and the New Woman', *Bram Stoker: History, Psychoanalysis and the Gothic*, ed. William Hughes and Andrew Amith (London: Macmillan, 1998), p. 80.
110. Kilgour, 'Vampiric Arts', p. 48.
111. Schaffer, '"A Wilde Desire Took Me"', p. 382.
112. Stoker cited in ibid., p. 389; Skal, *Hollywood Gothic*, p. 37.
113. Bram Stoker, 'The Censorship of Fiction', *Nineteenth Century* 64 (1908), p. 486. See also Bram Stoker, 'The Censorship of Stage Plays', *Nineteenth Century* 66 (1909), p. 985.
114. Schaffer, '"A Wilde Desire Took Me"', p. 384.
115. Ibid., pp. 395–6.
116. Ibid., p. 398. David J. Skal examines the depiction of Wilde in the popular press of the 1890s in relation to contemporary 'evolutionary anxiety', also discernible in *Dracula*: 'Wilde was repeatedly cartooned as a developed ape (or even, in one celebrated instance, a dinosaur), described explicitly as a slug, sea-creature, etc. Vampirism, homosexuality, and general "decadence" were thus popularly conceptualized as a kind of horrid evolutionary backsliding'. Skal, *V is for Vampire*, p. 221.
117. Schaffer, '"A Wilde Desire Took Me"', p. 398.
118. Ibid., pp. 398–9.
119. Stoker, *Bram Stoker, Dracula*, p. 73.
120. Schaffer, '"A Wilde Desire Took Me"', p. 399.
121. Ibid., p. 400.
122. Ibid., p. 392. Schaffer also highlights the fact that Wilde and Stoker competed for the attention of Henry Irving, Wilde's favorite actor. Schaffer, '"A Wilde Desire Took Me"', p. 392.
123. Belford, *Bram Stoker*, pp. 246–7.
124. *The Evening News* cited in Schaffer, '"A Wilde Desire Took Me"', p. 408. See also H. Montgomery Hyde, *The Trials of Oscar Wilde* (New York: Dover, 1962), p. 18.
125. Schaffer, '"A Wilde Desire Took Me"', pp. 406–7.
126. Nina Auerbach, 'Dracula: A Vampire of Our Own', *in Dracula*, ed. Glennis Byron, New Casebooks (London: Macmillan, 1999), pp. 163–4.
127. Farson, *The Man Who Wrote Dracula*, p. 152.
128. Schaffer, '"A Wilde Desire Took Me"', p. 409.
129. Ibid., p. 398.
130. Ibid., pp. 388–9, 401–2.
131. Ibid., p. 404.
132. Ibid., p. 405.
133. Ibid., pp. 398–9, 401; Stoker, *Bram Stoker, Dracula*, pp. 51, 73.
134. Christopher Craft argues that the death of the vampiric Lucy Westenra also represents an assurance that 'vampirism [read homosexuality] may indeed be vanquished, that its sexual threat, however powerful and intriguing, may be expelled'. Craft, '"Kiss Me with Those Red Lips"', p. 185.
135. Schaffer, '"A Wilde Desire Took Me"', pp. 16, 414.
136. Ibid., p. 414.

137. Stannard wrote over ninety books in her lifetime.
138. *Who Was Who 1897–1915*, p. 493.
139. Florence Fenwick Miller, 'Character Sketch: John Strange Winter', *The Women's Signal*, January 30, 1896, p. 66.
140. Pearson, *The Life of Oscar Wilde*, p. 324.
141. Wilde, *Reviews*, pp. 166–7.
142. Wilde, *The Complete Letters of Oscar Wilde*, p. 857.
143. Ibid., p. 869.
144. John Strange Winter (Henrietta Eliza Vaughan Stannard), *A Seaside Flirt* (London: F. V. White, 1897), p. 26.
145. Ibid.
146. Ibid., pp. 98–9.
147. Ibid., pp. 27–8.
148. Ibid., p. 30.
149. Ibid., p. 41.
150. Stokes, *Oscar Wilde: Myths, Miracles, and Imitations*, p. 139.
151. Winter (Henrietta Eliza Vaughan Stannard), *A Seaside Flirt*, p. 47.
152. Ibid., p. 53. Dermott's 'unnatural' artistic interest in Wilmot recalls Gilbert Vincent's in Adela Buller in 'The World's Slow Stain' by Dixon, discussed in Part 2.
153. Ibid., p. 83.
154. Ibid., p. 79.
155. Winter (Henrietta Eliza Vaughan Stannard), *A Seaside Flirt*, p. 93.
156. Ibid., pp. 97–8. Simon Callow highlights Wilde's generosity and kindness and reports Ada Leverson's comment that Wilde 'rather resent[ed] friends who [were] not in actual need'. Callow also notes that 'on more than one occasion [Wilde] is credited with having cured toothache by conversation alone'. Simon Callow, *Oscar Wilde and His Circle* (London: National Portrait Gallery, 2000), p. 117.
157. Winter (Henrietta Eliza Vaughan Stannard), *A Seaside Flirt*, p. 112.
158. *The Adventures of John Johns* was the most successful of the twelve novels Carrel wrote between 1895 and 1914, reaching seventeen editions by 1929.
159. The articles Carrel contributed to the *Fortnightly* were 'The College of France' (January–June 1893) and 'English and French Manners' (January–June 1894).
160. In his preface, Carrel states, 'none of the characters here described are offered for imitation. They are but imaginary men and women moving on the stage of life'. Frederic Carrel, *The Adventures of John Johns* (London: T. Werner Laurie, 1929), p. i.
161. Harris's biographer Philippa Pullar asserts 'the character [of John Johns] is too calculating . . . Harris was not a businessman; he was spontaneous, emotional, uneasy, untidy and impatient, but never calculating'. Philippa Pullar, *Frank Harris: A Biography* (New York: Simon & Schuster, 1976), p. 90. For further discussion of the differences between Harris and Johns, see Alfred Armstrong, *The Adventures of John Johns (Book Review)*, available www.oddbooks.co.uk/harris/johnjohns.html, January 4, 2003, last accessed on July 18, 2007.
162. Parts of *John Johns* have been misappropriated by some Harris biographers to 'fill in the gaps' of his early London life, most notably by A. I. Tobin and Elmer Gertz in their *A Study in Black and White* (1931). Armstrong, *The Adventures of John Johns (Book Review)*; Pullar, *Frank Harris: A Biography*, pp. 89–90.

163. Pullar thinks it unlikely that Carrel knew Harris 'before 1893 when he first contributed to the *Fortnightly*. In a letter written to [Harris's wife] Nellie Harris, on March 29, 1932, A. R. Cluer [vigorously] refuted the [implication in *John Johns* that Harris used a woman to win his first editorial position]. "The story told about Frank Harris and the *Evening News* is a cruel and baseless calumny and the invention in the States of some spiteful and unscrupulous liar who could not have been in England in 1883 . . . I who first knew your husband in 1880 can assure you that this is a vile and lying libel"'. Pullar, *Frank Harris: A Biography*, p. 90.
164. Frédéric Poingdestre Carrel, letter to 'Cher Madame', n.d. uncat. (Clark) (translated from the French by Bruce Whiteman, February 6, 2003).
165. Carrel, *The Adventures of John Johns*, p. 240.
166. Ibid., pp. 240–1.
167. Ibid. Note the implication, already discussed in relation to *A Seaside Flirt* above and mentioned with regard to Joseph Conrad's 'The Return' below, that Wilde's lack of romantic interest in women resulted in more than one broken heart.
168. Ibid., p. 243.
169. Ibid., pp. 243–4.
170. Ibid., p. 244.
171. Ibid., p. 243.
172. Wilde, *The Complete Letters of Oscar Wilde*, p. 915.
173. Ibid., p. 895.
174. Allen wrote under several pseudonyms including 'Cecil Power' and 'J. Arbuthnot Wilson'.
175. Although the first six editions of *The Ballad* cited the author as 'C. 3. 3.' (Wilde's prison cell number), the work was widely recognized as Wilde's.
176. Another historically based character in *Linnet* is Holmes, the charlatan occultist who is based on the medium D. D. Home. Many other real people have been identified in Allen's fiction: John Ruskin appears as John Truman in *Babylon* (1885), Seeta Mayne in *The Devil's Die* (1887) is probably based on the novelist 'Ouida', Hugh Massinger in *This Mortal Coil: A Novel* (1888) is based on Andrew Lang, and the poetess 'Blackbird' in *Under Sealed Orders* (1894) is a fictional rendering of Amy Levy. See Peter Morton, *Grant Allen*, April 2002, Flinders University, available http://ehlt.flinders.edu.au/english/GA/GAHome.htm, April 17, 2002, last accessed on July 18, 2007.
177. Grant Allen, *Linnet: A Romance* (London: Grant Richards, 1898), pp. 38, 211.
178. Ibid., pp. 5, 79.
179. Ibid., p. 19.
180. Ibid., p. 178.
181. Ibid., pp. 32, 241.
182. Oscar Wilde, 'The Relation of press to Art: A Note in Black and White on Mr Whistler's Lecture, *Pall Mall Gazette*, 28 February 1885' *Aristotle at Afternoon Tea*, ed. John Wyse Jackson (London: Fourth Estate, 1991), p. 52; Wilde, *Collins Complete Works of Oscar Wilde*, p. 48.
183. Anonymous, 'Recent Novels (Book Reviews)', *The Times*, April 6, 1899.
184. Grant Allen, 'The New Hedonism', *The Fortnightly Review* 61 (1894), p. 379.
185. Ibid., pp. 389–90.
186. Grant Allen, 'The Celt in English Art', *The Fortnightly Review* 55 (1891), pp. 272–3. Richard Haslam contends that 'Allen's re-imagining of the Celt

gave Wilde a new focus for his aesthetic concerns, since the essays in [the latter's] *Intentions* were studded with paeans to imagination'. Richard Haslam, 'Oscar Wilde and the Imagination of the Celt', *Irish Studies Review* 11 (1995), p. 3.
187. Wilde, *The Complete Letters of Oscar Wilde*, pp. 469–70.
188. Josephine M. Guy and Ian Small, *Oscar Wilde's Profession: Writing and the Culture Industry in the Late Nineteenth Century* (Oxford: Oxford University Press, 2000), pp. 277–80.
189. Allen, *Linnet: A Romance*, p. 5.
190. Ibid., p. 11.
191. Ibid., p. 13.
192. Richard Le Gallienne, 'Grant Allen', *The Fortnightly Review* 72 (1899), p. 1025.
193. Allen, *Linnet: A Romance*, p. 34.
194. Hichens, *The Green Carnation*, pp. 181–2.
195. Grant Allen, 'The New Hedonism', p. 61. Soon after 'The New Hedonism' was published, an article in *The Humanitarian* by George Ives averred that Allen's article should have argued that *all* types of love and pleasure should be embraced. The *Review of Reviews* strongly condemned Ives's protest as a 'dissertation in praise of unnatural vice'. Although Wilde only heard about the *Review of Reviews* attack on Ives, who was a friend, he wrote to offer his support on October 22: 'When the prurient and the impotent attack you, be sure you are right'. Wilde, *The Complete Letters of Oscar Wilde*, p. 619.
196. Allen, 'The New Hedonism', p. 391.
197. Grant Allen, 'Introduction', *The British Barbarians: A Hill-Top Novel* (London: John Lane, 1895), p. vii.
198. Ibid., pp. vii, xvii–xviii.
199. Allen, 'The New Hedonism', p. 389.
200. Allen, 'Introduction', pp. xvii–xix.
201. Allen, *Linnet: A Romance*, p. 322.
202. Ibid., pp. 72, 211.
203. Ibid., p. 335.
204. Joseph Conrad, 'The Return', *Tales of Unrest* (London: Eveleigh Nash and Grayson, 1922), p. 176.
205. Ibid., pp. 176–7.
206. Ibid., p. 216.
207. Paul Kirschner, 'Wilde's Shadow in Conrad's "The Return"', *Notes and Queries* 40.4 (1993).
208. Ibid., p. 495. This final remark evokes Lord Henry Wotton's comment in *The Picture of Dorian Gray*'s that 'the one charm of marriage is that it makes a life of deception absolutely necessary for both parties'. Wilde, *Collins Complete Works of Oscar Wilde*, p. 20.
209. Kirschner, 'Wilde's Shadow in Conrad's "The Return"', p. 496.
210. Conrad, 'The Return', pp. 260–1. The cover of Wilde's *Poems* (1881) was printed with gold lettering on white parchment and featured an intricate flower pattern on the spine.
211. Wilde, *Collins Complete Works of Oscar Wilde*, p. 867.
212. Conrad, 'The Return', pp. 218–19.
213. Ibid., p. 216.
214. Ibid., p. 175.
215. Ibid., pp. 91, 176–7, 214.

216. Ibid., pp. 15, 32, 34, 209.
217. Ibid., p. 262.
218. Ibid., pp. 194–5.
219. Kingsley Widmer, 'Joseph Conrad', *British Novelists, 1890–1929: Traditionalists*, vol. 34, ed. Thomas F. Staley, Dictionary of Literary Biography (Detroit: Gale Research, 1985), p. 44.
220. Jeffrey Meyers, *Joseph Conrad: A Biography* (London: John Murray, 1991), pp. 224–5.
221. Ibid., p. 225.
222. Widmer, 'Joseph Conrad', p. 46. Like Wilde, Conrad also tended to live 'beyond his means' in order to maintain this image. Meyers, *Joseph Conrad: A Biography*, p. 204.
223. Joseph Conrad, *The Collected Letters of Joseph Conrad*, vol. 1, ed. Frederick R. Karl and Laurence Davies (Cambridge, UK: Cambridge University Press, 1983), p. 231.
224. Ibid., p. 405.
225. Ibid., p. 393.
226. Lawrence Graver, *Conrad's Short Fiction* (Berkeley: University of California Press, 1969), p. 37.
227. Ibid., pp. 34–7; Widmer, 'Joseph Conrad', p. 52.
228. Conrad, *The Collected Letters of Joseph Conrad*, p. 394; John Dozier Gordan, *Joseph Conrad: The Making of a Novelist* (Cambridge, MA: Harvard University Press, 1941), p. 253.
229. Conrad, *The Collected Letters of Joseph Conrad*, p. 386.
230. Ibid., p. 394.
231. Joseph Conrad, 'Author's Notes and Prefaces' *Joseph Conrad on Fiction*, ed. Walter F. Wright (Lincoln: University of Nebraska Press, 1964), p. 192.
232. Ibid., pp. 191–2.
233. Roderick, *In Mortal Bondage: The Strange Life of Rosa Praed*, pp. 107–8. Roderick presumably found this letter in the Praed papers he consulted while writing his book; it has not been published in collections of Wilde's letters.
234. Anonymous, *The Illustrated London News*, February 27, 1892.
235. This is generally thought to be the reason Praed had so much difficulty completing the novel, which she began in the early 1890s. Mareya Schmidt and Peter Schmidt, *Praed, Rosa (1851–1935)*, 1996, OzLit, available http://dargo.vicnet.net.au/ozlit/writers, March 28, 2003.
236. Clarke, 'Rosa Praed (Mrs. Campbell Praed)', p. 303; Schmidt and Schmidt, *Praed, Rosa (1851–1935)*. After Harward's death in 1927, Praed tried to contact her through the medium Hester Downed, who had reverted to her maiden name after a failed marriage to Dr Travers Smith. As related in Part 2, as 'Hester Travers Smith', Downed had published *Psychic Messages from Oscar Wilde* in 1924. Clarke, *Rosa! Rosa!*, pp. 203–4.
237. Clarke, *Rosa! Rosa!*, pp. 156–7; Clarke, 'Rosa Praed (Mrs. Campbell Praed)', p. 309.
238. Mrs Campbell Praed, *The Scourge-Stick* (London: William Heinemann, 1898), pp. 70, 92–3, 164, 269.
239. Ibid., p. 274.
240. Ibid., p. 117.
241. Ibid., p. 163.

242. Ibid., pp. 163–4.
243. Ibid., p. 164.
244. Ibid., pp. 164, 277.
245. Ibid., p. 274.
246. Ibid., pp. 163–6.
247. J. M. Collyer, 'New Novels (Book Reviews)', *The Athenaeum*, April 2, 1898, p. 432.
248. Anonymous, 'Atmosphere and Adventure (Book Reviews)', *Literature*, April 23, 1898; Clarke, *Rosa! Rosa!*, p. 158; Collyer, 'New Novels (Book Reviews)', p. 432.
249. Clarke, *Rosa! Rosa!*, p.155.
250. The author's most successful novel, *When It Was Dark* (1903), was written under the Thorne pseudonym.
251. The year 1898 was Gull's second year on the literary staff of Frank Harris's *Saturday Review*. He also worked as a journalist for the *Bookman* and the *Academy* and as an editor for *London Life*, the *Daily Mail*, and the *Daily Express* before giving up journalism to write novels full time. *Who Was Who 1897–1915*, p. 443.
252. Guy Thorne (Cyril Arthur Edward Ranger Gull), 'The Strand of Twenty Years Ago: Some Personal Reminiscences', *T. P.'s Weekly*, July 11, 1913.
253. Richards commissioned Gull to write a historical novel which the latter failed to produce; Richards the publisher also implied that Gull took money from him under false pretenses. Richards, *Memories of a Misspent Youth: 1872–1896*, pp. 187–8.
254. Ian Fletcher and John Stokes aver that Gull's biographical works 'are inhibited both by the comparative recentness of Wilde's fall and by [Gull's] lack of insight'. Ian Fletcher and John Stokes, 'Oscar Wilde', *Anglo-Irish Literature: A Review of Research*, ed. Richard J. Finneran (New York: The Modern Language Association of America, 1976), p. 67.
255. Anonymous (Cyril Arthur Edward Ranger Gull), *The Hypocrite*, 5th edn. (London: Greening, 1898), pp. 43, 47.
256. Ibid., pp. 1–2.
257. Ibid., pp. 10–11.
258. Ibid., p. 43, Wilde; *Collins Complete Works of Oscar Wilde*, p. 1244.
259. Anonymous (Cyril Arthur Edward Ranger Gull), *The Hypocrite*, p. 91; Wilde, *Collins Complete Works of Oscar Wilde*, p. 1128.
260. The name of this priest is Father Gray. Gull may have intended this name as an allusion to Wilde's *The Picture of Dorian Gray*; it is also interesting that Wilde's former disciple John Gray began training as a Catholic priest in October 1898 (the year that *The Hypocrite* was first published); he was ordained in December 1901. Gull may also have been aware of Wilde's visit to the fashionable London priest Reverend Sebastien Bowden while still a student at Oxford. A letter from Bowden to Wilde dated April 15, 1878, mentions Wilde's 'unexpected loss of fortune' (probably referring to the surprisingly meager inheritance that had recently been left to Wilde by his half-brother Henry Wilson). Ellmann, *Oscar Wilde*, pp. 83, 90–1. A similar conflict and frustrated familial monetary expectations are experienced by Gobion.
261. Anonymous (Cyril Arthur Edward Ranger Gull), *The Hypocrite*, p. 13.
262. Ibid., p. 35.

263. Ibid., pp. 20, 77, 129.
264. Ibid., p. 15.
265. Ibid., pp. 14, 26, 44, 86.
266. Ibid., pp. 18–19.
267. Ibid., pp. 37, 144.
268. Ibid., p. 52.
269. An editor's assistant at the *Pilgrim*, a shady character whose mistress is an open secret, is called 'Wild'. The location of the rooms Gobion first procures in London, 'in one of the quiet streets running from the Fleet Street end of the Strand to the Embankment', recall Wilde's first London residence in Salisbury Street.
270. Anonymous (Cyril Arthur Edward Ranger Gull), *The Hypocrite*, p. 58.
271. Ibid., p. 151.
272. Ibid., pp. 155–6. Wilde told his wife that he had a vision of his mother in jail the day before she died. Ellmann, *Oscar Wilde*, p. 467. It is possible that Gull heard of this from Leonard Smithers or through another mutual acquaintance.
273. Anonymous (Cyril Arthur Edward Ranger Gull), *The Hypocrite*, pp. 166–7.
274. Ibid., pp. 163–4.
275. Wilde, *Collins Complete Works of Oscar Wilde*, p. 471.
276. Leonard Cresswell Ingleby, *Oscar Wilde* (London: T. Werner Laurie, 1907), p. 349.
277. Anonymous (Cyril Arthur Edward Ranger Gull), *The Hypocrite*, p. viii.
278. Ibid., pp. vii–viii.
279. Gull also dismisses the New Woman in *The Hypocrite* as a 'sexless oddity'. Ibid., p. 80.
280. Ibid., p. ii.
281. Anonymous (Cyril Arthur Edward Ranger Gull), *Miss Malevolent* (London: Greening, 1899), p. xii.
282. Ibid.
283. Ibid., p. 158.
284. Ibid., p. 185.
285. Ellmann, *Oscar Wilde*, p. 132; Wilde, *Collins Complete Works of Oscar Wilde*, p. 864.
286. Anonymous (Cyril Arthur Edward Ranger Gull), *Miss Malevolent*, pp. 14–16.
287. Ibid., pp. 55–7, 61.
288. Ibid., p. 37. The matriarch of this set, Mrs Policarp, keeps a copy of Wilde's *Intentions* on her desk as an aid to epigrammatic inspiration.
289. Ibid., p. 71.
290. Anonymous (Cyril Arthur Edward Ranger Gull), *The Hypocrite*, pp. 58, 61.
291. Ingleby, *Oscar Wilde*; Leonard Cresswell Ingleby, *Oscar Wilde: Some Reminiscences* (London: T. Werner Laurie, 1912).
292. Gull avers that Wilde's interpretation of Christ in *De Profundis* and amoral views on art present a danger to the 'half-educated' masses. Ingleby, *Oscar Wilde*, pp. 60, 86, 344–5.
293. Ingleby, *Oscar Wilde*, pp. 4, 11.
294. Ibid., p. 5.
295. Ibid., p. 349.
296. Ibid., p. 51.
297. Ibid., p. 351.

298. Ingleby, *Oscar Wilde: Some Reminiscences*, p. 14.
299. Ibid., p. 12. In *Reminiscences*, Gull also reveals that he knew Wilde's brother Willie 'fairly well in his later days' and that he preferred Willie's gentler humor and conversation to his brother's sharper, more cerebral style.
300. Richard Aldington, *Life for Life's Sake* (London: Cassell, 1968), pp. 42–3.
301. Kemp et al., *Edwardian Fiction*, p. 427; Mark Meredith, ed., *Who's Who in Literature* (Liverpool: The Literary Year Books, 1930), p. 473.
302. Ibid., pp. 205, 9, 48.
303. Ibid., pp. 207, 9.
304. Wilde, *Collins Complete Works of Oscar Wilde*, p. 67.
305. Yorke (Susan Richmond Lee), *Valentine: A Story of Ideals*, pp. 198, 205–6, 22, 52.
306. Ibid., p. 210.
307. Ibid., p. 207.
308. Ibid., p. 226–7.
309. Ibid., pp. 203, 205.
310. Ibid., pp. 200–1.
311. Ibid., p. 164.
312. Ibid., p. 197.
313. Ibid., p. 198. There is an echo of Wilde's *The Importance of Being Earnest* in this passage. In Act One of *Earnest*, Lady Bracknell declares, 'Ignorance is like a delicate exotic fruit; touch it and the bloom is gone'. Wilde, *Collins Complete Works of Oscar Wilde*, p. 368.
314. Richard Ellmann sees Wilde's ostracizers as falling into two groups: 'those who could not bear his homosexuality and those who could not bear his requests for money'. Ellmann, *Oscar Wilde*, p. 551.
315. Wilde, *The Complete Letters of Oscar Wilde*, p. 1227.
316. Ibid., p. 1229.
317. Ellmann, *Oscar Wilde*, p. 92.
318. Goodman, *The Oscar Wilde File*, p. 151.

Conclusion

1. Goodman, *The Oscar Wilde File*, p. 79.
2. A flawed version of the complete *De Profundis* was first published by Wilde's son Vyvyan Holland in 1949. The first accurate transcription (taken from the original autograph manuscript) was published in Rupert Hart-Davis's 1962 edition of Wilde's letters.
3. After his imprisonment and before his death, Wilde had already stirred the sympathy of many *Daily Chronicle* readers with two letters pleading for the better treatment of children in English jails, which appeared on May 28, 1897 and March 24, 1898.
4. Ellmann, *Oscar Wilde*, p. 546.
5. Ransome pleaded justification and won the case.
6. Holland, 'Biography and the Art of Lying', p. 5.
7. Vance Thompson, 'The Two Deaths of Oscar Wilde', *The Leaflet* 1 (1930).
8. For an examination of Wilde's appearances in twentieth-century crime fiction, see Heike Haase, 'Oscar Wilde in Crime Literature', in *The Importance of Reinventing Oscar: Versions of Wilde during the Last 100 Years*, ed. Uwe

Böker, Richard Corballis, and Julie A Hibbard (Amsterdam, Netherlands: Rodopi, 2002), p. 136.
9. Fletcher and Stokes, 'Oscar Wilde', p. 44.
10. Small, *Oscar Wilde Revalued*, pp. 12–13.
11. Holland, 'Biography and the Art of Lying', p. 16.

For a comprehensive bibliography of works cited in this book, visit angelakingston.net

INDEX

References to plates are printed in bold.
References to dramatic depictions of Wilde and fictional depictions of Wilde's contemporaries are to those mentioned in this book.

Academy, 40, 145, 285 n251
Ackroyd, Peter, 229, 238, 241
  Dan Leno and the Limehouse Golem (1994), 241
  Last Testament of Oscar Wilde, The (1983), 229, 238
Adventures of John Johns, The (1897), 189–93, 203, 281 n158, 281 n160, 281 n161, 281 n162, 282 n163
aestheticism, 9, 13, 15–17, 18, 19, 20–3, 25–7, 28–9, 43, 44–5, 46, 48, 50, 51, 57, 58–59, 62, 64, 66, 69, 71, 79, 81, 82, 83–4, **86**, 94, 96–7, 102, 107, 114, 115, 119, 121, 122, 124, 130, 134, 136, 137, 141, 142, 144, 149, 150, 154, 155, 158, 160, 166, 176, 181–2, 185, 188, 194, 195, 196, 201, 205, 208, 209, 210, 218, 219, 222, 224, 226, 233, 254 n126, 257 n218, 257 n219, 282–3 n186
Affinities: A Romance of To-day (1885), 6, 12, 48–57, 69, **87**, 148, 226, 256 n177
Albemarle Club, 126, 157
Albert Edward, Prince of Wales (later Edward VII), 15, 46, 47, 124
Albery, James, 25

Where's the Cat? (1880), 25, 115, 250–1 n47, 273 n304
Allen, Grant, 4, 98, 101, 193–200, 282 n174, 282 n176, 282–3 n186, 283 n195
  British Barbarians: A Hill-Top Novel, The (1895), 194, 199–200
  'Celt in English Art, The' (1891), 196, 198, 282–3 n186
  Colour Sense: Its Origin and Development; An Essay in Comparative Psychology, The (1879), 196
  fictional depictions: Grant Allen in *The Silver Domino; or, Side Whispers, Social and Literary* (1892), 98
  For Maimie's Sake: A Tale of Love and Dynamite (1886), 196
  Linnet: A Romance (1898), 8–9, 193–200, 226, 282 n176
  'New Hedonism, The' (1894), 196, 199, 283 n195
  Physiological Aesthetics (1877), 196
  Woman Who Did, The (1895), 194
Amery, Leopold, *see* Y. T. O.
Arnold, Matthew, 42, 60, 98
  Literature and Dogma (1873), 60

A. T. D. (anonymous), 4, 25–7, 121, 251 n50
'O'Flighty' (1879), 25–7, 251 n50
Autobiography of a Boy: Passages Selected by His Friend, G. S. Street, The (1894), 135–8, 159, 226

Balcome, Florence, *see* Stoker, Florence
Beardsley, Aubrey, 2, 4, 4–5, 60, 77, **92**, 116, 154, 160–8, 216, 267 n143, 275 n10, 275 n13, 275 n17, 275 n21, 276 n28, 276 n33
  fictional depictions: Beardsley, Aubrey, in *The Confessions of Aubrey Beardsley* (1993), 240; Sporion in *The Story of Venus and Tannhauser* (1896), 275 n9; Tannhäuser in *The Story of Venus and Tannhauser* (1896), 161; *Story of Venus and Tannhäuser, The* (1896), **92**, 160–8, 226, 275 n9, 275 n10, 275 n13, 275 n15
Beckson, Karl, 84, 118, 128–9, 265 n99
Beerbohm, Max, 2, 4–5, 5–6, 59, 101, 115–20, 135, 138, 148, 154, 163, 265 n99, 266 n115, 266 n123, 266 n129, 267 n143, 267 n144, 267 n145, 267 n149, 267 n150, 268 n168, 270 n221, 272 n294
  '1880' (1895), 119
  'Ballade de la Vie Joyeuse' (1892), 119
  Christmas Garland, A (1912), 135, 270 n221
  'Lord of Language, A' (1905), 120
  'Peep into the Past, A' (1893 or 1894), 115–20, 126

Zuleika Dobson; or An Oxford Love Story (1911), 115
Benson, E(dward) F(rederick), 139, 271 n244
  Dodo: A Detail of the Day (1893), 139
Bentley, George, 52–3, 95, 100, 262 n5
Besant, Walter, 22–5, 58, 64, 94, 250 n35, 250 n40
  Monks of Thelema, The (1877), 22–25, 27, 30, 58, 116, 226
Blavatsky, Madame Helena
  fictional depictions: Madame Tamvasco in *Affinities: A Romance of To-day* (1885), 49, 53, 148, 256 n177; Madame Obnoskin in *The Charlatan* (1895), 148
Bloom, Harold, 229, 248 n16
Brookfield, Charles, 110–11, 265 n99, 271 n237
  The Poet and the Puppets: A Travestie Suggested by Lady Windermere's Fan (1893), 110–11
Broughton, Rhoda, 4, 41–6, 59, 74, **86**, 94, 98, 145, 254 n121, 254 n122, 256 n198
  fictional depictions: Broughton, Rhoda, in *The Silver Domino; or, Side Whispers, Social and Literary* (1892), 98
  Second Thoughts (1880), 41–6, **86**, 222, 226
'Brown Roses' (1896), 123, 173–4, 226
Buchanan, Robert, 4, 99, 148–53, 158, 226, 273 n314, 273–4 n319, 274 n322
  Blue Bells of Scotland, The (1887), 150–1
  Charlatan, The (1894), 148–53, 226, 255 n153
  Clarissa (1890), 151

'Dismal Throng, The' (1893), 152
Dr Cupid (1889), 151
'Fleshly School of Poetry, The' (1872), 150
God and the Man (1881), 273 n314
That Winter Night (1887), 150–1
Burnand, F(rancis) C(owley), 44–5, 254 n138
The Colonel (1881), 44–5, 63, 115, 273 n304

Carrel, Frederic, 4, 189–93, 222, 281 n158, 281 n159, 282 n163, 282 n164
Adventures of John Johns, The (1897), 189–93, 203, 281 n158, 281 n160, 281 n161, 281 n162, 282 n163
'Case of Identity, A' (1892), 85
Charlatan, The (novel) (1894), 148–53, 226, 255 n153
Charlatan, The (play) (1894), 148
Colonel, The (1881), 44–5, 63, 115, 273 n304
Conrad, Joseph, 200–7, 284
Almayer's Folly (1895), 200
Children of the Sea: A Tale of the Forecastle, The (1898), 200
Outcast of the Islands, An (1896), 200
'The Return' (1898), 8–9, 200–7, 282 n167
Corelli, Marie, 4, 5, 95–100, 104, 133, 146, 151, 172, 262 n5, 263 n40, 263 n46
'Shakespeare's Mother' (1889), 99
Silver Domino; or, Side Whispers, Social and Literary, The (1892), 95–100, 217, 226, 263 n46
Soul of Lilith, The (1892), 95
Cruso, Henry, *see* Y. T. O.
Cunliffe, Arthur, 4, 5–6, 111–14

'Ossian Savage's New Play' (1893), 111–14

Daily Chronicle, 96, 122, 287 n3
Davidson, John, 4, 116, 130–5, 269 n201, 269–70 n202, 275 n21
Baptist Lake (1894), 130–5, 226, 138
décadence/decadence (movement), 4, 8, 83, 93–5, 109, 126, 131, 135, 145, 152, 158, 160, 161, 167, 168, 178, 180, 199–200, 205, 206, 210, 214, 216, 219, 233, 279 n103, 280 n116
Denisoff, Dennis, 13, 144–5, 154, 155, 271 n240, 272 n286, 273 n314
Dixon, Ella Hepworth, 4, 101–11, 134, 187, 222–3
As I Knew Them: Sketches of People I Have Met on the Way (1930), 101, 110
My Flirtations (1892), 101–5, 264 n58
Story of a Modern Woman, The (1894), 101, 105–8
'World's Slow Stain, The' (1904), 101, 108–10, 127, 233, 281
Douglas, Lord Alfred (Bosie), 41, 77–8, 82, **90, 91**, 93, 106, 111–14, 138–48, 157, 163, 168, 189, 219, 227–8, 251 n66, 253 n117, 261 n328, 267 n143, 268 n168, 274 n1, 274 n322
fictional depictions: Flower, Beaufort (Beaufy), in *The Story of A Modern Woman* (1894), 106; Hastings, Lord Reggie, in *The Green Carnation* (1894), 138–48, 274 n1
on fictional depictions of himself, 148

Downed, Hester (formerly Hester Travers Smith), 130, 230, 284 n236
Doyle, Arthur Conan, 4, 49, 78–84, **88**, 123–30, 213, 226, 261 n328, 269 n192
   fictional depictions: Doyle, Arthur Conan, in *Arthur and George* (2006), 246; Doyle, Arthur Conan, in *Skullduggery* (1987), 239; Doyle, Arthur Conan, in *The Problem of the Evil Editor* (2000), 245
   Micah Clarke (1888), 79, 80
   Sherlock Holmes stories by Doyle: *Adventures of Sherlock Holmes, The* (1892), 124; 'Case of Identity, A' (1892), 85; 'Empty House, The' (1903), 84, 127–30, 226, 233, 243–4, 269 n191; 'Final Problem, The' (1894), 127; 'Greek Interpreter, The' (1894), 84, 123–6, 226; *Memoirs of Sherlock Holmes* (1894), 124; 'Noble Bachelor, The' (1892), 85; 'Red-Headed League, The' (1892), 124; *Sign of Four, The* (1890), 78–84, **88**; *Study in Scarlet* (1887), 78–9, 80, 83, 260 n316
   Sherlock Holmes fictions by writers other than Doyle, 229, 233, 237, 237–8, 238, 239, 240, 241, 242, 242–3, 243, 243–4, 244, 245, 269 n191
Dracula (1897), 2, 174–84, 226, 279 n93
Du Maurier, George, 25, 45, 46, 52

Ellmann, Richard, 7, 8, 11, 18, 43, 64, 65, 66, 71, 94, 115, 139, 144–5, 164, 175, 265 n99, 267 n143, 287 n314

'Empty House, The' (1903), 84, 127–30, 226, 233, 243–4, 269 n191

Fleming, George, *see* Fletcher, Julia Constance
Fletcher, Ian, 75, 166, 167, 168, 230, 247 n3, 254 n120, 257 n218, 275 n14, 276 n22, 285 n254
Fletcher, Julia Constance, 4, 17–22, **85**, 250 n29
   Mirage (1877), 17–22, **85**
   Truth About Clement Ker, The (1888), 21–2
Freedman, Jonathan, 63–4, 71, 72, 248 n16, 257 n209, 257 n219, 257 n224
Fortnightly Review, The, 189, 196

Gilbert, W(illiam) S(chwenck) and Sullivan, Sir Arthur, 45–6, 79
   Patience (1881), 45–6, 110
Gray, John, 77, 78, 124, 154, 244, 269–70 n202, 285 n260
'Greek Interpreter, The' (1894), 84, 123–6, 226
Green Carnation, The (1894), 2, 13, 138–48, 190, 198, 226, 263 n52, 271 n248, 272 n286, 272 n294, 274 n1, 276 n28
Grosvenor Gallery, 15, 21, 22
Gull, Cyril Arthur Edward Ranger, 4, 210–21, 285 n251, 285 n253, 285 n254, 286 n272, 287 n299
   Hypocrite, The (1898), 8–9, 210–17, 226, 285 n260, 286 n279
   Miss Malevolent (1899), 217–20
   Oscar Wilde (1907), 219–21, 285 n254, 287 n292
   Oscar Wilde: Some Reminiscences (1912), 219–21, 285 n254, 287 n299

When It Was Dark (1903), 285 n250

Haralson, Eric, 64, 68, 69, 71, 155
Harris, Frank, 31, 40, 60, 120, 145, 147, 157, 181, 189–93, 196, 251 n66, 281 n161, 281 n162, 282 n163, 285 n251
  fictional depictions: John Johns in *The Adventures of John Johns* (1897), 189–93, 281 n161, 281 n162, 282 n163; *Oscar Wilde: His Life and Confessions* (1916), 31, 120
Hart-Davis, Rupert, 7, 164, 287 n2
Harward, Susan, 48, 208, 284 n236
Hichens, Robert, 4, 4–5, 5–6, 138–48, 230, 271 n245, 272 n286, 272 n294
  Green Carnation, The (1894), 2, 13, 138–48, 190, 198, 226, 263 n52, 271 n248, 272 n286, 272 n294, 274 n1, 276 n28
  Yesterday: The Autobiography of Robert Hichens (1947), 139, 271 n244
Hirst, Francis, *see* Y. T. O.
Holland, Merlin, 6, 7, 8, 164, 231,
Holland, Vyvyan, 73, 110, 159, 279 n91, 287 n2
Housman, Laurence, 65, 164–5, 234
  Echo de Paris (1923), 164–5, 229, 234
  Hypocrite, The (1898), 8–9, 210–17, 226, 285 n260, 286 n279

Immaturity (1879), 27–41, 226, 251 n68, 252 n95
Ingleby, Leonard Cresswell, *see* Gull, Cyril Arthur Edward Ranger

Irving, Henry, 99, 175, 176, 177–8, 179, 180, 182, 278 n85, 280 n122

James, Henry, 4, 20–1, 42, 61–73, 79, 94, 95, 100, 101, 116, 144–5, 226, 230, 256 n198, 257 n209, 257 n219, 257 n224, 257–8 n225, 258 n226, 258 n231, 258 n243, 270 n221
  Ambassadors, The (1903), 63, 65, 72
  Art of the Novel, The (1907), 72
  'Author of "Beltraffio, The" ' (1884), 62, 64
  'Figure in the Carpet, The' (1896), 66
  Golden Bowl, The (1904), 63
  Portrait of a Lady (1881), 52, 62
  Roderick Hudson (1875), 16, 62
  Spoils of Poynton, The (1897), 62–3
  Tragic Muse, The (1890), 2, 61–73, 225, 226, 257 n209, 268 n166
  Turn of the Screw, The (1898), 65, 258 n237
Jopling, Louise, 24–5, 54–5, 73, **89**
  fictional depictions: Borlase, Christine, in *Affinities: A Romance of To-day* (1885), 11, 49, 54–5
  Twenty Years of My Life: 1867–1887 (1925), 54

Lane, John, 60, 154, 158, 169, 196
Langtry, Lillie (Mrs Edward Langtry, *née* Le Breton), 25, 58, 103, 137, 159, 204
Lee, Susan Richmond, 221–4
  Valentine: A Story of Ideals (1899), 221–4
Le Gallienne, Richard, 4, 101, 121–3, 131, 135–6, 173–96, 198, 217, 219, 226, 227

296 INDEX

Le Gallienne, Richard—*continued*
  'Brown Roses' (1896), 123, 173–4, 226
  Décadent to His Soul, The (1893), 122
  'On Some Recent Editions of Oscar Wilde' (1910), 173
  Romantic '90s, The (1925), 123
  'Woman's Half-Profits, The' (1894), 121–3, 173, 226
Leverson, Ada (Mrs Ernest Leverson, *née* Beddington), 4, 4–5, 104, 109–10, 119, 135, 142, 146, 148, 153–5, 159–60, 163, 190, 267 n143, 268 n168, 275 n13, 281 n156
  'Advisability of Not Being Brought up in a Handbag: A Trivial Tragedy for Wonderful People, The' (1895), 154
  'Afternoon Party, An' (1893), 154
  fictional depictions: Buller, Adela, in 'The World's Slow Stain' (1904), 109–10; Windsor, Mrs, in *The Green Carnation* (1895), 142
  'Minx, The' (1894), 154
  'Overheard Fragment of a Dialogue' (1895), 154
  'Suggestion' (1895), 153–5, 159
  'The Quest of Sorrow' (1896), 153, 155, 159–60
Linnet: A Romance (1898), 8–9, 193–200, 226, 282 n176
Lippincott's Magazine, 71, 72, 79, 80, 93, *see also* Stoddart, J(oseph) M(arshall)

Mahaffy, John Pentland, 15, 16, 17, 47
  fictional depictions: Mahaffy in *Ye Soul Agonies in Ye Life of Oscar Wilde* (1882), 47
Meredith, George, 5, **89**, 152

Mirage (1877), 17–22, **85**
Miss Malevolent (1899), 217–20
Monks of Thelema, The (1877), 22–5, 27, 30, 58, 116, 226
Murray, Henry, 148–53
  The Charlatan (1894), 148–53, 226, 255 n153
My Flirtations (1892), 101–5, 264 n58

'Noble Bachelor, The' (1892), 85
Nordau, Max, 40, 220, 279 n102
  Degeneration (1892), 40, 279 n102

'O'Flighty' (1879), 25–7, 226, 251 n50
Oscar Wilde (1907), 219–21, 285 n254, 287 n292
Oscar Wilde: Some Reminiscences (1912), 219–21, 285 n254, 287 n299
'Ossian Savage's New Play' (1893), 111–14

Pall Mall Gazette, 24, 31–2, 43–4, 48, 59, 74–5, 95, 146, 150–1, 195
Partridge, Sir Bernard, **90**, 102, 103, 263 n52
Pater, Walter, 16, 18, 21, 22, 42, 43, 47, 57–9, 62, 63, 73, 94, 101, 102, 117, 141, 148, 161, 257 n224, 261 n336
  fictional depictions: Langham in *Robert Elsmere* (1888), 57–9
Patience (1881), 45–6, 110
Pearson, Hesketh, 59, 252 n70
'Peep into the Past, A' (1893 or 1894), 115–20, 126
Poet and the Puppets: A Travestie Suggested by Lady Windermere's Fan, The (1893), 110–11
Portrait of a Lady (1881), 52, 62
Praed, Rosa (Mrs Campbell Praed, *née* Murray-Prior), 4, 5, 48–57,

87, 189, 207–10, 226–7,
   255 n150, 284 n233,
   284 n235, 284 n236
Affinities: A Romance of To-day
   (1885), 6, 12, 48–57, 69,
   87, 148, 226, 256 n177
'At Royat' (1888), 207
Scourge-Stick, The (1898), 57,
   207–10, 226–7
Pre-Raphaelites, 16, 18, 23, 43, 48,
   150
Punch, 25, 45, 46, **90**, 102, 145,
   146, 154, 158, 208, 251 n49,
   264 n58, 272 n292, 275 n13
   see also Burnand, F(rancis)
   C(owley), Du Maurier,
   George and Partridge,
   Bernard

Queensberry, Marquess of, 82, 111,
   146, 157, 164, 237–8, 245,
   261 n328, 274 n1
   fictional depictions: elderly
   gentleman in *The Green
   Carnation* (1894), 146,
   275 n1
'Quest of Sorrow, The' (1896), 153,
   155, 159–60

Raffalovich, Marc-André, 4–5,
   73–8, 95, 100, 103, 144–5,
   154, 163, 164, 230, 259 n287,
   259 n290, 260 n310
   L'Affaire Oscar Wilde (1895), 78
   Self-Seekers: A Novel of Manners
      (1897), 76, 77
   Thread and the Path, The (1895),
      77
   Willing Exile, A (1890), 73–8
real people in fiction, 5–6, 10–13,
   229
'Red-Headed League, The' (1892),
   124
'Return, the' (1898), 8–9, 200–7,
   282 n167
Rhymers' Club, 121–2, 130–2

Rice, James, 22–5
   Monks of Thelema, The (1877),
   22–5, 27, 30, 58, 116, 226
Robert Elsmere (1888), 57–60,
   272 n286
Roderick Hudson (1875), 16, 62
Ross, Robert, 4, 12, 32, 65, 72,
   101, 102, 110, 124, 135, 154,
   163, 164, 186, 192, 224,
   227–8, 239, 266 n123,
   268 n168, 271 n244
Rossetti, Dante Gabriel, 22, 26–7,
   45–6, 47, 117, 150, 254 n131,
   273 n314, *see also*
   Pre-Raphaelites
Ruskin, John, 15, 16, 22, 45–6, 47,
   184, 254 n126
   fictional depictions: Ruskin, John,
   in *Manly Pursuits* (1999),
   244; Truman, John, in
   Babylon (1885), 282 n176

Saturday Review, 6, 48, 59, 120,
   185, 285 n251
Savile Club, 24, 64
Schuster, Adela, 224, 265 n90
Schaffer, Talia, 177–84, 280 n122
Schroeder, Horst, 60, 275 n17
Scourge-Stick, The (1898), 57,
   207–10, 226–7
Seaside Flirt, A (1897), 184–9,
   203
Second Thoughts (1880), 41–6, **86**,
   222, 226
Shaw, George Bernard, 4, 5, 27–41,
   44, 134, 147, 155, 196, 226,
   236, 241, 251 n54, 251 n66,
   251 n67, 251 n68, 252 n70,
   252 n85, 252 n95, 253 n104,
   253 n110, 253 n113,
   253 n115, 253 n117,
   253 n119, 262 n27, 270 n221
   Arms and the Man (1894), 38
   fictional depictions: Smith,
   Robert, in *Immaturity*
   (1879), 28

Shaw, George Bernard—*continued*
  Immaturity (1879), 27–41, 226, 251 n68, 252 n95
  John Bull's Other Island (1904), 41
  'Quintessence of Ibsenism, The' (1890), 32, 38–9
  Widower's Houses (1892), 39
Sign of Four, The (1890), 78–84, **88**
Silver Domino; or, Side Whispers, Social and Literary, The (1892), 95–100, 217, 226, 263 n46
Sinfield, Alan, 8, 158, 274 n335
Small, Ian, 9–10, 197, 273–4 n319
Stannard, Henrietta, 4, 98, 184–9, 222–3, 226–7, 281 n137
  Bootle's Baby: A Story of the Scarlet Lancers (1885), 184, 185, 186
  fictional depictions: Stannard, Henrietta, in *The Silver Domino; or, Side Whispers, Social and Literary* (1892), 98
  Seaside Flirt, A (1897), 184–9, 203
  That Imp (1887), 185
Stetz, Margaret, 103, 104, 105, 107, 170
Stoddart, J(oseph) M(arshall), 72, 79, 82
Stoker, Bram, 4, 49, 174–84, 278 n78, 278 n82, 278 n85, 278 n87, 279 n91, 279 n102, 280 n122
  'Censorship of Fiction, The' (1908), 180
  Dracula (1897), 2, 174–84, 226, 279 n93
  Dracula/vampire fictions by writers other than Stoker, 234, 238, 240, 241, 242, 242–3
  fictional depictions: Harker, Jonathan in *Dracula* (1897), 182–4; Stoker, Bram, in

Supping with Panthers (1996), 241
Personal Reminiscences of Henry Irving (1906), 180, 278 n85
Stoker, Florence (Mrs Bram Stoker, née Balcombe), 174–84, 278 n79, 278 n82, 278 n85, 278 n86, 278 n87, 279 n91
Stokes, John, 2, 3, 187, 257 n218, 285 n254
Story of a Modern Woman, The (1894), 101, 105–8
Story of Venus and Tannhäuser, The (1896), **92**, 160–8, 226, 275 n9, 275 n10, 275 n13, 275 n15
Street, G(eorge) S(lythe), 4, 135–8, 116, 154, 270 n236, 271 n237
  The Autobiography of a Boy: Passages Selected by His Friend, G. S. Street (1894), 135–8, 159, 226
Study in Scarlet, A (1887), 78–9, 80, 83, 260 n316
Sturgis, Matthew, 8, 259 n290, 260 n310, 275 n17, 276 n28
'Suggestion' (1895), 153–5, 159

Tanitch, Robert, 2–3, 159
Tennyson, Lord Alfred, 47, 97, 175–6, 179, 214
  fictional depictions: Tennyson, Alfred, in *The Silver Domino; or, Side Whispers, Social and Literary* (1892), 98; Tennyson, Alfred, in *Ye Soul Agonies in Ye Life of Oscar Wilde* (1882), 47
Terry, Ellen, 25, 48–9, 99, 101, 103, 151, 175–6, 182, 204, 250–1 n47, 253 n110, 278 n86
Thorne, Guy, *see* Gull, Cyril Arthur Edward Ranger
Tragic Muse, The (1890), 2, 61–73, 225, 226, 257 n209, 268 n166

Travers Smith, Hester (*née* Downed), 130, 230, 284 n236
Psychic Messages from Oscar Wilde (1924), 130, 284 n236
Tree, Herbert Beerbohm, 115, 148, 154, 265 n99
Turner, Reginald (Reggie), 116, 119–20, 139, 147, 148, 154, 164, 266 n123, 272 n294
Turn of the Screw, The (1898), 65, 258 n237

'Under the Hill' (1896), *see The Story of Venus and Tannhäuser* (1896)

Valentine: A Story of Ideals (1899), 221–4
Victoria, Queen, 47, 95
Vyver, Bertha, 97, 100

Wales, Albert Edward, Prince of, *see* Albert Edward
Ward, Mary (Mrs Humphry Ward, *née* Arnold), 57–60, 74, 98, 145, 256 n198, 276 n28
fictional depictions: Ward, Mrs Humphry, in *The Silver Domino; or, Side Whispers, Social and Literary* (1892), 98
Robert Elsmere (1888), 57–60, 272 n286
Writer's Recollections, A (1918), 59
Ward, W(illiam) W(alsford) (Bouncer), 17–18, 21, 133
Weintraub, Stanley, 28, 161, 253 n104
Where's the Cat? (1880), 25, 115, 250–1 n47, 273 n304
Whistler, James, 22, 25, 45–6, 59, 122–3, 134, 147–8
Whitman, Walt, 50, 56, 150, 176, 179, 180, 196, 235

Wilde, Constance (Mrs Oscar Wilde, *née* Lloyd), 36, 48–50, 52, 53–5, 74, 76–7, **87**, 96–7, 109, 147, 159, 176, 189, 240, 275 n17, 278 n87, 286 n272
fictional depictions: fairy in *The Silver Domino; or, Side Whispers, Social and Literary* (1892), 96–7; *fiancée* of Vivian Dermott in *A Seaside Flirt* (1897), 189; Fountain, Judith, in *Affinities: A Romance of Today* (1885), 48–50, 52, 53–5, **87**;
Laylham, Daisy, in *A Willing Exile* (1890), 74, 76–7;
Wilde, Constance, in *The Case of the Pederast's Wife* (2000), 244; Wilde, Constance, in *The Coward Does It With A Kiss* (1990), 240
Wilde, Lady Jane Francesca, *née* Elgee (Speranza), 6, 36–7, 49, 99, 174, 278 n78
Wilde, Oscar
academic criticism of, 7–11, 225, 227–31
aestheticism, 9, 15–17, 18, 19, 22, 23, 25–7, 28–9, 33, 43, 44–6, 48, 50, 51, 57, 58–9, 62, 64, 66, 69, 76, 79, 81, **86**, 94, 96–7, 102, 103, 107, 114, 121, 122, 124, 132, 136, 137, 141, 144, 149, 154, 155, 158, 166, 176, 181–2, 188, 194, 195, 196, 201, 208, 210, 218, 219, 224, 233, 254 n126, 282–3 n186
appearance, 6, 17, 22, 34–5, 49–50, 51, 62, 66, 80, 81, **85**, **86**, **88**, **89**, **91**, 94, 96, 101, 103, 105, 106, 108,

Wilde, Oscar—*continued*
109, 111, 115–16, 120, 125, 127, 129, 132, 136, 140, 149, 159, 165–6, 167, 169, 170, 173, 181, 183, 186, 190–1, 194, 201, 208, 211, 212, 218, 222, 257 n209, 266–7 n129, 268 n168, 269 n191

arrogance and egotism, 17, 23, 31, 33, 43, 50, 51, 56, 74, 76, 94, 98, 102, 109, 119–20, 122, 124, 129, 133, 136, 137, 149, 154, 155, 169, 192, 193, 211, 222, 226, 238, 242

death, 2, 3, 8, 33, 116, 120, 215, 224, 226, 227, 228, 237, 238, 239

décadence/decadence, 3, 83, **90**, 93–5, 122, 126, 132, 145, 152, 158, 200, 206, 210, 214, 216, 219–20, 233, 271 n240, 279 n103, 280 n116

dramatic depictions: Bunthorne, Reginald, in *Patience* (1881), 45–6, 48; Darrell, Mervyn, in *The Charlatan* (1894), 148; Holmes, Sherlock, in performances by William Gillette (1899–1932), 261–2 n342; Keegan, Peter, in *John Bull's Other Island* (1904), 41; 'Poet of the Lily, The', in *The Poet and the Puppets: A Travestie Suggested by Lady Windermere's Fan, The* (1893), 110–11; Ramsay, Scott, in *Where's the Cat?* (1880), 25, 115; Streyke, Lambert, in *The Colonel* (1881), 44–5, 63; Wilde, Oscar in *Aristophanes at Oxford* (1894), 120–1; Wilde, Oscar, in *The Trials of Oscar Wilde* (1960), 230, 237

on dramatic depictions of himself, 46, 110–11

drinking, 33, 35, 40, 115–16, 136, 191, 211, 212

editor of *The Woman's World*, 4, 21–2, 57, 58, 65, 99, 101, 105–8, 172, 201–2, 207

fictional depictions: Amarinth, Esmé, in *The Green Carnation* (1894), 138–48, 198, 226, 276 n28; Bosanquet-Barry, Mr, in *The Story of a Modern Woman* (1894), 105–8; Brome, Cyprian, in *A Willing Exile* (1890), 73–8; Carington, Cecil, in 'Suggestion' (1895) and 'The Quest of Sorrow' (1896), 153–5, 159–60; Chaloner, Francis, in *Second Thoughts* (1880), 41–44, **86**, 222, 226; Colquhoun, Esmé, in *Affinities: A Romance of Today* (1885), 48–57, 69, 256 n177; Darrell, Mervyn, in *The Charlatan* (1894), 148–153, 226; Davenant, Claude, in *Mirage* (1877), 17–22, **85**; Dermott, Vivian, in *A Seaside Flirt* (1897), 184–9, 226–7, 281 n152; Dracula, Count, in *Dracula* (1897), 174–84, 226, 279 n102; editor in 'The Return' (1898), 200–7; editor of *The Fan* in *The Story of a Modern Woman* (1894), 105–8; elephant in *The Silver Domino; or, Side Whispers, Social and Literary* (1892), 95–100, 226; Gobion, Caradoc Yardly, in *The Hypocrite* (1898), 210–17, 219, 226, 285 n260, 286 n269; Hawkshaw, Patrick, in *Immaturity* (1879), 27–41,

43, 226, 252 n85; Holmes, Mycroft, in *The Greek Interpreter* (1894) and *The Empty House* (1903), 123–30, 226, 268 n166; Holmes, Sherlock, in *The Sign of Four* (1890), 'A Case of Identity' (1892) and 'The Noble Bachelor' (1892), 83–4; Horace in *The Adventures of John Johns* (1897), 189–93; Lake, Baptist, in *Baptist Lake* (1894), 130–135, 226; Leyden, Franklyn, in 'The Fifth Edition' (1896), 169–72, 226, 277 n59; Mandell, Gilbert, in *My Flirtations* (1892), 101–5: Moran, Colonel Sebastian, in *The Empty House* (1903), 127–130, 233, 243–4, 268 n179, 269 n190, 269 n191; Nash, Gabriel, in *The Tragic Muse* (1890), 61–73, 225, 257 n209, 268 n166; O'Flighty in 'O'Flighty' (1879), 25–7, 226; Paravel, Cosmo, in *The Scourge-Stick* (1898), 207–10, 226–7; Priapusa in *The Story of Venus and Tannhäuser* (1896), **92**, 160–8, 226; Redmond, Val, in *My Flirtations* (1892), 101–5; Rondel, Hyacinth, in 'The Woman's Half-Profits' (1894) and 'Brown Roses' (1896), 121–3, 173–4, 226–7; Rondelet, Paul, in *The Monks of Thelema* (1877), 22–5, 30, 43, 226; Savage, Ossian, in 'Ossian Savage's New Play' (1893), 111–14; Sholto, Thaddeus, in *The Sign of Four* (1890),

78–84, **88**, 125, 126, 261 n321; Spiridion in *The Story of Venus and Tannhäuser* (1896), 160–8, 226; Tubby in *The Autobiography of a Boy: Passages Selected by His Friend, G. S. Street* (1894), 135–8, 226; Vincent, Gilbert, in 'The World's Slow Stain' (1904), 108–10, 233, 281 n152; Wade, Fabian, in *Valentine: A Story of Ideals* (1899), 221–4; Waye, Guy, in *Miss Malevolent* (1899), 217–20; Wilde, Oscar, in 'A Peep into the Past' (1893 or 1894), 115–20; Wilde, Oscar, in *Ye Soul Agonies in Ye Life of Oscar Wilde* (1882), 46–7; Wood, Mr, in *Robert Elsmere* (1888), 57–61, 272 n286; Wood, Florian, in *Linnet: A Romance* (1898), 193–200, 226
on fictional depictions: of himself, 1, 12–13, 21–2, 23, 25, 46, 56, 60, 96, 146–7, 192, 207; of real people, 1, 12, 11–13, 225
and the ancient Greeks, 15, 16, 18–19, 23, 29, 33, 36–7, 43, 49–50, 56, 81, 126, 137, 143, 166, 191, 195, 213, 222
illustrated caricatures, 13, 25, 45, 46–7, **90**, 118, 145–6, 162, 168, 251 n49, 263 n52, 266 n129, 275 n21, 276 n22, 280 n116
on illustrated caricatures of himself, 25, 118, 162, 168
indolence, 29, 32, 125, 151, 154–5, 169–70, 194, 200, 218, 266 n115

Wilde, Oscar—*continued*
  intelligence, 35, 47, 66, 67, 83, 93, 94, 125, 126, 137, 149, 186, 187, 188, 193, 195, 198, 201, 211, 214, 216, 219, 220, 229
  journalism, 4, 27, 29, 31–2, 38, 43–4, 48, 57, 59, 97–8, 116–7, 169, 170, 214–5, 234, 247 n3, 286 n269
  kindness and generosity, 31, 67, 81–2, 98, 107–8, 140, 171, 188, 219, 220, 228, 238, 281 n156
  lecturing, 46, 48, 50, 73–4, 79, 81, 122, 136, 139, 141, 143, 149, 218, 260 n319
  and marriage, 19–20, 23, 29–30, 53, 55, 76, 96, 108, 123, 133, 142, 173, 175, 176, 195, 240, 244, 283 n208
  and money, 23, 30, 43, 53, 76, 117, 123, 132, 136, 160, 170, 174, 180, 192, 212, 213, 214, 228, 233, 265 n90, 265 n97, 287 n314
  at Oxford, 15, 16–23, 25–27, 32, 41–3, 47, 50, 57–9, 61, 62, 82, 105, 111, 114, 120–1, 133, 136, 148–9, 174, 195, 211–14, 224, 234, 245, 250 n27
  poetry, 16, 18, 21, 22, 23, 26, 29, 30–1, 32–3, 35, 36, 41, 43, 45, 46, 47, 50, 52, 53, 55, 56, 57–8, 62, 97, 101, 110, 111, 121–3, 136, 137, 153, 165, 169, 173, 175, 189, 190, 192, 193, 194, 196, 201, 202–3, 209, 217, 218, 220, 221–2, 223–4, 233, 233–4, 235, 258 n231, 263 n52, 267 n145, 283 n210: *Ballad of Reading Gaol, The* (1898), 101, 153, 165, 193, 258 n231, 267 n145; 'Dole of the King's Daughter, The' (1876), 18; 'Harlot's House, The' (1885), 202–: *Poems* (1881), 46; 'Ravenna' (1878), 21, 26; 'Rome Unvisited' (1881), 62
  plays, 23, 38–9, 40, 47–8, 94, 98, 100, 101, 106, 110, 111, 113–14, 115, 117, 119, 121, 122, 123, 138, 139, 147, 157, 158–9, 162–3, 165, 168, 176, 196, 202, 208, 215–16, 238, 253 n104, 257–8 n225, 265 n99, 271 n237, 274 n322, 287 n313: *Duchess of Padua, The* (1891), 47–8; *Ideal Husband, An* (1895), 110, 111, 257–8 n225, 265 n99; *Importance of Being Earnest, The* (1895), 23, 38, 115, 119, 147, 157, 158–9, 253 n104, 257–8 n225, 287 n313; *Lady Windermere's Fan* (1892), 39, 94, 101, 106, 110, 113–14, 117, 122, 123, 139, 176, 202, 208, 238; *Salomé/Salome* (1893/1894), 38–9, 98, 100, 110, 115, 117, 121, 122, 138, 162–3, 165, 168, 271 n237, 274 n322; *Vera; or, The Nihilists* (1883), 196; *Woman of No Importance, A* (1893), 40, 110, 113–14, 115, 215–16
  prone to gossip, 29, 34, 102, 103–4, 105, 106–7, 187
  Prose, 1, 12, 40, 57, 60–1, 65, 66, 70, 71–2, 77, 80, 93–4, 115, 118–19, 120, 121, 122, 127, 128, 140, 141, 151, 153, 160, 170, 177–8, 195, 196, 203, 220, 222, 227–8, 235, 242, 244, 253 n115,

254 n138, 267 n149,
271 n240, 271 n244,
273–4 n319, 279 n93,
282–3 n186, 283 n208,
285 n260, 286 n288, 286
n292, 287 n2; 'Canterville
Ghost, The' (1887), 57;
'Decay of Lying, The'
(1889), 12, 60, 65, 70,
254 n138; *De Profundis*
(1905–1962), 40, 120, 160,
220, 227–8, 253 n115,
267 n149, 271 n244,
286 n292, 287 n2; *Happy
Prince and Other Tales, The*
(1888), 57, 235; *House of
Pomegranates, A* (1891), 94;
Intentions (1891), 94, 115,
122, 282–3 n186, 286 n288;
'Lord Arthur Savile's Crime'
(1887), 57, 94; 'Nightingale
and the Rose, The' (1888),
203; 'Pen, Pencil and Poison;
A Study in Green' (1889), 1,
80, 271 n240; *Picture of
Dorian Gray, The* (1890,
1891), 66, 71–2, 77, 80,
93–4, 115, 118–19, 121,
127, 128, 140, 141, 151,
153, 170, 177–8, 195, 196,
222, 242, 244, 273–4 n319,
279 n93, 283 n208,
285 n260; 'Portrait of
Mr. W. H., The' (1889), 12,
60–1, 93; 'Rise of Historical
Criticism, The' (1908), 12;
'Soul of Man Under
Socialism, The' (1891), 32,
38, 94, 137, 196, 197
and religion, 1, 9, 18–19, 137,
154–5, 159, 212, 285 n260
sexuality, 1, 4, 7, 8–9, 11, 19,
20–1, 60–1, 64, 68–69, 71,
73, 74, 78, 84, 93, 95, 100,
104, 117, 129, 137, 139,
149, 143–4, 144–5, 155, 158,
162, 165–8, 178–84, 187–8,
199, 203, 204, 205, 209–10,
213–14, 226, 230, 231, 236,
239, 240, 241, 243, 248 n23,
258 n237, 261 n321,
271 n240, 274 n335,
279 n103, 280 n116, 287 n314
socialism, 1, 4, 32, 38–39, 94,
115, 137, 150, 196–7,
231
speech and conversation, 1, 11,
17–18, 22, 25, 28–9, 33, 34,
41, 43, 45, 49, 50, 51, 56,
60, 62, 63, 66, 67, 72, 74,
76, 79, 80, 81, 83, 101, 102,
103–4, 106, 108–9, 116,
120, 126, 132, 134, 138,
139, 140, 165, 167, 169,
170, 173–4, 188, 191, 194,
195, 197–8, 201, 203–4,
208, 209, 211, 213, 214,
218–19, 220, 222, 223,
234, 235, 242, 276 n40,
281 n156, 287 n299
and the supernatural, 49–52, 69,
70, 72, 130, 148, 150, 176,
228, 230, 234, 235–6, 237,
241, 242, 244
at Trinity College, Dublin, 15,
47, 73, 174, 245
and women, 8–9, 11, 19–21, 27,
30, 35–6, 43, 50, 55, 58, 69,
102, 103–5, 107–8, 109,
112, 124, 141–2, 142–3,
154, 159, 166, 170–1, 181,
184, 187–8, 191, 195, 203,
204, 207, 209, 212, 213,
219, 222, 223, 229,
282 n167
and youth, 20, 26, 36, 76, 102,
104, 112, 124, 132, 140,
143, 144, 158, 166, 175,
176, 213, 222, 223, 236,
241
Wilde, Sir William, 128, 129,
174, 213, 251 n67, 278 n78

Wilde, William (Willie), 31, 82, 140, 151, 174, 182, 261 n323, 287 n299
  fictional depictions: Teddy in *The Green Carnation* (1894), 140
Willing Exile, A (1890), 73–8
Winter, John Strange, *see* Stannard, Henrietta
Woman's World, The, see Wilde, Oscar, editor of *The Woman's World*
Wood, Marilyn, 41, 42, 254 n122, 254 n131
Woods, Margaret, 42, 44, 254 n126
'Woman's Half-Profits, The' (1894), 121–13, 173, 226
'World's Slow Stain, The' (1904), 101, 108–10, 127, 233, 281

Wotton, Mabel, 4, 13, 169–72
  'Fifth Edition, The' (1896), 169–72, 226, 277 n59
  Word Portraits of Famous Writers (1889), 13, 171–2

Yellow Book, The, 4, 116–17, 118, 119, 121, 130–1, 146, 153, 160, 163, 205–6, 275 n21, 276 n28
Ye Soul Agonies in Ye Life of Oscar Wilde (1882), 4, 46–7
Yorke, Curtis, *see* Lee, Susan Richmond
Y. T. O., 120–1
  Aristophanes at Oxford (1894), 120–1